Canada and the Challenges
of International Development and Globalization

Canada and the Challenges of International Development and Globalization

edited by Mahmoud Masaeli and Lauchlan T. Munro

University of Ottawa Press
2018

Les **Presses** de l'Université d'Ottawa
University of Ottawa **Press**

The University of Ottawa Press (UOP) is proud to be the oldest of the francophone university presses in Canada and the only bilingual university publisher in North America. Since 1936, UOP has been "enriching intellectual and cultural discourse" by producing peer-reviewed and award-winning books in the humanities and social sciences, in French or in English.

Library and Archives Canada Cataloguing in Publication

Canada and the challenges of international development and globalization / edited by Mahmoud Masaeli and Lauchlan T. Munro.

Includes bibliographical references.
Issued in print and electronic formats.
ISBN 978-0-7766-2636-9 (softcover)
ISBN 978-0-7766-2637-6 (PDF)
ISBN 978-0-7766-2638-3 (EPUB)
ISBN 978-0-7766-2639-0 (Kindle)

1. Canada–Relations–Developing countries. 2. Developing countries–Relations–Canada. 3. Globalization–Canada. 4. Globalization–Developing countries. I. Masaeli, Mahmoud, 1954-, editor II. Munro, Lauchlan T., 1961-, editor

FC244.T55C32 2018   327.710172'4   C2018-900963-2
                                                  C2018-900964-0

Legal Deposit: First Quarter 2018
Library and Archives Canada
© University of Ottawa Press, 2018

Printed and bound in Canada
Copy editing: Susan James
Proofreading: Robbie McCaw
Series text design and typesetting: Counterpunch Inc., Linda Gustafson
Cover design: Édiscript enr.

The University of Ottawa Press gratefully acknowledges the support extended to its publishing list by the Government of Canada, the Canada Council for the Arts, the Ontario Arts Council, and the Federation for the Humanities and Social Sciences through the Awards to Scholarly Publications Program, and by the University of Ottawa.

Dedication

To my family, whose constant support has been the main motive
in my humanistic academic journey.
M. M.

To my grandfather, Norman R. McDonald (1893–1971).
Some called him "NR" and some called him "Mac." Some called him
"Sergeant" and some called him "Judge."
But I think he really liked being called "White Owl."
L. T. M.

Table of Contents

Detailed Table of Contents

Foreword

Mahmoud Masaeli and Lauchlan T. Munro

The book is written by many different authors coming from a variety of social, cultural, and academic backgrounds. Among the authors, you will find people of all genders, Indigenous people, Anglophones, Francophones, and Allophones, people whose ancestors have lived in Canada for many generations, and those who came here as immigrants. The authors include established scholars, practitioners, and young researchers. As editors, we have deliberately recruited authors coming from a wide variety of academic disciplines and a wide variety of viewpoints. Students encountering international development and globalization for the first time will read in this textbook authors coming from almost all of the theoretical perspectives outlined in Table 1.1, found in Chapter 1, Canada as an Example of International Development and Globalization. Students of international development and global studies will thus be able to grapple with the important debates in this field right from the start of their studies. Students may wish to match the authors of each chapter with the various theories of international development and globalization that are discussed in Chapter 1. While we have imposed a common structure on the chapters and case studies, we have tried to let each author speak with her or his own voice. Our aim is not to give one version of how Canada affects (and is affected by) international development and globalization, but to give many versions. Readers are invited to send feedback to the editors, who wish to improve future editions of this textbook.

We wish to thank all those who have contributed to this book in various ways. We thank the authors for their dedication and their patience. We thank all the staff at University of Ottawa Press for accepting our proposal and for supporting us during the long road from idea to final publication. Thanks also to Taryn Husband-Ceperkovic for assistance in project management and to the two anonymous peer reviewers who, we hope, will find that we have corrected the problems and gaps they identified in the earlier draft that they read. We thank Athena Tzivanopolous for translating Chapter 8 from the original French. Finally, we thank the students in DVM1100 at the University of Ottawa over the past two years who have read and commented on many drafts of the chapters and case studies now published here.

How to Use This Textbook

Notes for Students, Professors, and Teaching Assistants

Lauchlan T. Munro

Who Is This Textbook for?

This textbook is designed primarily for use in first- and second-year undergraduate courses that deal with international development and globalization with a Canadian focus. The book links Canada to the story of international development and globalization, something that most textbooks of international development do not do. The book shows that modern Canada is itself the product of the same forces that have shaped and that continue to shape developing nations today as they navigate their way through a globalized world.

The book will also be useful as a supplementary text in courses on Canadian politics, international relations, international economics, and Canadian foreign policy. Anyone interested in Canada's role in the world may also want to read this book. There is enough material in the textbook to support two typical three-credit courses in a Canadian university.

How Is This Textbook Organized?

The book is designed in a modular fashion. In other words, except for the first three chapters, which should be read together, readers can dip into chapters and case studies in any order that they like. Those who wish to focus more on globalization, for example, may wish to concentrate on Chapters 3, 6, 7, and 13. Those who are more interested in international development, on the other hand, will want to focus their attention on Chapters 2, 4, 11, 12, and 14. Most chapters, however, combine international development and globalization. The modular structure allows teachers to arrange their courses in a wide variety of possible sequences, since chapters are written is such a way that they do not assume the reader has read the preceding chapter. (There are two exceptions. Chapters 1 to 3 should be read in order before the other chapters. And Chapter 10 builds explicitly on Chapter 9.)

Our textbook is divided into 15 chapters and 11 case studies. The chapters are longer, typically around 8,000 words, while the case studies are shorter, around 1,700 words. The case studies provide concrete examples of how Canada has dealt with (or not dealt with!) various issues over the decades. Case studies provide illustrations of the broader, sometimes more theoretical, materials that are in the chapters. Table 1.0, below, provides suggestions as to which case studies go best with which chapters. You will note that one case study may be relevant to several chapters.

Table 1.0

Book Chapters and Their Related Case Studies

Book Chapter	Case Studies Most Closely Related to that Chapter
Chapter 1: Canada as an Example of International Development and Globalization	All Case Studies
Chapter 2: International Development: An Overview of Definitions, Historical Evolution, and Debates	All Case Studies
Chapter 3: Globalization: Definitions, Debates, and Relation to International Development	Case Studies 1, 5, 6, and 8
Chapter 4: Canada's Aid Program since 1945	Case Studies 1, 4, 5, and 11
Chapter 5: Canada's Military and the Developing Countries since 1945	Case Studies 3, 4, and 10
Chapter 6: Canadian Immigration and Refugee Policies since 1945	Case Studies 5 and 10
Chapter 7: Development and Globalization: The Role of Canadian Civil Society	Case Studies 2, 5, 10, and 11
Chapter 8: Canada, Quebec, and La Francophonie	Case Study 5
Chapter 9: Challenging the Colonialism at the Heart of Western Development: A Decolonizing Perspective	Case Studies 2 and 9
Chapter 10: Development Colonialism in a Canadian Context	Case Studies 2 and 9
Chapter 11: A Canadian Way to Promote Democracy Abroad? Lessons from an Abortive Experiment	Case Studies 4, 5, 6, 7, 10, and 11
Chapter 12: Canada's Aid Program and the Private Sector	Case Studies 2, 6, and 8
Chapter 13: Canada and the "Emerging Economies": Not Aid, But Not Just Trade	Case Studies 1, 5, 6, and 8
Chapter 14: Canada and the Security-Development Nexus in Fragile and Conflict-Affected States/Situations	Case Studies 3, 4, 5, 7, and 10
Chapter 15: Our Role: A Moral Case for Helping or an Ethical Duty to Strive for Justice?	Case Studies 1, 3, 7, and 11

The book's modular structure also allows professors to organize their courses according to more specific themes or issues. **Table 2.0**, below, suggests various possible themes and the chapters and case studies most relevant to those themes.

Table 2.0

Possible Themes and Related Chapters and Case Studies

Possible Theme	Related Chapters	Related Case Studies
Civil society and development	7, 11, and 15	2 and 11
Colonialism and development	1, 2, 3, 8, 9, and 10	2, 8, 10, and 11
Emerging economies, emerging markets, and BRICs	3, 12, and 13	1, 6, and 8
Ethics and development	9 and 15	1, 2, 3, 7, 8, and 11
Global issues/global public goods	3, 6, 13, and 14	1, 3, 5, 6, 7, 8, and 9
Indigenous peoples	1, 2, 9, and 10	2, 8, and 9
Peace, security, and development	5, 11, and 14	3, 4, 7, and 10
Private sector/capitalism	1, 3, 10, and 12	1, 6, 8, and 9

How Are the Book Chapters Organized?

Each chapter in this textbook follows the same structure. This uniform structure is designed to make both teaching and learning from this textbook easier. For example, the reader is told at the beginning of each chapter what the chapter is all about, what the student is supposed to learn from it, and what new or specialized vocabulary will appear in the chapter. These first three elements will then be followed by the chapter contents. Each chapter is structured as follows:

- Overview
- Learning objectives for the chapter
- Key terms
- The chapter contents
- Questions for further learning
- Suggested readings
- Suggested videos
- Suggested websites
- Works cited

To help both professors and teaching assistants to focus their teaching efforts, each chapter has a set of "learning objectives," supported by "key terms" that may be new to students. The learning objectives spell out what students will be expected to know after reading the chapter. Key terms are spelled out since they have specific meanings in international development or globalization studies, and these meanings may differ from what the word means in everyday use.

After the main contents of the chapter, each chapter includes "questions for further learning"; professors and teaching assistants may wish to use these for small group tutorials or for written or in-class assignments. Students may also wish to use these questions for further learning in private study groups. Students who are particularly interested in the subject matter of a chapter may wish to consult the "suggested readings," "suggested videos," and "suggested

websites" that appear before the end of each chapter. Professors may wish to use these suggested readings, videos, and websites for supplementary or recommended readings in their course syllabus, in addition to the textbook itself. Students may also wish to consult these suggested readings, videos, and websites as they prepare class assignments or essays. The overview, key terms, learning objectives, and questions for further learning from each chapter will provide useful study aids for students as they prepare for exams.

How Are the Case Studies Organized?

Each case study follows the same structure. This allows students to make comparisons between case studies. Since the case studies deal with public policy issues, they are organized in three parts:

- Issue
- Action
- Impact

In other words, each case study takes on a given issue or problem in international development and/or globalization. It then discusses what Canada did (or did not do) and, finally, it discusses the impact of Canada's action, recognising that Canada's actions can have positive impacts, negative impacts, ambiguous impacts, or no impact at all.

This issue–action–impact structure is designed to give students a firm grasp on why an issue was important to Canada and the world, what Canada did on that issue (if anything), why it acted the way it did, and what the consequences were. The case studies represent a wide variety of issue areas, from international scientific cooperation to climate change to regional issues. These case studies are meant to provide concrete illustrations of actions taken in relation to the big issues addressed in the chapters. These case studies are also meant to show the complexities of a world in which there are often no easy or simple solutions to complex problems. On most of these issues, Canada is only one country amongst many that are interested; as a mid-sized country, Canada has limited resources, influence, and power. But there may also be scope for well-thought-out initiatives that bring positive results. The case studies have been identified to show a wide range of issues where Canada has been engaged, with a variety of actions and outcomes.

What Is This Book Designed to Tell Me?

If this textbook has a hidden agenda, it is to show that international development is not all about aid. Many undergraduates arrive in university programs of international development or globalization with the naïve notion that aid and development are virtually synonymous. Many students also believe that aid is the driving force of international development. They may wish to pursue a career in international development through various Canadian or international aid organizations. As editors, it is not our job to discourage idealism. But it is our job to convey to students the fact that the world is much more complex than that naïve worldview suggests. Canada interacts with the developing world not only, and not even primarily, through its aid program, which in any case is relatively small (about 26 cents out of every $100 earned by Canadians). Canada interacts with the developing world through trade, migration (in and out), military intervention (and not just peacekeeping), relations with our own Indigenous peoples, and high-level international political negotiations on everything from climate change to international peace and security to the regulation of the international economic system. Students have to be made aware of these facts, and this textbook seeks to do so.

Our textbook also seeks to debunk another myth, namely that development is a simple, harmonious process of steadily improving living standards for everyone. Clearly, such a process would be ideal, but it is not the norm. International development and globalization have historically been fraught with conflict and debate, and continue to be so today. There are big debates about how the benefits of development are shared, about whether new technologies are always good, about the obvious and increasing impact of humans on our natural environment, and about what role democracy, human rights, and domination play in this drama. The editors have deliberately selected authors, chapter themes, and case studies to bring such issues to light. Once again, our purpose is not to douse the flames of idealism. Our purpose is to begin the processes of helping students understand and grapple with a complex set of issues, where sometimes it is not a battle between right and wrong, but a conflict between different versions of the good. Hence, professors may wish to have students read chapters and/or case studies with contrasting views on a subject, and to organize class discussions around these debates.

List of Figures

List of Tables

List of Boxes

Part I

Introduction

Basic Concepts

1

Canada as an Example of International Development and Globalization

Lauchlan T. Munro

Overview

A century and a half ago, the average Canadian died at age 41; today, she will live 81 years. Back then, we were a lot poorer in material terms. Our government was a lot less democratic and the threat of political violence was common. Our social and political values were very different back then. Yet Canada evolved, some would say "developed," into the country we know today: more health, more wealth, more pluralist and democratic. That process of social, economic, and political change was highly disruptive, often contested, and sometimes violent. It has also been very incomplete, in that the fruits of prosperity and democracy have not been shared at all equally. But, if Canada can undergo such a long-term transformation, however incomplete, can other countries do the same? What is the best way to understand Canada's development and how it relates to the rest of the world? These are the questions that this chapter begins to address.

Key Terms

- capitalism
- colonialism
- dependency
- development
- economic nationalism
- Indigenous peoples
- institutions
- modernization
- modernizationism
- (neo) liberalism
- pluralism
- subaltern studies
- theory

Learning Objectives

By the end of this chapter, students will be able to:

- understand Canada as a former colony of two great powers, Britain and France, built on Turtle Island;
- describe in what ways Canada used to resemble today's "developing countries" and still does;
- describe in broad terms how Canada has developed socially, politically, and economically over the past three centuries;
- recognize and describe the main schools of thought concerning development and globalization in relation to Canada.

A Family History

The new country where the immigrant family arrived had a troubled past and an uncertain future. Less than two decades earlier, there had been a nasty war with the new republic to the south, and both capital cities had been burned to the ground. Six years after the immigrant family arrived in the new country, rebellions broke out as people demanded a more representative form of government. The rebellions were suppressed with violence, though the government did eventually concede to the rebels' demands. A decade later, the parliament building was burned down by a mob during a politically inspired riot.

The immigrant family were not destitute when they arrived in the new country, but they were not rich either. It is not clear why they left their old country. They had been tenant farmers on a large estate in their old country. Maybe the prospect of owning land in the new country enticed them to move; maybe they were unsure of their long-term prospects in the old country. For in the old country they had been members of an ethnic, linguistic, and religious minority, albeit a relatively privileged one. Their ancestors in turn had come to that old country from their country of origin 140 years earlier, as part of a government plan to stabilize a restive colony. As the immigrant family arrived in the new country, they still felt strong ties of allegiance to their country of origin that their ancestors had left a century and a half before, though none of them had ever been there.

The family's journey to the new country was difficult. The youngest daughter died during the three-month-long voyage and was buried at sea. Another daughter was born almost immediately upon arrival in the new country and was given the same name as the girl who had just died. Six more children followed over the next eight years. One of them died within weeks of being born.

The immigrant family settled just north of the capital city of the new country, the capital that had been burned down just years before. The government allocated them land on condition that they develop it; they had to clear land for cultivation, build a house and farm buildings, and dig a well. The children grew up in that area, went to school, married the children of other recent immigrants from the same ethnic, linguistic, and religious background, and in turn established their own families and businesses. The eighth child, a boy, married a young woman and took over the family farm from his ageing parents. At the age of 29, he volunteered for the local militia and helped fight off a raiding party from the pesky republic to the south, a country that was just emerging from its own vicious civil war.

When they took over the family farm, the eighth son and his wife took on a debt load that they were never able to shed. Years later, when he was 55 years old and she was 42, they went bankrupt and had to sell the farm. The government was then offering free land farther west and so the family piled all their belongings onto a train and went west. They tried farming for two years but the crops failed both years. The family almost starved and froze to death the first winter. They survived by their wits and thanks to government relief.

After two years, they gave up farming and moved into the nearest town, where the family diversified into several lines of business. The elder daughters went into teaching, the father into hardware sales; a son went into the transportation business. Soon the family was thriving and the eighth son became a leading figure in the local community. At the age of 75, he mounted a white horse and led the annual parade celebrating a great military victory by his ancestors back in the old country, a battle that had happened 225 years before. When he died by accidental poisoning four years later, hundreds attended his funeral, and the local newspaper reported that people of a great variety of religious faiths and ethnic origins were in attendance. His wife died the following year, aged 67.

The eighth son and his wife had eleven children. The youngest had her life saved when two doctors in Toronto discovered insulin as a treatment for diabetes. She became a schoolteacher and married a young lawyer. The young lawyer had served in the army in a great war overseas, working as an ambulance driver, taking the wounded from the front lines back to the field hospitals for treatment. He never spoke of his wartime experiences. Around 65,000 citizens of the new country died overseas in that terrible war. The lawyer welcomed clients who were not from the same ethnic, religious, or linguistic background as he was. He also worked with the Indigenous people of the land where he and his wife's family had settled, the people whose forebears had been displaced by that settlement. Not every lawyer was willing to take immigrants and Indigenous people as clients.

The schoolteacher and the lawyer got married in the middle of an economic boom, but shortly thereafter disaster struck. A decade-long economic crisis hit the country; the economy shrank by almost half, and a quarter of all adults were unemployed. Malnutrition became common. A large group of unemployed men announced their intention to ride the railway to the national capital to demand government relief; on arriving in a provincial capital, they were met with police gunfire. Hundreds were arrested and shipped off to detention camps in the bush. Then there was another terrible war on the other side of the world, in which another 44,000 citizens of the new country lost their lives.

The schoolteacher and the lawyer had one daughter, who became the first woman in the family's history to attend university. She got two degrees, worked for many years as a social worker, and had two sons with her first husband, an architect who had served in the navy in that second overseas war, before getting a divorce. The younger of those two sons is the author of this chapter.

Canada, Colonialism, Globalization, and the British Connection

In outlining my (maternal) family's history (McCullagh 1968), my objective is not to praise them or to claim that they were extraordinary. Many millions of Canadians could outline a similar history of migration, displacement, death, birth, marriage, divorce, failure, and success. Rather, I use my family's history to illustrate aspects of Canada's history over the last 180 or so years, namely how Canada today is a product of an earlier era of globalization and development. As the attentive reader may have detected, many of the characteristics of what we now call the "developing countries" were once—and to some extent still are—characteristics of Canada.

When my great-great-grandparents, Richard and Susannah Perry, arrived in what is now Toronto in 1831, Upper Canada (now called Ontario), it was a British colony. Upper Canada was poor compared to Britain; it was relatively cut off from global trade and was in many ways technologically backward. Infrastructure was weak and the colony's only institution of higher education was less than five years old. Women routinely died in childbirth and a third of all children died before their fifth birthday.

In fact, Upper Canada had many of the characteristics of what we now call a fragile state. The colony suffered from an unrepresentative government dominated by a few rich families; social and political tensions were high, as the elite resisted calls for reform. Open rebellion erupted in both Upper Canada and Lower Canada (now called Quebec) in 1837, and these rebellions were suppressed by gunfire, mass arrests, and a few hangings. Even after democratic reforms were introduced, rioters burned down the parliament building in Montreal in 1848.

There were also sharp social cleavages between people of different religions (especially between Protestants and Roman Catholics) and languages (English and French). For many years, my great-grandfather led the Orange Day parade in Estevan, Saskatchewan; the parade celebrates the victory of the Protestant King William of Orange over the Catholic King James at the Battle of the Boyne in Ireland in 1688. Participants in Orange Day parades have historically engaged in virulent anti-Catholic and anti-French rhetoric, as well as expressing loyalty to the British Crown. Such parades were common in rural Ontario towns and in Toronto until quite recently.

The colony also had to deal with a sometimes hostile and equally fragile neighbour, the United States. The Americans burned York (now called Toronto) to the ground in 1814, and British and Canadian troops did the same to Washington, D.C., a few months later. Civil War wracked the United States from 1861 to 1865. From 1866 to 1871, the Fenian Brotherhood, a group of Americans of Irish descent, conducted armed raids into Canada, hoping to stir up rebellion against the British Crown. My great-grandfather joined the anti-Fenian militia. Many an American politician dreamed of annexing the British colonies on America's northern border.

My great-great-grandparents came to Upper Canada from County Limerick, Ireland. Their ancestors had come to Ireland around 1690, as part of the British government's effort to implant settlements of loyal Protestants throughout Ireland, a country with a staunch Roman Catholic majority and a distaste for British rule. When the Perrys moved to Upper Canada in 1831, their arrival was facilitated by a British colonial government eager to settle the lands near the American border with the same sort of people, Protestants loyal to the British Crown. To facilitate that settlement, the colonial authorities took land from the Chippewa and Mississauga Nations. The legality of that land grab was dubious, and was not corrected until 1923.

When my great-grandparents Richard Perry II and his wife Sarah Jane Hunter Perry went bankrupt in Ontario in 1892 and moved west to what was then the Territory of Assiniboia (now Saskatchewan), their migration was facilitated by the government-subsidized Canadian Pacific Railway. The Perrys were given land in Assiniboia by the Canadian government, which had recently acquired the territory from the Hudson's Bay Company. The Government of Canada was eager to populate the Canadian prairies in order to deprive the Americans of any excuse to occupy "empty" lands. But the lands were not and had not ever been "empty"; the white settlers on the Canadian prairies were also meant to counterbalance the First Nations and Métis peoples who had recently been displaced from that land.

The process of "settling" the Canadian Prairies was a story of treaty making, displacement, and resistance. The First Nations and the Métis peoples negotiated treaties with the Crown; these treaties confined the Indigenous peoples to specific pieces of land ("reserves") in exchange for various payments and services. This author, for example, was born in the territory covered by Treaty No. 2 of 1871. At other times, and often in response to the Crown's broken promises and proven insensitivities, the First Nations and Métis resisted this displacement and resettlement. In 1870 and again in 1885, only seven years before the Perrys arrived in Assiniboia, there had been open warfare, as the Métis and the Cree resisted the tide of white immigrants. The Government of Canada used the new Canadian Pacific Railway, which it had helped create, to rush white troops from Ontario to suppress what it called "the Northwest Rebellion" in 1885. After several battles, the rebellion was crushed and its leader, the Francophone Métis Louis Riel, was arrested, tried in front of an all-white, all-Anglophone jury, and hanged. For the next 30 years, thousands of mostly white settlers arrived every year to settle the Canadian Prairies. Louis Riel became a martyr and a folk hero for the Métis and for many Francophones in Quebec.

My family's history is thus intricately intertwined with the history of British colonialism and imperialism, both in Ireland and here in Canada. Both my grandfathers served in the Canadian army in the First World War. In 1914, because Canada was still a British colony, albeit a self-governing one, Britain's declaration of war brought Canada into the war too. Though no one in my mother's family has lived in Britain since the seventeenth century, a strong sense of loyalty to Britain and to the Crown pervades my family. As the government of Prime Minister Stephen Harper (2006–2015) tried to reinvigorate Canada's historical links to the British Crown, it was people of ancestry like mine whom it was seeking to mobilize.

But the presence in Canada of large numbers of people of British descent is not the only legacy of British colonial rule in Canada. The most obvious legacy is linguistic: Canada's major language is English. We often use British, as opposed to American, spellings: labour, centre. The legal system in nine of ten provinces and in areas of federal jurisdiction is based on the English legal system; indeed, the *Constitution Act 1982* specifies that "the Common Law of England" forms part of the Canadian constitution. Our parliamentary form of government is a version of British parliamentarianism, called the Westminster system, named after the part of London where the British Parliament sits. The Westminster principle of responsible government, which makes the prime minister and cabinet responsible to Parliament and dependent on being able to maintain the confidence of Parliament, is also part of the *Constitution Act 1982*. Of all the Canadian provinces and territories, only Nunavut departs from the pure Westminster system. Created in 1999, Nunavut sought to incorporate Inuit principles of governance into the operations of its legislature.

There are other, very subtle, similarities with Britain that often get overlooked. The fact that the Canadian constitution insists on the primacy of the communitarian principle of "peace, order, and good government" reflects a British political tradition called Burkean conservatism, named after the eighteenth-century Anglo-Irish politician, journalist, and scholar Edmund Burke. Burkean political thought emphasizes the dangers of radical political experiments such as revolution and promotes the value of tradition and incremental change. Canada's Burkean tradition stands in sharp contrast to the Jeffersonian tradition in the United States, which gives primacy to the individualistic principle of "life, liberty, and the pursuit of happiness" and insists on the right of oppressed peoples to revolution. The vastly different attitudes in Canada and the United States towards the ownership and regulation of firearms, for example, can be traced to these two very different constitutional philosophies.

The Francophone Fact in Canada's History

It was in the St. Lawrence River valley, in what is now Quebec, and in parts of what we now call Canada's Atlantic Provinces, that settlers from France established the first permanent European settlements in Canada, starting in the 1600s. The French brought with them their language, their legal system, and the Roman Catholic religion, along with the latest European technologies of the time. They called the colony

New France, and they set about re-creating a French world in the New World.

The French settlers encountered the Indigenous peoples who had been on those lands for generations. The relations between the French settlers and the Indigenous peoples were varied. Sometimes they fought; often they traded and often they cooperated both politically and militarily. Sometimes they intermarried, giving rise to the Métis Nation. The French tried to convert the Indigenous peoples to Roman Catholicism; they had some success in this endeavour, but also met with strong resistance. The French settlers, like the British, often treated the Indigenous peoples as inferiors.

In the seventeenth and eighteenth centuries, the British established colonies along the east coast of North America, from Newfoundland in the north to Georgia in the south. Britain and France were then rivals. From the seventeenth to the early nineteenth centuries, the two countries fought many wars against each other, both in Europe and in their colonies. I was raised on stories of great British military and naval heroes like Marlborough, Nelson, Rodney, Wellington, and Wolfe, who had defeated the French. In North America, each side allied itself with different groups of Indigenous nations: the British with the Iroquois Confederacy and the French with the Huron Nation. In 1759, the Anglo-French conflict came to a head in North America. The British sent a quarter of their navy and a large army to conquer New France, which, with great skill and a little luck, they managed to do. The French nearly took it back the following year, but the peace treaty of 1763 left New France to the British. For the century that followed, Britain had a predominantly Francophone colony, which they initially called Quebec (1763–1791), then Lower Canada (1791–1841), then Canada East (1843–1867). Since 1867, it has been known as Quebec.

The British initially sought to accommodate their new Francophone subjects. The *Quebec Act of 1774* guaranteed the preservation of the French language and the French legal system in Quebec. The *Act* also allowed the free practice of Roman Catholicism and restored the Catholic Church's right to collect tithes from the population, making Catholicism the established church. While these concessions reassured the Francophones, they were unpopular in the Thirteen British Colonies to the south. When those Thirteen Colonies formed the United States of America and declared their independence from Britain in 1776, one of the grievances they cited was the *Quebec Act*. When American troops tried to capture Quebec in both the American War of Independence (1776–1783) and in the War of 1812 (1812–1815) the Francophones of Quebec welcomed their would-be liberators with gunshot and cannon fire. Being under British rule might be bad, but being under American rule promised to be worse.

Still, relations between the French-speaking Catholic population and their largely Protestant English-speaking neighbours remained strained for many decades. The commercial and industrial elites in Quebec were largely Anglophone, while the working classes were largely Francophone. The differences in language, culture, and religion created a gulf of mutual incomprehension and distrust which only began to diminish in the late twentieth century. Frustration exploded in the rebellion of 1837. The British government's attempt to understand the causes of the rebellion and to find solutions was a report by the British aristocrat Lord Durham. Every generation of Quebec schoolchildren since the 1840s has been taught to denounce the "Durham Report" as an example of English racism.

The Canadian Confederation

What finally forced the confederation of British colonies in North America was the real possibility that the United States, recently emerged from its own civil war, might annex the British colonies to the north. There was little love lost between the United States and Britain; not only was Britain the former colonizer of the US, but Britain had supported the Confederacy, the losing side in the American Civil War. Britain also hoped that its increasingly prosperous North American colonies would take up more of the burden of paying for administration and defence, while remaining part of the British Empire. Starting in 1864, negotiations for creating a confederation of the remaining British colonies in North American began in earnest. No women or Indigenous people were invited to take part in the negotiations.

When, in the 1850s and 1860s, the British government started to push its reluctant North American colonies into a confederation, the Francophone representatives insisted that the new country be a federal structure in which health, education, culture, language, family law, and property law should be devolved to the sub-national units, which became known as provinces. They also insisted that French be one of the two official languages, along with English. After some horse-trading over minority language rights, this was agreed to, along with a few other special guarantees for Quebec, including a minimum number of Quebec seats in the federal parliament.

The Dominion of Canada was born on July 1, 1867. The new country was a self-governing colony within the British Empire, with Britain retaining responsibility for foreign affairs and defence. In the new constitution, the Indigenous peoples (then called "Indians") were made the wards of the new federal government. The federal government also got responsibility for the national currency, the post office, international and interprovincial trade, and the organisation of a militia. It was not until 1931, with the *Statute of Westminster*, that the Government of Canada gained full control over foreign affairs and national defence.

Initially, four British colonies combined in 1867 to form the Dominion of Canada: Ontario, Quebec, New Brunswick, and Nova Scotia. Manitoba joined three years later. British Columbia joined in 1871, and Prince Edward Island in 1873. In 1870, Canada bought Rupert's Land from the Hudson's Bay Company; this huge tract of land encompassed what is now northern Quebec, northern Ontario, northern Manitoba, Saskatchewan, Alberta, and much of the northern territories. Alberta and Saskatchewan became provinces in 1905, and Newfoundland (now called Newfoundland and Labrador) joined in 1949, after the pro-Canada camp won a razor-thin victory in a referendum. The northern territories of Canada—the Yukon, Northwest Territories, and Nunavut—have yet to attain provincial status.

Turtle Island—North America from an Indigenous Perspective

But all that is history told from the standpoint of the colonial settlers. The human history of Canada really begins with the Indigenous peoples, who have been here for around 20,000 years, or roughly 40 times longer than the settlers. In many Indigenous traditions, North America is called Turtle Island. In an Ojibway version of the story, a great flood covered all the land. The turtle volunteered his back to be the land surface if only other animals could swim to the bottom and bring up soil. Many animals tried and failed; only the muskrat succeeded in bringing up a handful of soil, but he died in the attempt. The soil was then placed on the back of the turtle and Kitchi Manitou, the Great Spirit, caused it to grow and become fertile and soon all the animals were able to return to the land, which we now call Turtle Island. In this cosmology, the border between modern Canada and the United States is meaningless. That border, and the two nation-states that it helps to define, are the inventions of the settlers who came later.

Long before the arrival of the first European settlers in the seventeenth century, the Indigenous peoples of North America had built diversified economies and societies, with an often complex division of labour. They managed multiple livelihoods (farming, fishing, manufacturing, trade, hunting) in often challenging environments; to do so, they domesticated crops (e.g., beans, maize, pumpkins), developed technologies (e.g., canoes, kayaks, snowshoes), and played organized sports (e.g., lacrosse) that we still use today. They developed sophisticated and very diverse cosmologies and metaphysics. Their beautifully expressive art is a manifestation of those cosmologies. They had in-depth understanding of the medicinal and other properties of plants and of the ecology in which they lived. They did not see nature as a resource to be exploited; rather, they saw themselves as part of nature. They acquired detailed knowledge of the geography where they lived; the European "explorers" of North America were in fact usually led by Indigenous guides who already knew the landscape. In politics, the Indigenous peoples often devised large and complicated political units. The Iroquois Confederacy, to take just one example, lasted 200 years and was based on a form of democratic governance.

The Europeans who settled in Turtle Island starting in the seventeenth century did not see things that way. The saw the Indigenous peoples as pagans who did not accept the "true" (i.e., Christian) religion. European philosophers such as Rousseau and Hegel described the "Indians" of North America (whom they had never met) as "savages" who were living in a "state of nature," that is, in a state before civilisation. Even the terminology used by the British and French to describe the Indigenous peoples of Turtle Island was denigrating: Europe was divided into nations, while the "Indians" were divided into tribes; Europe had emperors, kings, and aristocrats, while the "Indians" had only chiefs and headmen; White people had history and medicine, while "Indians" had legends and witch doctors; Christianity was a religion requiring faith, but "Indians" had only myths and superstitions. This pattern of cultural denigration was, and remains, a large part of the process of the colonization of Turtle Island. The project of building the nation-state we now call Canada was started by the French and then taken over by the British; it is now being implemented by the multicultural,

Figure 1.1
Growth of GDP per capita, 1800–2012: Argentina, Canada, and China

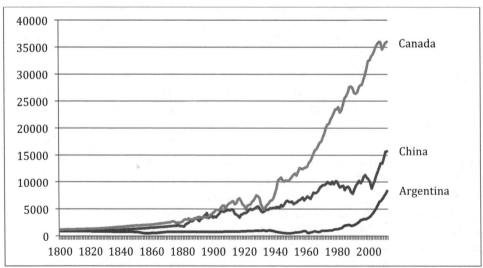

Source: www.gapminder.org

bi-lingual, Canadian state. But we can never forget that Canada was built on top of Turtle Island. In the year 1600, all of Turtle Island belonged to the Indigenous peoples; 400 years later, less than 4 percent of Turtle Island belongs to the Indigenous peoples. In 1600, there were several million Indigenous people on Turtle Island; by 1900, their number had been reduced to under half a million through war, displacement, and new diseases. (See Chapters 9 and 10, and Case Study 9.)

Canada Yesterday and Today

The Canada we know today is a very different country from the Canada that was cobbled together from various British colonies in the late nineteenth century. The population of Canada in 1867 was just below 3.5 million people; today, we are ten times that number. In 1867, the population was 80 percent rural; today, we are over 81 percent urban. With the shift from rural to urban life came a series of profound changes in how Canadians earn their livelihoods. Today, we are likely to work in manufacturing, service industries (restaurants, sales, transport, telecommunications), or knowledge-based industries (IT, research, higher education). In the nineteenth century, most people worked in the primary industries of farming, forestry, fishing, and mining. With the shift from rural to urban life has come a huge increase in our productivity, and with productivity has come greater wealth for almost everyone. On average, we have more disposable income, we live in bigger and more comfortable housing, and we routinely use technologies such as satellite TV, smartphones, and laptop computers that our grandparents never dreamed of.

Figure 1.1 (opposite) shows the increase in Canada's gross domestic product (GDP) per capita over the last 215 years, adjusted for inflation; GDP per capita is a measure of the total output

Figure 1.2
Average Life Expectancy for Argentina, Canada, and China, 1800–2012

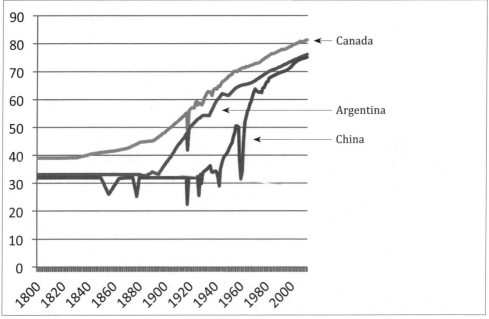

Source: www.gapminder.org

of an economy in a year, per head of population: in other words, average income. Canada's real GDP per capita grew little in the early nineteenth century, but then increased rapidly, much faster than the GDP per capita of other countries that started at similar levels of average income. Figure 1.1 also compares Canada with two such countries, Argentina and China. Today, Canada is one of the richest countries in the world.

We also live longer and healthier lives. In 1867, the average Canadian could expect to live only 41 years, while today average life expectancy is almost twice as long, 81 years. Canada has been more successful than other countries in raising its level of life expectancy, both in terms of improving life expectancy before other countries did and in terms of reaching a higher life expectancy than almost any other country. **Figure 1.2** (previous page) shows Canada's average life expectancy in comparison with Argentina and China.

Back in the nineteenth century, large numbers of people, especially children under five years of age, died of infectious diseases that have now disappeared in Canada or become extremely rare, such as measles, scarlet fever, polio, tetanus, and whooping cough. Even 50 years ago, these diseases were everyday occurrences that passed without public comment. As I wrote the first draft of this chapter, a minor outbreak of measles in Alberta was making national headlines. Once again, Canada has been more successful in reducing under-five mortality (the proportion of children who die before reaching their fifth birthday) than most other countries, as **Figure 1.3** shows. Most of these reductions in mortality, and the concomitant gains in average life expectancy, have been driven by improvements in public health—safe drinking water, sewage treatment, vaccination, better housing, improved nutrition—rather than by improvements in medical or hospital care.

The economic and demographic transformation of Canada over the last two centuries has had a profound impact on the natural environment. When Canada was a poor and

Figure 1.3
Under-five Mortality Rates for Argentina, Canada, and China, 1900–2012

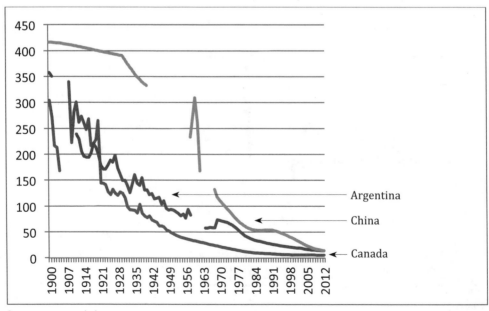

Source: www.gapminder.org

sparsely populated land 200 years ago, humans' impact on the natural environment was usually minimal, except in cities and a few densely populated areas like the St. Lawrence and Annapolis Valleys. The major exception to this rule was the fur trade. Starting in the seventeenth century, French colonists began exporting furs, principally beaver, from Canada to Europe. As the demand for felt hats grew in Europe in the late seventeenth and on into the eighteenth centuries, so too did the fur trade. Soon, the fur trade became a central feature of early modern Canadian history; it drove the European penetration of the interior of North America, it drove European and Métis settlements deeper into the continent; and it became a source of conflict between the British and the French. It also came to have a devastating effect on the natural environment, as beavers were hunted to near extinction in one region after another. In the nineteenth century, the fur trade shifted to buffalo hides as European demand for buffalo coats soared. For centuries, the Indigenous peoples of the Great Plains, the Sioux, Dakota, Lakota, Cree, and Métis, had hunted the buffalo, but they killed only what they could use and the hunt had been sustainable. With the introduction in the nineteenth century of modern firearms and the surge in European demand for buffalo hides, the buffalo were hunted to the brink of extinction. With the large buffalo herds destroyed, settlement of the western prairies by people like my great-grandparents could proceed.

As Canada became more industrialized and more widely and densely populated in the late nineteenth century, humans' impact on the natural environment grew more pronounced. Industrialization brought not only the benefits of manufactured products, but also the production of industrial waste: air, land, and water were increasingly polluted. A richer society based on consumption of goods and services led to the production of increasing amounts of garbage. The spread in the twentieth century of automobiles powered by fossil fuels created air pollution

and, ultimately, climate change. All these processes were driven by a mentality that viewed the natural environment as a "resource" that had to be "developed" or "exploited" and that viewed the air, land, lakes, and rivers as garbage bins into which humans could dump their waste. It is a worldview that is very far from the cosmology of Turtle Island and Indigenous ways of seeing humans as part of, rather than separate from, the natural environment. It was only late in the twentieth century that Canadians, and people in other rich industrialized countries, began to realize the environmental cost of their extractivist approach to development, and to realize the very real limits that the environment will eventually place on our economic and demographic growth.

How we govern ourselves has also changed a lot since the late nineteenth century. In 1867, only white male property owners could vote in federal elections. Most women got the right to vote in federal elections in 1917, but Canadians of Chinese and South Asian descent got the vote only in 1947 and 1948; Indigenous peoples got the right to vote in federal elections only in 1960. In 1921, Agnes Macphail became the first woman to be elected to the Canadian House of Commons, 54 years after the first federal election. In 1929, women were recognized as "persons" in our legal system for the first time. It was not until 90 years after Confederation that the first woman, Ellen Fairclough, took a seat at the federal cabinet table.

Discrimination on the basis of race, sex, religion, sexual orientation, or political creed was not outlawed in Canada until 1960, and similar protections did not become a constitutional requirement until the *Charter of Rights and Freedoms* came into force in 1982. Before then, racial and other forms of discrimination were not only common, but they were legal and widely accepted. For example, John Diefenbaker caused a scandal in 1957 when he became the first Canadian Prime Minister to refuse to join Ottawa's elite Rideau Club, where politicians, senior public servants, businessmen, and journalists met and networked. At that time, the

Rideau Club refused to admit Jews as members, and Diefenbaker refused to join a club that banned Jews. The Rideau Club admitted women as members only in 1978.

As a nation, we have also greatly altered the scope of behaviours that we have chosen to prohibit, or regulate. Sunday shopping and alcohol consumption were particular targets of Protestant religious groups a century ago, as they tried to regulate private behaviour in conformity with their own religious beliefs. Under pressure from religious leaders and the labour unions, the federal parliament in 1906 passed the *Lord's Day Act*, which not only forced almost all businesses to close on Sundays, but also prohibited most cultural, entertainment, and sporting events on Sundays. Some cities, notably Toronto, added municipal by-laws prohibiting people from playing amateur sports on Sundays. Quebec banned women from wearing shorts or skirts above the knee while in public. These laws were relaxed starting in the 1960s. The Supreme Court of Canada overturned the *Lord's Day Act* in 1985 in the face of fierce resistance from religious groups, provincial governments, and labour unions. Today, Sunday shopping is the norm in all provinces except Nova Scotia, and no one would dream of restricting sportspeople, amateur or professional, from playing on a Sunday.

The consumption of alcohol is subject to restrictions and taboos in most societies, but especially in Canada. The Protestant churches and affiliated groups like the Women's Christian Temperance Union fought hard to ban alcohol in Canada a century ago. From 1901 to 1948, Prince Edward Island was a "dry" province; the sale of alcohol was prohibited by provincial law. Ontario was dry from 1916 to 1927, and its taverns were not allowed to reopen until 1934. To this day, the sale of hard liquor in Ontario is a provincial government monopoly. Several First Nations communities have declared themselves dry.

The attempts at banning Sunday shopping, Sunday sports, and alcohol consumption are now viewed as historical curiosities, vain

attempts to impose a puritan form of Christianity on the whole population. But not all such attempts at religious indoctrination in Canada were so benign. Those same Christian churches were deeply involved in a federal government program to destroy Indigenous people's cultures and languages, called the Residential Schools system. Starting in 1876 and peaking around 1930, the federal Department of Indian Affairs (as it was then called) forcibly rounded up Indigenous children of school-going age and forced them to live in residential schools, often located hundreds of miles from their homes and families. The Indigenous children were forbidden to speak their own languages and were often subjected to psychological, physical, and sexual abuse. They were indoctrinated into the Christian religion and Western (basically British or French) ways of life. Indigenous children were taught to view their own cultural and linguistic heritage as inferior. The purpose, according to a deputy minister in charge of the department, was to "kill the Indian in the child." The result was a social and cultural devastation that the Truth and Reconciliation Commission of Canada has compared to a cultural genocide. The residential schools are now closed, the churches and governments involved have apologized, and an independent inquiry has issued a full and damning report. But the horrible legacy of residential schools will remain with us for generations.

As Canadians look at the beliefs and practices of other countries today, especially developing countries with social and religious practices very different from our own, we often denounce them as backward compared to our own modern values. The treatment of women in some predominantly Moslem countries has been a particular topic of commentary in recent years, as well as the predominance of religious schools in such countries and their restrictions on alcohol consumption and usury. Those who make such comments should remember that it was not so long ago that Canadian governments imposed their own version of strict Christianity on an often unwilling public.

In the 150 years since Confederation, our governments have grown a lot bigger, both absolutely and relative to the rest of the economy. In 1867, the federal government was responsible for the post office, banking, currency, weights and measures, interprovincial trade, harbours and railways, policing of the territories, and a very few other areas. Over the years, the federal government has added responsibilities for air transport, food safety, social security, financial regulation, environmental protection, foreign affairs, national defence, telecommunications, and national parks, to name just a few. The responsibilities of provincial and municipal governments have grown in a similar fashion. Today, spending by federal, provincial, and local governments accounts for roughly 42 percent of Canada's GDP.

Migration is a huge part of the story of Canada, whether you or your ancestors came as immigrants or whether you were amongst those, the Indigenous peoples, who were displaced to make room for the immigrants. Until the late nineteenth century, most immigrants came from Britain, France, or Ireland. The "founding peoples" of Confederation, the English, Scottish, Irish, and French, whose national symbols form the Canadian coat of arms (**Figure 1.4**), are still a major part of Canada's population. Much of Canada's political and economic elite still comes from people of those ethnicities. Only one Canadian prime minister to date, the Progressive Conservative John Diefenbaker (1957–1963), has been of something other than British, Irish, or French descent! Starting in the late nineteenth century, large numbers of immigrants started coming from central, eastern, and southern Europe, and from Asia. But after Diefenbaker's government removed the "colour bar" from the *Immigration Act* in 1961, immigrants to Canada have been increasingly non-white. China, the Philippines, South Asia, and the Caribbean now provide most immigrants to Canada. Recent immigrants from these "visible minorities" have mostly settled in the large cities, giving cities a demographic profile quite different from that of rural Canada.

Historically, there has been widespread racism amongst the white population against both the Indigenous peoples and the non-white immigrants. For many years, this racism was institutionalized and perfectly legal. Until 1924, for example, Chinese immigrants—and only Chinese immigrants—had to pay a head tax to enter Canada. Boatloads of Sikh and Jewish would-be immigrants were turned away by racist Canadian authorities in 1914 and 1939; the Jews on those boats had to return to Europe and most were murdered in Nazi concentration camps. Japanese Canadians were interned in camps and had their property confiscated in the Second World War. (See Chapter 6.)

Today, such racial discrimination is illegal. Successive Canadian governments, including the Conservative government led by Stephen Harper (2006–2015), have apologized for the Chinese head tax, the internment of Japanese Canadians, residential schools, and other past acts of institutional racism. The official policy of multiculturalism, instituted by the Liberal

Figure 1.4
Coat of Arms of Canada

government of Pierre Trudeau (1968–1979 and 1980–1984) in 1971, was enshrined in the *Charter of Rights and Freedoms* in 1982. Resisting some elements in his own party, Stephen Harper made it his mission to court non-white voters in his early years in power, with some success. In his later years as prime minister, however, Harper pivoted back to what he called "old stock" (i.e., white) Canadians and his government proposed (and sometimes enacted) a series of policies that essentially targeted people of colour, especially Moslems. In 2015, Harper's government was defeated by the Liberals, led by Justin Trudeau, who promised "sunny ways" and a more pluralist and inclusive society and a rejuvenated relationship with Indigenous peoples. Still, institutionalized racism remains deeply rooted in many parts of Canadian society, not least in the military, the police, and the criminal justice system. In many Canadian cities, your chances of being "randomly" stopped by the police increase dramatically if you are black, Indigenous, or Arab. If you are an Indigenous woman and you go missing, the police will likely not take your case as seriously as they would other missing persons cases. In the race to succeed Harper as Conservative Party leader in 2016–2017, several candidates ran on thinly veiled anti-immigrant platforms.

Canada and the Processes of "Development" and "Globalization"

Three things should be clear from this thumbnail sketch of Canadian history. The first is that Canada was not always the prosperous, stable, pluralist, and democratic country that it is today. Our ancestors used to be a lot poorer than we are today. Their lives were routinely cut short by diseases that are now extremely rare. They were less likely to go to school or to learn how to read and write. Materially, we are much more prosperous today than we were a century or two ago. The beliefs and practices of Canadians a century ago on issues such as race, gender,

sexual orientation, and religion do not come up to our current standards of what is acceptable in a modern pluralist democracy.

This process of a country getting richer, healthier, longer-lived, and more literate is often referred to as development. As it applies to the conscious effort to help poorer countries improve their lot, it is often referred to as "international development." Canada is today described by various sources as a "developed country," a "high income country," and a "high human development country." In essence, this means that Canadians have a high level of income per capita, long life expectancy, high levels of literacy, and low levels of absolute poverty such as starvation and destitution. The process of moving away from authoritarian forms of rule towards political democracy has been called "political development." There are many ways of looking at development and Chapter 2 will explain the main schools of thought and some of the debates around the term. To say that a country is "developed" is not to suggest that it has solved all its problems, or that it cannot improve further. It does mean, however, that both in relation to many other countries and in relation to its own past, the country has attained a high level of material prosperity and a high quality of life for its citizens, or at least for most of them.

The second thing that should be clear is that Canada's history is also full of violence; forced displacements; discrimination against women, Indigenous peoples, immigrants, people of colour/visible minorities, Catholics, non-Christians, LGBTQ people, and others; and social and political tensions based on class, race, nationality, religion, region, and language. Many of the challenges that Canada faces today—not least Canada's troubled relations with its Indigenous peoples, but also the seemingly eternal debates about Quebec's role in the Canadian confederation—have their roots in these old patterns of violence, displacement, discrimination, and political tensions.

The third thing that is clear from this thumbnail sketch of Canadian history is that our history is inextricably linked with key facts of global history: colonization, empire, international migration, international trade, and war. Canada has been shaped by all these. And, especially since the end of the Second World War, Canada has taken a lead role in shaping world history. In 1945, Canada was a founding member of the United Nations (UN). In 1949, Canada became a founding member of the North Atlantic Treaty Organization (NATO). In 1976, Canada became a member of the G7, the influential grouping of what were then the largest liberal democratic capitalist economies. Economically, too, Canada is now a big player on the world stage. Almost a third of the world's potash, an agricultural fertilizer, comes from Canada. Over 60 percent of the world's publicly traded mining companies have their shares traded on Canadian stock exchanges; this means that how Canada chooses to regulate, or not regulate, the mining industry has global consequences. Canada is and has always been part of the process of globalization.

So, if Canada can rise from being a marginal collection of colonies on the fringes of two empires, a place torn by social, religious, political, and ethnic tensions, a country whose relations with its neighbour were for decades tense and even violent, to being a stable, prosperous, pluralist, and democratic country living in peace with its neighbour, can other countries not do the same? How you answer that question depends a lot on how much importance you attach to each of the three points above.

And how you answer that question is important, for it is a key question in international development and globalization studies. Researchers, scholars, politicians, and pundits of various stripes have come up with very different answers to that question, based on their underlying theories of development.

In everyday speech, we use the word "theory" to mean a hunch, a guess, or a belief. That is not how the word is used in social science. In social science, a theory is an overarching explanation of a given phenomenon, a statement that lays out the most important factors at play and how they relate to each other. A theory seeks to explain how and why a system or a process unfolds the way it does, and what makes it work that way. In social science, theory is the highest form of knowledge.

One theory of development stresses the progress we have made, the step-by-step changes that have, over the long haul, allowed Canada to move up the ladder from a relatively poor, weak state with low life expectancy, primitive technology, and a non-representative form of government to our current status as wealthy, stable, pluralist, democratic country, with a capable and stable government, high levels of technology, and high levels of health and education. This theory of development is called **modernizationism**. Modernizationists believe that today's developing countries can move up the ladder of economic growth, social modernization, and democracy in much the same way that Canada did. Modernizationists come in two main varieties.

The first type, modernizationists trained in history, sociology, and (sometimes) political science, stress the role of changing values in promoting economic growth, social cohesions, and thus development. According to this view, certain social values are more conducive to economic growth and social cohesion than others. The American sociologist Talcott Parsons suggested that people in "traditional" societies valued immediate gratification, were oriented towards primordial loyalties like family or tribe, respected other people according to their inherited social status, and were community-oriented. As "traditional" societies become more "modern societies," Parsons suggested, people become more individualistic, more likely to save for the future, more oriented to general rules rather than primordial loyalties, and more likely to value individual achievement over inherited social status. From this view flows the notion that development is largely about changing social values, and that change and development come from within a society. It includes a view that development is a linear path from primitive to traditional to modern societies. Current writers such as Francis Fukuyama, Niall Ferguson, and Bernard Lewis promote the latest versions of this brand of modernizationism.

The second type of modernizationists are trained in economics (and sometimes political science); they believe that development is best promoted by making long-term investments in infrastructure (roads, railways, electrical grids, telecommunications networks, sewers, and water supply), and by adopting improved technologies for higher productivity. The American economist W.W. Rostow believed that there were five stages of development: "traditional society," "the pre-conditions for take-off," the "take-off" of economic growth, "the drive to maturity," and the "age of high mass consumption." This was a controversial view, including amongst economists.

Other modernizationists point out that political democracy almost always comes after the country has achieved a certain level of per capita income. Promoters of such views include Karl Deutsch and Seymour Martin Lipset. A variant led by political scientist Samuel Huntington emphasizes the need to maintain political order as a prerequisite for economic growth and development, even if that means authoritarian rule.

Mainstream economic theory emphasizes the positive role played throughout Canadian history by private enterprise and free markets, or capitalism, in the development of Canada. Such thinkers focus on the pursuit of the profit as a driver of economic decision making in both big and small businesses. They recall how entrepreneurs took risks, borrowed money, built businesses, and thereby created not only wealth for the owners of capital but also employment and prosperity for their employees. They stress the fact that most immigrants were attracted to Canada by the prospect of such economic freedom and the prospect of a higher material standard of living. They came from countries where certain types of people, such as ethnic minorities, were forbidden to practise certain professions; few such restrictions existed in Canada, making

it a more attractive place to live and work. Such authors often criticize government for unduly constraining Canada's private sector. These authors favour free trade on the grounds that it expands the markets for Canada's exports and allows Canadians to import the best products from abroad at the lowest possible prices. Such thinkers have historically been labelled as "liberals" (with a small "l"), or in more recent years, as "neoliberals." Many people who call themselves "conservatives" hold similar views. Most economists in Canada hold to some form of this theory. They draw for their inspiration on such early economists as Adam Smith and David Ricardo, as well as late-twentieth-century exponents such as Robert Bates, Peter Bauer, and Anne Krueger. Popularisers of this view inside Canada include Thomas d'Aquino, Kevin O'Leary, and the Fraser Institute.

A related theory stresses the importance of institutions in the development of Canada. Institutions are the formal and informal rules and customs that govern human behaviour. Some sets of institutions, for example private property, the rule of law, and an independent judiciary that enforces written laws, are conducive to economic growth, private enterprise, and social harmony. Such institutions are sometimes called "inclusive." Other types of institutions produce economic stagnation, social strife, and even economic decline, and are sometimes called "extractive." Such thinkers contrast the set of productive, inclusive institutions that rich, democratic countries like Canada have with weak or dysfunctional institutions in countries like the Democratic Republic of the Congo, where the government has historically done little more than exploit the general populace in order to enrich the ruling elites. These "neo-institutionalist" thinkers differ as to whether inclusive institutions can be built by conscious effort and design, or whether they evolve slowly, through Burkean experimentation and the happenstance of how critical moments in history get resolved. Daron Acemoglu, Douglass North, James Robinson, and Dani Rodrik are leading exponents of neo-institutionalism.

A very different way of understanding Canada's history is to emphasize our history as a colony, first of France, then of Britain, and finally, some would say, as an economic colony of the United States. According to this school of thought, throughout Canada's history, our economy has been built around producing staple products for export. These staple products were initially beaver pelts (seventeenth to nineteenth century) and buffalo hides (nineteenth century), but later lumber (nineteenth century) and wheat (nineteenth and twentieth century), and then fertilisers, metals, and petroleum (twentieth and twenty-first centuries). Because we have built our economy largely around the export of such primary (or "raw") commodities, our industrial growth has been stunted, and industry has been oriented to providing inputs into the staple industries or to providing minimal, first-stage processing of staple products, such as sawing lumber. Much of Canada's economic growth has been funded by foreign capital, initially British and later American. Foreign firms have dominated our economy. As a consequence of all these factors, Canada has not been a major creator of new technologies, but has paid to import these technologies from abroad; very few Canadian companies have become world leaders in their fields. This school of thought has several variants, but they all might usefully be grouped under the label of **economic nationalism**. Major thinkers in this uniquely Canadian brand of political economy are Stephen Clarkson, Harold Innis, Kari Polanyi Levitt, Abraham Rotstein, and Mel Watkins.

In the developing countries of the world, a related theory, which emphasizes the pernicious and continuing effects of colonialism, imperialism, and capitalism, is called **dependency theory** or "world systems" theory. In this view, development and underdevelopment cannot be understood without understanding the world economic system. Andre Gunder Frank, for example, states that "underdevelopment" is not an original or natural state of affairs; rather, today's underdeveloped economies are the products of capitalist imperialism, which fundamentally restructured those economies and societies for its own profit and benefit. Hence, the possibilities for growth and development in the Third World are constrained by the international economic system. Leading thinkers in this field include Andre Gunder Frank, Samir Amin, Walter Rodney (for dependency theory), Immanuel Wallerstein (for world systems theory), and Johan Galtung. In its cruder forms (Frank and Rodney), dependency theory has trouble explaining the recent rise of the BRICS (Brazil, Russia, India, China and South Africa) as increasingly wealthy and influential nations. (See Chapter 13). A more nuanced version of dependency theory promoted by Fernando Cardoso, Enzo Faletto and Peter Evans suggests that the Third World can experience development in the current system, but that we must understand the links between national and international factors affecting development.

A related theory is Marxism. Like dependency theory, Marxism says that capitalism is an exploitative system that generates inequality, exclusion, and crisis. But most Marxists also stress that capitalism was a revolutionary, indeed progressive, force in human history, given its capacity to accumulate capital, create new technologies, and drive economic growth. Older versions of Marxism are close to modernizationism in that they see development as a linear process of stages. Marxists who focus on the internationalization of capital and its effects are close to dependency theory. Prominent Marxists in development studies include Claude Ake, Bill Warren, and, of course, Karl Marx himself.

Less radical, more pragmatic, policy-oriented, and sometimes nationalist is the branch of development studies known as structuralist or heterodox economics. (Political) economists like Ha-Joon Chang, Celso Furtado, Gerald Helleiner, Richard Jolly, Raúl Prebisch, Dudley Seers, Frances Stewart, and Joseph Stiglitz do not neglect the importance of the colonial legacy, nor do they underestimate the highly imperfect nature of markets, capitalism, and the rules that govern the global economy. But they also stress the ability of proper government policies to overcome these problems, given time, political leadership, and pragmatism, especially if international institutions are reformed as well. They show that countries with initially similar starting points have produced vastly different development results, depending largely on the policies they have applied. An important variant of this school emphasizes that development is about creating human development and capabilities so that individuals can lead fulfilling lives; leading figures in this variant include Martha Nussbaum and Amartya Sen.

Drawing on continental European thinkers like Karl Marx, Sigmund Freud, and Michel Foucault, and emphasizing Canada's history of domination, oppression, exclusion, exploitation, and both overt and structural violence is yet another school of thought, called postmodernism. Postmodernist thinkers do not celebrate Canada as a stable, free, pluralist, and democratic society with a high material standard of living. Rather, they stress that violence, domination, exclusion, and inequality have been omnipresent in our history, starting with the first interactions between the European settlers and the Indigenous peoples. The precise targets of that domination and exclusion and the technologies of domination have changed over time. European settlers once tried to solve "the Indian problem" by providing Indigenous people with blankets tainted with smallpox, then they tried residential schools, and now they grind them down with a paternalistic bureaucracy in the name of "accountability." But the essence of our social, economic, and political systems remains domination, according to this interpretation of our history. Postmodernist thinkers include Arturo Escobar, Gustavo Esteva, James Ferguson, Gilbert Rist, and Vandana Shiva.

Postcolonialism combines elements from postmodernism, dependency theory, and subaltern studies (see below). In postcolonial thinking, as in postmodernism, relations of domination do not end with the formal political independence of a country or with the granting of formal political and civil rights. Like the dependency thinkers, postcolonial thinkers stress Canada's role in maintaining Western domination (which they often call "hegemony") over developing countries, usually in alliance with the great imperial powers such as France, the United Kingdom, and the United States. According to these thinkers, postcolonial hegemony is present inside Canada as well, notably in Canada's oppressive relations with its Indigenous peoples. Like subaltern studies, postcolonialism emphasizes the fact that people frequently resist efforts to impose postcolonial domination. Leading postcolonial thinkers include Mahmood Mamdani, Edward Saïd, and Ngũgĩ wa Thiong'o.

Feminist theory stresses the unequal gender relations throughout Canadian history, even after formal legal equality was achieved via the *Charter of Rights and Freedoms* in 1982. Gender-based violence, sexist stereotypes in the media, and informal rules in both society and the economy subordinate women (and girls) and subject them to a myriad of daily humiliations. In a form of analysis knows as "intersectionality," it is stressed that oppression based on gender frequently overlaps with other forms of oppression in our society, such as social class, ethnicity, and language. For example, the unexplained disappearances (i.e., murders) of hundreds of young Indigenous women in Canada require an intersectional analysis. In another example, Moslem women are often subject to sexism within their own communities and to Islamophobia from non-Moslems. According to the feminist theorists, no account of the "development" of Canada is complete without telling the story of women as the subjects, objects, and agents of that development, within the context of unequal gender relations. In a similar vein, other scholars and activists emphasize the role of homophobia in marginalising LGBTQ people throughout our history. Important feminist scholars working on international development include Bina Agarwal, Diane Elson, Devaki Jain, Naila Kabeer, and Martha Nussbaum.

An often neglected way to tell history is to tell it from below. Most accounts of the history, politics, and economics in Canada tell the stories of the leaders, the famous politicians, generals, businessmen (yes, usually men), activists, and scientists who have shaped our world. Our daily news follows this same pattern of focusing on the rich and powerful. But what would history look like from below, as told by the underlings, the ordinary farmers and workers, the unemployed and the homeless? What if history were written by the victims of progress and development, for example by those whose industries and livelihoods were destroyed by technological progress? How would the story of Canada differ if it were told from the perspective of Indigenous peoples? Or from the perspective of a woman trafficked into Canada for the purposes of the sex trade? Such studies, called subaltern studies, tell history as seen from below. They not only stress the victims of development, but they concentrate on the agency (i.e., the ability to act autonomously) of such people as they resist their oppression and struggle to realize their own dreams. Uma Kothari, Terence Ranger, and James Scott have written important works from a subaltern perspective; many of the authors classified as feminist, postmodernist, or postcolonial (see above) can also be classified as subaltern theorists. Related thinkers like Robert Chambers and Paolo Freire stress the need to empower the poorest members of society.

Finally, environmental theories of development believe that our current models of development, based on economic growth and increased consumption of goods and services, has been harmful to the natural environment. Environmentalists stress that our finite globe cannot accommodate infinite growth in the economy and the human population. Mainstream environmentalists believe that we need to protect the natural environment, especially by reducing our carbon footprint to put the brakes on climate change. They believe that a combination of better public policies (e.g., a carbon tax, more public transport, recycling), public education, and improved technologies (e.g., solar and wind power, electric cars) will be able to do this. More radical environmentalists question the whole development project; in this view, our industrial and consumerist society is the problem. Simply put, we are in danger of polluting ourselves out of existence. We must consume less and control human population growth. David Suzuki is the leading Canadian environmentalist; the UN's Intergovernmental Panel on Climate Change is the single most authoritative source on that issue. All these theories are laid out in **Table 1.1**.

Table 1.1

Theories of Development and Globalization

Name of Theory	According to This Theory...	
	The Main Barrier to Development Is	What Promotes Good Development Is
Modernization – Cultural Version	Traditional cultural values.	Modern social values.
Modernization – Economic Version	Lack of savings and investment.	Domestic and international investment.
Liberal (Free-Market) Economics	Excessive government regulation of the economy.	Private property rights and free enterprise.
Neo-institutionalism	Extractive institutions.	Inclusive institutions and rule of law.
Economic Nationalism	International capital and local structural rigidities.	National policies to counter international capital and promote local growth.
Dependency/ World Systems	International capitalism or the world system.	Socialist revolution; de-linking from the global economy.
Marxism	Inequality based on capitalist accumulation and crisis.	Capitalism (up to a point), then socialism.
Structuralist/ Heterodox Economics	Poor policies, unfavourable international context, local structural rigidities.	Pragmatic public policies at national and international levels.
Human Development and Capabilities	Lack of investment in health, education, nutrition. Gender inequality.	Investment in health, nutrition, education, gender equality, and social protection.
Post-modernism	Development is a myth.	It doesn't matter. Development is a myth.
Feminism	Patriarchy and misogyny.	Gender equality.
Subaltern Studies	Unequal power relations.	Empowering the subalterns, i.e., the poor and weak.
Post-colonialism	Unequal power relations based on colonial stereotypes and neo-colonial practices.	Development is a colonial myth that must be overthrown.
Mainstream Environmentalism	Lack of sustainability.	Sustainable lifestyles, environmentally friendly policies and technologies.
Radical Environmentalism	Development is the problem, not the solution.	Development is the problem, not the solution.

Our Analytical Focus Should Be On	The Main Policy Prescription Is	Economic Growth
Changing the traditional culture and promoting modernity.	To promote and embody modern values and practices.	Is desirable and is promoted by modern values.
Capital formation.	To promote public and private investment.	Is the key to development.
Ensuring the free functioning of the market economy.	To intervene in markets only when absolutely necessary.	Is the key to development.
Institutional change.	To build institutions that promote growth.	Is desirable.
How the national economy is structured by local and international forces.	Active regulation of the economy in the national interest.	Is desirable, if it promotes national development.
How global capitalism has created under-development.	De-linking from the global economy. Socialist economic planning to promote national development.	Is desirable, but only under socialism.
The material basis of society, patterns of accumulation.	Socialist revolution or a peaceful transition to socialism. Then central economic planning.	Is desirable but only up to a point, and then capitalism creates a crisis.
Finding where markets do and do not work, and why.	To correct market failures and promote human development and capabilities.	Is desirable, but growth is not the ultimate goal. Human development is the ultimate goal.
Finding ways to help individuals realize their full set of capabilities and so be free.	Development is about people, not things. Promote human development.	Is desirable, but growth is not the ultimate goal. Human development is the ultimate goal.
Understanding the many forms of domination.	State and market are both realms of domination. All policy is domination.	Is not interested in growth; economic growth is a form of domination.
Gendered social relations and how they interact with other forms of oppression.	To promote gender equality (and fight other injustices).	Can be a good thing, but who benefits from growth matters a great deal.
How subalterns resist oppression.	The state is part of unequal power relations.	May be alright but distribution of benefits is the key issue.
Studying how colonial power relations persist and how they can be resisted.	Not interested in policy prescriptions, but often critical of individual policy choices.	Is interested in growth only insofar as it affects power relations.
Humans as part of the biophysical environment.	Promoting sustainable lifestyles and green technologies.	Is the problem, at least in the way we have pursued growth till now.
Active regulation of the economy in the interest of the environment.	Abolishing consumer culture and smashing corporate power.	Is the problem.

Conclusion

Canada's history is a complicated one, and no single narrative, let alone a short chapter in a textbook, can do it justice. What is clear is that Canada has developed, in the sense of having undergone a series of profound economic, social, and political transformations, over the decades and centuries. The Canada we know today would be unrecognizable to our ancestors from even 50 years ago, never mind 100 or 150 years ago. At the same time, Canada has been deeply affected by, and now substantially affects, the flows of world history: overseas wars, intercontinental migration, long-distance trade, incoming and outgoing foreign investments, foreign aid, scientific discovery, and diplomacy. Canada is a country of international development and globalization.

Questions for Further Learning

- Write your own family history in five pages or less. If you are descended from immigrants, when, how, and why did they come to Canada? What was Canada like when they arrived? If you are an Indigenous person, how has your family been affected by the arrival of immigrants and settlers?

- How has Canada's history as a colony of both Britain and France affected the Canada we live in today? List at least five features of modern Canada that result directly from that dual heritage. What other countries have been colonies of both Britain and France? (There are three!)

- Women, Indigenous peoples, non-white immigrants. For each of these groups, describe their social, economic, and political situation in Canada in the late nineteenth century, around the mid-twentieth century, and today. What has changed and not changed? Why?

- Should Canada take a more activist role in international affairs? If so, how (e.g., militarily, economically, diplomatically)? Justify your answer. Compare the role you propose for Canada to the role(s) it has played in the past.

Key Terms

capitalism, p. 18

colonialism, p. 5

dependency, p. 19

development, p. 16

economic nationalism, p. 19

Indigenous peoples, p. 9

institutions, p. 18

modernization, p. 17

modernizationism, p. 17

(neo) liberalism, p. 18

pluralism, p. 3

subaltern studies, p. 21

theory, p. 17

Suggested Readings

So many books are published on Canadian history, politics, economics, and international relations that it is hard to keep any list up to date. Instead, I offer some enduring classics from different periods of our history:

Brown, George Williams, ed. 1950. *Canada*. United Nations Series, University of California Press, Berkeley, and University of Toronto Press, Toronto. (Leading Canadian scholars of the mid-twentieth century reflect on Canada in the aftermath of the Second World War.)

Colombo, John Robert. 1976. *Colombo's Canadian References*. Oxford University Press, Toronto. (Half dictionary, half encyclopedia, this book reflects the high tide of English Canadian nationalism.)

Truth and Reconciliation Commission of Canada. 2015. *Honouring the Truth, Reconciling for the Future: Summary of the Final Report of the Truth and Reconciliation Commission of Canada*. Truth and Reconciliation Commission of Canada, Ottawa. www.trc.ca. (The wrenching truth about Canada's relations with Indigenous peoples, now in an official report.)

Vallières, Pierre. 1969. *White Niggers of America*. McClelland & Stewart, Toronto. (Literally a call to arms in the name of militant Quebec nationalism.)

Wrong, George M., and H. H. Langton, eds. 1915. *Chronicles of Canada*. 32 volumes. Glasgow, Brook and Company, Toronto. (This represents one of the first attempts at a professional history of Canada. Many aspects of our self-image as a country are rooted in these books.)

Suggested Videos

Canada: The Story of Us – CBC: http://www.cbc.ca/2017/canadathestoryofus/
Engaging the World – Harpelle and Muirhead: http://engagingtheworld.ca/about/
Historica Canada's Heritage Minutes: https://www.historicacanada.ca/heritageminutes

Suggested Websites

Assembly of First Nations: http://www.afn.ca/index.php/en
Canada's History: http://www.canadashistory.ca/home.aspx
Canadian Association for the Study of International Development: https://www.casid-acedi.ca/
Government of Canada: https://www.canada.ca/home.html
See also
Indigenous and Northern Affairs Canada: https://www.aadnc-aandc.gc.ca/
Canadian Heritage: http://www.pch.gc.ca
Global Affairs Canada: www.international.gc.ca
Library and Archives Canada: http://www.bac-lac.gc.ca
Government of Quebec: http://www.gouv.qc.ca/portail/quebec/pgs/commun/?lang=en.
Historica Canada: https://www.historicacanada.ca/

Works Cited

McCullagh, Violet (Perry). 1968. *The Pioneering Perrys*. Private printing, Winnipeg.
www.gapminder.org for all statistics in this chapter.

Notes

2 International Development

An Overview of Definitions, Historical Evolution, and Debates

Mahmoud Masaeli

Key Terms

international development

Cold War

economic growth

modernization theory

moral responsibility to help

human development

dependency theory

neoliberalism

Sustainable Development Goals

Overview

"Development" is a contested term. It stands for different ideas, theories, policies, programs of action, and practices by scholars, policy makers, strategists, practitioners, and institutions that promise a better life for all. The vagueness in the meaning of the concept urges fundamental questions. What is the precise meaning of development? Whose condition of life must be improved through development? What does improvement stand for, and in what sense? Who is the subject of development? Does it embrace the condition of life of those whose distinct voice has been stifled by the predominant discourse of development? The main goal is to argue that international development, as a Western enterprise, was constructed for specific purposes. In the beginning, the post–Second World War condition, this enterprise was firmly associated with the Cold War policies of the West. For this reason, the mainstream view of international development essentially reflects the worldview and the interests of Western countries.

Learning Objectives

By the end of this chapter, students will be able to:

- understand the main concepts and theories of development applied in the international sphere.
- explain the main assumptions of a wide range of the theories of international development.
- understand how different theories present the needs of their own time and conditions, to what degree these theories have been successful in achieving their promises.
- evaluate the different theories by looking at the conditions in which they have been applied.
- criticize the structural constraints pertinent especially to the mainstream theories of development.

Theory and Practice of Development: From National to International

The emergence of the discipline of international development after the Second World War is marked by three characteristics. First, theorists and practitioners of development reoriented their own understanding and conception of development as a means of achieving a better life from the domestic sphere to the international domain. The main argument in favour of this reorientation derives from modernization theory, in accordance with which science and technology end suffering from economic stagnation and backwardness. Since colonial rule did not seek to improve the standards of living of the colonized peoples, the urgent question for the leaders of the newly independent countries after 1945 was how to modernize the country and achieve rapid economic growth. At the same time, and with the purpose of winning the hearts and minds of the people of these developing countries, the leaders of advanced societies led by the United States initiated technical assistance programs to help those countries in their aspiration for economic progress and prosperity (Truman 1949). In this context, economic development became a major subject in international relations.

The second characteristic is related to the emergence of a new moral outlook urging assistance programs for people of developing countries in the post–Second World War context. This moral outlook had its roots in the classical liberal tradition of the eighteenth century, encouraging entrepreneurial spirit as the engine of economic growth for prosperity.

Implicit in this spirit is the cardinal importance of freedom and democratic atmosphere for economic progress. Since this path to a prosperous life was presumed to be universal in scope and breadth, it was assumed to be inspiring for all societies, regardless of their own cultures and identities. Accordingly, liberal nations were feeling morally responsible to share their own development experience and scientific achievements with others to boost their economic growth as the gateway to prosperity (Ekbladh 2010; Rist 2008).

The Christian faith was at the heart of this sense of moral responsibility to help. As a central theological doctrine, Christianity requires all believers to assist their brothers and sisters to overcome their hardships. This progressive social perspective from Christianity requires that believers commit themselves to the protection of equal dignity of all human beings, and for this purpose to take necessary measures to eliminate servitude, deprivation, and poverty (Schweiker 1995). Indeed, the religious duty of believers serves the attainment of the common good of all without distinction. This moral duty in Christianity requires practical actions by the believers to do their best to improve the condition of life of disadvantaged people. Moral responsibility to assist those who are in hardship is intrinsic in a living Gospel.

In addition, Christians are individually called to make God the centre of their being. Believers in the Christian faith should be transformed by the healing presence of God, and allow God to continue to work through their spirit to heal the whole world. This is a moral mission toward all others, especially the poor, whether they are the sinners or the righteous. Indeed, the Bible commands believers to focus on the ultimate goal of the faith to free people from hardship (Gosnell 2014).

The two sources of moral thoughts, moral liberalism and Christian morality, cast a powerful light on the issues of poor living conditions, underdevelopment, and poverty in the former colonies. However, this powerful outlook toward assisting developing countries deviated from its original promise and soon turned toward a distorted meaning of moral responsibility. The West, including the former colonizers, assumed that the only responsibility incumbent on them was a *moral responsibility to help* and not *a duty to justice*. In addition, such responsibility to assist developing countries in attaining a prosperous life remained limited to only economic growth, without regard for social, political, and human development. This growth was seen to be promoted through foreign aid programs and interventionist policies. To put it in a nutshell, from its inception, international development was tailored in economic growth motivated by a moral responsibility to help, and through generous Western foreign aid programs.

By their liberal spirit, Western liberal societies are committed to the freedom and well-being of the others. This commitment is accomplished through help. *Moral responsibility to help is what we owe to others.*

The third characteristic is the relationship of international development with the Cold War (1946–1989), the ideological and strategic rivalry between the capitalist, liberal democratic West (including Canada) and the Communist world led by the Soviet Union. Indeed, and from the beginning, international development was implanted as a strategic plan to make developing countries conform to Western liberalism as a way of reducing the threat of communism. This agenda by the United States, which was the leading power after the Second World War, aimed to link the economic growth of developing countries with the security concerns of the Cold War in international politics. With its European and other allies, the United States initiated aid programs, technological assistance, and foreign investment in developing countries. Aid was supposed to ensure that developing countries directed their course of life from the colonial condition toward economic growth. Economic growth, it was believed, would bring political stability in the post-colonial world and a safe environment of collaboration with Western liberal democracies. This aspiration was especially stimulated by the fear in the West of the influence of communism in the vulnerable political condition of newly independent countries. Development programs were, indeed, instrumental in maintaining the peaceful world order against the threats of communism (Latham 2011).

We must embark on a bold new program for making the benefits of our scientific advances and industrial progress available for the improvement and growth of underdeveloped areas. (Truman 1949).

The moral responsibility to help, foreign aid programs, and alliance-making formed the mainstream approach in international development from the time of its inception in the late 1940s. However, this view of development was not immune to criticisms and challenges. Influenced by the ideology of socialism, a group of developing countries refused to align with the West. In addition, starting in the 1970s, the emergence of alternative perspectives depicting development as a multidimensional process involving social, political, and cultural aspects, and human development, began to challenge the mainstream perspective of development as economic growth. It is worth noting that these alternative voices were echoed by development ethicists proposing a deeper and more constructive understanding of the realities of developing countries. Accordingly, international development from the end of the Second World War until the mid-1970s was oriented in three basically contradictory directions:

1. the Western-inspired and liberal mainstream theory of development as growth,
2. the socialist and nationalistic views of development, and
3. alternative approaches, including ethical visions of development.

This split in development perspectives merits further historical analysis. The beginning of the mainstream theories of international development traces back to US President Harry Truman's inaugural address on January 20, 1949:

> The United States is pre-eminent among nations in the development of industrial and scientific techniques. The material resources which we can afford to use for assistance of other peoples are limited. But our imponderable resources in technical knowledge are constantly growing and are inexhaustible.
> I believe that we should make available to the peace-loving peoples the benefits of our store of technical knowledge in order to help them realize their aspirations for a better life. And, in cooperation with other nations, we should foster capital investment in areas needing development. (Truman 1949)

Truman further reminded his listeners that the failure in his program would make vulnerable communities susceptible to communist takeover; in Truman's view, vulnerability to communism was caused by backwardness. A brief analysis of the statement discloses the relationship of this plan of action with the political atmosphere of the Cold War era. Truman's plan did not derive primarily from humanitarian concerns. Rather, the United States undertook this mission for political and economic purposes. Politically speaking, through aid programs, the US president wanted to confront the challenge of communism. Furthermore, from an economic perspective, the United States wanted to boost its own economy through the establishment of links with developing countries instead of the then war-devastated economy of Europe (Pierce 2007).

Truman's international development proposal also signalled the emergence of a discourse that saw developing countries as inferior in capability. This vision latent in Truman's speech is that the West is a saviour. The saviour is on a mission to help other countries that, due to internal reasons, are not able to overcome their problems. In addition, if developing countries are not assisted in their process of economic growth, they may become threats to the West by joining the Communist bloc. By giving foreign aid to these countries, the West can maintain a peaceful and stable international order and promote prosperity at the same time. Truman's 1949 speech marked the beginning of a discourse that set up a binary distinction between "the West and the Rest," as **Table 2.1** illustrates. This binary has only recently started to go out of fashion. (See Chapter 13.)

In the 1960s, a more sophisticated perspective of development appeared in the international community. In fact, at a time of massive unrest caused by the post-colonial rupture, the United Nations proclaimed the 1960s as the Development Decade. However, this initiative was still largely aligned with the mainstream view of development as economic growth propelled by foreign aid. The decade was nonetheless full of emotion and promise, as several dozen African, Caribbean, and other countries cast off their colonial status and made their own way in the world, often inclined to follow socialist prescriptions for the better life. To prevent what the West saw as the disaster of socialism, there was a need for an accelerated aid program in the form of funds and know-how from technologically advanced and economically rich countries.

Table 2.1
The West–Rest Binary

Western Societies (The West)	Developing Countries (The Rest)
Scientifically advanced and innovative	Traditional and backward
Economically developed and industrialized	Unable to produce the basic necessities of life
Technological knowledge	Illiteracy and impoverishment
Prosperous and affluent	Suffering from poverty
Progress and constant growth	Retrospective and stagnant
Free society and democracy	Vulnerable and prone to communism
Democratic and justice-advocating	Despotic and politically backward
Peace-loving and law-abiding	Potentially aggressive and a threat to international peace

Shadowed by the Cold War rivalry that reached its zenith in the 1960s, American President John F. Kennedy (1961–1963) undertook a mission, one that was similar to Truman's a decade earlier. In his inaugural address, Kennedy suggested accelerated aid programs and technological assistance to "those peoples in the huts and villages of half the globe struggling to break the bonds of mass misery" (Kennedy 1961). He further emphasized that the West must pledge its best efforts to help developing countries help themselves. According to this new plan for international development, decolonizing countries were seen as deserving of more assistance in their road to economic growth through partnership with the West. The strategic considerations are obvious in this plan, even though it was labelled by the United Nations as the First Decade for Development. In a time of heated ideological/strategic confrontation between the free world and the Communist bloc, the slogan to help the developing countries in their economic development was a very attractive promise. The Western-led aid programs for rapid economic growth became a powerful discourse around which alliance making was justified.

> There is no escaping our obligations: our moral obligations as a wise leader and good neighbor in the interdependent community of free nations—our economic obligations as the wealthiest people in a world of largely poor people, as a nation no longer dependent upon the loans from abroad that once helped us develop our own economy—and our political obligations as the single largest counter to the adversaries of freedom. (Kennedy 1961)

In line with this justification for more urgent measures against both ascendant nationalism and spreading communism, Walt Whitman Rostow, an American economist, presented his vindication of economic growth for developing countries. In his book, *The Stages of Economic Growth*, published in 1960, economic growth, mediated through modernization, is imperative in development. Rostow suggested that development was indispensable for prosperity and that each nation must pass through five stages of economic growth, as shown in **Figure 2.1**.

To develop, developing countries must leave traditional social relations and enter into the preconditions for take-off via installation of infrastructure supported by foreign assistance. Following this stage, the take-off in economic growth takes place and drives the country into the stage of maturity. The ultimate stage in the attainment of economic development is the age of mass consumption. Rostow suggested

Figure 2.1
Rostow's Stages of Economic Growth

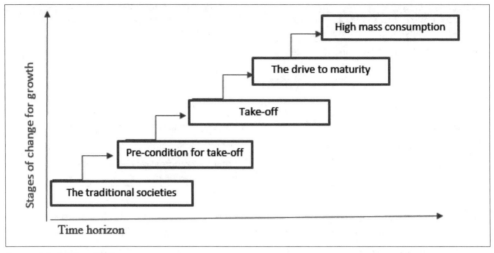

Source: Adapted from Rostow, 1971.

that this mediated process of economic growth requires technological modernization and social evolution. In this model, development for a better life is portrayed with a purely economic face, since the ultimate goal of development is mass consumption.

Rostow's theory of economic growth established significant elements for the development of nations: endogenous motivation in development; the critical importance of entrepreneurial spirit, investment, and the accumulation of capital; and the role of science and technology in development. However, the theory suffered from several limitations and weaknesses. Rostow's theory ignored the structural causes of underdevelopment and uneven development. Lack of attention to cultural complexities, which differ from society to society, disregarding of the discriminatory nature of the international system, grounding economic growth on the false dichotomy between modern and traditional, reducing the meaning of development to the sole materialist dimension of consumption, and formulating a one-size-fits-all solution are among the weaknesses of Rostow's work.

If a nation can produce adequate goods and services, generate a sufficient and growing supply of products, accumulate capital, and distribute the fruits of its own production in a relatively equitable manner, that nation is considered "developed," in the modernization theory of the 1950s and 1960s.

Viewing development as synonymous with economic growth became less popular in the 1970s, as the view began to grow that development should be defined as the satisfaction of *basic human needs*. The argument behind this model of development is simple: if development is the development of human beings, then human beings and their needs must be the focus of development programs. Thus, development is not synonymous with economic growth (Alston 1979; Lederer 1980); employment, poverty, and income distribution are important too. And basic needs are not restricted to income and other materialistic criteria. People need a just condition of life, marked by the fair distribution of wealth, goods, and services. More particularly, the most basic needs of people must be met in order to allow them to be capable of achieving long-term physical well-being, which means being freed from absolute poverty. There must be minimum resources available to people, including sufficient nutritional food, adequate shelter, decent clothing, education, protection from disease, and physical security.

> The human needs approach says that, first and foremost, development must mean meeting people's *basic needs*: employment, sufficient food, adequate shelter, decent clothing, health, nutrition, education, and security.

The basic needs approach was embraced by the International Labour Organization conference on World Employment in 1976, which proposed that the satisfaction of basic human needs must be the overriding objective of national and international development policy. In its Declaration of Principles, the World Employment Conference argued that past development strategies in most developing countries had not led to the eradication of poverty and unemployment. Major shifts would be needed in both national and international development strategies to ensure full employment and adequate income for the poor as quickly as possible. The basic needs approach came with an emphasis on the public policy dimensions of development. Indeed, the basic needs approach required turning the view of development upside down by pointing out that development is essentially a bottom-up construct that combines economic growth with social equity policies.

The basic needs approach reflected a shift in the meaning of development, since this approach suggested non-materialist needs—including personal security, nutrition, education, and health care—as basic needs that must be met. This focus on the human dimension of development was confirmed by the World Bank and other international institutions. Robert McNamara, the president of the World Bank

Group (1968–1980), announced increased lending for basic needs and employment in a famous speech in Nairobi in 1974. He said that the primary goal must be policies that address the absolute poor of the world, helping them to access basic needs. This is required for fundamental human dignity. With a view to the need to meet the basic needs of the poorest population of the world, the development debates in the 1970s and 1980s shifted towards the alleviation of poverty through addressing basic needs. This shift was later embraced by the United Nations Development Program and the World Bank.

In spite of its richness and depth, the basic needs approach still suffered from certain weaknesses. The first was that the approach remained largely restricted to economic factors. Cultural and social complexities of different nations were ignored. The second problem was that the state was in charge of development and not the individuals whose dignity must be addressed, and those in charge of the state might not be interested in the needs of the poor; the basic needs approach was politically naive. The third weakness was that development was still understood in terms of moral responsibility to help rather than doing justice to the systematically oppressed status of citizens of developing countries. Finally, the fourth weakness with the approach was that the oppressive and discriminatory structure of the international system was ignored.

> Development is a process which enables human beings to realize their potentials, build self-confidence, and lead lives of dignity and fulfillment. It is a process that frees people from the fear of want and exploitation. (Julius Nyerere 1990)

Accordingly, starting in the 1980s, a fundamental shift in the development debates came to the fore: good development as *human development*. Amartya Sen, the Nobel Peace Prize laureate in economics, heralded the human development approach (Sen 1999). Human development is a normative (ethical) approach that extends the meaning of development beyond the one-sidedness of material prosperity and instead lays out a multidimensional and multi-sectoral process of socio-cultural and politico-economic changes aimed at human well-being and freedom. That is, development is seen as a process rather than an idea, a theory, and/or policies and programs aimed at helping others attain a better material life. Human development, instead, involves enhancing people's quality of life. Accordingly, the human development approach reflects a move beyond policy measures improving people's material prosperity toward enlarging people's capability in attaining their own sense and model of the better life. Although the basic needs approach was a human-centred view extending the meaning of development beyond the material restrictiveness of that view, people continued to play a passive role in the determination of their own well-being. The human development approach (and a closely related version, the capability approach) completes the basic needs version of development and grounds it upon an active human-focused definition of development.

> From the perspective of the human development and capability approach, development means freedom. Indeed, it is human development. Human development is concerned with achieving the richness of human life. The ultimate goal of development is to *enlarge people's choices.*

The newness of the human development approach lies in its humanist assumption; development is for human beings, so it must be defined by human beings themselves. Economic growth, high income, and welfare policies aiming at addressing people's needs are all instrumental for the higher goal of achieving a qualified life. Hence, human development indicates that the process of people's deliberative participation in their own well-being is a categorical imperative without which a qualified life cannot be defined. In this sense, human development depends on people's freedom. But, freedom is not a theoretical term defined in its legal sense. Rather, it is an actualized freedom; the capability to act with full agency. Freedom is not the maximization of the range of choices. Nor is it direct control by individuals or groups of the means of production and distribution of the wealth. It is rather a real possibility to give meaning to life and enhance its quality. That is the reason why Sen argues that development means freedom: "someone who acts and brings about change, and whose achievements can be judged in terms of her own values and objectives, whether or not we assess them in terms of some external criteria as well" (1999). This freedom as the essence of human well-being means "a person is free to do and achieve in pursuit of whatever goals or values he or she regards as important" (1999).

Human development is concerned with achieving the richness of human life, rather than the richness of the economy in which human beings live. This *human-centred* approach in development involves people's democratic participation in development. The United Nations Development Program (UNDP) envisaged human development as an evaluative space to measure people's functioning capability in portraying their own well-being. For this purpose, the UNDP initiated the Human Development Index (HDI) (see **Figure 2.2**) to assess the development of a country based on its people's capability as the ultimate goal of development. The Index is instrumental in the assessment of national policies for improving their nationals' capabilities. The HDI is calculated using the country's achievement as the key dimension in human development, including a long and healthy life, being literate and knowledgeable, and having a decent standard of living.

Nevertheless, the HDI does not reflect inequalities, poverty, human security, and

Figure 2.2
The Human Development Index

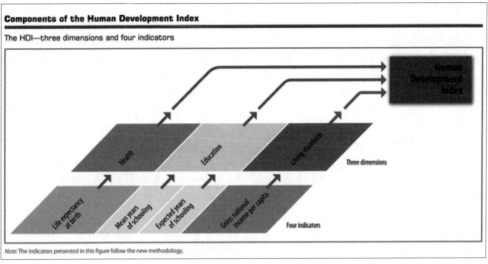

Components of the Human Development Index

The HDI—three dimensions and four indicators

Note: The indicators presented in this figure follow the new methodology.

Source: UNDP.

empowerment. The Human Development Report Office offers the "other composite indices as broader proxy on some of the key issues of human development, inequality, gender disparity and human poverty" (http://hdr.undp.org/).

> **The basic objective of human development is to enlarge people's choice to make development mere democratic and participatory. (UNDP, *Human Development Report* 1991)**

The human development and capability approach brings a wealth of human values to development theories. This includes the following:

- Income, economic growth, and welfare policies are instrumental in good development.
- Good development is human-centred. Human beings are the undeniable and most important sources of development.
- In addition to addressing people's basic needs, development programs must

be concentrated on people's actualized freedoms (the capabilities) as well as the natural environment of local communities. Correspondingly, it is deeply cultural and endorses diverse values in different local settings.

- It is an open-ended process of exploring human potentials in widening their choices. It is a work-in-progress and a continuous endeavour for assessing the quality of life. Therefore, it is the best alternative to the theory of economic growth.
- It extends beyond the basic needs of the poorest in the world and embraces the development of both developing and developed societies (http://hdr.undp.org/).

In summary, although international development in its contemporary understanding is a Western liberal gambit with political dimensions, in the process of its evolution it was gradually influenced by humanitarian ideas. By the 1990s, development turned into the human development and capability approach. International institutions adopted human development as the means of measuring poverty reduction in different countries, while as a matter of public policy it was a powerful tool to assess the quality of life in different countries. Nevertheless, the mainstream view of development remained loyal to the market-centred perspectives inherited from the classical economics of the eighteenth and nineteenth centuries.

Opposite Winds Blow

Nevertheless, the theory of international development was confronted by critical approaches essentially originating mostly from Marxist philosophy. The best known of this critical approaches are the dependency theories interrogating the mainstream on what the causes of unequal development in the world are. Emerging in the 1960s, dependency theories criticized the theory of modernization and argued that the development of Western countries was the outcome of their colonialist policies and their stripping of wealth and natural resources from the colonized societies. The main argument of these theories is that from the sixteenth century onwards, colonizing powers have structured the world economy around the unequal division of markets, labour, tasks, and benefits. Accordingly, underdevelopment has structural causes. The international political economy and the dependency of developing countries on the developed north must be analyzed in terms of historical colonialism, imperialism, and domination. Thus unequal development requires a *historical* and *structuralist* analysis of the diffusion of capitalism. Dependency theories took hold in the 1960s and 1970s, notably because of the burgeoning revolutionary atmosphere in Latin America.

Dependency had its roots in the structural economics of the United Nations Economic Commission for Latin America (UNECLA), especially the influential 1950 report by the commission's director, Raúl Prebisch, on "The Economic Development of Latin America and Its Principal Problems" (UNECLA 1950). Structuralist economists such as Prebisch from Argentina and Celso Furtado from Brazil situated the causes of underdevelopment and unequal development in the structure of the international political economy around the European theory of modernization and the diffusion of capitalism. Prebisch in particular asserted that the terms of international trade would move steadily against developing countries that produced primary (i.e., unprocessed) products for export, and in favour of the advanced countries that exported manufactured goods. The policy solution, therefore, was to promote the industrialization of the developing countries through active government intervention to build the national economy. The proposed policies were both nationalist and interventionist.

The first-generation dependency scholars went further. They not only pointed an accusing finger at European modernization, but they also came right out and called modernization the mechanism of dependency and imperialism. For them, the development of the West took place around the unfair structure of the world economy that the dependency of developing countries was formed around. From the 1500s onward, European accumulation of capital was attained through the extraction of wealth (natural resources and capital) from the colonies. The result was devastating: the underdevelopment of colonies. The mechanism of dependency continued even after colonialism ended. Correspondingly, the world was structured around the First World industrialized manufacturers and the underdeveloped producers.

Where are the fruits of the unfair world division of labour, tasks, markets, and trade policies? Dependency argued that the international division of labour and trade has enabled Western countries to establish mastery over the world economy and reap such fruits. Moving beyond Prebisch's argument about the declining terms of trade, dependency theorists, using Marxist economics, insisted that international trade was "unequal exchange" (Wallerstein

Figure 2.3
Dependency Theory: The Metropolis-Satellite Model

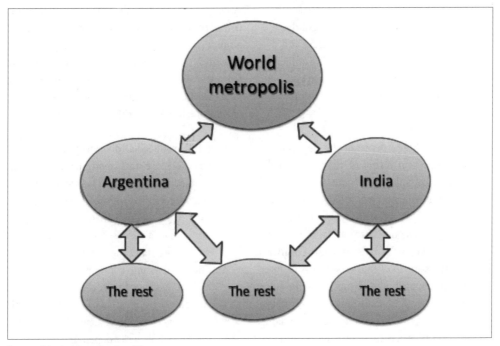

Source: Adapted from Frank, 1966.

1979). Unequal exchange enabled the First World industrialized manufacturers to exploit producers. Dependency has therefore been caused by the unequal exchange between the core (Western, industrialized) countries, and the peripheral (developing) countries. Developing countries must therefore reject not only liberal market-based theories but also orthodox Marxist proposals based on class struggle and state socialism, and instead invent their own path to development. The first step to development is to break down all imperialistic dependencies. The policy prescriptions of the dependency school were socialist revolution and de-linking of the developing countries from the international economic system.

The dependency argument was put forward in its most radical version by Paul Baran (Ghosh 2001; Magdoff 2003) and Andre Gunder Frank (Frank 1966). In an atmosphere prone to revolution in the developing world, their neo-Marxist account became known as Dependency Theory

(capital D and T). Using a model that showed metropolitan-satellite relationships (see **Figure 2.3**) between the developed and underdeveloped countries, Frank argued that the First World (the developed, industrialized countries) had attained its development through the underdevelopment of others. Indeed, Frank showed that the contemporary status of underdevelopment in most parts of the world was the historical product of past colonialist practices between the satellite underdeveloped and the now-developed metropolitan countries (Frank 1966). These relations of unequal dependency were an essential part of the structure and development of the capitalist system on the world scale as a whole, as Frank saw it. Moving away from dependency of the peripheries to the core countries toward mutual, but deeply unequal, dependency relationship in a metropolitan-satellite model, Frank concluded that the development of the West was a result of the underdevelopment of the satellites.

I hope that better confirmation of these hypotheses and further pursuit of the proposed historical, holistic, and structural approach may help the peoples of the underdeveloped countries to understand the causes and eliminate the reality of their development of underdevelopment and their underdevelopment of development. (Frank 1966)

Dependency Theory depicted the dependency of the satellites in terms of their historically imposed weak, vulnerable, and subordinated status in the international political economy. Satellite countries may produce considerable surpluses, but a significant portion of their surplus is drained off by metropolitan countries through the control of markets; terms of international trade; and related mechanisms, rules, and regulations. In addition, metropolitan countries have established a benefit-making relationship between their own elites and the comprador bourgeoisie ruling classes in the satellite countries (Frank 1966). As the predatory ruling class, the comprador bourgeoisie represents the greedy benefits of the capitalist forces in its own country, and by this representation consolidates its own parasitic status by siphoning off the wealth of the country. This is why, even though satellite countries have freed themselves from colonialism, the world imperialistic structures has continued to keep them in a state of dependency. In other terms, the old colonial dominations have been replaced with new economic and commercial dependencies. In Frank's view, this condition was ripe for revolutionary policies and it was time for the satellite countries to break the chains of dependency.

Another version of the neo-Marxist Dependency Theory, called World-Systems Theory, was produced by the American Marxist sociologist Immanuel Wallerstein. Having been divided around a *world-system* of core-periphery dependency structures, Wallerstein suggested that the capitalist world was marked by a single division of labour. This system is by its nature socio-economic and has created its own structures, borders, and members. Life within this system is essentially self-contained; hence the competition and struggle for profit-taking among the forces in the system is handled in a consistent manner (Wallerstein 1979). Formed from the sixteenth century, this centreless capitalist world system has been further developed around the following considerations:

1. It has produced a "division of labour" based on core states, peripheral areas, and semi-peripheral areas. The peripheral areas are marked with single-crop economies, a labour-intensive mode of production of raw materials. They depend heavily on the core states for their survival.

2. The world-system contains a capitalist market governed by the core states, whose complex economies have led to their domination over peripheral areas. The power of the core states varies depending on their capacity to function in the whole system. The system manifests a hierarchy of occupational tasks, in which tasks requiring higher levels of skill and greater capitalization are reserved for higher-ranking areas.

3. The world-system has no single political centre. Rather, it is a multiplicity of political systems that have given capitalist states the freedom to manoeuvre to maximize their profits. This structurally capitalist system has made it possible to constantly expand and flourish over the past four centuries.

4. The core states require different kinds of knowledge to maintain their predominance over the peripheral areas.

5. The system is susceptible to a set of complex crises, since it generates both the protective forces of the market and the forces of change.

6. Accordingly, the system must be analyzed by the methodology of holism if one wants to explore its complexity and historical evolution from the beginning of its construction. (Wallerstein 1979)

By portraying this picture of underdevelopment, *World-Systems Theory* brings sociology to the centre of international development and defines the analysis of the imperialistic characteristics of the world system as the starting point in the study of uneven development. The theory presents a thoughtful view of dependency, while tackling its roots going back five hundred years to the beginning of capitalism. However, in an era of global interconnectedness and transformations, the world-system theory has been able to redefine its theoretical assumptions by transforming them from the core-periphery to the global north-south division. From a reviewed perspective, the old world system is becoming lifeless, and instead a new global system is forming that is defined and controlled by the means of hegemony over strategic information. In this system, the better life is marked by the new concepts and patterns of competition, ability to control information, and the willingness and ability to move along with rapid global transformations.

> **The way a country is integrated into the capitalist world system determines how economic development takes place in that country. (Wallerstein 1979)**

It must be noted that dependency theory (small d and t) is like an umbrella covering different versions of dependency theory (see **Figure 2.4**). The first one is Dependency Theory (capital D and T) and refers to the main view of dependency by Cardoso, Faletto, and Frank. The second one is the World-Systems Theory by Wallerstein. The third version is the dynamic dependency theory of Thomas Gold. The fourth version is known as the regularization theory of Destanne de Bernis, influenced by Antonio Gramsci.

Figure 2.4
Versions of Dependency Theory

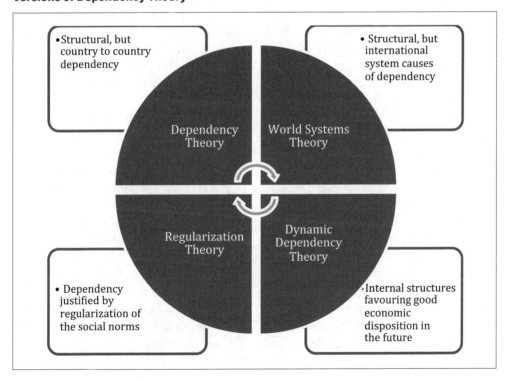

- Structural, but country to country dependency

- Structural, but international system causes of dependency

Dependency Theory

World Systems Theory

Regularization Theory

Dynamic Dependency Theory

- Dependency justified by regularization of the social norms

- Internal structures favouring good economic disposition in the future

Development Is Restructured!

By the mid-1980s, four different views were prevalent in international development studies: the liberal mainstream perspective, which was still interpreting development in terms of economic growth and material satisfaction; the basic needs model, which was near its expiry date; the human development model, which was just beginning to coalesce; and the Dependency/World-Systems Theories, which were struggling in the changing atmosphere. However, none of the four contending theories were able to offer a solution to the economic stagnation, inflation, and political instability that was making life difficult in the Western world in the 1970s and early 1980s. From the mid-1970s, the Western capitalist economies suffered slow economic growth, high unemployment, low productivity, and high inflation. In addition, the revolutionary atmosphere caused by Marxist movements and radical religious movements created a state of uncertainty for the post–Second World War liberal capitalist consensus in the West.

The reaction was natural. A group of liberal (pro-market) economists had already formed around the teachings of Friedrich von Hayek (1899–1992) and Milton Friedman (1912–2006). They joined forces with the right-wing political elites in the West and formed an alliance to end the political and economic turbulence (Jones 2012). With the arrival of Margaret Thatcher as prime minister of the United Kingdom and of Ronald Reagan as president of the United States, the main leaders of the Western world were fully in this camp. Much of the impetus for liberal (pro-market, anti-state) economic reforms, however, came from the managers and economic elites representing the interests of corporations. There was an important element of class struggle. In a time of perceived social and economic collapse in the West, "the upper classes everywhere felt threatened . . . The upper classes had to move decisively if they were to protect themselves from political and economic annihilation" (Harvey 2005). It was also a time to capture the minds of Western citizens by displaying the failure of the Keynesian economic model of state intervention and the inherent evils of communism, which were said to be pushing Latin American and Africa into turbulence.

Business groups, right-wing politicians, conservative think-tanks, and influential religious groups formed a union to move history in its "proper" direction: the free-market economy aligned with freedom and democracy. Politically speaking, neoliberalism (as the movement came to be called) argued for the end of history and the victory of liberal democracy as the ultimate stage of the evolution of human society (Fukuyama 1993). In this context, propaganda became colourful and all means of justification were used to support the neoliberal proposal. Milton Friedman, one of the intellectual fathers of this new wave, passionately defined the return to the free market capitalism (Friedman 1962). He suggested that people removed from the discipline of the market lost their independence and became undesirably dependent on government programs. "The record of history is absolutely crystal clear: there is no alternative way, so far discovered, of improving the lot of the ordinary people that holds a candle to the productive activities that are unleashed by a free enterprise system" (quoted in Butler and Friedman 2011).

The neoliberal revolution of the 1980s and 1990s asserted that development policy must do whatever necessary to integrate local markets and societies within the global capitalist system. "There is no other alternative," said UK's Prime Minister Margaret Thatcher.

The (neo)liberal revolution of the 1980s and 1990s sought to control inflation, weaken trade unions, control government spending, and reduce the economic activities of governments everywhere. Though it was controversial in the West, this new (neo)liberal project gained in credibility after the collapse of communism in the former Soviet Bloc and the end of the Cold War in 1989–1991 removed the main ideological rival to capitalism. The collapse of Soviet communism created over a dozen new countries and freed several more; Western countries quickly tried to guide these countries to liberal capitalist democracy.

John Williamson of the Peterson Institute for International Economics coined the term "Washington Consensus" to describe the standard set of policy prescriptions that were then promoted by the International Monetary Fund, the World Bank, and the US Treasury, all based in Washington, D.C., as cures for Latin American economies plagued by inflation, slow growth, and balance of payments problems (Williamson 2004). Williamson's Washington Consensus contained ten key sets of policies:

1. Fiscal discipline
2. Re-ordering public expenditure priorities
3. Tax reform
4. Liberalizing interest rates
5. Competitive exchange rate
6. Trade liberalization
7. Liberalization of inward foreign direct investment
8. Privatization
9. Deregulation
10. Securing property rights

The term "Washington Consensus," however, quickly came to be used in the more general sense of referring to any strongly market-based approach to economics and public policy. Such market-based economic policy reforms typically included the following:

i. Reducing the role of the state as a producer of goods and services and giving greater power to the free market, with little or no care for any social damage caused.
ii. Abolition of state monopolies and privatization of state-owned enterprises producing goods and services. Banks, key industries, railroads, toll highways, electricity and gas supply, telecommunications, schools, and hospitals were often privatized.
iii. Deregulation of markets, including labour markets, to allow greater competition.
iv. Reform of the welfare state to promote the spirit of individual initiative and to punish laziness.
v. Atomization of society by undermining aspirations for the common good and communal ties and by encouraging individuals to find solutions for their own well-being.
vi. Undermining of trade unions and other vehicles that promote working-class interests.
vii. Technological change, freer international and internal trade, flexible labour markets, and the end of lifetime employment.
viii. Attempts to restrict state intervention to its core responsibilities of maintaining a police force and standing army, administering justice, undertaking public works, and protecting members of the community who cannot be held responsible, such as children.
ix. Promoting civil and political rights and democratic values abroad. The proposal is determinedly depoliticized.

The Washington Consensus, in either the strict (Williamson 2004) sense or in its more popular sense as a set of pro-market policies, quickly become contentious, especially in the areas of trade liberalization and elimination of subsidies. This new dispute was led by Joseph Stiglitz, the former chief economist at the World Bank and a Nobel Laureate in economics. He argued that the Washington Consensus was unlikely to promote the development of the poorest countries in the world. Stiglitz argued that any future consensus cannot be made just in Washington. Rather, any new framework for poor countries must provide better and greater adaptation to the circumstances of the countries involved (Stiglitz 2005 and 2008).

Stiglitz and others argued that Washington Consensus policies produced only limited growth. In addition, even when growth did occur, it was not equitably shared. Accordingly, imperative in such a framework is an emphasis on the importance of equity and employment. He also suggests a balancing of the role of government and markets that promotes and regulates markets, provides institutional and physical infrastructure, and promotes education, innovation, and technology. Stiglitz (2005) concluded that the intellectual framework for thinking about policies provided by the Washington Consensus was badly flawed. Accordingly, the *Post-Washington Consensus* suggested alternative frameworks encompassing the historical experience of the countries that grew faster, while addressing the issues of sustainability and equality.

From Millennium Development Goals to Sustainable Development Goals: Worldwide Solutions?

Sixty-five years after the advent of international development as a concept and of international aid as a set of practices, and having gone through the stages of the rise and fall of a variety of theories and policies, poverty and the extreme gap between the haves and have-nots remain tragic features of human life. As a transmittable human evil with roots either in natural brutality or in man-made structures (or both), poverty shocks the conscience of human beings. The World Bank reports that the number of people living on less than $1.25 per day has decreased from half of the citizens in the developing world in 1981 to about one fifth in 2015. However, most of the progress made in reducing poverty has come in Asia, and statistics show that extreme poverty still persists. Sub-Saharan Africa still accounts for one-third of the extreme poverty in the world. The

poverty persists not only in the lack of material well-being of the poor, but also takes a more extreme form through illiteracy, malnutrition, social inequality, cultural and traditional attitudes, and corruption in the system. Added to these malaises, there is the burden of international debt, especially for African countries.

But, since economic growth targeted the material side of the life, it did not necessarily translate into greater well-being for the poor; this is exactly what Amartya Sen and the basic needs theorists had predicted. In addition, the rate of economic growth was very slow in many places, while the deprivation resulting from complex socio-cultural barriers and structural causes persisted in the developing world. Neoliberalism, the ideology of the free market and the spirit of capitalism, is often accused of making the situation worse.

To initiate sustained efforts to end poverty, to make the world more inclusive and equitable, and to create a shared future in accordance with common human values, the United Nations in its 2000 summit unanimously adopted the Millennium Declaration (UN 2000). The Millennium Declaration contained a statement of values, principles, and objectives for the international agenda for the twenty-first century. The Millennium Forum, which brought together representatives of more than a thousand non-governmental and civil society organizations, also became engaged in a series of consultations over the issues of poverty eradication and the protection of vulnerable people. Drawn from the Millennium Declaration and the consulting forum, the Millennium Development Goals (MDGs) served as a blueprint for measuring progress in development among the countries in the world. The goals are indeed the manifestation of the long-term search to find an effective and permanent solution to world poverty. The goals draw heavily for their inspiration from the basic needs theorists and from the human development and capabilities approach to development. The main goal, MDG1, called for the halving of poverty in the world within

15 years and the eradication of extreme poverty. The MDGs were:

Goal 1: Eradicate extreme poverty and hunger
Goal 2: Achieve universal primary education
Goal 3: Promote gender equality
Goal 4: Reduce child mortality
Goal 5: Improve maternal health
Goal 6: Combat HIV/AIDS, malaria, and other diseases
Goal 7: Ensure environmental sustainability
Goal 8: Develop a global partnership for development

The MDGs were not without their critics, however. The lack of an explicit human rights framework was one criticism. From the other side, (neo)liberals criticized the MDGs' lack of attention to wealth creation and the role of markets in producing and distributing goods and services. And only one MDG applied to the developed countries, MDG8.

The MDGs reached their date of expiration in 2015. While much progress had been made, there still remained a long way to go to reach several of the goals. The difficulties involved in reaching the MDGs were apparent well before the target date of 2015. The Rio+20 sustainable development summit in Brazil in 2012 asked UN member states to implement measures for Sustainable Development Goals (SDGs) to carry the MDG agenda beyond the 2015 deadline. There was a global consultation on the post-MDG global agenda in 2015. An innovation in this consultation was the responsibility of the member states to provide evidence-based inputs, analytical thinking, and field experience. The world prepared itself to define and implement political measures in support of the new agenda: the Sustainable Development Goals. The dream came gradually true, when in August 2015 the 193 member states of the United Nations reached a consensus on the new agenda on sustainable development in a report

Figure 2.5
The Sustainable Development Goals, 2015

Source: http://www.un.org/sustainabledevelopment/news/communications-material/

titled "Transforming our World: The 2030 Agenda for Sustainable Development" (UN 2015). In endorsing that agenda, the UN General Assembly adopted 17 goals for sustainable development (see **Figure 2.5**, previous page). The UN Deputy Secretary-General underlined that Sustainable Development Goals are essential for a safe and secure future that brings prosperity, opportunity, and human rights to all.

A novel feature of the new agenda lies in a global consensus to set the goals for both people and the planet. The SDGs take the effects of climate change on oceans, forests, and biodiversity into account. Taking this more holistic view, the SDGs assert in effect that good development must be sustainable development. A remnant of the idea of the development ethicists from early 1950s, who argued that the ultimate goal of development must be human flourishing, the SDGs promise a view of good development that could potentially provide a better life for all and build a firm foundation for stability and

peace everywhere in the world. (This meaning of development will be presented in Chapter 15.) Goals listed on the roster of this ambitious but promising agenda targeted elimination rather than reduction of poverty and more attention to health, education, gender, and inequality. These goals are cosmopolitan in scope and apply to all countries and all people, which is a significant departure from the MDGs and the West-Rest binary.

Steps taken after adoption of the SDGs show considerable promise in terms of raising public awareness around the SDGs. The critical importance of this issue lies in the low level of public awareness of MDGs when they were adopted in 2000. The UN Development Program has now held Social Good Summits in more than a hundred countries since 2015, running parallel with the Sustainable Development Summit. This is an important initiative, since the realization of the SDGs depends on everyone being aware of their responsibility.

Conclusion

Development is a vague and contested term. It has been defined differently for varied goals in a multiplicity of settings. Basically, and in the mainstream theorizing of the term, development means economic growth, modernization, and meeting people's basic needs. In whatever sense the term is defined, the fact is that the conceptualization and definition of development is derived from modern rationalization of social relations aimed at ending human suffering and attaining a better life. However, determining the meaning of the better life is itself a matter of philosophical, ethical, and political debate. Some theorists understand the idea of a better life in terms of material well-being; hence economic development is for them the road to the better life. Others believe that the better life is a matter of normative articulation, which entails human development. Some believe in the reforms in the existing economic systems as the road to the better life, while others consider the existing systems essentially as holding back good development. There are others who believe that development as the means of attaining the better life is a multidimensional and multi-purpose term that must be precisely defined in light of the historical conditions of societies and their needs. A group of neo-Marxist theorists argue that the better life for nations will be attained when their relationship of dependency on the advanced Western societies is broken down, while (neo)liberals assert that development can only take place in the context of increased international trade and international investment flows. Still others understand development as freedom, as enlarging people's choices. For them, then, the better life is a matter of a journey passing through the democratic processes of deliberate participation and contribution. Each of these pathways to the better life defines development instrumentally for portraying their own purposive life. That is why the literature of development reflects a vast range of definitions, policies, programs, and strategies, and their application. For this reason, the conception of development is not free from cultural values and political considerations. This is especially true of the post-Second World War theorization of development. However, the theorizing of the conception of development in the most recent decades has gone through deliberative arguments to portray the concept as human development and then initiate global programs for its implementation and application.

Questions for Further Learning

- What do you understand by the word "development"? Draw a picture of your own concept of development.
- What dimensions must be taken into account to define the term development? Should these dimensions be understood from the perspective of modernization theory and/or the theory of economic growth, or do we need a more comprehensive definition?
- What makes human development distinct from the other theories of development?
- Do you agree that we seek freedom not for itself but for its ability to allow us to develop ourselves?
- Are the (neo)liberal measures helpful for the development of the southern societies, or are they detrimental for them? What evidence exists to support your stance?

Key Terms

Cold War, p. 29

dependency theory, p. 37

economic growth, p. 28

human development, p. 29

international development, p. 28

modernization theory, p. 28

moral responsibility to help, p. 28

neoliberalism, p. 40

Sustainable Development Goals, p. 43

Suggested Readings

Cooper, Frederick, and Randall Packard, eds. 1997. *Development Theory and Social Science*. Berkley CA: University of California Press.

Crush, Jonathan, ed. 1995. *Power of Development*. London: Routledge.

Crain, William. 2005. *Theories of Development: Concepts and Applications*. Upper Saddle River, NJ: Pearson Prentice Hall.

Black, Maggie. 2002. *The No-Nonsense Guide to International Development*. Oxford: New Internationalist Publications.

Escobar, Arturo. 1995. *Encountering Development: The Making and Unmaking of the Third World*. Princeton: Princeton University Press.

Grabowski, Richard, Sharmistha Self, and Michael P. Shields. 2007. *Economic Development: A Regional, Institutional, and Historical Approach*. Armonk, NY: M.E. Sharpe.

Haynes, Jeffrey. 2008. *Development Studies: Short Introductions.* Cambridge, UK: Polity Press.

Isbester, John. 2006. *Promises Not Kept: Poverty and the Betrayal of Third World Development.* Bloomfield: Kumarian Press.

Kingsbury, Damien. 2012. *International Development: Issues and Challenges.* New York: Palgrave Macmillan.

Munck, Ronaldo, and Denis O'Hearn, eds. 1999. *Critical Development Theory.* London: Zed Books.

Rist, Gilbert. 2001. *The History of Development: From Western Origins to Global Faith.* London: Zed Books.

Williams, David. 2012. *International Development and Global Politics: History, Theory and Practice.* New York: Routledge.

Suggested Websites

Human Development and Capability Association: https://hd-ca.org/

The U.N. Sustainable Development Knowledge Platform: https://sustainabledevelopment.un.org/hlpf/2016

Center for Global Development: www.cgdev.org

Global Development Network: www.gdnet.org

International Development Ethics Association: https://developmentethics.org/

Canadian Association for the Study of International Development: https://www.casid-acedi.ca/

International Development Evaluation Association: https://ideas-global.org/

The Communication Initiative Network: http://www.comminit.com/global/

Devex: https://www.devex.com/

Development Classifieds: http://www.comminit.com/ci-classifieds

Suggested Videos

US Agency for International Development video overview, https://www.youtube.com/watch?v=F2HWjbvWnoc

Religion and Social Change in Protestantism and Liberation Theology, http://study.com/academy/lesson/religion-and-social-change-in-protestantism-and-liberation-theology.html

Rostow's stages of growth, https://www.youtube.com/watch?v=k9j69VpmBKk

Modernization Theory: Definition, Development, and Claims, http://study.com/academy/lesson/modernization-theory-definition-development-claims.html

Dependency Theory, https://www.youtube.com/watch?v=RoMLdFlta1E

Amartya Sen on human development and capabilities, https://www.youtube.com/watch?v=OQ-Gb8oHTgk

Works Cited

Alston, Philip. 1979. *Human Rights and the Basic Needs Strategy for Development.* London, England: Anti-Slavery Society.

Butler, Eamonn, and Milton Friedman. 2011. *A Concise Guide to the Ideas and Influence of the Free Market Economist.* Hampshire: Harriman House.

Ekbladh, David. 2010. *The Great American Mission: Modernization and the Construction of an American World Order.* Princeton: Princeton University Press.

Emmanuel, Arghiri. 1972. *Unequal Exchange: A Study in the Imperialism of Trade.* New York: Monthly Review Press.

Frank, Andre Gunder. 1966. "The Development of Underdevelopment." *Monthly Review.* September.

Friedman, Milton. 1962. *Capitalism and Freedom.* Chicago: University of Chicago Press.

Fukuyama, Francis. 1993. *The End of History and the Last Man.* New York: Avon Books.

Furtado, Celso. 1976. *Economic Development of Latin America: Historical Background and*

Contemporary Problems. Cambridge: Cambridge University Press.

Ghosh, B. N. 2001. *Dependency Theory Revisited.* Aldershot, UK: Ashgate.

Gosnell, Peter. 2014. *The Ethical Vision of the Bible: Learning Good from Knowing God.* Madison, WI: IVP Academic.

Harvey, David. 2005. *A Brief History of Neoliberalism.* Oxford: Oxford University Press.

Jones, Daniel Stedman. 2012. *Masters of the Universe: Hayek, Friedman, and the Birth of Neoliberal Politics.* Princeton: Princeton University Press.

Kennedy, John F. 1961. "Inaugural Address." Delivered at Washington, D.C., on 20 January. https://www.jfklibrary.org/Asset-Viewer/BqXIEM9F4024ntFl7SVAjA.aspx

Latham, Michael. 2011. *The Right Kind of Revolution: Modernization, Development, and US Foreign Policy from the Cold War to the Present.* Ithaca: Cornell University Press.

Lederer, Katrin, ed. 1980. *Human Needs: A Contribution to the Current Debate.* Cambridge: Oelgeschlager, Gunn & Hain.

Magdoff, Harry. 2003. *Imperialism without Colonies.* New York: Monthly Review Press.

Nyerere, Julius. 1990. *The Challenge to the South: the South Commission under the chairmanship of Julius Nyerere.* Oxford: Oxford University Press.

Pierce, Anne. 2007. *Woodrow Wilson and Harry Truman: Mission and Power in American Foreign Policy.* New Brunswick, NJ: Transaction Publishers.

Prebisch, Raúl. 1971. *Change and Development: Latin America's Great Task: Report Submitted to the Inter-American Development Bank.* New York: Praeger.

Rist, Gilbert. 2008. *The History of Development from Western Origins to Global Faith.* New Delhi: Academic Foundation.

Rostow, Walt. 1971. *The Stages of Economic Growth.* 3rd ed. Cambridge: Cambridge University Press.

Schweiker, William. 1995. *Responsibility and Christian Ethics.* Cambridge: Cambridge University Press.

Sen, Amartya. 1999. *Development as Freedom.* New York: Anchor Books.

Stiglitz, Joseph. 2008. *The Washington Consensus Reconsidered: Towards a New Global Governance.* New York: Oxford University Press.

———. 2005. *Lectures on the Post Washington Consensus.* São Paolo, Brazil, 22 August.

Truman, Harry. 1949. "Inaugural Address." Delivered at Washington, D.C. on 20 January. https://www.trumanlibrary.org/whistlestop/50yr_archive/inagural20jan1949.htm

UN. 2000. *United Nations Millennium Declaration.* (A/55/L.2). New York: United Nations.

———. 2015. *Transforming our World: The 2030 Agenda for Sustainable Development.* (A/RES/70/1). New York: United Nations.

UNDP. 1991. *Human Development Report, United Nations Development Programme.* Oxford: Oxford University Press.

UNECLA. 1950. *The Economic Development of Latin America and Its Principal Problems.* New York: UN Economic Commission for Latin America.

Wallerstein, Immanuel. 1979. *The Capitalist World Economy.* Cambridge: Cambridge University Press.

Williamson, John. 2004. "A Short History of the Washington Consensus." Paper commissioned by Fundación CIDOB for the conference "From the Washington Consensus Towards a New Global Governance." Barcelona, Spain, September 24–25.

Notes

3

Globalization

Definitions, Debates, and Relation to International Development

Stephen McBride and Stephanie Tombari

Key Terms

globalization

neoliberalism

sustainable development

developing states

Overview

This chapter introduces the concept of globalization in relation to international development. It explores the theoretical approaches to the study of globalization, and offers frameworks for analyzing the impact of economic globalization in the neoliberal period on developing and developed states. In particular, it compares the view of development offered by international organizations with the process by which today's developed states achieved their economic goals. Few, if any, of today's developed states did so by the processes now recommended for developing states, or under conditions imposed by constitution-like arrangements incorporated in international treaties. Unsurprisingly, some developing states have looked for alternative pathways, and developed states have looked for ways to exploit global rules to their own advantage. The challenge for developing countries is rendered more complex by the intersection of economic and environmental crises which makes sustainability, as well as economic development, a priority.

Learning Objectives

By the end of this chapter, students will be able to:
- identify and explain various concepts of globalization and the main theoretical orientations to the study of globalization and international development.
- compare and analyze the effects of neoliberal globalization, new constitutionalism, and structural adjustment programs) on developing and developed states.
- identify examples of, and opportunities for, resistance to the global trade regime by developing states.
- reflect on the interaction between the need for economic development and environmental sustainability.

What is Globalization?

Globalization has been a contested term since first rising to prominence in the 1980s (Hoogvelt 1997). Scholars have debated the novelty of globalization—whether it is a relatively new phenomenon of the late twentieth century or the evolution of an ongoing process that first began with exploration and trade 500 years ago. Similarly, there have been disputes about whether increased internationalization, which most seem to agree is a feature of the late twentieth century, is truly global, or whether it is a more limited regional phenomenon. Other debates centre on the type of globalization— often depicted as "neoliberal" for reasons to be developed further in the chapter—and whether other types are possible.

"(T)he specificities of interpreting global processes depend partly on whether focus is on the sociology, the economics, or the politics of globalization" (Kothari, Minogue, and DeJong 2002, 17; see also Hoogvelt 1997). So while "globalization" is not a single process or product of the Internet or finance capitalism, for example, the way globalization is conceptualized often depends on the lens through which it is being understood. It's important to keep in mind that focusing on one aspect of globalization for the purpose of study does not mean that the sociological, economic, or political processes operate independently of one another.

Similarly, Appadurai (2006, 588) argues that the global cultural economy is a "complex, overlapping, disjunctive order" that can no longer be understood using traditional development models of "core" and "periphery" states, or of consumers and producers. (See Chapter 2 and Chapter 13.) Instead, the global economy is a product of "disjunctures" between economics, sociological or cultural influences, and national and international politics. Appadurai thus proposes that globalization be examined across five dimensions, or "scapes" of "global cultural flow": ethnoscapes, technoscapes, financescapes, mediascapes, and ideoscapes (588–89).

Ethnoscapes are concerned with the mobility of people such as migrants, tourists, guest workers, refugees, and other persons, whose movements, personal relations, and expectations affect production and policies between and within states. A mother in India moves her family to the United Kingdom for a new job; a man in Saskatchewan moves to Switzerland to be closer to his partner; a Mexican father spends summers working on an Ontario tomato farm. But whereas highly skilled and professional workers from advanced industrialized "Western" states tend to move across national borders with relative ease, less skilled workers from developing states face tighter restrictions on immigration from developed countries (Hanson 2010). (See Chapter 6.)

Technoscapes are the increasingly borderless links between high and low technology, mechanical and informational technology, and the speed with which these technologies travel. For example, a blue jeans production chain may link a sewing factory in China with a fabric maker in India and a distribution company in Texas, all based on instructions from shareholders in New York. The uneven distribution of technoscapes is a result not only of traditional economies of scale, but also of complex relationships between instantaneous money flows, political opportunities, and the availability of low-wage labour (Appadurai 2006, 589–90).

Financescapes encompass the flow of capital, the range of speculative financial instruments, and the daily spikes in currency exchanges that with blinding speed can—and have—created both wealth and crisis for states, corporations, and individuals. So while development can still be described by traditional indicators like gross domestic product, financescapes are deeply disjunctured by technology; thus financescapes (and resulting changes in ethnoscapes) must be examined in terms of the distribution and speed of high and low technology: "How is one to make a meaningful comparison of wages in Japan and the United States or of real estate costs in New York and Tokyo, without taking sophisticated account of the very complex fiscal and investment flows that link the two economies through a global grid of currency speculation and capital transfer?" (590).

Mediascapes are the production and distribution of information through online media and other channels—such as news reports, magazines, documentaries, books, movies, music, and social media—with varying degrees of access across states, as well as the actual content of information that interprets and reflects ideas back into the world. The ways we think about other places in the world are largely facilitated by media: to someone living in Montreal, rural Bangladesh may be imagined as poor and regressive, as Western mediascapes collide with ethnoscapes (and ideoscapes). Moreover, information that was available only to the educated and wealthy few a century ago, and even then largely at the local level, is now available instantly to people in many different parts of the globe. However, while information is certainly more widely accessible than it was ten years ago, 4.6 billion people, over half the world's population, still lack Internet access (see A Human Right, n.d.).

Finally, *Ideoscapes* consist of the political ideologies and counter-ideologies that have shaped,

and are shaping, the political economies of the world. The "master narratives" derived from the Enlightenment, such as "freedom," "rights," and "democracy," as well as religious teachings from Christianity, Islam, and Buddhism, were "constructed with a certain internal logic and presupposed a certain relationship between reading, representation and the public sphere" (Appadurai 2006, 591). Disjunctures between ideological terms and images have increased over time with exploration and technology, and this has led different nation-states to selectively organize their polities according to their own values, norms, and cultures. But while political ideologies can be useful societal organizing principles, they can also be punitive in nature. For example, the (uneven) spread of neoliberal thinking, which suggests that corporate taxes and government regulation should be minimized or eliminated to stimulate private sector growth, continues to seem like "common sense" even after the global financial crisis in 2008–2009 and despite austerity measures that have cut social spending and public sector jobs.

These views identify the complex range of activities associated with modern globalization. There is a huge literature on globalization and this has triggered various attempts to categorize and simplify it. Here, keeping in mind the sociological, political, and economic aspects of globalization identified above, we look at two of these efforts as a way to make sense of a very complex concept: Dobuzinskis's (2000) *Three Worlds of Globalization* and Hoogvelt's (1997) *Globalization and the Postcolonial World*. Then we turn to the way globalization has been institutionalized in modern political economy before exploring issues of international development, including structural adjustment, the rise of the emerging economies (including the BRICS—Brazil, Russia, India, China, and South Africa), and, finally, issues of sustainable development.

Conceptualizations of Globalization

Three worlds of globalization

Globalization has attracted normative assessments of whether or not it is a "good thing." Corresponding to these normative arguments are empirical judgements about whether it is a useful term or whether what the term describes actually exists; thus, some have written about the myth of globalization (Hirst, Thompson, and Bromley 2009) and other myths associated with it, such as the myth of the powerless state (Weiss 1997). A number of years ago Dobuzinskis (2000) sought to make sense out of all this by depicting "three worlds of globalization," each of which contain empirical (factual) and normative (values-based) judgements.

The first of these, the "World I" approaches, are uncritical and see globalization as a logical and welcome development of "welfare enhancing" market forces. Setting markets free, in this view, is good for all countries and individuals, rich and poor. International trade organizations that promote market integration are thus depicted in much international relations scholarship as mutually beneficial, leaving all parties as least as well off as they would have been without the agreements. Essentially, this view is hostile toward the state in either of its commonsense meanings—first, as a system of government and, second, as a territorial entity possessing legal sovereignty. Thus economic liberals may value a strong state at the national level for limited purposes such as law and order, defence, and protection of property rights. Beyond that, state intervention is regarded with suspicion as market-inhibiting. Extending this view to the global level finds a similar set of imperatives. National security concerns and protecting business interests, where possible, are acceptable areas of state activity, but it is desirable to keep the state away from activities that control capital movements or impose too many restrictions on trade. To the extent, then, that it erodes national boundaries and state capacity to intervene in markets, globalization is regarded positively in this world view.

"World II" viewpoints concede globalization's new and significant characteristics, and see it as inevitable and thus something to which governments and citizens must adapt, regardless of whether it is positively or negatively assessed. From this perspective, national governments continue to be important, though increasingly their decisions may be shaped or determined by global actors, whether international organizations or transnational capital. Since states are less capable than they were previously to assert themselves in the international arena, much of what they do consists of attempting to position themselves favourably in order to take advantage of opportunities brought by globalization, and limit the damage of its negative effects. The term "competition state" has been coined to describe the economic version of this strategy (Cerny 2005). Here the state (in meaning one—system of government) actively attempts to make its territory (state in meaning two—nation-state) attractive to investors, both domestic and foreign, on the theory that investment drives economic growth and thus prosperity. The strategy can come in many different varieties, two of which are illustrated here. A low road strategy, for example, would offer a low-paid, closely controlled labour force as an asset for competitive investment. Alternatively, by investing in education and training, a state might follow a high road competition state strategy with the high quality of its labour force as a point of attraction to potential investors. Either way, the state is active but adaptive in the face of forces it hopes to influence but cannot control.

"World III" encompasses the critics of globalization. Many are from the political left and point to globalization as the product of powerful class-based social forces and as a phenomenon that accordingly creates winners and losers along class lines. From this standpoint, globalization is ideologically suspect in that "it appears to justify the spread of Western culture and of capitalist society by suggesting that there are forces operating beyond human control that are transforming the world" (Waters 1995, 3). Other critics come from the political right, often the so-called "alt-right," who construct nationalist and xenophobic mythologies in which immigrants and foreigners loom large as causes of economic and cultural decline. Fuelled by such sentiments, as well as by a perception among many that they had been "left behind" by economic globalization, the Brexit referendum and the election of Donald Trump in 2016 show that right-wing criticisms of globalization are on the rise.

Yet, disputed as this terrain may be, there is little doubt that the world's political economy is actually in a process of transformation. The various "takes" on the phenomenon of globalization represent efforts to portray and understand that process and will form the background to our analysis.

Three models of the political economy of globalization and development

Hoogvelt (1997) also maintains that there are three vantages from which pundits, supporters, and critics view globalization. Hoogvelt explicitly links the three models of globalization to international relations theories: realism, institutionalism, and structuralism. Realism gives primacy to the nation-state and interstate politics, arguing that states use their political power to interfere in the international market for self-interest (Hoogvelt 1997, 7). Realism asserts that the international system is based on hegemony and balance of power. In this view, globalization is likely the creation of (powerful) states and their interests will be reflected in the norms and institutions of the global era, just as the interests of powerful states were in previous eras. Conversely, developing states with weak political systems and leaders have little say in international politics and economics.

Institutionalism or pluralism is descended from the liberal economic theories of Adam Smith (1723–1790), whereby "increasing economic interdependence forces states to develop and pursue policies of rational self-interest which lead to greater economic cooperation between them rather than to conflict" (Hoogvelt 1997, 8). Cooperation is thus both necessary and largely beneficial for the economic growth of all participating states. And while nation-states have managed to develop under different degrees of political and/or religious freedom, they tend to embrace (willingly or, some argue, by coercion) the capitalist economic model of production in order to be "equal" participants in the global political economy. Further, the stability of the global system is guaranteed by supranational organizations such as the United Nations, the World Trade Organization (WTO), and the International Monetary Fund (IMF). In this view, developing states have the opportunity to develop and grow their economies through a liberalized trading system in which their comparative advantage will convey benefits.

The third model, structuralism, relies on Marxist theories of political economy, including dependency theory, whereby the capitalist system of production has resulted in a highly organized class-based world order, and an unequal system of core, periphery, and semi-periphery states (Hoogvelt 1997, 9). (See Chapter 1 and Chapter 2.) In this model, the global political economy is called structuralist "because it challenges the assumption that national societies constitute 'independent' units whose development can be understood without taking into account the systemic ways in which these societies are linked to one another in the context of an ever expanding network of material (economic) exchanges" (Hoogvelt 1997, 8). As in the realist view, the results of the global economy for weaker states are in this view typically negative. However, the enduring class-based structure, the rise of neoliberalism, and the assault on the labour movement by political and economic elites has resulted in less for the middle and working classes in developed states as well.

Institutionalizing Globalization

Attempts to impose some order on the complexities of globalization occur in the real world as well as in the world of academic theories. The dominant ideology and policy paradigm of our era is often called neoliberalism. Neoliberal thinking about the global economy found its clearest expression in what was called the Washington Consensus, which shaped relations between the developed and developing worlds from the 1980s onwards. (See Chapter 2 for a description of the Washington Consensus.)

John Williamson, who has been seen by some as an architect of the policies adopted by the Washington Consensus, denied that the Washington Consensus represented "an extreme and dogmatic commitment to the belief that markets can handle everything" but conceded that this was how the term had later come to be used (Williamson 2000, 252). These developments set the scene for neoliberal convergence, or what might be termed the "There Is No Alternative" hypothesis put forward by British Prime Minister Margaret Thatcher (1979–1990).

Just as neoliberal ideas have become predominant, global institutions have been established to lock in these neoliberal views of the economy at both national and global levels. Often described as "new constitutionalism," "quiet constitutionalism," or "disciplinary neoliberalism," the main trends are shown in **Box 3.1**.

Policy Convergence and Divergence

Together, ideas and institutions like those of the Washington Consensus and new constitutionalism suggest a one-size-fits-all model of development. Pushed by the leading states and international organizations, developing countries face intense pressures to adopt this conventional wisdom. Thus, globalization may have many dimensions, but there have been concerted efforts to assign primacy to the economic dimension and, within it, to the neoliberal view of how the economy should be organized.

Notwithstanding these pressures, there is scope for national variation; the neoliberal order is not monolithic (Kahler and Lake 2003; Weiss 2005; Brenner, Peck, and Theodore 2010). There is variation—indeed, resistance—across geographical, ideological, and political spaces. Explanations of why some states may be less compliant with pressures of neoliberal globalization than others include:

1. the presence of leftist governments and labour unions (Boix 2000; Coleman 2001; Garrett 1998)
2. cultural or social solidarity (Teichman 2007; Rose 1993; Drezner 2005; Deacon 2000; Flockhart 2004)
3. the shift from a bipolar to multipolar world (Drezner 2005; Porter and Webb 2008)
4. "strategic activism" by developing capitalist states. (Weiss 2005)

To the extent that developing countries reject neoliberal policy advice and rely on their own states to further their development, they are following the pattern by which today's developed countries undertook their own development. (See **Box 3.2**.)

Box 3.1

Political Globalization: The New Constitutionalism

(McBride 2011, 19–40)

In the era of neoliberal globalization, political economists have noted efforts to entrench the new world order by means of binding and enforceable provisions of international economic agreements that, in certain respects, have the qualities of domestic constitutions (Gill 1992; Clarkson 1993; McBride 2005). Indeed, many constitutional experts have been blinded to the impact of non-traditional measures, such as trade agreements, on national constitutions when considered as the formal and informal rules and values that establish political institutions in the way they operate. To create profitable opportunities for capital, the neoliberal state reshaped institutions and engaged in "accumulation by dispossession" (Harvey 2003) in a number of ways. Privatization, deregulation, labour flexibility, capital mobility, and free trade are important weapons in the neoliberal policy arsenal. Limiting democratic governance through concentrating power in institutions that are well insulated from popular pressure is at the core of its institutional design. This has been referred to as "quiet constitutionalism" or "new constitutionalism" because it consists of "efforts to insulate important economic agencies and agents from popular scrutiny and accountability, and thus to narrow democratic control of the economy" (Gill 1992, 269; Hirst, Thompson, and Bromley 2009).

Thus, neoliberalism has constructed new institutions that provide a constitutional framework for the accumulation strategy associated with economic globalization.

Neoliberal rules insulate (private) capital from governmental (public) regulation. Key powers are institutionally located in ways that are remote from popular pressure and democratic influence. These locations are designed to be minimally accountable, or not accountable at all, to popular representatives. Furthermore, the agreements are designed to lock in the neoliberal content of globalization by embedding rules in international agreements that will be very difficult to change in the future. Finally, in many cases public authority is replaced by private authority, or by a sharing of authority that was formerly exercised exclusively by public actors.

The result has been a considerable network of institutions of global economic governance that, taken collectively, undermine or usurp national constitutions, and in the process create a two-tiered world of constitutional rights: rights for transnational corporations at the global or regional levels, but no general political or social rights at these levels. The new constitution that is created is not complete, and there are certainly signs of resistance to it. These may be expected to intensify if economic recovery from the 2009 economic crisis is prolonged.

The impact of the new constitution on national policy capacity may be inversely related to level of development; that is, it may have more impact on less developed countries. Its reach is thus hierarchical, and it can be seen as one instrument by which the developed countries dominate the less developed countries.

Box 3.2

Development as Associative–Dissociative Processes

(McBride 2005, 28–29)

In a major historical survey of issues of development, Senghaas (1985, 27) identified two broad strategic responses used by semi-peripheral countries in their dealings with hegemonic or core powers. The first, called associative, implied an open acceptance of the "challenge and adapting to the superior economy through division of labour. This amounts to the free trade position." The second, called dissociative, consisted of "attempting to develop the domestic economic potential in the shelter of more or less far-reaching protectionist measures, international competitiveness not being the guiding criterion for development promotion." Senghaas notes (1985, 40) that among countries which actually achieved development, albeit later than the leading powers, consistent pursuit of the free trade option was the exception rather than the rule. In most "a non–free trade posture played a major part in the broadening and deepening of the industrialization process." These countries followed what Senghaas terms an associative-dissociative sequence of development. This means that their development

> began with an upswing in export growth (a predominantly associative phase), the agricultural, silvicultural and mineral resources of the societies in question being

devoted mainly to exports. In a later phase a dissociative development policy was pursued, corresponding with the well-known pattern of industrialization through import substitution: the substitution by local products of, at first, formerly imported consumer goods, and later, of basic, capital and engineering goods. In the long-term, development of this kind led to a comprehensively associative free-trade posture, which, however, was not adopted until decades after the start of modern development, for the most part not until decades after the Second World War. (Senghaas 1985, 32)

Based on this account of how states have developed, the problem with the neoliberal policy consensus is obvious. It recommends a particular development strategy that few if any of the developed countries followed in their own economic histories. Through new constitutionalist measures, it seeks to preclude developing countries from following strategies that in the past did lead to successful economic development. From this perspective, then, it seems reasonable to depict the consensus neoliberal ideas and their associated institutions as being part of a system of power designed to preserve the existing global hierarchy.

Structural Adjustment Policies and International Organizations

International financial institutions (IFIs) such as the International Monetary Fund (IMF), World Bank, and Inter-American Development Bank have been strong promoters of economic liberalization in developing states. Biersteker (1992) illustrates how the IMF and

World Bank promoted liberalization via both external pressures and normative exhortation, taking advantage of a global recession in the advanced industrial world from 1980 to 1983 that provoked depression in the developing world, which then created new opportunities for the diffusion of neoliberal ideas. Domestic elite interests within African, East Asian, and Latin American countries, critical of past policies and high national debts, became champions of IMF and World Bank "best practices" for liberal reform. Successful liberalization in East Asian countries bred greater demand in other countries for more liberalization (Biersteker 1992, 122–24).

But the specific policy prescriptions put forth by the IFIs were basically non-negotiable: developing and newly industrialized countries that got too far into debt were required to abide by structural adjustment programs. Despite the willingness of some states to liberalize and deregulate their economies, the strict policy prescriptions of the IMF and World Bank, and the various punishments for non-compliance—including denial of access to US markets—illustrate how the IFIs coerced developing countries to follow the neoliberal path prescribed under the Washington Consensus (Harvey 2003). The WTO has significant coercive influence among international organizations over both developed and developing countries, albeit to a lesser degree for the former (Weiss 2005). Gensey and Winham (2008) point out that state autonomy is weakened when a state (voluntarily) joins the WTO, including states considered global economic powers. Indeed, Canada has found itself on the receiving end of WTO rulings, to the detriment of Canadian culture: the magazine industry lost preferential treatment after the WTO rejected Canada's claim that its efforts were aimed at protecting Canadian culture and national identity (Gensey and Winham 2008, 50). To be sure, the United States has more "room to manoeuvre" (Weiss 2005) within the WTO than Canada, in part because it is the organization's chief architect. As such, the US can force open capital markets through the WTO (and IMF) when it appears that doing so will benefit US financial institutions (Harvey 2003). "Taiwan and Singapore were forced to sign on to the WTO, and thereby open their financial markets to speculative capital, in the face of US threats to deny them access to the US market" (Harvey 2003, 71).

Developing Countries' Resistance to Neoliberalism

Nevertheless, developing countries, even small ones, have resisted such global pressures.

The Left in Latin America

In Uruguay a left-wing coalition government took office in 2005 and began the task of recovering from the side effects of the Argentinian financial crisis of the early 2000s. This had left Uruguay, a small country of some 3.5 million people, in recession. Ten years later, the Frente Amplio or left-wing coalition was still in office. It could point to an impressive economic record in which real wages increased 46.6 percent from 2005 to 2013, real minimum wages increased almost 250 percent during the same period, coverage under the government health plan and defined benefit pension plan rose from 59 percent in 2005 to 76 percent in 2013, poverty declined from 38 percent of population in 2005 to 10 percent in 2013, and extreme poverty declined from 5 percent in 2005 to 0.04 percent in 2013. Inequality, as measured by the Gini coefficient, also declined from 0.45 in 2004 to 0.38 in 2013 (Pugh 2014).

The Frente Amplio has held the presidency and majorities in both chambers of the legislature since first coming to office in 2005. Uruguay is not alone, but is part of a regional anti-neoliberal trend, with friendly governments in Argentina, Bolivia, Brazil, Ecuador, and Venezuela. In addition, there is vastly increased cooperation through the Union of South American Nations (Telesur 2014) and the Mercosur Parliament; such organizations have helped small countries to resist or ignore pressure from the IFIs.

Bolivia's leftist government since 2006 has also achieved a significant transformation in that country. Measures include the nationalization of oil, gas, and mineral resources; transfers of income to the Indigenous majority; cutting poverty by 32 percent; and an expanded education system that claims to have wiped out illiteracy. To minimize foreign interference, the US ambassador and several US government agencies, along with the IMF, were expelled.

Brazil, too, showed a successful, albeit limited, alternative to global neoliberal policy prescriptions under the Brazilian Workers' Party from 2003 to 2016. That government's social policies saw a reduction in poverty by 55 percent over 12 years and a reduction in extreme poverty by 65 percent. Unemployment fell to record low levels and per capita income growth was healthy (Ismi 2014–15, 37). Notwithstanding that track record, the elected president, Dilma Rousseff, was impeached and removed from office in 2016 and replaced by a neoliberal government that capped public spending for the next 20 years. Clearly, this represents a dramatic U-turn in Brazilian policy. Whether it will prove to have such longevity is less clear.

Still, the global shift to a multipolar world, precipitated by the rise of Brazil, Russia, India, China, and South Africa (BRICS) has enabled states to resist pressure from international organizations (Drezner 2005; Porter and Webb 2008). This is because, in a multipolar world, there are more sites for regulatory harmonization and competition (Drezner 2005). Certainly, the rapid growth of China, India, and other "emerging economies" over the last 30 years represents a partial redistribution of power away from the traditional developed countries, who must now listen to these emerging/developing countries more than they did before. (See Chapter 13.) This redistribution has gone so far that many emerging/developing countries have been incorporated into an important new global forum, the G20, which in some respects has replaced the G7/G8 as the leading forum for coordinating international economic policy.

Others, contemplating the rise of the BRICS, along with declining poverty rates and, more contentiously, inequality, argue that these facts represent a success story for neoliberal globalization, since many of these fast-growing emerging countries have indeed liberalized their economies and embraced free trade and closer economic integration.

Manipulating the new constitutionalism

Apart from resistance to the recommended neoliberal model, others have pointed to the potential for countries to position themselves differently within the global economy and to take advantage of the possibilities within the new constitutional architecture. Strong states use "strategic activism" to make room to manoeuvre within the WTO and the global economy generally (Weiss 2005). The shift in investment from production and products, which are "sticky" areas under WTO regulations, to technology and knowledge research has made it possible for these states to use legitimate WTO regulations to support domestic economies (Weiss 2005, 724). In other words, instead of constraining the scope of state activism, the tighter rules of WTO stimulate a more proactive approach to industrial governance: "in spite of some obvious restrictions on traditional (especially subsidy-intensive) industry policy, there remains ample scope for domestic industry promotion" (Weiss 2005, 729).

However, and returning to the theme of hierarchy within the global order, these openings are more available to developed rather than developing countries, as Weiss's discussion of the WTO's Agreement on Subsidies and Countervailing Measures makes clear: "Rich nations as a group have carved out a multilateral order which best suits their current development trajectory—one that diminishes space for promoting industries critical to their climb up the development ladder, while increasing scope for sponsoring the technology-intensive sectors now critical to securing national prosperity" (Weiss 2005, 724).

In other words, while developing states have ended subsidies and tax barriers as conditions of WTO membership, developed states have uncovered other WTO regulations that make subsidies for the wealth-increasing technology and knowledge industries legitimate. Thus in the face of "best practices" promoted and pushed by international organizations, but which have zero-sum implications for developing states: "If, for example, we find that the WTO proclaims free trade but actually delivers unfair trade in which the richer countries maintain their collective advantage over the poorer, then we should not be surprised. This is typical of imperial practices" (Harvey 2005, 133).

The interaction between the neoliberal view of development in the era of globalization, favoured by powerful states and the IFIs in which they are dominant, is a complex one. Some developing states, notably the BRICS, have made significant advances within the context established by neoliberalism, though not by slavishly following its recommendations. Others, including some small Latin American countries, have sought to challenge the model and seek alternative routes to development, demonstrating that, in the slogan of the World Social Forum, "Another World is Possible."

Whether by seeking to develop by following neoliberal recommendations or by seeking alternatives, developing countries face the challenges posed by the existing international hierarchy and its institutional architecture, as well as the dilemmas posed by periodic crises of the global system, such as the financial crisis of 2008–2009. They also face a new challenge, one that was not a consideration in the period when today's developed states were adding industry and advanced technology to their economies. This is the challenge of climate change and, more broadly, environmental sustainability.

Global governance and sustainability

While climate change is decidedly an international issue, there is no world organization that can enforce regulations to reduce greenhouse gas emissions. (See Case Study 8.) This state of affairs "leaves the environment falling between cracks of regimes" (Doern et al. 1999).

Moreover, WTO rules tend to make it harder to improve environmental standards across the board (Drezner 2001). A number of international trade cases already illustrate this obstacle to green development strategies. In Ontario, the government introduced a green energy strategy designed to replace carbon-intensive energy production with clean and renewable energy and, at the same time, ensure that a proportion of the jobs created by the strategy were homegrown (McBride and Shields 2013). However, Japan and the European Union objected to the "local content" regulations that were likely needed to sustain political support for a strategy that would produce greener but more expensive energy. The case at the WTO produced a ruling that local content provisions were contrary to international trade law (Sinclair and Trew 2015).

Similarly, US complaints prompted China to end its subsidies for wind-generated electricity; the United States has successfully challenged Chinese subsidies three times at the WTO (USTR 2011). However, the dispute between the United States and China continues. In May 2012, the US Commerce Department announced that it would be imposing duties to counter alleged dumping of Chinese-made solar panels. Shortly afterwards, China requested consultations at the WTO alleging the US duties were contrary to WTO rules.

Aaron Cosbey (2011) has argued that the WTO dispute settlement process is the wrong place to forge international consensus on policy measures to support renewable energy, which is essentially an environmental issue, not a trade issue. Such cases pit trade against the environment and pose the issue of whether trade law can or should outweigh legitimate environmental concerns. So far it seems trade law has prevailed.

Sustainable Development and Globalization

These cases highlight a rather unsatisfactory debate about how to deal with the environmental crisis in a context where the usual imperatives towards economic development also apply. Since the latter part of the first decade of this century, the idea of a "green economy" has been advanced as a solution to deal with the convergence of several global problems: food price volatility, natural disasters, climate change, increases in inequality, and the 2008–2009 global financial crisis (Benson, Bass, and Greenfield 2014). A truly "green economy" must reduce social and income inequality as much as it reduces greenhouse gases. But the green economy remains a contested concept. "A number of transition paths (to a greener, more sustainable future) are currently being envisaged. But the question of which ideas and values will prevail, and shape policy and practice partly depends on which worldviews inform public opinion and policy processes" (UNRISD 2012, 3).

For example, the World Economic Forum emphasizes "greening economic growth [as] the only way in which sustainable, inclusive development can be achieved that will satisfy the basic needs of 9 billion people and provide them with equal rights to material prosperity. A key challenge is the urgent need to reduce carbon emissions . . . Another imperative is the need to increase natural resource productivity to meet unprecedented demands for clean water, food and urban development" (World Economic Forum, n.d.).

This view of "greening" growth—rather than seeking alternatives to unfettered production and consumption—has largely been informed by familiar neoliberal policy prescriptions: making carbon a tradable commodity, avoiding regulation, and promoting voluntary corporate social responsibility while limiting action to the confines of the global trade regime. Power relations remain important, and the influence of the advanced economies on international agencies means that few, if any, UN agencies suggest real structural change. Instead, policy recommendations for a green economy—even one that pays attention to social goals—emphasize existing economic policies, the power of technology to solve problems, sustainable consumption, and the free market to adjust environmental costs. The "green economy" has thus been framed as a "win-win" for stakeholders, including business and environmentalists (Jacobs 2012; Tombari 2016). So while the (so-called) "green" or "greening" economies of the world may have different policy interpretations, they may also be a project within the larger neoliberal agenda, rather than an effort to halt climate change, create jobs, and reduce social and income inequality.

To some extent, the Paris Agreement on Climate Change, signed by 195 countries including Canada in November 2015 (see Case Study 8), represented a response to these concerns, since it addressed the urgent need for action on climate change while recognizing that economic development goals must also be met. And though President Donald Trump announced his intention to withdraw the United States, one of the world's largest greenhouse gas emitters, from the Paris Agreement in June 2017, US states and municipalities have promised to meet the Paris targets without the federal government.

Conclusion

The chapter opened by surveying globalization as a complex process of many dimensions. We noted academic attempts to classify, and thereby simplify, what is a voluminous and wide-ranging, multifaceted debate about the nature and implications of this phenomenon. The "order" imposed on globalization is a helpful academic device. Several of the concepts or interpretations that are described here have noted that hierarchical social relations are embedded within globalization. In turning to real-world efforts to institutionalize global relationships, we noted efforts to privilege the economic dimensions as opposed, for example, to the environmental ones. However, these attempts to institutionalize a particular vision of economic globalization, in which a particular model of the road to development is singled out, have also encountered resistance. Debates about what is the best development strategy for developing countries look far from being over. That said, the whole concept of economic development is complicated by the looming environmental crisis expressed in concerns over climate change and the need to limit carbon emissions. Although there is much talk of greening the economy, it remains unclear how traditional development concerns such as the need for more growth, more income, more production, and more jobs can be reconciled with the need for environmental sustainability. Globalization has certainly changed the world, but it has not solved all its problems.

Questions for Further Learning

- In the era of globalization, does the state still play a key role in orchestrating economic development?
- To what extent is the neoliberal "one size fits all" model of economic development appropriate for developing countries today?
- In what ways might economic development be sustainable?

Key Terms

globalization, p. 50

neoliberalism, p. 54

sustainable development, p. 61

Gini coefficient, p. 57

developing states, p. 50

Suggested Readings

Fine, Ben, Jyoti Saraswati, and Daniela Tavasci, eds. 2013. *Beyond the Developmental State*. London: Pluto Press.

Gill, Stephen, and A. Claire Cutler, eds. 2014. *New Constitutionalism and World Order*. Cambridge: Cambridge University Press.

Klein, Naomi. 2014. *This Changes Everything: Capitalism vs. the Climate*. Toronto: Simon & Schuster.

McBride, Stephen. 2005. *Paradigm Shift: Globalization and the Canadian State*. 2nd ed. Fernwood Publishing: Halifax.

Suggested Videos

Naomi Klein on Global Neoliberalism. https://youtu.be/sKTmwu3ynOY

China: Role Model for Asian Development: Asia Global Institute. https://youtu.be/5XjSrsv1itk

What is Sustainable Development? United Nations. https://youtu.be/masQeEG5FX4

COP21 video message from United Nations Secretary-General Ban Ki-moon. https://youtu.be/4tnIyAOKnBw

Paris Agreement Explained: Selwin Hart, UN. https://youtu.be/o6Rovrp-SCs

What Is Globalization? Wissenswerte. https://www.youtube.com/watch?v=30TLyPPrZE4

What Is New about Post-1980 Globalization? Noam Chomsky. http://www.youtube.com/watch?v=AHJPSLgHemM&feature=related

Suggested Websites

World Social Forum: www.forumsocialmundial.org.br/index.php?cd_language=2

World Economic Forum: http://www.weforum.org/

World Trade Organization: www.wto.org

International Institute for Sustainable Development: http://www.iisd.org/

Heterodox Economists' Newsletter: http://www.heterodoxnews.com/n/htn176.html#art-17592186054871

Works Cited

Appadurai, Arjun. 2006. "Disjuncture and Difference in the Global Cultural Economy." In *Media and Cultural Studies: Key Works*, rev. ed., edited by Meenakshi Gigi Durham and Douglas M. Kellner. Oxford: Blackwell Publishing.

Benson, Emily, Steve Bass, and Oliver Greenfield. 2014. "Green Economy Barometer: Who Is Doing What, Where and Why? Backgrounder Paper." *Green Economy Coalition*. Retrieved from http://pubs.iied.org/pdfs/16573IIIED.pdf?

Biersteker, Thomas. 1992. "The 'Triumph' of Neoclassical Economics in the Developing World: Policy Convergence and Bases of Governance in the International Economic Order." In *Governance without Government: Order and Change in World Politics*, edited by James Rosenau and Ernst-Otto Czempiel. Cambridge: Cambridge University Press.

Boix, Carles. 2000. "Partisan Governments, the International Economy, and Macroeconomic Policies in Advanced Nations, 1960–93." *World Politics* 53 (1): 38–73.

Brenner, Neil, Jamie Peck, and Nik Theodore. 2010. "After Neoliberalization?" *Globalizations*, 7 (3): 327–345.

Cerny, Philip. 2005. Different Roads to Globalization: Neoliberalism, the Competition State, and Politics in a More Open World.

Clarkson, Stephen. 1993. "Economics: The New Hemispheric Fundamentalism." In *The Political Economy of North American Free Trade*, edited by Ricardo Grinspun and Maxwell Cameron. New York: St. Martin's Press.

Coleman, William. 2001. "Agricultural Policy Reform and Policy Convergence: An Actor-Centred Institutionalist Approach." *Journal of Comparative Policy Analysis: Research and Practice* 3 (2): 219–241.

Cosbey, Aaron. 2011. "Renewable Energy Subsidies and the WTO: The Wrong Law and the Wrong Venue." *Subsidy Watch* 4.

Deacon, Bob. 2000. "Eastern European Welfare States: The Impact of the Politics of Globalization." *Journal of European Social Policy* 10 (2): 146–161.

Dobuzinskis, Laurent. 2000. *Three Worlds of Globalization.*

Doern, G. Bruce, Margaret Hill, Michael Prince, and Richard Schultz. 1999. *Changing the Rules: Canadian Regulatory Regimes and Institutions.* Toronto: University of Toronto Press.

Drezner, Daniel. 2001. "Globalization and Policy Convergence." *International Studies Review* 3 (1): 53–78.

———. 2005. "Globalization, Harmonization, and Competition: The Different Pathways to Policy Convergence." *Journal of European Public Policy* 12 (5): 841–859.

Flockhart, Trine. 2004. "Masters and Novices: Socialization and Social Learning through the NATO Parliamentary Assembly." *International Relations* 18 (4).

Garrett, Geoffrey. 1998. *Partisan Politics in the Global Economy.* Cambridge: Cambridge University Press.

Gensey, Guy, and Gilbert Winham. 2008. "International Law, Dispute Settlement, and Autonomy." In *Global Ordering: Institutions and Autonomy in a Changing World*, edited by Louis Pauly and William Coleman. Vancouver: University of British Columbia Press.

Gill, Stephen. 1992. "Economic Globalization and the Internationalization of Authority: Limits and Contradictions." *Geoforum* 23 (3): 269–84.

Hanson, Gordon. 2010. "International Migration and the Developing World." In *Handbook of Development Economics* (Volume 5), edited by Dani Rodrik and Mark Rosenzweig. Amsterdam: North-Holland.

Harvey, David. 2003. *The New Imperialism.* Oxford: Oxford University Press.

———. 2004. "The 'New' Imperialism: Accumulation by Dispossession." *Socialist Register*, no. 40, 63–87.

———. 2005. *A Brief History of Neoliberalism.* New York: Oxford University Press.

Hirst, Paul, Grahame Thompson, and Simon Bromley. 2009. *Globalization in Question.* 3rd ed. Oxford: Polity Press.

Hoogvelt, Ankie. 1997. *Globalization and the Postcolonial World: The New Political Economy of Development.* Baltimore: The Johns Hopkins University Press.

A Human Right. n.d. [website]. Retrieved from http://ahumanright.org/

Ismi, Asad. 2014/15. "Left Parties Win Important National Elections in 2014." *CCPA Monitor* December/January.

Jacobs, Michael. 2012. "Green Growth: Economic Theory and Political Discourse." Working Paper No. 108. London: Grantham Research Centre for Climate Change and Environment, London School of Economics and Political Science.

Kahler, Miles, and David Lake. 2003. *Governance in a Global Economy: Political Authority in Transition.* Princeton: Princeton University Press.

Kothari, Uma, Martin Minogue, and Jocelyn DeJong. 2002. "The Political Economy of Globalization." In *Development Theory and Practice: Critical Perspectives*, edited by Uma Kothari and Martin Minogue. Houndmills, UK: Palgrave.

McBride, Stephen. 2005. *Paradigm Shift: Globalization and the Canadian State.* 2nd ed. Halifax: Fernwood Publishing.

———. 2011. "New Constitutionalism: International and Private Rule in the New Global Order." In *Relations of Global Power: Neoliberal Order and Disorder*, edited by Stephen McBride and Gary Teeple. Toronto: University of Toronto Press.

McBride, Stephen, and John Shields. 2013. "International Trade Agreements and the Ontario Green Energy Act: Opportunities and Obstacles." In *Climate@Work*, edited by Carla Lipsig-Mummé. Halifax: Fernwood.

Porter, Tony, and Michael Webb. 2008. "Role of the OECD in the Orchestration of Global Knowledge Networks." In *The OECD and Transnational Governance*, edited by Rianne Mahon and Stephen McBride. Vancouver, University of British Columbia Press.

Pugh, Paul. 2014. "Uruguay: More than 'Country of the Year.'" *Progressive Economics Forum*. Retrieved from http://www.progressive-economics.ca/2014/02/23/paul-pugh-on-uruguays-fitting-recognition/.

Rose, Richard. 1993. *Lesson-drawing in Public Policy: A Guide to Learning across Time and Space*. Chatham, NJ: Chatham House.

Senghaas, Dieter. 1985. *The European Experience: A Historical Critique of Development Theory*. Leamington Spa: Berg Publishers.

Sinclair, Scott, and Stuart Trew. 2015. "International Constraints on Green Strategies: Ontario's WTO Defeat and Public Sector Remedies." In *Work in a Warming World*, edited by Carla Lipsig-Mummé and Stephen McBride. Montreal, Kingston: McGill-Queen's University Press.

Teichman, Judith. 2007. "Multilateral Lending Institutions and Transnational Policy Networks in Mexico and Chile." *Global Governance*, no. 13, 557–573.

Telesur. 2014. "UNASUR: Integrating South America." Retrieved from http://www.telesurtv.net/english/telesuragenda/UNASUR-20141203-0029.html.

Tombari, Stephanie. 2016. *The Green Publicity State: Sustainability, Austerity and the 'Green Economy' in Michigan and Ontario, 2007–2012*. Ph.D. thesis, Hamilton,: McMaster University. https://macsphere.mcmaster.ca/bitstream/11375/18954/2/Tombari_Stephanie_L_201603_PhD.pdf.

UNRISD. 2012. *From Green Economy to Green Society: Bringing the Social to Rio+20*. Geneva: United Nations Research Institute for Social Development.

USTR. 2011. *China Ends Wind Power Equipment Subsidies Challenged by the United States in WTO Dispute*. Washington, D.C.: Office of the United States Trade Representative.

Waters, Malcolm. 1995. *Globalization*. London: Routledge.

Weiss, Linda. 1997. "Globalization and the Myths of the Powerless State." *New Left Review*, no. 225, 3–27.

———. 2005. "Global Governance, National Strategies: How Industrialized States Make Move to Room under the WTO." *Review of International Political Economy* 12 (5): 723–749.

Williamson, John. 2000. "What Should the World Bank Think about the Washington Consensus?" *The World Bank Research Observer* 15 (2).

World Economic Forum. n.d. "Climate Change and Green Growth: An Introduction." Retrieved from http://www.weforum.org/issues/climate-change-and-green-growth.

Notes

Part II

Canada and the Developing Countries since 1945

4 Canada's Aid Program since 1945

Hunter McGill

Overview

The issue for this chapter is: "How did Canada become a provider of foreign aid?" The chapter takes an historical approach, with special treatment of gender and tied aid as examples of policy issues. The various components and mechanisms for delivering Canada's aid program are explained, as well as their variations over time. Connections between aid policy and overall foreign policy are explained, as well as the efforts to coordinate Canadian aid with the aid of other traditional donor countries.

Key Terms

development cooperation

foreign aid

gender

Official Development Assistance (ODA)

tied aid

Learning Objectives

By the end of this chapter, students will be able to:

- understand the origins of foreign aid.
- understand the evolution of North-South relations from foreign aid to development assistance and then to development cooperation.
- appreciate the various components and mechanisms of Canada's foreign aid.
- understand the connections between aid and other elements of Canada's foreign policy.
- understand Canada's place in the global development cooperation environment.

Beginnings

Histories of foreign aid tend to start in the mid-1940s with the creation of the World Bank and the International Monetary Fund (IMF) by countries meeting in Bretton Woods, New Hampshire, in July 1944. Reflecting the location of that meeting, the two organizations have come to be known as the Bretton Woods institutions. The political leaders of the Allied countries, including Canada, foresaw an end to the Second World War (1939–1945) and with rare foresight identified the need for mechanisms to deliver financial and technical assistance to countries in Europe to help them rebuild their devastated economies (Conway 2012). In parallel, the same countries plus others were working on the creation of the United Nations, culminating in the San Francisco Conference of June 1945, which was to serve as a political venue for the achievement of sustainable peace and security in the world. (See Case Study 1.)

As a major participant in the Second World War, and sharing the view that new institutions, both political and financial, were needed to promote economic growth and stability in the world, Canada was an important actor at the meetings in Bretton Woods and San Francisco. In 1944–1945 the great colonial empires of Britain and France still held sway. The countries of South and Southeast Asia and of Africa did not exist as independent entities and the largest "developing" country, China, was in the throes of a civil war that ended only in 1949. Thus the dialogue about the purposes of these new postwar institutions took place in a rather exclusive club of like-minded Western countries. From 1945 to 1950, their experience was based on their work in the reconstruction of war-shattered Europe. In looking at the needs of what US President Truman called the underdeveloped regions of the world (see Chapter 2), the countries called "developed" had little if any experience with development, and the theoretical frameworks that grew after 1960 were not available to planners, negotiators, and decision-makers.

The international scene began to shift soon after 1945, as the Cold War started and the Soviet Union extended its political dominance over Eastern Europe. At the same time, the British and French colonial empires began to disintegrate. Following long struggles, India and Pakistan (which then included Bangladesh) gained independence from Britain in 1947, followed by Burma and Ceylon (now Sri Lanka) in 1948. These newly independent countries quickly became members of the United Nations and the Commonwealth. Canada supported the move for independence for these countries, and agreed to provide economic aid through the Colombo Plan for Cooperative Economic Development in South and Southeast Asia, named for the capital of Ceylon, where the negotiations to create the program concluded in 1950. The countries involved in the first meetings to define the parameters of the Colombo Plan were Australia, Britain, Canada, India, New Zealand, Pakistan, and Ceylon. The Colombo Plan laid the foundations for today's system of aid or development cooperation.

Around the same time, in Southeast Asia, French colonies struggled for independence. French Indochina was the site of brutal wars in Vietnam, Laos, and Cambodia as France sought to maintain control. The result was the partition of Vietnam, with a Communist regime in the north and a US-affiliated government in the south, and significant political turbulence in Cambodia and Laos over several decades. (See Chapter 14.) Indonesia achieved its independence from the Netherlands in 1949 after a war of independence. The initial remit of the Colombo Plan did not extend to these countries and they were not included to any significant extent in Canada's first foreign aid programming. As the Colombo Plan evolved, however, the Southeast Asian countries came under its auspices.

The Colombo Plan Experience and Aid in the 1950s

Canadian motives for involvement in the Colombo Plan were varied. A major influence was concern about the spread of communism in Asia, in light of the recent Communist takeovers in Eastern Europe. The Korean War (1950–1953) erupted between the Communist north and the American-backed south while the Colombo agreements were being finalized. There was a significant push from Britain to find ways of burden-sharing with respect to its post-independence commitments to the new nations of South Asia, at a time when Britain was under enormous fiscal and foreign exchange pressures. But the overarching driver for the developed Commonwealth countries was recognition of the need to address poverty and to reduce the enormous gap between rich and poor countries.

Aid provided through the Colombo Plan concentrated on capital investment for infrastructure in the energy, transportation, and large-scale water and sanitation sectors. Projects included hydro-electric dams, large irrigation schemes, and railway lines. This fit well with the centrally planned economic development approach adopted by the recipient countries, through successive versions of national five-year plans. Also, the aid was largely financed with loans, though for the most part these were given on what are called "soft" terms, via subsidized interest rates with long repayment periods. The intent was to support economic growth which would then generate the income to allow the loans to be repaid. The projects were designed using the donor countries' national experience, without much consideration for distinctive local factors, and most of the high value-added inputs (machinery, equipment, technical expertise) came from the donor countries themselves in an arrangement called tied aid.

Selling the idea of Canadian aid to distant, recently independent countries that had until then been the responsibility of Britain was a rather difficult undertaking. On the political side, the British Empire was being transformed into the Commonwealth of Nations. For the Canadian proponents of participation in the Colombo Plan, led by Lester Pearson as Secretary of State for External Affairs (1948–1957), it was a hard sell in Ottawa, as the federal cabinet was divided. Canada's initial financial commitment was for $400,000 for technical assistance, though within a year the amount had been raised to $25 million for capital (infrastructure) assistance. Interestingly, the prevailing view among senior officials at the time was that the need for this aid was going to be short term, an attitude shaped by the experience of postwar reconstruction in Europe.

Examples of Canadian projects provided under the Colombo Plan included the Warsak Dam in Pakistan, the Trombay nuclear research reactor and the Kundah hydro-electric project in India, and a fishing project in Sri Lanka. Canadian aid also included scholarships for students to attend Canadian universities and colleges. While these students were supposed to return home on graduating, many chose to remain in Canada and become citizens. This represented a loss of human capital to the developing country in question, but a gain for Canada.

Early in the 1950s, as South Asia experienced serious drought and crop failures, Canada,

Australia, and the United States introduced food aid into their assistance programs. As well as meeting the recipient country's food needs, food aid was justified on the basis of easing the recipient's foreign exchange shortages, thus enabling the recipient country to import inputs for investment and growth. From a modest start in 1951, food aid grew to account for 46 percent of Canadian Official Development Assistance (ODA) by 1959, most of it wheat and other grains; much of the growth in Canadian food aid occurred during the Diefenbaker government (1957–1963), whose political support was based in the grain-growing Prairie provinces. From 1954 on, non-food commodities were also included in the range of products funded with aid; items in this category included aluminum, steel, fertilizer, wood pulp, and newsprint. For both food and non-food commodities, the products supplied were sold on the local market and the proceeds deposited in a "counterpart" fund in local currency, which was drawn upon to finance the local costs of development projects. At least this was the theory, though over the years the practice proved to be irregular and the management of the funds politically challenging.

In the late 1950s, the British colonies in the Caribbean prepared to gain independence and join the Commonwealth. Ambitiously, the English-speaking countries of the Caribbean attempted to put together an economic and political union called the West Indies Federation, and for this they sought Canada's help. Beginning in 1958, Canada participated in the West Indies Aid Program. Among the activities Canadian aid supported were vessels for an inter-island shipping line and associated harbour facilities, and the institutional foundations for what became (and remains) the University of the West Indies. A number of the Federation member countries turned to Canada for help with other forms of aid, including in the education field, and in the construction of roads and bridges, notably in the latter case in Jamaica.

In parallel with these steps to create bilateral (country-to-country) aid programs, Canada was making commitments to the UN system for multilateral aid. A range of government departments in Ottawa provided technical expertise to institutions such as the UN Children's Fund, the UN Food and Agriculture Organization, the World Health Organization, the Office of the UN High Commissioner for Refugees, and the UN Educational, Scientific, and Cultural Organization. Support took the form of grants, technical assistance (Canadian experts), and training programs. (See Case Study 5.)

During the 1950s, foreign aid put a greater emphasis on bricks-and-mortar infrastructure and less on human capacity development than might have been appropriate. As the basic needs school rose to prominence in the late 1960s (see Chapter 2), this infrastructure-heavy approach to development drew increasing amounts of criticism. Furthermore, and in hindsight, the timeframes used in planning this aid effort were almost absurdly short, given the development challenges being addressed, but there was little if any precedent to guide decision-making. Finally, much of the assistance, both capital and technical, was centrally planned and imposed and gave little consideration of the needs and wishes of the populations it was intended to help.

African Independence

As the 1960s dawned, the British, French, and Belgian colonial empires in Africa began to dissolve. Ghana gained independence in 1957, and was followed by Nigeria in 1960 and Sierra Leone in 1961, and then in the early 1960s by Malawi, Tanzania, Uganda, Kenya, and Zambia, and later Botswana, Lesotho, and Swaziland. Most of French West Africa gained independence in 1960, as did the Belgian Congo (now the Democratic Republic of the Congo). All of these countries, following the lead of the newly independent Asian countries, joined the United

Nations and became clients of the World Bank, whose mandate had been enlarged to include assistance to non-European nations. The former British colonies became members of the Commonwealth. The equivalent grouping of former French colonies, La Francophonie, was not created until 1970. (See Chapter 8.) Motivated in part by this large influx of newly independent states into its membership, the UN General Assembly designated the 1960s as the UN Development Decade.

Extending Canada's foreign aid to the new and, for the most part, very poor[1] African countries was made easier by political links through the Commonwealth. The newly independent English-speaking countries in Africa, as had been the case in South Asia, had retained governmental structures inspired by the British Westminster system of government (see Chapter 1). Thus, many practices could be transported from donor countries like Britain, Canada, and Australia to the ex-colonies. As the newly independent countries strove to meet their new leaders' promises of access to education, a significant element of Canadian aid took the form of volunteer teachers who went overseas for placements of a year or more. (See Case Study 11.)

Before the Liberal Pierre Trudeau became prime minister in 1968, Canadian aid went mostly to English-speaking Commonwealth countries or through the multilateral channels of the UN. That began to change in 1968, with the mission led by former federal cabinet minister Lionel Chevrier to francophone Africa. Chevrier's mandate was to build diplomatic and other relationships between Canada and the former French colonies, then still firmly within France's neocolonial sphere of influence (see world-system's theory, in Chapter 2), based largely on language and aid. In the space of a few weeks, Chevrier visited most of the francophone countries of West and North Africa and established the foundation for cooperation programs

that still exist. The initial impetus for Ottawa's engagement with francophone Africa stemmed from domestic issues inside Canada, notably Quebec's push for greater visibility internationally. (See Chapter 8.) Despite the rushed and politicized start to the Canada–francophone Africa relationship, these assistance programs survived and matured into long-term programs of cooperation that still exist today.

Organizational Change

Around the same time, important changes were being made in Canada to design, manage, and deliver foreign aid. Starting in 1951, Canada's aid program was managed by the Technical Cooperation Service, which was later turned into the International Economic and Technical Cooperation Division, and then the Economic and Technical Assistance Branch in the Department of Trade and Commerce, where it was something of an organizational orphan. Throughout this period, policy oversight was in theory exercised by External Affairs, and budgetary control by the Department of Finance. In 1959, Canada's aid program came under the External Aid Office (EAO) in the Department of External Affairs and many of its early employees came from Canada's diplomatic corps. The head of the office was Herbert Moran, who had been Canadian High Commissioner to Pakistan and was thus familiar with Canada's Colombo Plan aid. Among the significant developments in the EAO in 1961 and 1962 was the recruitment of staff with developing country experience and suitable knowledge from outside the ranks of the public service, to complement the personnel from External Affairs and the Department of Finance.

Internationally, the so-called international architecture of aid and related agencies was also evolving in the 1960s. The UN Development Program (UNDP) was created in 1966. The World Bank's mandate had been enlarged to include assistance to the newly independent

---

1. Measured in terms of gross national product per capita.

nations, though the Bank's instruments and a new facility for issuing "soft" loans were added in 1960. Canada, as a member of the World Bank's executive board, was and is eighth in terms of voting power, reflecting its financial contribution. Control over the policy positions that Canada would adopt at the World Bank was and is firmly in the hands of the Department of Finance, not External Affairs or its successors.

In a parallel development, in 1960 the Development Assistance Group was set up at the Organisation for Economic Co-operation and Development (OECD), an intergovernmental body based in Paris and grouping the world's leading market-based economies. Within a year, this Group became the OECD Development Assistance Committee (OECD-DAC, or simply DAC), set up to coordinate and facilitate resource flows from OECD member states to developing countries to support the latter's economic development. Canada was one of the eight founding member countries of the DAC. The DAC continues to play an important role as the custodian of the definition of what counts as aid (technically called "Official Development Assistance" or ODA), and as the forum where the major donors conduct reviews of each other's aid programs. The DAC reviews, done every four or five years, provide a valuable snapshot of member countries' performance against the global aid targets, against the objectives they have set for themselves, and in comparison with other aid donors.[2]

On his retirement as Canadian prime minister in 1968, Lester Pearson was asked by the president of the World Bank to lead a high profile panel to propose a path for international cooperation. The result was a report titled *Partners in Development* (Commission on International Development 1969); the report contained, among other things, a proposal that donor countries should provide 0.7 percent of their gross national product (GNP) annually

as aid by 1975, " . . . but in no case later than 1980." This target (often called "the 0.7 target") was agreed to by the United Nations General Assembly in 1970 when it designated the 1970s as the Second Development Decade. The target has been endorsed by multiple international declarations since then. But only six countries have ever achieved this target; Canada has never been one of them.

In 1968, the Trudeau cabinet passed an order-in-council to create the Canadian International Development Agency (CIDA) to replace the EAO. From the beginning, therefore, CIDA lacked a legislative mandate; the question of whether CIDA should have its own legislation has been an issue ever since. Maurice Strong was named as CIDA's first president. CIDA was placed under the Secretary of State (Minister, in today's terms) for External Affairs. The new CIDA had a higher profile and a larger budget than its predecessor and Strong, with his personal connections to Prime Minister Trudeau, set out to raise Canada's profile internationally. Throughout the 1970s, CIDA saw growth in budgets and staffing levels, especially for the Africa programs.

In parallel, young Canadians with an awareness of global poverty, inequality, and injustice were establishing civil society organizations (CSOs) to work in developing countries at the grass-roots level. Among the organizations created at this time were Canadian University Service Overseas (now CUSO), World University Service of Canada (WUSC), the Canadian Hunger Foundation, Centre d'études et de coopération internationale, and the Unitarian Service Committee (now USC Canada). Many of the early participants in these CSO programs, notably ex-CUSO volunteers, were recruited by CIDA when they returned to Canada from overseas. The Canadian Council for International Cooperation (CCIC) was established in 1968 as the national umbrella organization for non-governmental organisations. CCIC now has around 80 member organizations. (See Chapter 7 and Case Study 11.)

---

2. Declaration of interest: The author of this chapter used to work for both CIDA and the OECD-DAC.

Starting in the late 1960s, CIDA started to provide substantial financial support for projects and programs designed and implemented by the CSOs themselves. Reflecting the growth of civil society's efforts to assist developing countries, in 1972 CIDA created a new division to work in partnership with CSOs. But the CSOs were not silent partners; they often criticized CIDA and the Canadian government for perceived shortcomings and failings, notably Canada's perennial failure to reach the 0.7 target. The relationship between the Canadian government and Canadian CSOs working on international development has at times been fraught.

In 1970, Canada established the International Development Research Centre (IDRC). Unlike CIDA, IDRC was created by an Act of Parliament. Funded by Canada but with an international board of governors, IDRC was created to " . . . initiate, encourage, support and conduct research into the problems of the developing regions of the world and into the means for applying and adapting scientific, technical and other knowledge to the economic and social development of those regions" (*IDRC Act*, 1970). In marked contrast to CIDA, IDRC did not engage in much tied aid (see below), and instead focused most of its support on researchers and innovators in developing countries, but not necessarily recipient country governments. (See Case Study 6.)

Storming and Norming

Starting in the 1950s, the UN organized a series of conferences on issues related to international development. Many of these conferences fell prey to Cold War politics and/or the politics of decolonization. The developing countries formed a loose coalition known as the Group of 77 or G77. The G77 often went into these conferences with political agendas linked to decolonization, the elimination of apartheid in South Africa (see Case Study 2), the plight of the Palestinians (see Case Study 10), or nuclear disarmament. A common demand from the G77 was

that the donor countries achieve the 0.7 target as an indication of their commitment to development. Canada, like many donor countries, was usually represented at these conferences by technical specialists who were looking at how to articulate targets to be agreed upon and how to achieve them. The result was considerable friction and dissension in many international conferences during the Cold War (1946–1989).

In 1979–1980, the Independent Commission on International Development Issues (also called the Brandt Commission) tried to unblock the impasse in global discussions on cooperation and raise the profile of the complex set of issues covered by international development. Its report, titled *North-South: A Programme for Survival*, called for renewed efforts to achieve 0.7 percent and to go beyond it to 1.0 percent of GNP; the report also sought increased predictability in aid flows, and based the case for development assistance and cooperation on both the moral rationale and the mutual interests of donor and recipient countries. The report introduced the terminology of North (donors) and South (recipient countries). In Canada, the Liberal government reacted by setting up a parliamentary task force. (See below re the Breau report.)

The World Commission on Environment and Development (also known as the Brundtland Commission) highlighted the close links between international development and environmental sustainability. The key contribution of the Commission's 1987 report, *Our Common Future*, was its definition of "sustainable development" as a form of development that had to " ... meet the needs of the present without compromising the ability of future generations to meet their own needs." The Brundtland Commission benefited from considerable Canadian influence. Maurice Strong, first president of CIDA, was a Commission member and James McNeill, former senior Canadian environmental official, was Secretary General. (See Case Study 8.) IDRC holds the Brundtland Commission's archives.

Table 4.1

Major International Development Conferences, 1975–1996

1975	World Conference of the International Women's Year
1976	UN Conference on Human Settlements (Habitat I)
1978	International Conference on Primary Health Care
1980	Second World Conference on Women
1985	Third World Conference on Women
1990	World Conference on Education for All
1990	World Summit for Children
1992	International Conference on Nutrition
1992	UN Conference on Environment and Development
1993	World Conference on Human Rights
1994	International Conference on Population and Development
1995	Fourth World Conference on Women
1995	World Summit for Social Development
1996	Second UN Conference on Human Settlements (Habitat II)

As the Cold War and its associated (post-) colonial conflicts wound down in the 1980s, the prospects for international collaboration improved. There followed a succession of UN-sponsored conferences (see **Table 4.1**) on issues and themes such as environment, women, education, and social development. The objective of these conferences was to engage all governments to support policies and commit resources to make progress on issues seen as crucial to international development. These conferences laid the foundations for the UN Millennium Declaration and the Millennium Development Goals (MDGs) of 2000, and for the Sustainable Development Goals (SDGs) of 2015. (See Chapter 2.)

Two Key Issues in Development Assistance

The following two key issues in development assistance have been selected from a range of topics, to illustrate how Canada has dealt with subjects closely linked to effective development assistance.

Women in development/gender equality

The challenge of Women in Development, (WID) later re-defined as gender equality, serves as an example of Canada's leadership within its development cooperation programs. The World Conference of the International Women's Year held in Mexico City in 1975 served as a stimulus for reflection and debate within aid agencies. Beginning in 1976, CIDA committed to supporting equality between men and women in development using a "Women in Development lens." WID was understood as recognising the importance of involving women in all stages of development, both as actors and as decision-makers. Over time, however, it became evident that development policies and programs were not gender-neutral and that women and men had different needs, interests, and roles; successful development required taking gender equality into consideration. The initial policy and programming framework for WID had set out the rationale for involving women in all stages of project and program planning and implementation, as actors and decision-makers as well as beneficiaries. A WID directorate was established within

CIDA in 1983, one of the first donor agencies to do so. With experience, and reflecting the broader understanding of gender inequality, CIDA re-examined its approach and in 1995 issued its "Policy on Women in Development and Gender Equity."

In 1999 CIDA published its "Policy on Gender Equality," generally seen as the high point of Canada's engagement with gender and development. This policy identified gender equality as a cross-cutting theme, to be factored into all of CIDA's policies, projects, and bilateral, multilateral, and civil society programs. The policy directed that Canada's development cooperation efforts were to take into account the differentiated needs, perspectives, interests, and roles of women and men in development. The policy stated, "For poverty reduction to be achieved, the constraints that women and girls face must be eliminated." The policy was seen at the time as setting the standard for other donor countries.

Since 1999, however, the policy has not been revisited. Meanwhile, other donors and the international community have identified steps that should be taken to ensure that current gender equality activities reflect improved knowledge and good practice for sustainable development results. Under the Harper government (2006–2015), there appears to have been a move away from CIDA financing activities directly linked to gender equality, and a subtle but clear shift away from using the term "gender equality" in favour of "equality between men and women." Some analysts have noted that recent flagship Canadian ODA initiatives, such as the 2010 Muskoka Initiative for Maternal, Newborn and Child Health, did not incorporate the full range of women's reproductive rights; the initiative tended to categorize women as mothers and to portray mothers and pregnant women as victims. The Liberal government elected in 2015 has added a greater recognition of women's rights to sexual and reproductive health into the Muskoka Initiative.

Tied aid

The OECD defines "tied aid" as "offering aid on the condition that it be used to procure goods or services from the provider of the aid" (OECD, n.d.). In other words, Canadian tied aid means that recipient countries must purchase a certain proportion of goods and services for their aid program from Canadian suppliers. Early aid programs, such as the Colombo Plan, involved very high levels of tied aid. Examples of tied aid were railway locomotives, turbines and generators for hydro-electric plants, and Canadian teachers and teams of experts. Like all donors, Canada began providing aid with the best of motives but without much understanding of the newly independent, post-colonial, poor countries. The initial belief was that the recipient country lacked key inputs and what better way to meet this need than to supply capital and human inputs from the advanced donor economy?

Assessments of the impact of tied aid have concluded that tied aid involves a significant additional cost to the recipient. For capital equipment, tied aid imposed a cost penalty of around 30 percent in terms of the value of the assistance received, as compared to sourcing the same item from the lowest-cost supplier in the world (Bhagwati 1985.) In the case of tied technical assistance, the cost of the personnel from the donor country was far higher than local or third country staff, due to higher salaries, special allowances to recruit and retain the specialists, and the dependence element tying the recipient to the donor rather than building local capacity.

The issue of tied aid figured in several of the parliamentary reviews of Canada's aid and government responses in the 1980s and 1990s, but little progress was made. The argument in favour of tied aid, usually presented by trade officials and organizations of exporters, was that tied aid and its benefits to Canadians (jobs created, markets established/maintained) built domestic political support for the foreign aid program.

In 2001 the member states of the OECD-DAC agreed to untie all their bilateral aid to the least-developed countries (LDCs), an agreement amended in 2006 and 2008 to include non-LDC highly indebted countries. The Nordic donor countries had already untied their bilateral programs to these recipients and were the drivers of this policy shift. Canada supported the 2001 DAC agreement. At that time, around 50 percent of Canadian bilateral aid was tied and 6 percent partially untied. By 2007, Canadian untied bilateral aid had risen to 69 percent, the balance being technical cooperation and humanitarian aid. In 2008, Canada agreed to fully untie its food aid effective immediately, and to fully untie all of its bilateral (non-food) aid by 2013. The assessment by the DAC, in its 2012 peer review of Canadian development cooperation, suggests that full untied aid compliance by Canada is difficult to verify, as data are not clear and available in a timely way.

Canadian Aid Expenditures

According to the OECD-DAC, Official Development Assistance (ODA) is aid that is

i. provided by official agencies, including state and local governments ... ; and
ii. each transaction of which:
    a) is administered with the promotion of the economic development and welfare of developing countries as its main objective; and
    b) is concessional in character and conveys a grant element of at least 25 per cent (calculated at a rate of discount of 10 per cent). (OECD, n.d.)

In other words, ODA must be provided by the government and can be made up of grants or "soft" loans with lower than market interest rates. Government aid through CSOs counts as ODA. However, aid provided by individuals or non-governmental bodies like philanthropies

or churches does not count as ODA. The 0.7 target is measured using ODA as a percentage of gross national product.

The only quantitative target for aid that has been agreed to by donors is the 0.7 target proposed by the Pearson Commission and accepted by the UN General Assembly in 1970. Canada's level of effort against the 0.7 target is illustrated in **Figure 4.1**.

Using CIDA data, based since 1960 on the OECD reporting rules, there was a steady though sometimes erratic increase in the ODA:GNP ratio from 1950 to the early 1970s. The ODA:GNP ratio then stayed above .4 percent for two decades. But from the early 1990s, budget cuts brought on by the federal government's fiscal crisis steadily eroded the ODA:GNP ratio, until it bottomed out at 0.22 percent in 2001–2002. The ODA:GNP ratio then recovered somewhat as the succeeding governments of Paul Martin and Stephen Harper respected then-Prime Minister Jean Chrétien's 2002 commitment to double ODA by 2010.[3] As part of the subsequent deficit reduction measures in 2012, the Harper government then made cuts to ODA. When the government of Justin Trudeau announced its new, feminist policy on international assistance in June 2017, it refused to allocate any additional funding to ODA. Since ODA will not be increasing and since the economy is likely to grow, Canada's ODA:GNP ratio is expected to fall in the coming years.

Up to 1986, Canada's aid program was composed of "soft" loans and grants, the former for capital or infrastructure projects and the latter for technical assistance and training. Gradually, the share of loans in Canada's aid program diminished as the World Bank and other regional development banks assumed the responsibility for soft lending. This shift to grant aid also reflected the international consensus

---

3. The commitment was to double the absolute number of dollars spent on ODA, not to double the ODA:GNP ratio. Since Canada's economy grew between 2001 and 2010, the ODA:GNP ratio increased, but did not double.

that many LDCs simply could not afford to take on more debt and in fact were having difficulty repaying their existing debt. This shift was also based on the evidence that even very concessional loans were not contributing to the economic growth expected, especially in the case of loans taken out for social sector investments such as education, health, and water and sanitation infrastructure. The result was that Canada, along with other DAC members, agreed to provide aid to LDCs in the form of grants only.

From the start of Canada's aid program, most of Canadian development assistance flowed through bilateral or multilateral channels. (Government funding of CSOs is a third channel.) Bilateral aid goes from Canada directly to the recipient, on a country-to-country basis, whereas multilateral aid is channelled through international organizations such as the UN or World Bank. No Canadian government policy document has ever set out a rationale for the ratio between the multilateral and bilateral channels for aid, and for technical and other reasons it is difficult to determine any particular policy-driven pattern in the distribution of

Canada's bilateral vs. multilateral aid expenditures over time. Since the question of aid effectiveness came to the fore around 1990, the distribution of Canadian aid between bilateral and multilateral channels has fluctuated between 62:38 in 1997 and 79:21 in 2009.

Canadian Aid Strategies

Over the decades the Canadian government has published a number of aid strategies, usually in response to international commissions (e.g., Brandt, Brundtland), parliamentary reviews, or changes of government in Ottawa.

The 1975 "Strategy for International Development Cooperation" was prepared at the instigation of then CIDA president, Paul Gérin-Lajoie. (See Chapter 8.) His ambition was to obtain agreement for a timetable to achieve the 0.7 target and to link aid to non-aid policy issues, notably trade and market access for developing countries. Since his strategy went beyond aid to other policy areas that affected developing countries, he used the term "development

Figure 4.1

Canada's Official Development Assistance as a Percentage of GNP, Various Years

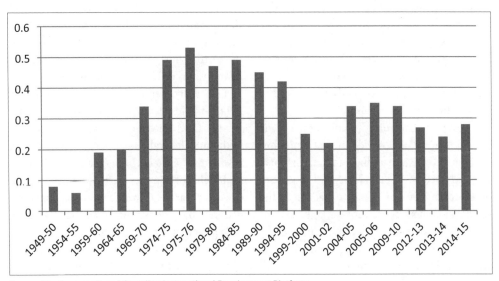

Source: Morrison, 1998, and Canadian International Development Platform.

cooperation." There was also pressure from outside CIDA to reduce the number of bilateral aid recipient countries and focus more effort on the LDCs. Elsewhere in the Canadian government, however, there were calls to use the aid program more to support Canadian exports. The end product, after close to two years of intensive interdepartmental discussions, was approved by Cabinet in 1975. Other issues included the 0.7 target, selection of bilateral aid recipient countries reflecting a needs-based approach (see Chapter 2), some steps to untie bilateral aid, programming priorities to favour certain sectors and themes, and the share of aid to be delivered through multilateral and other channels. The strategy also contained a commitment to share information on international development with the Canadian public.

In 1980, the Parliamentary Task Force on North-South Relations, chaired by Herb Breau, published its report. Coming soon after the Brandt Commission report, the remit of the task force was to look at the spectrum of relations between developed and developing countries. The task force held public hearings and received evidence from civil society, business, and a range of government departments and agencies, and one of its findings was that public understanding of the aid program and support for the program were both lacking and needed. The report of the task force called for an integrated, comprehensive public policy for cooperation, increased volume of aid, greater untying of bilateral aid, concentration of bilateral assistance in fewer countries, and an increase in funding for Canadian CSOs.

The next parliamentary examination of Canada's aid came in 1987, by the House of Commons Committee on External Affairs and International Trade, chaired by William Winegard. The work of the committee was in part a reaction to the Ethiopian famine of 1984–1986 and the extraordinary media attention given to that event, which in turn led to an unprecedented public awareness of poverty in Africa. The core messages of the committee's report, titled *For Whose Benefit?*, covered the need for a coherent focus of Canadian aid on assisting the poorest peoples and countries, building human and institutional capacity in developing countries, untying aid, factoring in human rights considerations, decentralizing Canada's aid delivery, and increasing Canadian public awareness and support.

Less than one year later, in 1988, the Mulroney government issued *Sharing our Future: Canada's Aid Strategy.* The Winegard report appeared to have had some influence in terms of the decentralization of aid management, a timetable for increases in aid volumes, an emphasis on human resource development, especially the role of women, more emphasis on poverty alleviation, sensitivity to human rights in selecting recipient countries, and expanded public outreach. There was some movement on untying Canadian bilateral aid. Progress toward the 0.7 percent target was pushed into the next decade. The strategy stated that Canadian development assistance supported Canada's foreign policy objectives, such as global peace and security, social justice, and a strong international trading system, but it did not enshrine this in an overarching statement. The 1988 Strategy did set out an "ODA Charter of Principles and Priorities." This charter captured three of the Winegard report's points: assisting the poorest, ensuring that development priorities came first, and helping partner country populations help themselves, plus a mention of "partnership" as the foundation for Canada's relationships with the developing world.

One year after the release of *Sharing our Future*, the Mulroney government (1984–1993) cut the ODA allocation budget by 13 percent in the 1989 federal budget, as part of an overall cost-cutting exercise. The cut to ODA represented almost a quarter of all federal expenditure cuts that year. As Canada's gross national product grew by 7 percent in 1989, the ODA:GNP ratio plummeted by 0.04 percent. See Figure 4.1.

1993 was CIDA's 25th anniversary. It was also the year of transition from the Progressive Conservative government of Brian Mulroney to the Liberal government of Jean Chrétien (1993–2003). And it was the year CIDA had three presidents: Marcel Massé, Jocelyne Bourgon, and Huguette Labelle. The new government started a review of Canada's foreign policy and gave the job to a special joint House of Commons–Senate committee reviewing Canadian foreign policy. The report of the committee had a chapter dedicated to international assistance, which recommended six measures for action:

1. Clarify CIDA's mandate, especially its lack of a legislative mandate.
2. Distinguish between the government's aid objectives and trade objectives.
3. Reform policy conditionality regarding structural adjustment (see Chapters 2 and 3).
4. Target aid.
5. Improve the achievement of results.
6. Maintain Canadian public support for the aid program.

There was little coverage of how much aid Canada should give ("aid volume") beyond a recommendation that ODA levels be stabilized.

The government's response came out in 1995 under the title *Canada and the World*. This was a comprehensive look at Canada's foreign policy, with a chapter dedicated to aid. This government stated that an effective development assistance program had to emphasize sustainability, human development, and poverty reduction, but did not make aid to the poorest the primary purpose of the program. Priority was to be given to basic human needs, women in development, human rights/democracy/good governance (see Chapter 11), private sector development (see Chapter 12), the environment, and infrastructure services. A legislated mandate for CIDA was rejected, and no commitment on aid volume was made, beyond a vague undertaking to move toward the 0.7 target when fiscal conditions permitted. Geographic concentration of Canadian bilateral aid was also rejected.

By mid-decade, however, with global ODA expenditures beginning to grow, Canada and other DAC member countries decided that it was time to examine the contribution aid could play in contributing to economic growth and poverty reduction in support of the efforts of the developing countries themselves. A process of reflection and analysis at the DAC resulted in the publication in 1996 of a statement of commitment called *Shaping the 21st Century: The Contribution of Development Cooperation*. As well as formalising the commitment of donor countries to a partnership with recipient (developing) countries, the statement set out a series of goals that became the basis for the Millennium Development Goals (MDGs). Canada was an active player in the process, which usefully went beyond setting input targets expressed in budgetary terms and emphasized results and development goals. An area of notable attention from Canada, reflecting policy emphasis over the previous 15 years, was gender equality.

Three weeks after the release of *Canada and the World*, the Liberal government brought in massive spending cuts in response to a looming debt crisis. The 1995 federal budget included a 20.5 percent cut in the aid budget. The Departments of National Defence and Foreign Affairs were also heavily cut; by disproportionately cutting "the three D's" (defence, diplomacy, and development), departments that that did not provide services to Canadians at home, the Chrétien government hoped to minimize the political impact of the cuts. Among the many CIDA programs affected, the Public Participation Program, which had responsibility for supporting development education in Canada, was eliminated altogether. Canada's ODA:GNP ratio went from 0.42 percent in 1995 to 0.34 percent in 1997. After the federal government's finances moved back into surplus, and notwithstanding the attention generated by the MDGs, the growth in Canadian aid budgets was modest from the late 1990s to 2012. Canada's commitment to increase ODA was expressed in carefully qualified terms, with much of the emphasis placed on aid to LDCs in sub-Saharan Africa.

In 2005, the Liberal government of Paul Martin (2003–2006) produced a document called *Canada's International Policy Statement: A Role of Pride and Influence in the World* that covered diplomacy, development, defence, and international trade in a comprehensive framework. The document was intended to reflect the trend seen in other donor countries, placing aid in the broader context of Canada's links with the global community. This approach held out the promise that development cooperation would be given equal weight with political and commercial relationships. The International Policy Statement was quietly dropped after the 2006 federal election brought Stephen Harper's Conservatives to power.

Under the Harper government there were no comprehensive statements published about aid, development cooperation, or foreign policy. There were significant shifts in the bilateral assistance, with the program concentrated on fewer and different countries, and a shift away from poor sub-Saharan African countries and in favour of middle-income Latin American countries. But the changes were announced in ministerial speeches and press releases, not in grand policy statements. Similarly, increased flows through multilateral channels were not communicated in policy announcements linked to changes in the global enabling environment or to any strategic assessment of Canada's international objectives. In 2012 the Conservative government signalled that all of Canada's international engagements, including development cooperation, would be utilized to advance Canada's national economic interests.

The Harper government made much of its Muskoka Initiative on maternal, newborn, and child health. (See above.) The Harper government on several occasions announced increases in the Canadian financial commitment to this initiative, beyond the initial 2010 contribution of $1.25 billion. At the 2014 review conference in Toronto, the Canadian financial support was announced as $3.5 billion. What is not known is whether this was additional funding or whether these funds

were taken from other parts of the ODA budget. Equally unclear is what was achieved in the form of sustainable development results.

Under the Harper government in particular, there were a number of ministerial announcements about the importance of the private sector in development. (See Chapter 12.) While ODA alone will not meet all the external finance needs of developing countries, and while foreign direct investment and remittances represent important financial flows, foreign aid will continue to be crucial for the public finance needs of many poor countries, especially LDCs. It is still not clear what place the private sector will occupy in the range of Canadian aid mechanisms in the near future. In its 2017 budget, the Liberal government of Justin Trudeau announced the creation of a "development finance institution," that is, a bilateral development lender. Up till now, Canada was the only G7 country not to have such an institution.

In parallel, and though it is difficult to track due to the opacity of government reporting, there was a shift in the treatment of Canada's development CSOs under the Harper government. Several Canadian CSOs that had received CIDA funding for decades found their government funding was withdrawn and had to cease operations. (See Chapter 7.) Since 2008, non-governmental organisations have had to respond to calls for proposals to support objectives and parameters set by CIDA. For some analysts, this represents an explicit instrumentalization of CSOs, changing them from partners to contractors.

Global Rebuilding and Re-engagement

As the 1990s drew to a close, with the work to shape the UN Millennium Declaration and the Millennium Development Goals coming to its conclusion, aid officials in a number of donor countries were thinking about the arguments required to support requests for budget increases. While political endorsement of the

MDGs was given in 2000, commitment of the means to achieve them had to be wrung out of the finance ministries in donor country capitals. The core of the argument for bigger aid budgets was the promise to make aid more effective. This was the birth of the "aid effectiveness agenda."

Consequently, DAC members set out to identify how aid could be more effective. This process resulted in a watershed agreement in 2005 where the heads of aid agencies, along with donor government ministers, senior representatives of key multilateral institutions (World Bank and UN Development Program (UNDP)), and representatives of developing countries, signed the Paris Declaration on Aid Effectiveness (see **Table 4.2**). Several of the provisions of the declaration posed problems for Canada, as they called for ownership by the partner developing country of the development cooperation process, the use of the partner (i.e., recipient) country's budgetary systems, and mutual accountability. Canada had difficulty with these elements of the aid effectiveness agenda because they required decentralisation of authority at a time when the trend in Canada was to greater centralisation and tighter political control.

A follow-up meeting held in Accra, Ghana, in 2008 included parliamentarians from a number of participating countries, and the presence of some civil society organizations as observers. In 2011, in Busan, South Korea, a further ministerial meeting took place, with an even larger group of participants, including some non-traditional/emerging donors such as Brazil, China, and India. (See Chapter 13.) A major

evaluation was presented, with the core message that not much progress had been made in achieving the goals of the Paris Declaration, and that the donors had made less progress in meeting the Paris Declaration criteria than the developing countries had. At the end of the meeting the participants agreed to the Busan Partnership for Effective Development Cooperation, under the slogan "From effective aid to cooperation for effective development."

In 2012, in its peer review of Canada's development cooperation policies and programs, the OECD-DAC, with peer reviewers from the Netherlands and France, noted the absence of a clear strategy in Canada for implementing the commitments of the Paris Declaration. They also noted also that Canada's 2009 effectiveness action plan was weak, in that it did not apply to parts of the government other than CIDA, that it focused on efficiency and domestic accountability and did not give priority to areas needing the most attention, such as aid predictability, alignment, and harmonisation of Canadian efforts with those of partner countries and other donors (OECD/DAC 2012).

In 2008, the Parliament of Canada passed a private member's bill called the *Official Development Assistance Accountability Act*. In a minority Parliament, the governing Conservatives voted against the bill, but it passed anyway, with support from three opposition parties. The *Act* proposed a simple framework and rationale for Canadian ODA. The structure and purpose of the legislation drew from the Paris Declaration. It set out three "tests" for Canada's ODA, that it should

Table 4.2
Principles of the Paris Declaration on Aid Effectiveness, 2005

Ownership of the development cooperation relationship by the partner developing country
Alignment of aid with partner countries' strategies and systems
Harmonization and coordination by donors
Management for development results
Mutual responsibility, accountability, and transparency

a) contribute to poverty reduction,
b) take into account the perspectives of the poor, and
c) be consistent with international human rights standards.

The *Act* required the government to report annually to Parliament on how aid expenditures met these tests. After initial attempts at compliance with the reporting requirement in 2009, 2010, and 2011, the annual reports to Parliament became little more than lists of expenditures by various departments, agencies, and Crown corporations, under a covering note to the effect that the disbursements meet the requirements of the *Act*.

Recent Organizational Developments

In 2012, as part of the Deficit Reduction Action Plan, the Harper government announced that it was shutting down the International Centre for Human Rights and Democratic Development (known as "Rights and Democracy"). Rights and Democracy had been created as a Crown corporation with all-party support in 1988. The closure followed a turbulent period at the organization as certain governors attempted to impose a policy agenda that was resisted by other members of the board. (See Chapter 11.)

As part of the 2013 federal government budget package, it was announced that CIDA would be merged with the Department of Foreign Affairs and International Trade (DFAIT) to create the Department of Foreign Affairs, Trade and Development (DFATD). This step caught many people, including senior CIDA and DFAIT officials, completely by surprise. The rationale was that amalgamation would produce coherence and greater effectiveness of Canadian aid and foreign policy, and was consistent with practice in other donor countries. No targets for the improvements sought were set and the amalgamation process was prolonged, with little information made public regarding the process and the shape of the "new" organization. The position of Minister for International Cooperation was retained, as part of a triumvirate of ministers with Minister for Foreign Affairs and Minister for International Trade.

With the installation of the new Liberal government in November 2015, several important changes were made to Canada's aid program, as part of the initiative to show that "Canada is back" on the world stage. DFATD was changed to Global Affairs Canada. In a precedent-setting move, the mandate letters for all new ministers, including the minister of international development, were published. Chief among the new minister's objectives were to help the poorest and most vulnerable, support implementation of Agenda 2030 for Sustainable Development, champion the values of governance, pluralism, diversity, and human rights; continue the Maternal, Newborn and Child Health initiative, including reproductive rights and health care for women; and assist countries vulnerable to climate change.

In May of 2016 the Liberal government launched an International Assistance Review, covering ODA as well as other forms of support to developing countries not covered by the definition of ODA. This review began with extensive on-line consultations lasting three months. In June 2017, the Trudeau government released *Canada's Feminist International Assistance Policy* (Government of Canada 2017), taking as its starting point Sustainable Development Goal 5—achieving gender equality and empowering all women and girls. The policy is structured around six action areas:

1. Gender Equality and the Empowerment of Women and Girls
2. Human Dignity
3. Growth That Works for Everyone
4. Environment and Climate Action
5. Inclusive Governance
6. Peace and Security

Though the policy sets out increases for support to LDCs and to sub-Saharan African countries, it does not commit to any increases in the ODA budget. Thus it is expected that Canada's ODA:GNP ratio will drop below 0.25 percent as of 2017.

Conclusion

It is difficult to summarize 70 years of public policy making and government programming in one paragraph. From tentative beginnings with the Colombo Plan, through engagement with newly independent countries in Africa and the Caribbean, plus sporadic links with some Latin American countries, Canada's bilateral aid program has grown and shrunk, chiefly in reaction to domestic, mostly fiscal, considerations. In multilateral aid, until quite recently, Canada has participated in the full global range of institutions and initiatives, as part of an unstated foreign policy principle of joining all organizations that would have Canada as a member and committing, at least rhetorically, to international development campaigns and programs. From a peak in the 1980s of reaching out to Canadians and encouraging their involvement in aid activities, the trend for the last 20 years has been to inform Canadians less and less about their aid program. From flirting with poverty reduction as the purpose of Canadian development assistance, recent governments have been increasingly explicit about using the aid program to advance national economic interests. At the start of a new era in global engagement through the Sustainable Development Goals, the impression is of a steady decline in Canada's commitment to and ability to shape international development cooperation efforts, shifting from a systemic, comprehensive attitude to an episodic, transactional approach. The launch in 2016 by the new Liberal government of a review of international assistance held out some promise of an overarching strategy for Canadian aid, and an improvement in performance. But we have seen such reviews come and go in the past, often with little practical effect. The policy announcement, however, while making an important commitment to a feminist international assistance program, made no undertaking for budget increases to realize the goals set out.

Questions for Further Learning

- How has Canada performed as an aid donor compared to other donor countries?
- What are the respective merits and drawbacks of bilateral, multilateral, and civil society channels of aid?
- How has the international aid effectiveness initiative evolved and how has it influenced Canadian aid?

Key Terms

development cooperation, p. 70

foreign aid, p. 70

gender, p. 76

official development assistance (ODA), p. 78

tied aid, p. 71

Suggested Readings

Brown, Stephen, ed. 2012. *Struggling for Effectiveness: CIDA and Canadian Foreign Aid*. Kingston and Montreal: McGill-Queen's University Press.

Brown, Stephen, Molly den Heyer, and David Black, eds. 2016. *Rethinking Canadian Aid*. Ottawa: University of Ottawa Press.

Commission on International Development. 1969. *Partners in Development: Report of the Commission on International Development, Chairman Lester B. Pearson*. New York: Praeger Publishers.

Development Initiatives. 2013. *Investments to End Poverty: Real Money, Real Choices, Real Lives*. Bristol, UK: Development Initiatives.

Global Affairs Canada. 2017. *Canada's Feminist International Assistance Policy*. Ottawa: Global Affairs Canada.

Government of Canada. 2016. *Canada's International Assistance Review: Discussion Paper*. Ottawa: Government of Canada.

LePan, Douglas. 1979. *Bright Glass of Memory: A Memoir*. Toronto: McGraw Hill-Ryerson.

Morrison, David R. 1998. *Aid and Ebb Tide: A History of CIDA and Canadian Development Assistance*. Waterloo, ON: Wilfrid Laurier University Press.

Muirhead, Bruce, and Ron Harpelle. 2010. *IDRC: 40 Years of Ideas, Innovation, and Impact*. Waterloo, ON: Waterloo University Press.

United Nations. 2015. *Sustainable Development Goals: 17 Goals to Transform Our World*. New York, United Nations.

Suggested Videos

Canadian Council on Africa: Official Development Aid for Africa. https://www.youtube.com/watch?v=MwhkVj7xcFY

CBC, Power and Politics: Canada's Feminist Aid Policy 2017. https://www.youtube.com/watch?v=x9tx7j4YvFs

Jeffrey Sachs on official development assistance. https://www.youtube.com/watch?v=r3mOgerixTA

Michael Clemens: Does aid cause growth? https://www.youtube.com/watch?v=yV9jDPqSAT0

OECD-DAC on rethinking development finance. https://www.youtube.com/watch?v=csWQBsJhmVI

Suggested Websites

Canadian International Development Platform: http://cidpnsi.ca/

Commitment to Development Index, Center for Global Development: https://www.cgdev.org/commitment-development-index

Development Co-operation Directorate, Organisation for Economic Co-operation and Development: www.oecd.org/dac/

Development Initiatives: www.devinit.org

Global Affairs Canada – Development: www.international.gc.ca/development-developpement/index.aspx?lang=eng

Works Cited

Commission on International Development. 1969. *Partners in Development: Report of the Commission on International Development, Chairman Lester B. Pearson*. New York: Praeger Publishers.

Conway, Martin. 2012. *The Sorrows of Belgium: Liberation and Political Reconstruction, 1944–1947*. Oxford.

Government of Canada. 2017. "Canada's Feminist International Assistance Policy." Ottawa: Global Affairs Canada. http://international.gc/world-monde/issues_development-enjeux_developpement/priorities-priorites/policy-politique.aspx?lang=eng.

Independent Commission on International Development Issues ("The Brandt Commission"). 1980. *North-South: A Programme for Survival*. Cambridge, MA: MIT Press.

OECD. n.d. "Tied Aid." Found on http://www.oecd.org/dac/untied-aid/ on 3 April 2017.

OECD. n.d. "Official Development Assistance—Definition and Coverage." Found on http://www.oecd.org/dac/stats/officialdevelopmentassistancedefinitionandcoverage.htm on 3 April 2017.

OECD/DAC. 2012. *Canada: Development Assistance Committee (DAC), Peer Review* 2012. Paris: OECD.

World Commission on Environment and Development ("The Brundtland Commission"). 1987. *Our Common Future*. Harmondsworth, UK: Penguin.

5 Canada's Military and the Developing Countries since 1945

Casey Brunelle

Key Terms

asymmetric warfare

humanitarian intervention

multilateral middle power

NATO

peacekeeping

peacemaking

soft power

global terrorism

War on Terror

Overview

This chapter explores the evolution of Canada's military from the Second World War to the beginning of the twenty-first century, with a particular focus on its experiences in developing countries. From a young and relatively inexperienced country in the late nineteenth century, Canada developed rapidly throughout both World Wars as a middle power with considerable military prowess. Following extensive participation in the Korean War, Canada adopted a multilateral stance of geopolitical mediation, contributing troops, support, and financing to UN peacekeeping efforts throughout the Cold War. Setbacks in the 1990s led to a re-think, and since 2001 the War on Terror has brought a re-assertion of the use of Canadian military force overseas. The domestic and international drivers of the various changes in Canadian military policy are explained.

Learning Objectives

By the end of this chapter, students will be able to:

- explain the evolution of Canada's military from the end of the Second World War into the modern era.
- critically discuss the identity of Canada as an originator of the concept of peacekeeping, whether this identity is justified as an international symbol, and how it has evolved into the modern era.
- discuss how the politicization of foreign policy has influenced the identity and the evolving role of Canada's military in developing countries.
- understand the importance of military operations as an extension of a country's foreign policy, and how such an extension functions as part of a country's broader international development agenda.

Introduction

In the wake of powerful experiences, both successful and tragic, during the humanitarian interventions in the 1990s, Canada saw a dramatic shift in its role as a provider of soft power alternatives throughout the early twenty-first century. Asymmetric military operations in Afghanistan and Libya, as well as more recent participation in the US-led coalition against ISIL (Islamic State of Iraq and the Levant) in Iraq, have contributed to this change in Canada's international identity. This chapter examines the role of Canada's military over the last 70 years, as both an indicator of, and catalyst to, Canada's broader foreign policy approaches in developing countries. While not a comprehensive history of Canada's military operations, this chapter details the key engagements and deployments of the armed forces as they apply to this key institution, both within and beyond the borders of Canada.

What Is the Issue?

Historically, Canada's military has been widely celebrated for its adaptability of doctrine and fluidity of operations. While no doubt less intentional, the political and civilian institutions that direct and oversee the modern Canadian Armed Forces (CAF) on expeditionary missions in developing countries mirror at least some of that fluidity in terms of prescribed policies. Significant shifts in foreign policy since the end of the Second World War—such as the role of Canada being a multilateral middle power during much of the Cold War (1946–1989) shifting to becoming a key player in the US-led War on Terror since 2001—bring about the need to deconstruct Canada's military experiences in developing countries as an extension of broader Canadian development agendas. Are these differing experiences reconcilable, or, in terms of traditional national identity and current geopolitical climate, are these shifts in Canada's foreign policy inherently opposed to one another's means and objectives, for both developing countries and Canada itself?

A Brief History of Canada's Military in Developing Countries, 1945–present

1945–1968: A crossroads for Canada and the world

Just as it had less than two decades earlier, Canada emerged from the Second World War (1939–1945) as a country and a people forcibly matured by the trauma of conflict. Having participated extensively in the Allied effort against the Axis powers of Nazi Germany, Fascist Italy, and Imperial Japan, Canada in 1945 possessed one of the world's largest military forces, with hundreds of thousands of soldiers, sailors, and airmen and -women.

Within just weeks of the end of the war in Europe, however, a period of rapid demobilization resulted in Canada's military hardware being sold off, decommissioned, and returned to almost pre-war levels, while regular personnel levels within the army, navy, and air force declined dramatically. With the scars of conflict still fresh and the participation of all global powers in the United Nations appearing as a means to maintain global peace, it was felt in Ottawa that the need for a standing army was no longer in touch with the geopolitical reality and by 1947 the permanent force of Canada's military numbered only several thousand (Johnston and Harris 1992).

As early as 1944, the Western Allies (the US, the UK, and Canada) consciously identified their long-term opponent as their then wartime ally—the Soviet Union. To differing degrees, leaders such as British Prime Minister Winston Churchill and US President Franklin D. Roosevelt saw the Soviet Union as a looming threat, one they would have to address promptly following the eventual surrender of Nazi Germany. In the conferences between the "Big Three" (Stalin from the Soviet Union, Churchill and later Attlee from the UK, and Roosevelt and later Truman from the US) at Yalta and Potsdam in February and July 1945 respectively, the differing strategic ambitions of the Western Allies and the Soviet Union became increasingly evident. With the common enemy of Nazi Germany now defeated, US President Truman had only hinted to Stalin about an unspecified "powerful new weapon" likely to be used in the case of continuing Japanese resistance. The detonation of US atomic bombs over Hiroshima and Nagasaki in August 1945 not only brought about a final defeat for the Axis Powers, but also radically shifted the dynamic between the one-time allies of the West and the Soviet Union.

The deteriorating geopolitical situation between the West and the Soviet Union in occupied Germany climaxed with the Berlin Blockade of 1948–1949. The subsequent resolve demonstrated by the US, UK, France, and their allies hardened even further against Soviet desires to force Eastern Europe under communist rule (Miller 1998). The success of Western air power in resupplying the blockaded population of West Berlin, accelerated further by the introduction of the revalued Deutsche Mark in the Western occupation zones, cemented the seemingly diametric opposition between the capitalist and communist camps. By the time of the first Soviet atomic weapons test in August 1949, the geopolitical climate that would define the next four decades was erected in ideological terms, with its physical counterpart, the Berlin Wall, not far behind.

It is important to understand the events in Europe immediately following the Second World War when considering an evaluation of the evolving role of Canada's military in developing countries. Like those of its allies, Canada's military was forced to rapidly adapt at the onset of the Cold War from "warfighting" to military deterrence, training, and advising.

The establishment of the North Atlantic Treaty Organization (NATO) in April 1949 represented a doctrinal turning point for Canada's military, especially in terms of the strategic concept of the collective defence for the alliance's member states. Little more than a political association until the onset of the Korean War the next year, NATO represented the first permanent military alliance. While NATO was certainly founded with a public and self-image of an alliance of Western liberal democracies, some states that did not adhere to that criterion were nonetheless welcomed into the alliance by virtue of geopolitical necessity: Portugal was a founding member in 1949, while Turkey and Greece joined in 1952.

Canada in Korea

Canada's defence mandate would be drastically changed yet again with its participation in the Korean War (1950–1953). Following the North Korean invasion of South Korea, the post–Second World War belief in the maintenance of world peace through UN mechanisms and nuclear deterrence was dismissed. Canada's military joined a large military force aimed at preventing what the West saw as the communist world's effort to spread its influence by force, resulting in a rapid remobilization and an increase of military expenditures to 2.7 percent of Canada's gross domestic product (Johnston and Harris 1992).

Canada was the third-largest contingent of the first 16 nations that were called to "collective action to resist aggression" in the Korean Peninsula (Wood 1966). This was the first major military intervention undertaken by the United Nations. Four months after the UN Security Council resolution in June 1950 authorizing the use of force to end the North Korean invasion, Canadian troops landed in Pusan, South Korea. The Canadian section of the front was a zone approximately 50 kilometres long to the north of the South Korean capital of Seoul. Major Canadian engagements included Operation Killer in February 1951 and the Battle of Kapyong in April 1951 against a joint Chinese–North Korean offensive (Johnston and Harris 1992).

The Korean War represented a modest return to the necessity of conventional ground forces, in a budding age of nuclear deterrence and what was soon to be termed "mutually assured destruction" between the nuclear-capable superpowers. Some 516 Canadians died during the conflict, 312 as a direct result of combat, and Canadian troops remained in South Korea for three years following the cessation of hostilities (Wood 1966). In the span of these six years, over 25,000 Canadians served in Korea, and those who served there and died are honoured at the National War Memorial in Ottawa and at a special memorial statue nearby.

With the stalemate between Communist and United Nations forces, the termination of hostilities through the 1953 armistice, and the corresponding lack of a clear victory, initial enthusiasm in Canada for supporting the UN mission gradually died down. Canada's military once again entered a period of demobilization.

Canada and the Suez Crisis

While on a much smaller scale than the Korean War in terms of absolute military involvement, the Suez Crisis of 1956–1957 is an event more readily identified throughout the world as a key part of Canada's emergent national identity. For reasons more complex than this chapter can cover, the outcomes of the crisis separate Canadian history between two broad sections in time and space—the first being a world dominated by the "Old Europe" colonial great powers and the second being a world of charting an uncertain course of self-definition, self-determination, and self-realization for Canadians as a people and a country (Carrol 2009). The implications for Canada's military, especially in terms of its experiences in developing countries, cannot be overstated when it comes to the political role that Canada played within the Suez Crisis, and the tone that set for the events of the following decades.

During the Cold War, complicated geopolitical dealings between the Soviet and Western spheres of influence had become commonplace by the mid-1950s. Large-scale investments and military training programs by the competing superpowers were intended to woo newly independent developing countries in Africa and Asia. The Suez Canal in Egypt represented a focal point of this competition. The canal was important because it reduced the length of ocean voyages between Asia and Europe dramatically for both civilian and military traffic.

Following overtures to the Soviet Union by Egyptian nationalist President Gamal Abdel Nasser, the UK and US withdrew their financial and technical aid in the construction of the vital Aswan Dam project in southern Egypt. When Nasser responded unilaterally by nationalizing the Suez Canal, British, French, and Israeli forces responded with an invasion of Egypt. With both the Soviet Union and the US applying pressure on the UK, France, and Israel to withdraw their forces, Canadian Secretary of State for External Affairs Lester Pearson, worked to resolve the crisis through the UN (Carrol 2009). Proposing the establishment of a UN mediation contingent, composed of multinational forces, Pearson's efforts resulted in the establishment of the first true UN peacekeeping force, thus initiating a long tradition for both the UN and Canada that continues into the twenty-first century, although with a significantly altered breadth and scope.

Personnel from Brazil, Canada, Colombia, Denmark, Finland, India, Indonesia, Poland, Sweden, and Yugoslavia formed the first UN Emergency Force (UNEF) in 1956. Commanded by Canadian General E.L.M. "Tommy" Burns, the emergency contingent was pre-approved by Nasser, although he objected to the use of Canadian troops with "British-sounding" names like the Queen's Own Rifles, the employment of the Union Jack emblazoned on Canada's national ensign, and challenged Canada as the neutral actor it professed to be[1] (Carrol 2009; Marteinson and McNorgan 2000). (See Chapter 1.)

The UNEF task force was outfitted with equipment much less "potent" than what its Canadian commander had originally desired, with little armour or heavy weaponry to support its delicate role in mediating and negotiating between the combat-experienced and motivated militaries of Egypt, France, Israel, and the UK (Marteinson and McNorgan 2000). With financial pressure from the two superpowers (the US and the USSR), the British, French, and Israeli contingents withdrew from their positions, signifying a symbolic victory for Nasser and the nationalist Arab movement. (See Case Study 10.) Regardless of the strategic political claims, however, the Suez Crisis laid the groundwork for the first peacekeeping experiment and thus represents one of the key transition moments in the UN's complex role within the Cold War, particularly in relation to developing countries.

The theory and practice of peacekeeping, as it was originally conceptualized by the UN in the mid-1950s, was an *ad hoc* necessity to mitigating potentially violent outcomes of the early-mid Cold War. UN peacekeeping has come to be identified as having begun with Pearson's innovative solution to the Suez Crisis. Hillmer and Rawling (1992, 451) aptly describe the politically contentious process of this mandate:

Peacekeeping had not been envisaged by the founders of the United Nations. The charter states as a first principle that the UN seeks to "maintain international peace and security." It makes provision for a potentially powerful Military Staff Committee and calls upon member nations to keep military forces ready to combat aggression. Yet the international organization was never able to agree on such an arrangement, and its central body, the Security Council, was paralyzed from the start by Cold War tensions between the Soviet Union and the United States, each with a veto to prevent the taking of any measure it did not favour. Except in 1950, when the Council took advantage of a Soviet absence to move quickly against North Korea, it was impossible to get the United Nations behind concerted, substantial commitments to collective security. Thus a new concept, peacekeeping, lurched into view as a response to the world's many messy quarrels. Lester Pearson and others hoped that it would give time, a breathing space, so that real peace could be manufactured. All too often, however, peacekeeping became an end in itself.

Canada in Sub-Saharan Africa

A key event in post-colonial African history is the Congo crisis of the 1960s, along with the UN peacekeeping intervention in Congo, which lasted from 1960 to 1964. A detailed historical overview of the Congo Crisis, the murder of the first Congolese prime minister, Patrice Lumumba, and the entanglements of superpower influence in the conflict, is beyond the scope of this chapter, but it is important to note the evolution of the UN Operation in the Congo (ONUC) from a peacekeeping force of nearly 20,000 personnel to a military force, whose rules of engagement extended beyond mere self-defence.

---

1. When he became prime minister in 1963, with Canada's centennial year of 1967 approaching, Pearson pushed for the adoption of a distinctly Canadian national flag, devoid of colonial symbols. The new red-and-white mapleleaf flag was officially unveiled in February 1965.

The mandate of the ONUC was both to oversee the withdrawal of Belgian military personnel and mercenaries from southern Congo, where Katangan rebels had staged an insurrection against the newly independent Congo, and to provide broader military assistance, so as to ensure stability of the region. ONUC's chief of staff, Brigadier-General Jacques Dextraze, was one of the nearly two thousand peacekeepers that Canada provided over the course of the mission's four-year duration, primarily in the role of logistics support and communications. Canada's contribution to ONUC was not without controversy; the Soviet Union stated that such a contingent was inappropriate because Canada and Belgium were allies in NATO (Dorn 2013).

While the mission was terminated in June 1964 before a sustainable peace could be retained in the country, ONUC did indeed succeed in overseeing the reintegration of the secessionist Katanga region into the Congo and, more broadly, the mission represents the first explicit deployment of UN military power for peacekeeping entirely within a sovereign state. Canada's participation in ONUC was due to overwhelming domestic public concern, rather than strategic machinations by Prime Minister John Diefenbaker's government (1957–1963). This was not the case for Canada's military assistance missions in Ghana and Tanzania, under the relatively interventionist government of Lester Pearson (1963–1968) (Dorn 2013).

During the rapid decolonization in sub-Saharan Africa, many newly independent states were in need of the professionalization of their militaries; at the same time, these newly independent countries sought to avoid the political and ideological entanglements involved in depending on either former colonial powers or the two superpowers to provide such training (Donaghy 2012). In the 1960s, Tanzania and Ghana were two examples where Canadian specialists helped train the new countries' militaries, through different means and with significantly varying outcomes (Kilford 2009). With perhaps naïve hopes, Canadians officials made

the argument that providing such assistance, as an end to itself, would prevent a potentially violent escalation in the East–West dichotomy that was brewing at the height of the Cold War (Godefroy 2002).

As one of the first former colonies to gain its independence in sub-Saharan Africa, Ghana was relatively wealthy, faced no external threats, and had little major internal unrest at the time (Kilford 2009). Its president, Kwame Nkrumah, was a key player in the Non-Aligned Movement (NAM) and sought the participation of middle power countries, such as Canada, who possessed effective military experience, but also a minimal amount of colonial baggage with its shared colonizer, the UK.

From 1961 to 1973, Canada provided military assistance to Ghana through a small team of advisors and the provision of equipment (Godefroy 2002). In 1966, the Canadian-trained military in Ghana overthrew President Nkrumah and his government in a coup d'état. The US, long weary of Nkrumah's antagonistic rhetoric towards the West, took comfort both in the coup and the fact that it had happened largely without their intervention. With a new Ghanaian government in place that was more amenable to Western geopolitical desires, the Canadian military training program increased in scope. By 1973, however, and following another coup by the Ghanaian military in 1972, renewed pressures in Ottawa to reduce funding of the program resulted in its termination (Jeffery 2013).

On the other side of the continent, Canadian military assistance to the newly independent Tanzania began in 1964 and, at its peak, included nearly 90 commissioned and non-commissioned Canadian officers (Jeffery 2013). Unlike the case in Ghana, Canadian assistance in Tanzania was not readily received with optimism and compliance in Ottawa, but Prime Minister Pearson eventually mandated an assessment team to be dispatched to the country in 1961 (Kilford 2009). The program enabled the creation of the Tanzanian *National*

Defence Act, doctrinal developments, and operational advisement. As a result of increasing Soviet and Communist Chinese involvement in the southern African region, and Canada's inability to sway Tanzania to join the Western sphere of influence, the Canadian mission was terminated after just five years (Godefroy 2002).

With internal political instabilities in the participant countries and in light of the persistent backroom dealings of ideologically driven superpower blocs, Canada terminated its military missions in both countries, thereby reducing long-term outcomes and largely wasting the personnel and financial investments that Canada contributed to both countries. With the election of Pierre Trudeau in 1968 and the repositioning of Canada as a multilateral middle power, the interventionist policies of Canada's military in the developing countries of the world would be shifted once again to meet evolving geopolitical demands.

1968–1991: Canada as a multilateral middle power

When Prime Minister Pierre Trudeau came to power in 1968, he immediately announced a complete overhaul of Canada's national defence and foreign policy priorities. (See Chapter 4.) Trudeau felt that, increasingly, the latter drove the former, and that the one-sixth of the national budget spent on defence left little fiscal room to sustain the sweeping social service reforms brought about by the previous government, including universal health care and old-age pensions (Kilford 2009).

Adamant that military aid and arms sales were not essential to the viability of the developing world, especially when there were no clear external threats present in those countries to which Canada had made such contributions, Trudeau was clear in his desire to not have Canada become entangled in the geopolitical machinations of the ideologically driven Cold War (Kilford 2009). When his government published the 1971 *Defence White Paper*, it was evident that the military assistance that had defined Canada's experiences in developing countries in the 1960s was no longer a priority.

The catalyst behind the strategic readjustment of Trudeau's foreign policy was not just the changing nuclear balance between the Soviet Union and the West, but also reportedly the emergence of China as a nuclear power and the growing economic power of Japan and Europe. The results of the *White Paper*, while perhaps well intentioned, gravely damaged the morale of Canada's military, which had already been shaken following the unification of its army, navy, and air force in February 1968 (Lotz 1990). The report, requesting a military of "versatile forces and multi-purpose equipment rather than a high degree of specialization," set out the four key priorities for the Canadian Forces as the following:

- the surveillance of Canada's own territory and coast-lines, i.e., the protection of sovereignty;
- the defence of North America in cooperation with US forces;
- the fulfilment of such NATO commitments as may be agreed upon; and
- the performance of such international peacekeeping roles as Canada may from time to time be asked to undertake. (Macdonald 1971: 16)

An emphasis in the *White Paper* was placed upon the past successes, and ongoing future potential, for the newly unified Canadian Forces to aid in the advancement of developing countries through means beyond conventional combat roles, with a special focus on disaster-relief efforts and technical training. Examples of such peace-oriented missions included contributions to earthquake response in Peru, providing relief following flooding in Pakistan, and humanitarian flights for refugees in eastern India.

In a major departure, the 1971 *Defence White Paper* announced a distancing from the Pearson-era notion of internationalism as a matter of inherent obligation for Canada's military, and facilitated the selling off of significant pieces of military hardware, including Canada's last air-craft carrier, reducing the role of nuclear-armed F-104 Starfighter aircraft in Europe, and reducing the number of personnel in both the regular and reserve forces (Kilford 2009). Trudeau ushered in a major shift in strategic thinking by suggesting that Canada, rather than being the "smallest of the large powers," was, in fact, the "largest of the small powers" (Radwanski 1978, 183).

While Canada stayed out of military partici-pation in the US-led Vietnam War (1955–1975), it readily provided the US with military equip-ment throughout the conflict and allowed around 7,000 Canadians to volunteer for ser-vice in the US military. Approximately 133 Canadians were killed in action, including the son of famed military veteran and soon-to-be Chief of the Defence Staff (1972–1977) General Jacques Dextraze.

From 1954 through 1973, Canada served in the International Control Commission (ICC), the body established to oversee the implemen-tation of the Geneva Accords that ended the First Indochina War (1946–1954) and broke French Indochina into Cambodia, Laos, and Vietnam. Composed of one NATO country (Canada), one Soviet ally (Poland), and a non-aligned country (India), the ICC was a Cold War balancing act. It suffered from a lack of respect by both sides of the Cold War, as well as a lack of funding and staff (Thakur 1984). Unable to exercise its mandate effectively as the Second Indochina War (1955–75) ("the Vietnam War" to Americans) escalated during the 1960s, the ICC was ultimately disbanded in March 1973. It was succeeded by the International Com-mission of Control and Supervision. Canada remained a member of that commission, along-side Hungary, Indonesia, and Poland, until the US had begun its withdrawal from Vietnam in 1973, after which it was replaced by Iran, then a US ally. (See Chapter 14.)

In the lead-up to the 1971 *White Paper*, the Canadian Military Assistance Committee (MAC) produced a report in summer 1969, attempting to persuade the new Trudeau government that military assistance programs in developing countries were indeed in line with Canada's evolving foreign policy strategies:

> small, selective program of military assis-tance can increase the effectiveness of Cana-dian policy in the developing world, and can contribute to Canadian efforts to prompt economic and social progress, provided that such a program remains minor in scale, and is made complementary to the much larger Canadian economic aid program. (Interde-partmental MAC 1969)

In line with the review's desire to avoid putting all the "eggs in one basket," as the Commit-tee described the military assistance program in Tanzania, the review recommended Can-adian military assistance in a dizzying number of countries. The list of proposed missions included Burma, Ceylon (now Sri Lanka), Indo-nesia, Kenya, Malaysia, Singapore, Thailand, Uganda, Zambia, and others, but did not take into account geopolitical factors, and Trudeau received the review's recommendations with scepticism. Ultimately, the review requested only $500,000 "to provide on request some modest, carefully evaluated advisory training assistance to Malaysia and Singapore" (Inter-departmental MAC 1969, 2). In the end, the committee was granted $100,000 per year for two years for training programs in Malaysia and Singapore. While Trudeau remained convinced of the irrelevance (if not detriment) of such mis-sions to broader Canadian foreign policy strat-egies, the committee took the financial grant as a modest victory, although the shifting pri-orities for the military in developing countries continued to be made increasingly evident.

Canadian contributions to multiple UN peacekeeping missions took place through the 1960s to the 1980s, in contentious places like Cyprus (1964–present), Israel–Syria (1974–present), Lebanon (1978), Sinai (1981–present), and Namibia (1989–1990). Given the size of the Canadian contribution, finding sustainable funding for such UN operations continued to be a factious topic within both the military high command and Parliament.

By the early 1990s, the end of the Cold War and the collapse of the Soviet Union provoked debate about the continued need for NATO in a potentially unipolar world and, with it, Canada's commitment to the collective defence agreement therein. The role of Canada's military in developing countries was on the verge of yet another significant change in strategy, inputs, and, most particularly, outcomes.

1991–2001: The post–Cold War surge in peacekeeping

In the early post–Cold War period, the scope and breadth of Canada's participation overseas in peacekeeping and military assistance were indeed notable. Canada's performance in this period was also marked by great controversy and even outright tragedy in Somalia, Rwanda, and the former Yugoslavia.

This section will briefly discuss these three cases as definers, whether deliberate or not, of Canada's military experiences overseas during the 1990s. These high-profile instances of well-intentioned, but ultimately inadequate, responses led to a period of self-reflection and reassessment for the mandate of peacekeeping and the role that Canada might play in its implementation in developing countries. As of early 2017, this legacy has resurfaced in a discussion held in the aftermath of the Afghanistan deployment and on the eve of a potential return to conventional UN peacekeeping mandates.

Canada in the former Yugoslavia

The United Nations Protection Force (UNPRO-FOR) was the first of several UN peacekeeping missions in Croatia and Bosnia and Herzegovina during the Yugoslav Wars of the 1990s. These wars resulted from the breakup of the former state of Yugoslavia (1918–1991). The UNPROFOR mandate ran from February 1992 until March 1995, and the mission ended with

restructuring into several individual missions in Macedonia and Croatia, as well as NATO and EU missions in Bosnia and Herzegovina. As the UN commander in Sector Sarajevo, Canadian Lieutenant-General Lewis MacKenzie was appointed chief of staff for the UN peacekeeping mission and, when hostilities broke out in April 1992, he employed his UN force to open Sarajevo Airport and facilitate the provision of humanitarian aid. During this period, the UN Security Council passed over 70 resolutions related to the former Yugoslavia.

While Canadian and other UN peacekeeping forces felt increasingly "ineffective, if not useless" to stop the constant violations of ceasefires, the deployment of 2,500 Canadian troops and the adept usage of the media by General MacKenzie helped save some of those targeted for ethnic cleansing (Dorn 2005, 14). During a Croatian attempt to take the Serbian-controlled Medak Pocket, 875 Canadian peacekeepers exchanged heavy fire with Croatian forces, driving them off through defensive measures. The engagement, which became known as Canada's "Secret Battle," took place shortly after the Somalia Affair (see below) came to light, and was not recognized by the Canadian government until ten years later, largely for political reasons (Dorn 2005). With the failure of Dutch UN peacekeepers to prevent the massacre of 8,000 Bosnian Muslim men and boys by Serb troops in 1995, and the decisive victory of Croatian forces in Operation Storm in August 1995, the US-brokered Dayton Agreement of 1995 ended UNPROFOR's mandate, and restructured the mission based on the changed political geography. Canada kept a force of over 1,000 troops in Bosnia until 2000. Canada also participated in the much-debated NATO bombing campaign in Kosovo during 1998 and 1999 against Serbian forces.

Elevated to the status of an international celebrity, General MacKenzie retired from the military upon his return to Canada in 1993. In the time since, he has written extensively on his experiences as commander of Sector Sarajevo, and served as a vocal opponent to NATO involvement in the former Yugoslavia in the latter half of the 1990s.

Canada in Somalia

In 1990, the Somali dictator Siad Barre was overthrown in a popular uprising. His regime was replaced by a bewildering array of warring factions and Somalia spiralled into famine and civil war. The international community stepped in to help restore order and deliver humanitarian relief with the UN Operation in Somalia (UNISOM). The Canadian contribution included the deployment of 1,400 troops and a helicopter unit in December 1992. Soldiers from the Canadian Airborne Regiment (CAR) were considered to be among the military's elite. They were also reportedly disgruntled with the mandate of the UNISOM mission and its reportedly "weak" rules of engagement (Dawson 2008).

Canada's participation in UNISOM reached its nadir with the deaths of two Somali nationals at the hands of CAR paratroopers. The first incident was the fatal shooting of an unarmed Somali on 4 March 1993, following a decision by Captain Michel Rainville, characterizing tampering with, and petty theft of, military equipment as "sabotage," a rebranding that purportedly enabled the use of deadly force to defend Canadian assets (Dorn 2005). The second incident came on 16 March, when Canadian soldiers captured Shidane Abukar Arone hiding in a portable toilet across from the Canadian base. In the hours that followed, multiple CAR paratroopers tortured and eventually killed the teenager, taking multiple pictures of the acts, while his screams could reportedly be heard across the base (Dawson 2008). Both the soldiers and commissioned officers responsible for the incident were charged in a court martial, with various sentences being passed in an episode that shocked the Canadian public and, in the words of the subsequent Department of National Defence inquiry, saw "a proud legacy dishonoured" (Dorn 2005, 13).

This Somalia Affair, as it came to be known, provoked the resignations of senior soldiers, including Chief of the Defence Staff Jean Boyle, the disbanding of the Canadian Airborne Regiment, and a severe embarrassment for the nation and its military. The Somalia Affair saw the beginning of the "Decade of Darkness," a period of dramatic downsizing of Canada's military personnel and defence spending from 1994 to 2003. The Decade of Darkness paralleled Canada's retreat from participation in peacekeeping missions (Kasurak 2013). (See Chapter 4.) Regardless of whether Canada's operational objectives were accomplished in Somalia, the political disaster that was the Somalia Affair resulted in a bleak aftermath for Canadian internationalism in the years following the end of the Cold War. Its record for peacekeeping significantly tarnished by the CAR's atrocities, the Canadian government, like much of the developed world, adopted what was dubbed the "Somalia syndrome," that is, the belief that "multilateral interventions to thwart starvation, genocide, the forced movement of peoples, and massive violations of fundamental rights are no longer politically or operationally feasible" (Weiss 1995, 171).

Canada in Rwanda

With the operation in Somalia being phased out in an atmosphere of political and strategic failure, the tensions arising in the central African country of Rwanda saw the establishment of the United Nations Assistance Mission for Rwanda (UNAMIR). It is impossible to discuss the role of Canada in Rwanda without an examination of the UN Force Commander, Major-General Roméo Dallaire. UNAMIR was established on 5 October 1993 by Security Council Resolution 872, its mandate to monitor the ceasefire between rival factions, to process the repatriation of refugees, to assist in mine clearance, and to coordinate humanitarian assistance. Canada participated in the mission from December 1993 until February 1996, with 112 military personnel providing logistics support to UNAMIR at any given time.

Despite having no prior experience in peace-keeping management, Dallaire diligently set up the UNAMIR mission as per direction from UN Headquarters in New York City. When the mass slaughter of approximately 800,000 Tutsi and moderate Hutu began over the course of 100 days in April 1994, the restrictive rules of engagement for UN forces and limited operational strength of UNAMIR's mission left the peacekeepers largely helpless to stop the genocide. After the torture and murder of ten Belgian peacekeepers, Dallaire used his multinational forces to set up areas of "safe control" in and around the capital, Kigali. Using UN credentials to dissuade and repel attacks by the Interahamwe militia, Dallaire and his forces were credited with saving 32,000 people. While Canada was the only country to send additional troops to reinforce UNAMIR during the genocide itself, they numbered only 30 and proved entirely inadequate to make any strategic difference (Dorn 2005).

In the wake of the genocide, General Dallaire returned to Canada with severe post-traumatic stress disorder and, with the overwhelming support of the Canadian public, became a senator and ardent advocate for humanitarian causes, particularly child soldiers and conflict resolution. For their courage and leadership throughout the unrest, Canadian Generals Dallaire and Guy Tousignant and Major Brent Beardsley were awarded the Meritorious Service Cross. Several years after UNAMIR's failure to prevent the genocide in Rwanda, UN Secretary-General Kofi Annan admitted some responsibility for the tragedy in 1999. Both the UN's weaknesses in the former Yugoslavia and the so-called Somalia Syndrome were cited as the leading factors for the extremely cautious response by the UN Security Council to the Rwandan genocide (Dorn 2005). The shortcomings of both the UN and its member states in permitting the Rwandan genocide to take place either through inaction, at best, or direct facilitation, at worst, remains one of the worst failures of peacekeeping.

There were also impacts on the Canadian military, in addition to the Decade of Darkness. The controversy emerging from the atrocities committed in Somalia and the collective failure to prevent mass slaughter in Rwanda and the former Yugoslavia provoked a decline in Canadian peacekeeping during the late 1990s and early 2000s. During this time, Canada made only relatively minor contributions to peacekeeping operations in Sierra Leone (1999–2005), the Democratic Republic of the Congo (1999–present), East Timor (2000–2002), Haiti (2004), and Sudan (2005–2009). Canada, the country that helped invent peacekeeping, effectively turned its back on the concept as an operational priority.

2001–2017: Geopolitical Shifts and the War on Terror

The strategic failures in Somalia, the former Yugoslavia, and Rwanda, and subsequent questions surrounding the role of peacekeepers in general, prompted a significant pause for self-reflection by both the international community and Canada. As the so-called Decade of Darkness came to a close, the purported threat of global terrorism, and the corresponding evolution from a dynamic of "peacekeeping" to peacemaking brought about yet another dramatic shift in geopolitical priorities for Canada and its military.

The period since 2001 has been marked by Canada's participation in major combat missions in Afghanistan, Libya, and Iraq. At the same time, the Canadian Forces remain an active contributor to global humanitarian and security operations. The Royal Canadian Air Force supported the French-led Operation Serval in Mali (2013–2014) and the Canadian Armed Forces' Disaster Assistance Response Team (DART) has seen service in major disaster relief operations in Honduras (1998), Turkey (1999), Sri Lanka (2004), Pakistan (2005), Haiti (2010), and the Philippines (2013).

Canada in Afghanistan

The 11 September 2001 attacks by on the US (called "9/11") dramatically changed defence priorities not just for Canada and NATO, but for the entire world. The al-Qaeda operatives responsible for 9/11 were trained in camps in Taliban-controlled Afghanistan (Wallin and Dallaire 2010). In an unprecedented step that required NATO members to affirm their collective security approach, the US invoked Article 5 of the NATO Treaty, under which an attack on one member country is considered to be an attack on all. (See Case Study 4.) In response, the Canadian Armed Forces deployed to Afghanistan in October 2001. In what was eventually to become the longest combat mission in Canadian military history, the war in Afghanistan saw a shift in national identity for Canada's soldiers, as the face of international peacekeeping turned into hardened combat veterans on the front lines of the US-led War on Terror.

With NATO forces operating in Afghanistan only days after the 9/11 attacks, the creation of the International Security Assistance Force (ISAF) in December 2001 provided the Alliance with legitimacy by means of a UN-mandated mission, with implementation overseen by NATO. In the month before the US-led invasion of Iraq in March 2003, the Liberal government in Ottawa voted to extend Canada's participation in Afghanistan, a tactic widely seen as being a method to avoid becoming entangled in the Iraq invasion.

By 2006, Canadian personnel had been redeployed from the Afghan capital of Kabul to the southern Afghan region of Kandahar, the birthplace of the Taliban movement and one of the most dangerous provinces in Afghanistan. Engaged in asymmetric warfare against Taliban insurgents, Al-Qaeda operatives, and their allies, Canadian soldiers saw some of the fiercest fighting since the Korean War and, on 13 March 2008, the by then Conservative government in Ottawa voted, with Liberal backing, to extend the combat mission past February 2009 until 2011.

After extending the mission twice, Ottawa announced a termination of combat operations in July 2011, with a training mission taking its place until late 2013. On 15 March 2014, the last Canadian soldiers departed from Afghanistan and a formal recognition of Canada's deployment was performed in Ottawa on 9 May 2014, in what was described as a "National Day of Honour." In total, 158 Canadian soldiers, one diplomat, and four civilians were killed during the twelve-year deployment.

The Afghan mission saw Canada embrace the "3D" approach to foreign policy in which defence, diplomacy, and development agencies work closely together. This has sometimes been controversial. (See Chapters 11 and 14 and Case Study 4.)

Canada in Libya

From March to November 2011, the Canadian Army, the Royal Canadian Air Force, and the Royal Canadian Navy were given the mandate to prevent Libyan government forces loyal to embattled leader Muammar Gaddafi from carrying out attacks against anti-Gaddafi forces and civilians. As part of NATO's larger Operation Unified Protector, enabled by UN Security Council Resolution 1973, Canada dispatched special operations personnel, multi-role aircraft, and two navy frigates throughout the deployment, while Canadian Lieutenant-General Charles Bouchard acted as NATO's operational commander.

With the operational objectives achieved by October, Libya's new, post-Gaddafi government requested an extension of the mission until the end of the year, but the UN Security Council voted to end NATO's mandate. The government of Prime Minister Stephen Harper hosted a victory parade in Ottawa.

While the mission marked a decisive Canadian victory over Gaddafi's forces, the strategic outcomes of the conflict have been less satisfactory. Much like Somalia after the fall of Siad Barre, Libya has descended into a civil war between competing factions of the new government, Islamist extremist groups, and tribal militants.

Canada in Iraq/Syria

The latest—and possibly most contentious—case of Canada's military being deployed overseas is Operation Impact, the Canadian contribution to the military intervention against the Islamist extremist group known as the Islamic State in Iraq and the Levant (ISIL). Following rapid and dramatic territorial gains in Iraq by ISIL in the spring and summer of 2014, a number of international coalitions were established to counter ISIL's growing influence.

In September 2014, as a combined effort with its NATO allies and several Sunni Gulf states, Canada deployed six CF-18 fighter jets, an air-to-air refueller, two surveillance aircraft, 700 support personnel, and approximately 69 special operations forces to act as advisors to Iraqi and Kurdish forces. On 30 March 2015, Parliament voted to expand the mission's scope to include combating ISIL in Iraq. Following the Liberal Party's victory in the 2015 federal election, the new prime minister, Justin Trudeau, announced his intention to withdraw Canada's aircraft from the conflict, while reinforcing its role in training and advising Iraqi and Kurdish ground forces. As of April 2017, important gains have been made against ISIL in Iraq, largely by local Iraqi and Kurdish forces with international support.

Future direction of Canada's peacekeeping efforts

In the year after Justin Trudeau's Liberals took over the government in November 2015, it has been widely rumoured that Canada would return to peacekeeping as a major priority for the Canadian Forces. By the end of 2016, there has been significant effort put into planning such a mission, possibly in Mali or the Central African Republic (MacCharles and Campion-Smith 2016). The idea of pivoting back to UN peacekeeping reflects a line of thinking embraced by other developed nations, such as Germany, the Netherlands, and the UK. With over 125,000 UN troops deployed today, more than three times the number deployed during the supposed golden age of peacekeeping around 2000, the traditional doctrine of peacekeeping will have to change just as drastically as the threats and vulnerabilities it seeks to safeguard against. (See Chapter 14.) Whether such a shift can be effectively implemented in an age of macroeconomic woes, geopolitical instability, and a resurgence of nationalist ideologies in developed states remains yet unclear. Moreover, the election of Donald Trump as US president may result in American pressure on Canada to do something other than peacekeeping with its military.

Either way, a whitewashed, blind optimism based on pride in Canada's past participation in UN peacekeeping missions will do little good. We need to understand clearly what the needs, objectives, and likely dangers are when it comes to such contextually sensitive mandates as peacekeeping operations.

Conclusion

As a military administered by an elected civilian government, the Canadian Armed Forces are inherently a utility through which the implementation of domestic and foreign policy may come to practical fruition. Since the end of the Second World War, changing defence priorities and strategies have resulted from both internal changes (change in government in Ottawa, fiscal crisis) and external changes (the end of the Cold War, the 9/11 attacks), or typically a combination of the two. The story of Canada's military in developing countries is one of complex geopolitical demands, the supply of prescribed solutions, and the influence of both known and unknown contextual factors.

Whether as the "largest of small powers" or the "smallest of large powers," the history of Canada and its military is one that is, for the most part, internally proud and externally respected across the globe. It is inevitable that implementation of foreign policy through military means—whether in terms of combat or humanitarian relief—is never received with universal praise or admiration. But in playing their part in a dizzying number of combat missions, peacekeeping mandates, and humanitarian and disaster relief responses, the men and women of Canada's military have consistently reinforced the reputation of the Canadian Armed Forces as an effective, compassionate, and resolute entity in the face of bleak and trying geopolitical situations. Where Canada has come up short, as in the Somalia Affair, it is vital to document and deconstruct the actions of a small group or even the individual as an indicator of underlying power dynamics within the larger organization, whether by evaluating the atrocities committed by individuals in the Canadian Airborne Regiment in Somalia or the institutional ineffectiveness of peacekeeping missions in the wake of acute humanitarian crises. Typically, these failings, whether intentional or not, are the catalysts for broader political outcomes and, most particularly, the catalysts that form the opinions about Canada in the developing countries it seeks to aid.

It is impossible in a single chapter to discuss in detail the Canadian military operations and the many Canadian contributions to UN peacekeeping missions in developing countries in their entirety since 1945. Nor can the ongoing participation of Global Affairs Canada, the Royal Canadian Mounted Police, and other law enforcement, security, and intelligence organizations as part of Canada's foreign and development policy be discussed in a chapter of this length. In order to gain a better understanding of how the experiences of Canada in developing countries shape its domestic and foreign policy, or are a product of them, a detailed personal exploration of the above organizations is strongly recommended to the reader.

Questions for Further Learning

- Is it accurate (or fair) to suggest that UN peacekeeping is a "Canadian innovation"? If so, how has this suggestion contributed to Canada's identity as a geopolitical actor? How has such an identity evolved as the number of Canadian peacekeepers and Canadian-led peacekeeping missions decreased dramatically around the beginning of the twenty-first century?

- Is the shift from "peacekeeping" (e.g., Suez) to "peacemaking" (e.g., Afghanistan) a deliberate decision of Canadian foreign policy, or is it more consistent with a broader and more gradual change in the geopolitical priorities of developed countries following the end of the Cold War?

- Does heightened Canadian participation in combat operations, such as the US-led campaign against ISIL in Iraq, damage Canada's historical reputation as a multilateral middle power, or does such a shift simply build upon a still-developing legacy of foreign affairs?

- Discuss what you think should be the role of countries like Canada, being historically a middle power. Do you believe that paradigm shifts, such as the War on Terror, necessitate a divergence from this traditional agenda and its legacy, towards one of more direct military action?

Key Terms

asymmetric warfare, p. 100
humanitarian intervention, p. 90

multilateral middle power, p. 90
NATO, p. 91
peacekeeping, p. 93

peacemaking, p. 90
soft power, p. 90
global terrorism, p. 99
War on Terror, p. 90

Suggested Readings

Byers, Michael. 2012. "After Afghanistan: Canada's Return to UN Peacekeeping." *Canadian Military Journal* 13 (1).

Dallaire, Romeo. 2003. *Shake Hands with the Devil: The Failure of Humanity in Rwanda*. Toronto: Random House Canada.

Kilford, Christopher. 2010. *The Other Cold War: Canada's Military Assistance to the Developing World 1945–1975*. Kingston: Canadian Defence Academy Press.

McCullough, Colin. 2016. *Creating Canada's Peacekeeping Past*. Vancouver: University of British Columbia Press.

Tremblay, Yves, ed. 2000. *Canadian Military History since the 17th Century*. Proceedings of the Canadian Military History Conference, Ottawa, 5–9 May, 2000.

Trudgen, Matthew. 2012. "A Canadian Approach: Canada's Cold War Grand Strategy, 1945–1989." *Journal of Military and Strategic Studies* 14 (3&4): 1–27.

Suggested Videos

3World Media. (2009). "Waging Peace: Canada in Afghanistan." http://www.wagingpeacefilm.com/About_the_Film.html

The Agenda with Steve Paikin. (2010). "After Afghanistan: Peacekeepers or war makers?" https://www.youtube.com/watch?v=w-Cp1ZooinA

The National. (2016). "Canada's peacekeepers face a troubled world." https://www.youtube.com/watch?v=7EcymA9bFro

UMKC. (2013). "Global Role of UN Peacekeepers." https://www.youtube.com/watch?v=xPK7sVZNje4

United Nations. (2013). "UN Peacekeeping Is." https://www.youtube.com/watch?v=jAXVbtdBu1o

United Nations. (2009). "In the cause of Peace: Honouring 60 years of UN peacekeeping." https://www.youtube.com/watch?v=rqYuRh78-_4

Suggested Websites

Canadian Global Affairs Institute (formerly Canadian Defence and Foreign Affairs Institute): http://www.cgai.ca/

Department of National Defence and Canadian Forces: http://www.forces.gc.ca/en/index.page

North Atlantic Treaty Organization (NATO): http://www.nato.int/ North Atlantic Treaty Organization (NATO)

Project Ploughshares: http://ploughshares.ca/

Stockholm International Peace Research Institute: https://sipri.org/ Stockholm International Peace Research Institute

UN Peacekeeping: http://www.un.org/en/peacekeeping/

UN Security Council: http://www.un.org/en/sc/

Works Cited

Carrol, Michael. 2009. *Pearson's Peacekeepers: Canada and the United Nations Emergency Force, 1956–67.* Vancouver: University of British Columbia Press.

Dawson, Grant. 2008. "Success in Failed States: Canadian Military Strategy in Somalia and the Implications for Afghanistan." *The Journal for Conflict Studies*, no. 28.

Donaghy, Greg. 2012. "The Rise and Fall of Canadian Military Assistance in the Developing World, 1952–1971." *Department of Foreign Affairs and International Trade* 4 (1): 74–84.

Dorn, Walter. 2005. "Canadian Peacekeeping: Proud Tradition, Strong Future?" *Canadian Foreign Policy* 12 (2): 7–32.

———. 2013. "The UN's First 'Air Force': Peacekeepers in Combat, Congo 1960–1964." *The Journal of Military History*, no. 77, 523–556.

Godefroy, Andrew. 2002. "The Canadian Armed Forces Advisory and Training Team 1965–1970." *Canadian Military History* 11 (3): 31–47.

Hillmer, Norman, and William Rawling. 1992. "United Nations Peacekeeping Operations." In *We Stand on Guard: An Illustrated History of the Canadian Army*, edited by John Marteinson. Montreal: Ovale Publications.

Interdepartmental MAC. 1969. "Canadian Military Assistance to Developing Countries—A Review by the Interdepartmental Military Assistance Committee." Ottawa: Library and Archives Canada.

Jeffery, Mike. 2013. *The Future of Foreign Military Training*. Strategic Studies Working Group Papers. Canadian Defence & Foreign Affairs Institute and Canadian International Council.

Johnston, William, and Stephen Harris. 1992. "The Post-War Army and the War in Korea." In *We Stand on Guard: An Illustrated History of the Canadian Army*, edited by John Marteinson. Montreal: Ovale Publications.

Kasurak, Peter. 2013. *A National Force: The Evolution of Canada's Army, 1950–2000*. Vancouver: University of British Columbia Press.

Kilford, Christopher. 2009. *The Other Cold War: Canadian Military Assistance in the Developing World.* Kingston: Canadian Defence Academy Press.

Lotz, Jim. 1990. *Canadians at War*. London: Bison Books Ltd.

MacCharles, Tonda, and Bruce Campion-Smith. 2016. "Canadian Soldiers Appear Headed to Mali." *Toronto Star*. Retrieved 20 December 2016, from https://www.thestar.com/news/canada/2016/11/26/canadian-soldiers-appear-headed-to-mali.html.

Macdonald, Donald. 1971. *Defence in the 70s.*

Minister of National Defence. Ottawa: Information Canada.

Marteinson, John, and Michael McNorgan. 2000. *The Royal Canadian Armoured Corps: An Illustrated History.* Toronto: Royal Canadian Armoured Corps Association.

Miller, Roger. 1998. *To Save a City: The Berlin Airlift 1948–1949.* Air Force History and Museums Program.

NATO. "About NATO." Retrieved 1 November 2015, from http://www.nato.int/.

Radwanski, George. 1978. *Trudeau.* Toronto: Macmillan Company of Canada.

RAND Corporation. "Asymmetric Warfare." Retrieved 1 November 2015 from http://www.rand.org/topics/asymmetric-warfare.html.

Thakur, Ramesh. 1984. *Peacekeeping in Vietnam: Canada, India, Poland, and the International Commission.* Edmonton: University of Alberta Press.

UN. "What is Peacekeeping?" United Nations Peacekeeping. Retrieved 1 November 2015 from http://www.un.org/en/peacekeeping/.

Wallin, Pamela, and Romeo Dallaire. 2010. *Where We Go From Here: Canada's Mission in Afghanistan.* Interim Report. Special Study on the National Security and Defence Policies of Canada. Ottawa: Senate Standing Committee on National Security and Defence.

Weiss, Thomas. 1995. "Overcoming the Somalia Syndrome: 'Operation Rekindle Hope?'" *Global Governance* 1 (2): 171–187.

Wood, Herbert Fairlie. 1966. *Strange Battleground: The Operations in Korea and Their Effects on the Defence Policy of Canada.* Ottawa: Queen's Printer.

Notes

6 Canadian Immigration and Refugee Policies since 1945

Bruno Gélinas-Faucher and Delphine Nakache

Key Terms

immigration

multicultural society

nativism

Order-in-Council

refugee

regulation

xenophobia

Overview

Canadian immigration policies have evolved over time, shaped by various social, political, and economic factors. Following Confederation in 1867, Canada opened its doors to mass settlement of the prairies. However, at the turn of the nineteenth century, this open-door approach gradually gave way to more restrictive measures that discriminated on the basis of race, ethnicity, and national origin. In the second half of the twentieth century the discriminatory clauses in immigration laws slowly gave way to racially neutral criteria, such as skills and education. Canada also came to adopt a more favourable attitude towards refugees, first by offering a *de facto* refuge to individuals displaced by humanitarian crisis following the Second World War, and later by joining the *1951 Refugee Convention*. The transformation of Canada's immigration and refugee policies culminated in the adoption of a modern legislative framework that now prohibits discrimination and recognizes the importance of immigration for the development of Canada.

Learning Objectives

By the end of this chapter, students will be able to:

- understand the major transformations that the Canadian immigration system has undergone, and the key factors influencing these changes.
- describe the major role of immigration in the development of the country over time.
- describe how Canada benefits from immigration.
- know the key criteria used when accepting immigrants and offering protection to refugees in Canada.

Introduction

If is often said that Canada is a "land of immigrants," referring to the millions of newcomers who have settled in the country and helped build the nation. In essence, this expression aptly describes the crucial role that immigration has played in the development of the country. And this contribution continues today; in fact, it has become more apparent than ever.

For example, in 2013, foreign-born immigrants represented close to 21 percent of Canada's population, the highest proportion among the G8 countries (Migration Policy Institute 2013). Still, this proportion is expected to rise in the coming years. According to Statistics Canada, one in four people in this country will have been born outside Canada by 2031 (2010, 1). This coincides with the increasingly important role of immigration with regard to the Canadian economy. Due to population ageing, it is estimated that by 2031 half of the working-age population (that is, the population aged 15 to 64) will be composed of first- or second-generation immigrants (Statistics Canada 2010, 20).

Canada's immigrant population is also more diverse than ever before. Historically, most immigrants came from Europe and the United States, but today Canada's immigrant population reports close to 200 countries as a place of birth (Statistics Canada 2013, 7). Over time, immigrants and their descendants have added to the nation's ethnic and cultural composition and Canada is now officially recognized as a multicultural society, accepting and encouraging all Canadians citizens, regardless of their language, religion, racial, or ethnic origins. In 1971, Canada was the first country in the world to adopt multiculturalism as a policy. Canada's approach to multiculturalism has evolved over the years and is embedded within a broad legislative framework. In 1982, the *Canadian Charter of Rights and Freedoms* was adopted. Section 15 of the Charter recognizes that all Canadians are guaranteed equality before the law and equality of opportunity regardless of their origin, while section 27 protects minority groups in Canada and incorporates the notion of religious diversity and the protection of "different" religious beliefs. In 1988, the *Canadian Multiculturalism Act* came into effect, the first multiculturalism law in the world. The *Act* acknowledges multiculturalism as a fundamental characteristic of Canadian society and its objective is to preserve and enhance multiculturalism in Canada to assist in the preservation of culture and language in, among other things, reducing discrimination and promoting culturally sensitive institutional change at the federal level.

Importantly, Canada's modern legislative framework governing the admission of immigrants also clearly recognizes the essential contribution of immigration to the country's development. For example, the fundamental objectives of Canadian immigration policy listed in the *Immigration and Refugee Protection Act* (hereinafter IRPA 2001) include the following:

- To permit Canada to pursue the maximum social, cultural and economic benefits of immigration;

- To enrich and strengthen the social and cultural fabric of Canadian society, while respecting the federal, bilingual and multicultural character of Canada;
- To support the development of a strong and prosperous Canadian economy, in which the benefits of immigration are shared across all regions of Canada;
- To see that families are reunited in Canada;
- To promote the successful integration of permanent residents into Canada, while recognizing that integration involves mutual obligations for new immigrants and Canadian society.

Equally important, the stated goals of the IRPA 2001 with respect to refugees explicitly recognize Canada's international commitments regarding human rights and the fundamental humanitarian character of refugee protection.

The importance of these objectives should not be minimized, especially as they stand in sharp contrast to some of the policies of exclusion and racialization that characterized Canadian immigration policies for much of the twentieth century. In fact, it was only in 1962 that new regulations were implemented with a view to dismantling Canada's discriminatory immigration policy. Even then, we had to wait until 1976, when new legislation was enacted, to have an immigration policy totally exempt from any racial criteria. It is also worth noting that Canada finally ratified the *Convention Relating to the Status of Refugees* in 1969, that is, 18 years after it was adopted by the United Nations and 15 years after it came into force. In ratifying that Convention, Canada expressed for the first time its willingness to assume the international legal obligations attached to the protection of refugees. Obviously, as laudable as the objectives enunciated in Canada's modern legislation might be, they should not be taken as guaranteeing flawless immigration programs or governmental action, and the current debates surrounding recent immigration measures serve as a constant reminder that our system is far from perfect.

This chapter provides an overview of the historical events that gave rise to the present Canadian immigration and refugee policies. We first look at the broad characteristics of the prevailing immigration policies from the time of Confederation until the end of the Second World War. This is important to understand the critical transformations that took place from the 1950s on, which are addressed in the second part of this chapter. We then turn to a presentation of the current immigration system and its main characteristics.

In the Beginning: 1867–1945

Confederation and the development of the Canadian West

In the early days of Confederation, immigration was seen as a crucial tool to develop the new Dominion of Canada, mostly through agriculture and the settlement of the vast western prairies of what is now Alberta, Manitoba, and Saskatchewan. In fact, the use of immigration as a means of land development was so evident at that time that the subjects of immigration and agriculture were treated under the same heading in the *Constitution Act, 1867*. Thus, in its earliest stage, Canada pursued an active immigration policy aimed at facilitating the settlement of European farmers and farm-labourers in the Canadian West. It was hoped that, in the long run, the settlement of the West would provide a market for goods produced in the rest of the country, as well as supplying Canada with agricultural products for consumption and for export. Settlement of the prairies would also deter American expansion to the north.

However, recruitment of immigrants in the first three decades following Confederation proved somewhat disappointing: the Canadian economy was weaker than expected and Canada had trouble competing with the United States in attracting European emigrants. The

Figure 6.1
Pamphlet Advertising The Last Best West

Source: National Archives of Canada, File No. C-30620, June 16, 2010.

tide eventually turned in 1896. To achieve mass settlement of the Prairies, the new Liberal government of Wilfred Laurier (1896–1911) launched an intensive recruitment campaign (see **Figure 6.1**), portraying the Canadian Prairies as "The Last Best West"—this was a reference to the United States, where land on the Great Plains was becoming less available and more expensive to settlers. Canada's grant of free or cheap land as part of the recruitment campaign, coupled with a booming Canadian economy, succeeded in attracting an unprecedented number of immigrants.

During that period, immigration also became an important source of workers for labour-intensive companies essential to the economic prosperity of the country, such as mining and forestry. To finish the final section of the transcontinental railway in British Columbia in the 1880s, an estimated 15,000 Chinese workers were brought to Canada.

Canada's intensive efforts to promote immigration at the turn of the twentieth century were successful. More than three million people

Figure 6.2
Growing Number of Immigrants from 1896 to 1914

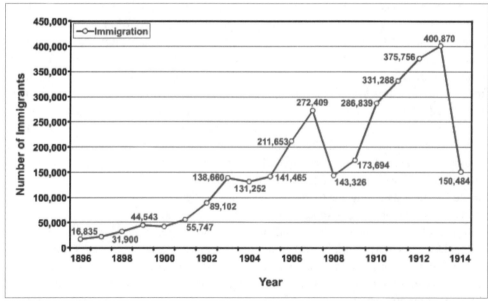

Source: F.H. Leacy, ed., 1983, Historical Statistics of Canada, 2nd ed., Ottawa: Statistics Canada, Series A-350.
http://www.canadianhistory.ca/iv/1867-1914/interactivewindow/immigration_1896-1914.html

came to Canada between 1896 and the start of the First World War in 1914. However, as Canada was becoming a more mixed society due to the new groups of settlers, social tensions and racism grew in Canadian society. As time went on, the government would increasingly distinguish which ethnic groups would be allowed to immigrate to Canada (see **Figure 6.2**, opposite), and racialization would become a central feature of Canada's immigration policies.

The beginning of the racialization of immigration

The steady increase in immigrants to Canada at the turn of the twentieth century coincided with strong growth of the national economy. In a way, economic interests prevailed over other considerations and kept the doors open for both European and non-European immigrants. However, the arrival of more than three million "foreigners" with various cultures, languages, and ethnicities in such a short period of time started causing some tension among the Canadian population. Moreover, starting in 1907,

an economic recession exacerbated the already growing hostility towards Asian immigrants, especially on the west coast.

A symptom of this sentiment, the Asiatic Exclusion League was formed in Vancouver in 1907. The League was created under the auspices of labour unions and included prominent politicians in its membership. On September 7, 1907, a rally in support of the League in Vancouver escalated into a violent and destructive anti-Asian riot (see **Figure 6.3**) that caused severe damage to the areas known as Chinatown and Japantown. After the incident, many politicians demanded that Asian immigration be limited. In the following years, the federal government adopted various measures aimed at prohibiting targeted groups from immigrating to Canada.

One of the most famous measures in this area was the "continuous journey regulation," which prohibited the landing of any immigrant who did not come to Canada by continuous journey from the country of which they were natives or citizens. Immigrants were required to

Figure 6.3

Damage Resulting from the 1907 Anti-Asian Riots in Vancouver

Source: Public Archives of Canada.

purchase a through ticket to Canada from their country of origin; otherwise they were denied entry. With the sea routes of the early 1900s, this created in practice a significant barrier to South Asian immigration, since the main immigration routes from those countries did not offer direct passage to Canada (see **Figure 6.4**). While Indian immigrants were officially British subjects, and thus able to claim privileged legal status in Canada, the government used this rule to indirectly restrict their arrival without having to justify their exclusion on the basis of race, nationality, or ethnic origins.

The continuous journey regulation famously came under the spotlight in 1914, when the *Komagata Maru* steamship arrived in Vancouver with 376 travellers from India who were mainly Sikh, with some Muslims and Hindus. The passengers were denied entry because their voyage had not been "continuous." However, the passengers refused to leave, and were confined to

Figure 6.4
Cartoon Encouraging the Exclusion of Chinese Immigrants, 1907

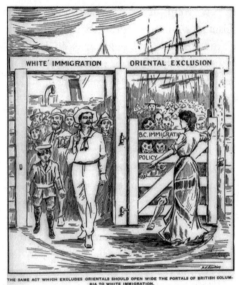

Source: Vancouver Public Library, Special Collections. *Saturday Sunset* newspaper, August 24, 1907.

Figure 6.5
Passengers on Board the *Komagata Maru*, 1914

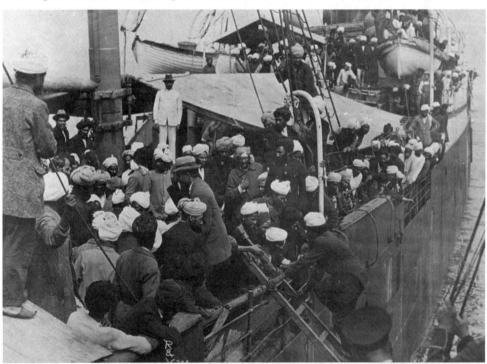

Source: Library and Archives Canada, under the reproduction reference number PA-034014.

the ship for more than two months while the legality of the continuous journey regulation was challenged in court. The Supreme Court of British Columbia eventually upheld the legality of the regulation, and the *Komagata Maru* was forced to leave Canadian waters and return to India (see **Figure 6.5**, opposite). Between 1910 and 1920, only 112 Indian immigrants gained entry into Canada (Johnston 1984, 7; Rahim 2014, 88–91).

The federal government also turned its attention to migrants of Japanese origin. Similarly to Indian immigration, Canada could not specifically prohibit Japanese individuals from immigrating because Britain had signed a trade treaty with Japan that secured the rights of Japanese to enter, travel, or reside in any part of the British dominions. (Canada's defence and foreign relations were managed by Britain until 1931; see Chapter 1.) Nevertheless, in 1908, Canada successfully concluded with the Japanese government what it called a "gentlemen's agreement," specifying that the maximum annual number of Japanese immigrants admitted to Canada could not exceed 400.

Many other measures directly targeted Chinese immigrants. The first laws came from the provincial legislature of British Columbia, where the xenophobic and racist attitudes towards them were most pronounced. Thus, between 1878 and 1908, the province passed multiple laws aimed at stopping or deterring Chinese immigration. While some laws purported to impose explicit prohibitions on the entry of Chinese immigrants, others imposed entrance requirements (such as proficiency in

Figure 6.6
Chinese Head Tax Certificate

Source: Vancouver Public Library, Special Collections, VPL 1773, head tax document courtesy of Linda Jang.
http://langaraprm.com/2005/culture/redressing-the-past-of-the-lo-wah-kui-chinese-canadians-demand-compensation-for-past-injustices/

a European language) that in effect excluded many of them. Still other laws imposed discriminatory burdens on those who had already been admitted; for example, by disqualifying them from working in particular sectors and from participating in political decision making (Galloway 1997, 10).

The language used in some of these laws clearly demonstrates the xenophobic stereotypes that then prevailed. For example, the preamble of the *Chinese Regulation Act, 1884* underlined how Chinese were "not disposed to be governed by our laws; are dissimilar in habits and occupation from our people; evade the payment of taxes justly due to the Government; are governed by pestilential habits; are useless in instances of emergency; habitually desecrate graveyards by the removal of bodies therefrom; and generally the laws governing the whites are found to be inapplicable to Chinese, and such Chinese are inclined to habits subversive of the comfort and well-being of the community."

While some of these laws did not pass constitutional muster because they encroached on federal powers, the federal legislature eventually joined the crusade and endeavoured to discourage Chinese immigration by passing the *Chinese Immigration Act* in 1885. The *Act* imposed became known as a "head tax," a fixed fee of $50 charged to each Chinese individual entering Canada (see **Figure 6.6**, previous page). This amount was gradually increased to $100 in 1900 and $500 in 1903. The policy culminated in 1923 with Parliament imposing an outright ban on Chinese immigration.

The list of governmental discriminatory measures would not be complete without a mention of the multiple efforts aimed at preventing the settlement in Canada of "Black people" living in the United States. First, it is reported that the Canadian government took steps to disseminate false propaganda in the United States. For example, Black people requesting information from a Canadian immigration agent on how to immigrate to Canada often received in response a letter mentioning

the poor conditions awaiting Black settlers in Canada. For those who decided to make their way to the border, the Canadian government instructed immigration officials to "selectively" enforce immigration regulations. As a result, Black people were classified as unfit for admission on medical grounds. This policy culminated in 1911 with the government adopting an Order-in-Council (i.e., a regulation adopted by the federal Cabinet) that prohibited "any immigrants belonging to the Negro race, which race is deemed unsuitable to the climate and requirements of Canada." While the Order was never officially inscribed in the immigration legislation, it is nevertheless a powerful indication of the government's attitude towards Black settlement in Canada.

The First World War and the Great Depression, 1914–1939: Perpetuating intolerance

The start of the First World War in 1914 only exacerbated the hostility towards "foreigners." The general intake of immigrants slowed significantly, and entry was barred altogether for immigrants from enemy countries such as Germany, Italy, and Ukraine (who at the time had Austro-Hungarian citizenship). The "enemy aliens" who were already in Canada experienced great hardship, facing internment or deportation on suspicion of conspiring against the government, and losing the right to vote in 1917 under the *Wartime Elections Act* (Kelley and Trebilcock 1998, 169–175).

During the interwar period (1919–1939), immigration policies became even more restrictive, especially through the Great Depression of the 1930s. With millions of Canadians unemployed, immigrants were seen as competing for scarce jobs and contributing to the depression of wages. The government reacted by adopting further exclusionary policies that dramatically restricted new entrances and by implementing widespread deportations. As time passed, the grounds for deportation became more varied and arbitrary:

Immigrants, along with their dependents, could be deported for a number of stated reasons: criminality, medical causes, being a "public charge," or for "other civil causes," a catch-all category which covered political deportations of radicals and union organizers ... Following large-scale immigration in times of economic expansion, deportation served as a stabilizing mechanism in times of depression, when immigrants could not find work and became charges on the public welfare or were politically troublesome. (Whitaker 1991, 13)

Between 1930 and 1935, the government officially deported more than 28,000 persons, almost as many as had been deported in the previous 20 years (Whitaker 1991, 13).

Closed doors for Jewish refugees fleeing Europe in the 1930s

It is in this context of opposition to immigration that Canada dealt, at the end of the 1930s, with a growing number of people fleeing Europe following the rise to power of Hitler and the Nazi Party in Germany. While Jews had already in the 1920s faced tighter restrictions when they attempted to enter Canada, they were similarly turned away when they sought asylum from Nazi persecution. The Canadian government demanded a massive capital requirement of Jewish immigrants ($20,000 by 1938), which of course many could not display. In 1940, an Order-in-Council prohibited entry of nationals of countries at war with Canada, ensuring that few German and Eastern European Jews could escape to Canada.

A famous event illustrating this tragic period is the fate of the passengers of the steamship *St. Louis* in 1939. The 907 Jews fleeing Nazi Germany aboard the ship were denied sanctuary in Cuba, the United States, and Canada. The ship ultimately sailed back to Germany, where many of the passengers died in concentration camps.

The Second World War

Canada's record grew even uglier during the Second World War. Anti-Asian sentiment reached its peak with the confiscation of property and forcible relocation of the Japanese-Canadian population of the west coast to internment camps established in the interior (see **Figure 6.7**, overleaf). Many of the internees were Canadian citizens by birth. Despite strong reservations by leading members of the RCMP and of the armed forces, it was argued that people of Japanese ancestry would pose a security threat due to their loyalty to their country of origin, which was at war with Canada. However, as Kelley and Trebilcock explain, "it was not the legitimacy of these fears that prompted the government to strip the Japanese Canadians of their properties and their rights to reside freely in the country. The war ignited deep prejudices against those of Japanese ancestry that had been smouldering in British Columbia since the turn of the century" (1998, 255). Many Japanese immigrants were also deported at the end of the war.

Summary to 1945

In sum, following an open-door policy driven by economic considerations at the end of the nineteenth century, the first half of the twentieth century was dominated by cultural, racial, and ideological criteria that became key features for the selection of potential immigrants. This discrimination was driven by both nativism and xenophobia among the Canadian population, and received official sanction in immigration laws and policies. Nativism is a policy of favouring native-born inhabitants as opposed to immigrants; xenophobia is a fear or hatred of foreigners or strangers or of anything that is strange or foreign.

Figure 6.7
Internment Camp for Japanese-Canadians in British Columbia, 1945

Source: Jack Long/National Film Board of Canada/Library and Archives Canada/PA-142853.

A Time of Transformation: 1945–1978

The period following the end of the Second World War brought about progressive changes in Canada's immigration policy. The discriminatory clauses in immigration laws slowly gave way to racially neutral criteria, such as skills and education. Canada also started adopting a more favourable attitude towards refugees, first by offering a *de facto* protection to individuals displaced by humanitarian crises following the Second World War, and later by joining the 1951 *Refugee Convention*. Ultimately, the

transformation of Canada's immigration and refugee policies was a slow process that resulted from a variety of factors. This process of transformation culminated in the enactment of the *Immigration Act*, 1976.

From "absorptive capacity" to progressive liberalization

Following the Second World War, the Canadian economy once again enjoyed widespread growth and prosperity. The rapid economic expansion across the country created a high demand for skilled labour that immigration could satisfy. The postwar period was also characterized by social changes that affected attitudes toward immigrants. This incremental change was closely related to the economic boom; with low unemployment rates, the perception that immigrants were competing for jobs inevitably diminished. Coupled with greater education among Canadians and a growing aversion to xenophobia following the horrors of the Second World War, Canadian society slowly became more tolerant (Kelley and Trebilcock 1998, 311 and 313).

The Canadian government thus gradually opened its frontiers to an increasingly diverse foreign labour workforce. But the embrace was still cautious, with the government only ready to accept immigration based upon what it called the "absorptive capacity" of the Canadian economy and society. In a famous speech in the House of Commons in 1947, Liberal Prime Minister Mackenzie King (1921–1926, 1926–1930, and 1935–1948) described the government's new approach to postwar immigration, including the need to respect this absorptive capacity and the changing attitude towards discrimination:

> The policy of the government is to foster the growth of the population of Canada by the encouragement of immigration. The government will seek ... to ensure the careful selection and permanent settlement of such numbers of immigrants as can advantageously be absorbed in our national economy ...
>
> With regard to the selection of immigrants, much has been said about discrimination. I wish to make it quite clear that Canada is perfectly within her rights in selecting the persons whom we regard as desirable future citizens. It is not a "fundamental human right" of any alien to enter Canada. It is a privilege. It is a matter of domestic policy ... This does not mean, however, that we should not seek to remove from our legislation what may appear to be objectionable discrimination.

However, the Prime Minister was also quick to point out:

> [T]he people of Canada do not wish, as a result of mass immigration, to make a fundamental alteration in the character of our population. Large-scale immigration from the orient would change the fundamental composition of the Canadian population. Any considerable oriental immigration would, moreover, be certain to give rise to social and economic problems of a character that might lead to serious difficulties in the field of international relations. The government, therefore, has no thought of making any change in immigration regulations which would have consequences of the kind. (House of Commons Debates 1947, 2644–46)

The prerogative for selection of potential immigrants was thus still at the centre of the government's new policy. The aim was mainly to admit immigrants who could be "easily assimilated" into mainstream Canada and who would not alter the fundamental makeup of the country. Despite this ambivalent approach, some discriminatory clauses in the immigration legislation were progressively altered and removed. Thus, the *Chinese Immigration Act* of 1923 was repealed in 1947. The contribution of Chinese Canadians during the Second World War, Canada's admission to the United Nations as a member state in November 1945, and pressure exercised by the Committee for the Repeal of the Chinese Immigration Act (a group created in 1946 and supported by both Chinese-Canadians and non-Chinese-Canadians) were important factors that propelled this evolution. Despite this important step forward, it took some more time before other progressive measures were adopted.

In fact, immigration policies did not take a defined and consistent direction until the 1960s. In the meantime, a new immigration act was passed in 1952, which largely reiterated and codified previous discriminatory practices and perpetuated the *status quo*. Like previous legislation, it provided for the refusal of admission on the grounds of nationality; ethnic group; geographical area of origin; peculiar customs, habits, and modes of life; "unsuitability" with regard to the climate; and probable inability to become readily assimilated. The *Act* also included a new restriction prohibiting homosexuals from entering Canada. Importantly, however, the *Act* granted a very large degree of discretion to the minister. This would have far-reaching implications in the following years.

At first, the immigration minister's wide discretionary powers were used to effectively operationalize the government's discriminatory policy. In 1956, for instance, a regulation was passed that organized the four categories of persons allowed to immigrate into a hierarchy of most- to least-welcome national origins:

> [a]t the top were unsponsored British subjects from the United Kingdom and the white Commonwealth, as well as those of American and French origins; second were unsponsored immigrants from specified Western European countries; third were a broad range of sponsored relatives from Europe, America and a few middle eastern countries; at the bottom was a residual category designed to restrict Asians to sponsor close relatives without indicating that intention openly. (Whitaker 1991, 17–18)

However, a few years later, these powers proved to be an invaluable tool in transforming immigration policies.

Under the Progressive Conservative government of John Diefenbaker (1957–1963), a new regulation was adopted in 1962, beginning the process of putting an end to racial immigration policies. New independent immigrants were now to be selected based only on their skills and means of support, rather than race or national origin. The adoption of the new regulation by Cabinet, rather than through legislation, at that time allowed the introduction of a more inclusive immigration policy, since Parliament might not have approved such radical changes. But discrimination was not completely eliminated by the new regulation, since a clause was added that prohibited immigrants from certain nationalities—mainly Asians and Africans—from sponsoring more distant relatives. Nevertheless, the 1962 regulation was an important step toward more inclusive immigration policies.

This important change in immigration policy can be partly explained by the paradigm shift in human rights protection that had developed over time, both in Canada and internationally under the leadership of the United Nations.[1] Most notably, Diefenbaker's *Canadian Bill of Rights* (S.C. 1960, c. 44) had become law two years before the new immigration regulation. That legislation prohibited federal laws and governmental actions from discriminating on the basis of race, colour, national origin, religion, or sex. Consequently, discriminative policies favouring certain immigrants on the basis of ethnicity and national origin became difficult to justify (Knowles 1997, 152).

The 1960s was a decade of economic expansion, when skilled labour was in great demand. However, "the economic recovery of Europe had sharply reduced Canada's major source for skilled labour. Educated, skilled workers could only be found in large number in precisely that part of the world traditionally restricted the most by Canadian law and practice: Asia" (Whitaker 1991, 19). Thus economic needs and an increasingly tolerant political culture led to the adoption of a new immigration regulation in 1967.

The 1967 regulation introduced the points system for the first time, a lasting feature of the Canadian immigration framework,

---

1. The Canadian jurist John Humphreys was the main author of the UN's *Universal Declaration of Human Rights* of 1948.

marking the removal of the last of racial discrimination. Under this new system, immigrants were assigned points according to certain objective criteria relating to their ability to successfully settle in Canada, such as education, skills, and resources. From that point on, the removal of racial or national barriers allowed immigration to Canada to become increasingly diverse in terms of country of origin. Immigration from countries in Asia, the Caribbean, Latin America, and Africa increased significantly. This represented a major shift from the traditional pattern of immigration that had historically favoured Europe and the United States. In fact, in the 1940s and 1950s, immigration to Canada was made up almost entirely of immigrants from Europe. This situation changed dramatically, as shown in **Table 6.1**:

Table 6.1

Changing Immigration Pattern Following the Removal of Racial and National Barriers

Immigrant Arrivals by Countries of Last Permanent Residence, 1967-1991											
Period		Europe	United States	Central/ South Americas	Caribbean	Asia	Africa	Australia	Oceania	Not stated	Total
1968-1972	Nbre	387,670	114,615	24,863	53,100	112,584	22,014	18,656	0	3,622	737,124
	%	52.6	15.5	3.4	7.2	15.3	3	2,5	0	0.5	100
1973-1977	Nbre	324,131	102,141	63,598	86,627	216,837	42,748	10870	7937	0	854,889
	%	37.9	11.9	7.4	10.1	25.4	5	1.3	0.9	0	100
1978-1982	Nbre	196,546	49,407	36,262	39362	236,596	21,946	6,438	4,502	232	591,291
	%	33.2	8.4	6.1	6.7	40	3.7	1.1	0.8	0	100
1983-1987	Nbre	124,344	36,214	56,442	39,079	226,326	24,027	2,774	3,771	38	513,015
	%	24.2	7.1	11	7.6	44.1	4.7	0.5	0.7	0	100
1988-1992	Nbre	237,666	33,686	91061	59,911	545,410	70,744	4,771	8,534	0	1,051,783
	%	22.6	3.2	8.7	5.7	51.9	6.7	0.5	0.8	0	100
1993-1995	Nbre	126,509	19,433	39,119	36,599	418,016	45,255	3,476	3,791	0	692,198
	%	18.3	2.8	5.7	5.3	60.4	6.5	0.5	0.5	0	100
1968-1995	Nbre	1,396,866	355,496	311,345	314,678	1,755,769	226,734	46,985	28,535	3,892	4,440,300
	%	31.5	8	7	7.1	39.5	5.1	1.1	0.6	0.1	100

Source: http://www.justice.gc.ca/eng/rp-pr/csj-sjc/jsp-sjp/rpo2_8-dro2_8/t2.html#sec1

To this day, immigration from developing countries continues to exceed that from European or other developed countries. In 2014, the top five source countries for immigration to Canada were the Philippines, India, China, Iran, and Pakistan (see **Table 6.2** and **Figure 6.8**).

Table 6.2
Canadian Permanent Residents by Source Area

Total by Source area										
Source area	2005	2006	2007	2008	2009	2010	2011	2012	2013	2014
Africa and the Middle East	46,082	48,974	46,890	49,512	55,035	64,778	57,938	56,446	62,229	62,175
Asia and Pacific	141,483	130,445	116,386	122,743	122,519	141,440	125,118	133,854	132,134	133,764
Europe and the United Kingdom	40,626	37,007	37,322	37,621	38,209	36,800	29,587	32,034	30,712	30,176
United States	8,394	9,613	9,463	10,190	8,995	8,141	7,676	7,891	8,501	8,496
South and Central America	24,749	24,676	26,011	26,550	26,869	28,818	27,855	27,172	24,950	24,948
Source area not stated	906	923	680	626	542	703	570	501	497	844
Category not stated	2	2	1	2	1	7	3	5	0	1
Total by Source area	262,242	251,640	236,753	247,244	252,170	280,687	248,747	257,903	259,023	260,404

Source : http://www.cic.gc.ca/english/resources/statistics/facts2014/permanent/08.asp

Figure 6.8
Canada: Permanent Residents by Top Source Countries, 2012–2014

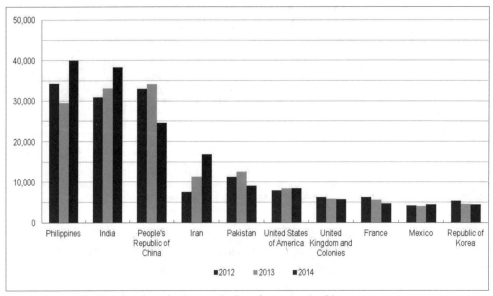

Source: Library and Archives Canada, under the reproduction reference number PA-034014.

A new approach to refugees?

The period following the Second World War saw Canada accepting several groups for resettlement who faced political, racial, and religious discrimination abroad. These refugee groups included 37,000 Hungarians after the Soviet Union crushed the Hungarian revolution (1956–1957) and 12,000 Czechoslovakian refugees fleeing the Soviet invasion of their country (1968–1969) (Whitaker 1991, 18). But Canada waited until 1969 to ratify the 1951 *UN Convention Relating to the Status of Refugees* (the 1951 *Refugee Convention*), which is the central feature of today's international regime of refugee protection. The 1951 *Refugee Convention* defines a refugee as a person who

> owing to a well-founded fear of being persecuted for reasons of race, religion, nationality, membership of a particular social group or political opinion, is outside the country of his nationality, and is unable to, or owing to such fear, is unwilling to avail himself of the protection of that country. (Article 1)

The Convention sets out the rights and duties of individuals who are granted refugee protection as well as the responsibilities of States that grant asylum.

However, two important points must be made regarding Canada's response to refugees. First, Canada's motivation was not purely humanitarian, to say the least. For example, when immigration officials were sent to refugee camps in Germany and Austria in 1947, they selected people for resettlement on the basis of their economic potential, ethnic origin, and ideological views, often rejecting communists and Jews. Similarly, most of the Hungarians and Czechs who were resettled in the 1950s and 1960s were young and highly skilled (Jones and Baglay 2007, 7–8). This intake of skilled immigrants capable of performing physically demanding work was in turn often a response to labour shortages in particular industries. Second, immigration law at that time did not distinguish between refugees and other types of immigrants. Parliament had not created any special category of refugees, but the large discretionary powers of the immigration minister allowed him to simply grant permits when he saw fit. Refugees were thus admitted on a case-by-case basis, usually by suspending the application of normal immigration rules. Overall, the situation in the decades following the Second World War is aptly summarized by Jones and Baglay:

> Through the 1940s, 1950s, and 1960s, there was little evidence in Canada's refugee policy of a stable long-term approach to assisting people in need. Although Canada admitted groups of refugees from various countries, all arrangements were made on an ad hoc basis and were most often motivated by economic considerations. (2007)

It is no surprise, then, that it took 18 years for Canada to ratify the 1951 *Refugee Convention*. At that time, "the open-ended refugee definition and non-refoulement principle [contained in the 1951 *Refugee Convention*] ran contrary to its interests of immigration control and the ability to turn away undesirable migrants" (Jones and Baglay 2007, 9). However, the more liberal stance on immigration and refugee admissions, coupled with the emergence of humanitarianism and internationalism as distinct features of Canadian foreign policy, ultimately prompted the government to ratify the 1951 *Refugee Convention*.

In the years immediately following Canada's ratification of the 1951 *Refugee Convention*, several new groups of refugees were admitted to the country. For example, Canada admitted 8,000 Ugandan Asians expelled by President Idi Amin Dada between 1972 and 1973; 7,000 Chileans fleeing the military coup after 1973; 10,000 Lebanese fleeing civil war between 1976 and 1978; and 60,000 Southeast Asians (the Boat People) and 12,000 Poles fleeing Communist regimes between 1979 and 1981. It is also interesting to note that during the 1970s, one of the largest groups of individuals admitted to Canada as refugees consisted of Americans avoiding conscription and deserters refusing to participate in the Vietnam War. (See Chapters 5 and 14.) It is estimated that between 30,000 and 40,000 of them fled to Canada (Jones and Baglay 2007, 9). Despite Canada's renewed role following ratification, however, refugees were still not recognized as a distinct class within the Canadian legislative framework.

A modern immigration system: Immigration Act, 1976

The slow process of transformation in immigration and refugee policies after the Second World War culminated with the enactment of the *Immigration Act, 1976*. The *Act* represented a significant shift in Canadian immigration law and was unprecedented in many ways.

First, it was the first immigration legislation to clearly outline the fundamental principles and objectives of Canadian immigration policy. This was important, not only because it illustrated a clear and coherent long-term direction, but also because these objectives embodied the transformation that had characterized immigration policies since the end of the Second World War. The new objectives included the promotion of Canada's demographic, economic, cultural, and social goals; family reunification; and the fulfilment of Canada's human rights international obligations, including treatment of refugees and non-discrimination in immigration policy. It was the first time since Confederation that the legislative framework unequivocally stated that any person seeking admission to Canada on either a permanent or temporary basis was subject to standards of admission that did not discriminate based on race, national or ethnic origin, colour, religion, or sex.

In line with these objectives, the second significant innovation of the 1976 *Immigration Act* was the creation of a distinct class for refugees. As discussed earlier, the admission of refugees had previously been determined on an *ad hoc* basis. The *Act* now created specific criteria for refugee protection that implemented the definition of refugees found in the 1951 UN *Refugee Convention*. This meant that refugees were now selected and admitted separately from immigrants. The *Act* also went further and allowed persecuted and displaced persons who did not strictly fall under the refugee definition to be admitted nevertheless on humanitarian grounds. Alongside the new refugee class, the *Act* also recognized two other classes of individuals eligible for permanent resident status: independent (i.e., economic class) immigrants, selected on the basis of the points system; and a family class, which included immediate family members sponsored by Canadian citizens and permanent residents.

Finally, the third important element of the *Act* was a provision that imposed a mandatory responsibility on the government to plan future immigration policies. For example, the government was now required to set annual target numbers for different classes of immigrants to be admitted to Canada. The *Act* also required the government to consult with the provinces regarding the planning and management of Canadian immigration.

Today, these important features still characterize Canada's modern immigration legislative framework. At the time, the *Act* was regarded—both domestically and internationally—as a progressive piece of legislation and received widespread approval from public and private interest groups, the media, and academics (Kelley and Trebilcock 1998, 380).

The 1980s and 1990s

Despite the modern immigration framework created by the *Immigration Act* of 1976, many more challenges were encountered in the following decades. For example, starting in the 1980s, the number of people applying for refugee status grew to proportions never before envisaged. The processing system was unable to cope with the increasing demand and the backlog in refugee determinations increased dramatically. In the realm of public opinion, many refugee claimants were accused of "abusing" the system, looking for a way around the regular immigration regulations. This issue was dramatically illustrated in the late 1980s, when two boats irregularly transporting Sikh and Tamil migrants landed on Canada's Atlantic coast and their passengers claimed refugee status. This effectively sparked a national outcry, and the government argued that illegitimate claimants were trying to "jump the queue" to try to benefit from potential lenient measures aimed at clearing the backlog of refugee claims that had accumulated. This eventually led to a tightening of refugee regulations and procedures. Deportation of rejected asylum seekers was made easier.

Paralleling this trend was a period of increased legal protections for non-citizens. Thus, following the adoption of the *Canadian Charter of Rights and Freedom* in 1982, many constitutional challenges to the immigration and refugee legislative framework were raised, with a view to imposing stricter constitutional limits on the power of government and Parliament in the field of immigration. For example, in the case of *Singh vs. the Minister of Employment and Immigration*, the Supreme Court of Canada recognized that refugee claimants could benefit from the protection of the Charter. The Court also ruled that section 7 of the Charter required an oral hearing in the refugee status determination process. The *Singh* decision had a significant impact on refugee law in Canada, pushing the federal government to create the Immigration and Refugee Board in 1989 in order to provide an oral hearing for all refugee claimants.

Another landmark event during that era was the adoption in 1988 of the *Canadian Multiculturalism Act*. Several years earlier, Liberal Prime Minister Pierre Trudeau (1968–1979 and 1980–1984) had announced multiculturalism as an official government policy, and the *Act*, passed under Progressive Conservative Prime Minister Brian Mulroney (1984–1993) now provided a legislative framework for that policy. In a nutshell, the *Act* recognized multiculturalism as a fundamental characteristic of

Canadian heritage and identity, with an integral role in shaping Canada's future (s. 3(1)(*b*)). The *Act* specifically acknowledges the freedom of all members of Canadian society to preserve, enhance, and share their cultural heritage, while promoting the participation of all communities in the continuing evolution and shaping of all aspects of Canadian society. To achieve that goal, the *Act* made it an official policy of the Government of Canada to, among other things, eliminate any barrier hindering that participation, ensure that all individuals receive equal treatment and equal protection under the law, and foster the recognition and appreciation of the diverse cultures of Canadian society. It also imposed obligations on federal institutions to that effect.

These important developments did not stop the resurgence of an anti-immigration backlash during the 1980s and 1990s. Yet, with the advent of strong human rights protections, some of the measures adopted in the past to give effect to this swing in public opinion or to respond to economic downturns were no longer viable options. Overt racial discrimination in the selection of immigrants (or in any other public policy) was no longer constitutional. Even as immigration re-emerged as a topic of public debate, governments found themselves uneasily suspended between growing public unease about immigration and the reality that Canada would require more immigrants to compensate for the ageing population of the future.

The *Immigration and Refugee Protection Act* of 2001 and the Current Immigration System

In the mist of the ambivalent context that prevailed at the time, a process of immigration reform began in 1996 with the appointment by the Liberal government of Prime Minister Jean Chrétien (1993–2003) of a three-person panel to review all aspects of immigration law, policies, and practices. Moreover, in March 2000, the

Senate Standing Committee on Citizenship and Immigration contributed to the debate with a report titled *Refugee Protection and Border Security: Striking a Balance*. Interestingly, this report was itself prompted by dramatic events that had captured the public's attention. As explained in the report:

> In the summer of 1999, the arrival off the shores of British Columbia of four boats carrying 599 migrants placed a spotlight on Canada's immigration and refugee laws. The migrants, mostly Chinese and including a number of teenagers, arrived in leaky boats amid truly horrible conditions. None had travel or identity documents, and most made refugee claims when apprehended (2000, Introduction, par. 1).

The report noted that this phenomenon was becoming international. The discussion following the report eventually led to the adoption of the *Immigration and Refugee Protection Act, 2001* (IRPA 2001), which replaced the *Immigration Act* of 1976.

This IRPA 2001 retained much of the framework from the 1976 *Act*, including many of the principles and objectives underlying the country's immigration and refugees system. It also retained the previous division between the family, refugee, and economic classes of immigrants. Importantly, however, the *Act* tightened the

Figure 6.9
Canada's 2016 Immigration Plan Levels

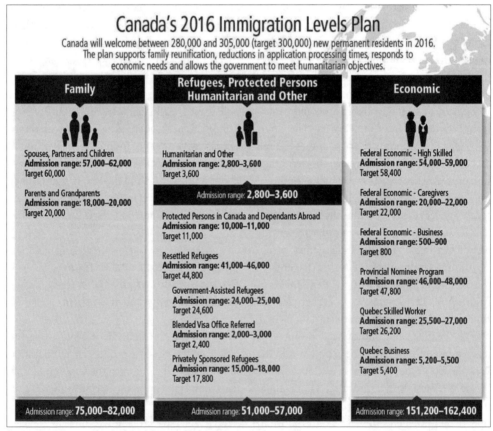

Source: http://news.gc.ca/web/article-en.do?nid=1038699

eligibility requirements for refugees and skilled immigrants and increased penalties for people smuggling and trafficking. The IRPA 2001 provided the government with broadened powers to arrest, detain, and deport foreign nationals and permanent residents on the suspicion that they might be, or could become, a security threat (Crépeau and Nakache 2006). Between 2002 (implementation of the IRPA 2001) and 2014, the number of new immigrants per year fluctuated between 220,000 and 260,000. In 2015, Canada admitted 271,845 new permanent residents, which represented the highest admissions level since 2010. Since 2016 (see **Figure 6.9** opposite), the government has established 300,000 as a new baseline for permanent resident admissions per year (Immigration, Refugees and Citizenship Canada [IRCC] 2016).

Table 6.3
Canada's Immigration Plan for 2017

Immigration Category	2017 Target	2016 Target	Percentage Difference, 2016 to 2017
Economic Includes applicants and accompanying family members in federal programs in the Express Entry system; the Provincial Nominee Program; business immigrants; caregivers; and skilled workers and business immigrants selected by Quebec.	172,500	160,600	+7.41%
Family Includes sponsored spouses, partners, and children, and parents and grandparents	84,000	80,000	+5%
Refugee and Humanitarian Includes resettled refugees (government assisted and privately sponsored), protected persons who become permanent residents, permanent residents selected on humanitarian and compassionate grounds, for reasons of public policy, and in the Permit Holder Class.	43,500	59,400	-26.77%
Target range	280k–320k	280k–305k	+4.92% (higher range)
Target	300,000	300,000	No change

Source: http://news.gc.ca/web/article-en.do?nid=1145319

Between 2008 and 2015, the federal government made changes to many aspects of its immigration and refugee policy, either by amending the *Act* or by adopting a series of regulations or Ministerial Instructions (Nakache and Kinoshita 2010). These changes were characterized (among other things) by an increased emphasis on temporary migrant workers, a reduction in immigration opportunities from abroad for skilled immigrants and members of the family class, the imposition of multiple penalties (see Table 6.3) on refugee claimants, and increased grounds of inadmissibility and removal. Despite their potential "impact on both the social and economic fabric of Canada and how the country is perceived by potential immigrants from around the world" (Alboim and Cohl 2012), the measures were criticized for having been adopted with limited public consultation and support.

The election of Justin Trudeau's Liberals in 2015 signals further change for Canada's immigration and refugee policies. During the electoral campaign, the Liberals opposed many of the above changes brought forward by the previous Harper Conservative government (2006–2015), and they promised a new immigration plan (see **Figure 6.9**), which included reuniting more families and providing a place of refuge for those fleeing persecution.

The Syrian Refugee Crisis

As history shows, refugee policies in Canada have occasionally been shaped in reaction to events that captured the public's attention. The most recent example in this cycle is the Syrian refugee crisis that entered the spotlight during the 2015 federal election campaign. The civil war in Syria has raged since 2011, and at the time of the election campaign an unprecedented four million registered Syrian refugees had left their country (United Nations High Commissioner for Refugees, n.d.). (See Case Study 4.)

Despite the sheer magnitude of the Syrian crisis, what really transformed the issue into a ballot question was the grisly photograph of three-year-old Alan Kurdi's lifeless body washed up on a Turkish beach. As the family were trying to make their way to Greece, the young boy, along with his mother and brother, drowned

when a rubber dinghy carrying the Kurdi family capsized off the Turkish coast. The photograph received extensive media coverage around the world. When it became known that the Kurdis had family in British Columbia who were trying to help them come to Canada, the Syrian refugee crisis became an unexpected campaign issue, galvanizing debate over whether the country was doing enough to help address the major humanitarian crisis. The Trudeau Liberals pledged that they would resettle 25,000 Syrian refugees by the end of 2015, and they were elected to power. As of December 2016, the new government had resettled 37,402 Syrian refugees since November 2015 (see the IRCC page "#WelcomeRefugees: Key figures"). Though 2016 was an unprecedented year, planned admissions for resettled refugees in 2017 are still significant (double the number in 2015 and preceding years) and will see a substantial increase in privately sponsored Syrian refugees (Immigration, Refugees and Citizenship Canada, 2016). Canada's response to the Syrian refugee crisis can be seen as a landmark, set alongside other important moments in the country's history of refugee protection. The mechanics of Canada's response also bears resemblance to many changes in immigration policies that were prompted by dramatic events that captured the public's attention, such as the Boat People in 1979–80.

Conclusion

People often fear that immigrants will take their jobs, be a burden on public services, create social tensions, and even increase criminal activity. In some cases, xenophobia arises, especially when certain groups foment fears and insecurities. This can even lead to outbreaks of violence towards immigrants. If this description describes the situation in many countries today, it also certainly describes Canadian society in the first half of the twentieth century.

Today, however, the current social context allows us to reflect critically on Canada's past immigration policies. Some formal apologies have even been made by the government to various ethno-cultural communities affected by wartime discriminatory measures and immigration restrictions applied in Canada. As stated by then-Prime Minister

Harper in 2013, "[t]he wartime measures and immigration restrictions experienced by those communities mark an unfortunate period in our nation's history. The policies were race-based and inconsistent with values that Canadians hold today."

This reflection, however, is the result of an important transformation in our society. Canada's immigration and refugee policies have evolved and changed over time, shaped by evolving social, political, and economic factors, as well as by society's beliefs about race, desirability, and integration. For a good part of its history, overt racial discrimination in the selection of immigrants was a structural feature of Canadian immigration policy. The contrast with today's immigration framework is a measure of the progress that has been made. But this is certainly not the end; immigration and refugee policies will continue to be regularly re-assessed in light of changing realities. New events such as the current Syrian refugee crisis will constantly cause the re-examination of Canadian society and Canadian immigration policies.

Questions for Further Learning

- How did Canada's immigration policies in the first half of the twentieth century compare to those of similar countries at that time, such as Australia, the United States, and Great Britain?
- Does the social context that prevailed in Canada in the first half of the twentieth century bear a resemblance to the situation in some of today's newly industrialized countries, such as South Africa, Malaysia, or Brazil?
- Do you feel that you are well-informed regarding the changes that are currently taking place in the field of refugee and immigration laws and policies?
- Do you think Canada is doing too much or should do more to respond to the current Syrian refugee crisis?

Key Terms

immigration, p. 108   Order-in-Council, p. 114   regulation, p. 109

multicultural society, p. 108   refugee, p. 109   xenophobia, p. 115

nativism, p. 115

Suggested Readings

Abella, Irving, and Harold Troper. 1982. *None Is Too Many: Canada and the Jews of Europe, 1933–1948*. Toronto: Lester & Orpen Dennys.

Adachi, Ken. 1991. *The Enemy that Never Was: A History of Japanese Canadians*. Toronto: McClelland & Stewart Inc.

Canadian Charter of Rights and Freedoms, Constitution Act, 1982, Part I.

Canadian Multiculturalism Act, R.S.C., 1985, c. 24 (4th Supp.).

Con, Harry, et al. 1982. *From China to Canada: A History of the Chinese Communities in Canada*. Toronto: McClelland and Stewart Limited.

Dewing, Michael. 2009. *Canadian Multiculturalism*. Library of Parliament, Publication No. 2009-20-E. Ottawa: Parliament of Canada.

Fleras, Augie, and Jean Leonard Elliott. 1992. *Multiculturalism in Canada: The Challenge of Diversity*. Scarborough: Nelson Canada.

Hawkins, Freda. 1988. *Canada and Immigration:*

Public Policy and Public Concern. 2nd ed. Montreal and Kingston: McGill-Queen's University Press.

———. 1991. *Critical Years in Immigration: Canada and Australia Compared.* 2nd ed. Montreal and Kingston: McGill-Queen's University Press.

IRPA. 2001. *Immigration and Refugee Protection Act.* S.C. 2001, c. 27.

Knowles, Valerie. 2000. *Forging our Legacy: Canadian Citizenship and Immigration, 1900–1977.* Ottawa: Public Works and Government Services Canada.

Roberts, Barbara. 1998. *Whence They Came: Deportation from Canada 1900–1935.* Ottawa: University of Ottawa Press.

Roy, Patricia. 1989. *A White Man's Province: British Columbia Politicians and Chinese and Japanese Immigrants 1858–1914.* Vancouver: University of British Columbia Press.

———. 2003. *The Oriental Question: Consolidating a White Man's Province, 1914–1941.* Vancouver: University of British Columbia Press.

Tan, Jin, and Patricia Roy. 1985. *The Chinese in Canada.* Ottawa: Canadian Historical Association.

Ward, Peter. 1978. *White Canada Forever: Popular Attitudes and Public Policy Toward Orientals in British Columbia.* Montreal: McGill-Queen's University Press.

Wayland, S. V. 1997. "Immigration, Multiculturalism and National Identity in Canada."*International Journal of Group Rights* 5 (1): 46–47.

Suggested Videos

Canadian Museum of Immigration at Pier 21 online resource: "Canadian Immigration Process Online Game." http://www.virtualmuseum.ca/ Exhibitions/Pier21/eng/home-accueil-eng.html

CBC's *The National*: "New Challenges for Syrian Refugees in Canada." https://www.youtube. com/watch?v=VU7uttRJskE

Official video of Immigration, Refugees and Citizenship Canada: "Making Economic Immigration Work for Canada." https://www.youtube. com/watch?v=a4FCtrlosG8&index=5&list =PLA40417703AAB47D8

Official video of Immigration, Refugees and Citizenship Canada: "Canada welcomes Syrian refugees: A look back." https://www.youtube. com/watch?v=2Pqzq3ldBTs

Official video of Immigration, Refugees and Citizenship Canada: "Discover the achievements of the Community Historical Recognition Program." http://www.cic.gc.ca/english/ department/media/multimedia/video/ chrp-achievmnt/chrp-achievmnt.asOfficial video of Immigration, Refugees and Citizenship Canada: "Refugees building a new life in Canada: Winnipeg and Charlottetown." https:// www.youtube.com/watch?v=xHjlzlS _7Ns&list=PL9D5CCC7CCBCFA4C4&index=2

Official video of Immigration, Refugees and Citizenship Canada: "Resettling to Canada: Welcoming Syrian Refugees." https://www.youtube. com/watch?v=AedTWebJJnM&list= PL9D5CCC7CCBCFA4C4&index=5

Video excerpt from a 2015 election debate where leaders exchange views on the topic of refugees. Length: 3:07. http://globalnews.ca/ video/2227488/trudeau-and-mulcair-attack -harper-on-refugee-crisis

Suggested Websites

Canadian Council for Refugees: http://ccrweb.ca/ en/home

Canadian History Portal: http://www .canadianhistory.ca/

Canadian Museum of Immigration at Pier 21: http://www.pier21.ca/

Immigration, Refugees and Citizenship Canada: http://www.cic.gc.ca/

International Migration Outlook. OECD's annual publication analyzing recent developments in migration movements and policies in member countries: http://www.oecd-ilibrary.org/ social-issues-migration-health/international -migration-outlook_1999124x

The Canadian Immigration Historical Society:
http://cihs-shic.ca/

The Office of the United Nations High Commissioner for Refugees: http://www.unhcr.org/

#WelcomeRefugees: Canada resettled Syrian
refugees: http://www.cic.gc.ca/english/refugees/
welcome/index.asp /

Works Cited

Alboim, Naomi, and Karen Cohl. 2012. "Shaping
the Future: Canada's Rapidly Changing Immigration Policies." Toronto: Maytree Foundation.

Canadian History Portal. n.d. *1867–1914: Fitful
Growth*. Retrieved from http://www.canadian-
history.ca/iv/1945–1967/policy/refugees.html.

———. n.d. *1914–1945: World War II*. Retrieved
from http://www.canadianhistory.ca/iv/1914
–1945/wwii/index.html.

Crépeau, François and Delphine Nakache. 2006.
"Controlling Irregular Migration in Canada:
Reconciling Security Concerns with Human
Rights Protection." *IRPP Choices* 12 (1).

Dewing, Michael. 2009. *Canadian Multiculturalism*.
Library of Parliament, Publication No. 2009-20-
E. Ottawa: Parliament of Canada.

Galloway, Donald. 1997. *Immigration Law*.
Toronto: Irwin Law.

Immigration, Refugees and Citizenship Canada.
2016. *2016 Annual Report to Parliament on
Immigration*. Ottawa: Government of Canada.
ISSN 1706-3329. Catalogue Number Ci1E-PDF.

Johnston, Hugh. 1984. *The East Indians in Canada*.
Ottawa: Canadian Historical Association.

Jones, Martin, and Sasha Baglay. 2007. *Refugee Law*.
Toronto: Irwin Law.

Kelley, Ninette, and Michael Trebilcock. 1998. *The
Making of the Mosaic: A History of Canadian
Immigration Policy*. Toronto: University of
Toronto Press.

King, William Lyon Mackenzie. 1947. "Immigration." Parliament of Canada. House of Commons. 20th Parliament, 3rd Session, May 1.

Knowles, Valerie. 1997. *Strangers at Our Gates:
Canadian Immigration and Immigration Policy,
1540–1997*. Toronto: Dundurn Press.

Migration Policy Institute. 2013. *Top 25 Destination Countries for Global Migrants over Time*.
Retrieved from http://www.migrationpolicy.org/
programs/data-hub/charts/top-25-destination-
countries-global-migrants-over-time.

Nakache, Delphine, and Kinoshita, Paula J. 2010.
"The Canadian Temporary Foreign Worker
Program: Do Short-Term Economic Needs
Prevail Over Human Rights Concerns?" IRPP
Study No. 5.

Rahim, Abdur. 2014. *Canadian Immigration and
South Asian Immigrants*. Bloomington, IN:
Xlibris Publishing.

Senate Standing Committee on Citizenship and
Immigration. 2000. *Refugee Protection and
Border Security: Striking a Balance*.

Statistics Canada. 2010. *Projections of the Diversity
of the Canadian Population* (Catalogue no.
91-551-X). Ottawa: Minister of Industry.

———. 2013. *Immigration and Ethnocultural Diversity in Canada* (Catalogue no. 99-010-X2011001).
Ottawa: Minister of Industry.

The Constitution Act, 1867, 30 and 31 Vict., c. 3.

United Nations High Commissioner for Refugees.
n.d. *Syria Regional Refugee Response: Inter-
agency Information Sharing Portal*. Retrieved
from http://data.unhcr.org/syrianrefugees/
regional.php.

Whitaker, Reg. 1991. *Canadian Immigration Policy
since Confederation*. Ottawa: Canadian Historical Association.

Notes

7

Development and Globalization
The Role of Canadian Civil Society

Ian Smillie and Julia Sánchez

Key Terms

advocacy

Canadian civil society

civil society
organizations (CSOs)

fundraising

government funding

humanitarian action

Non-Governmental
Organizations (NGOs)

North-South

public engagement

volunteers

Overview

This chapter explores theories of voluntary action and charts the evolution of Canada's international development organizations since the 1960s. The chapter discusses the engagement of CSOs with Canadians through fundraising, development education, and advocacy. It describes the change from a hands-on approach by Canadian CSOs in developing countries to one of partnership with a growing range of Southern counterparts. It deals with issues around government funding of CSOs and problems of dependency. The chapter explores the phenomenon of apparently successful micro-NGOs. There is a growing role for South-North CSO advocacy around broader development issues related to trade, the environment, governance, and human rights. The concept of "helping" and "capacity building" will be challenged as never before by changing needs and realities, by Southern CSOs, and by the need for new ways of explaining "development" to a willing but poorly informed Canadian public.

Learning Objectives

By the end of this chapter, students will be able to:

- understand the terminology, history, and theories of international voluntary action.
- trace the evolution of Canadian organizations working internationally.
- follow the changing role of Canadian civil society organizations in development.
- look to the challenges ahead in government relations, funding, and ways of working.

Terminology, History, and Theories of Non-Governmental Action

A lot of effort has gone into naming and renaming Non-Governmental Organizations (NGOs) working in the field of international development. There have been many variations on the NGO theme, partly because "NGO"—the name that has stuck for so long—is a negative. That is perhaps not surprising. *Non-governmental* can actually mean something positive: not bureaucratic, not slow, not rigid, not distant from the people they work with. The favoured term today among Canada's international development community, however, is Civil Society Organization (CSO).

This term too has limitations. *Civil society* is a bit like the word *downtown:* the boundaries are not well defined. *Civil society* refers to all of the organizations and institutions that are not part of government or the private sector. The organizations that work on issues relating to international development are a sub-set of civil society writ large, so there is bound to be confusion with a term that can be applied correctly to Save the Children, Ducks Unlimited, and the Dominion of Canada Rifle Association. With that *caveat* in mind, this chapter will lean towards "CSO," but "NGO" and other terms will creep in from time to time.

The idea of humanistic service, of course, predates all modern terminology. It can be found in the ancient Code of Hammurabi, the Confucian code of ethics, Greek philosophy, Jewish law, Buddhist thought, Hinduism, the Bible, and the Qur'an. Organized charitable activity in countries like Canada has distant roots in the Dark Ages and Middle Ages, when the Christian church was the organizer of hospitals, schools, and universities. (See Chapters 2 and 15.)

Theories about the voluntary sector abound. One theory focuses on the failure of government and the private sector to meet the demand that voluntary associations provide. The rise of European charities in the late nineteenth and early twentieth centuries was a response to needs that governments were unable or unwilling to meet until the advent of German and French welfare programs of the 1880s and 1890s, and the British pension, health, and unemployment insurance schemes that came in before the First World War. The obverse can be seen in countries where philanthropy and voluntarism are weak. Here we have "voluntary failure" in which a weak voluntary ethic allows the state to usurp or bypass civil society.

In his landmark book, *Making Democracy Work: Civic Traditions in Modern Italy*, Robert Putnam (1993) demonstrated the importance of civil society to democracy and development. Reviewing 500 years of Italian history, he showed that impoverishment and poor governance in the Italian south resulted not so much from climate or lack or resources but from an absence of the vibrant civil society organizations that existed in the Italian north and which had, over time, become an essential part of development and democratic governance. Civil society organizations served as a supplement to the state, as a complement, as a watchdog on state excess, and as a kind of societal glue bringing people together in overlapping circles of common cause and voice.

Seeing themselves reflected in Putnam's mirror, international development NGOs adopted the civil society terminology for themselves. The idea of civil society, however, was not new. Hegel and Gramsci wrote about it, and in his 1835 opus, *Democracy in America*, Alexis de Tocqueville remarked on the eagerness with which Americans, especially those on the frontier, created new *associations* for every conceivable purpose: welfare, education, health, self-improvement, self-protection, and of course, politics. This was an integral part of American democracy.

Students of the voluntary sector have created different "stages" to describe its evolution. David Korten (1990) wrote about *first generation organizations* dealing with relief and welfare. *Second generation organizations* focus on self-reliant local development. *Third generation organizations* take a more systemic approach, going beyond one-off projects and "local" activities. Korten saw *fourth generation organizations* as "people's movements" of the type one finds among Indigenous people and labour movements. In this typology, organizations "graduate" from the simple to the complex, from a charity ethic to something more political.

Samuel Martin (1975) saw a different typology. Martin's Stage One is *community-based voluntarism*. People get together to deal with a problem: widows and orphans, a school, a bridge. This is the community-based organization of Biblical times, of the Old West, of almost every village today in India and Africa and Latin America. Stage Two—*institutionalization*—grows out of necessity because of greater needs. The voluntary ethic remains, but the work is better organized and more systematic. Stage Three—*professionalization*—happens when organizations grow and when higher standards become necessary. Professional staff, managers, and accountants are required to do the work properly. At this stage, government may recognize the value of such organizations and may, along with growing levels of regulation, provide some elements of support and funding. For Martin, the final stage was the *welfare state,* in which voluntary organizations would no longer be required because their services would now be provided by government. The ultimate welfare state, the Soviet Union, did away with all voluntary organizations. The state provided all services, but at the same time it eliminated the aspects of civil society that Putnam found so essential to development and democracy: its voice, and its ability to act as watchdog and to hold the state accountable.

Critics of international development NGOs paint a less flattering, more contentious portrait. One school of thought sees them as purveyors at home of a paternalistic view of poverty, delinking it from power relationships in the South and between South and North. Dependent upon government funding, they are seen as part of a neoliberal agenda promoting economic liberalization, privatization, free trade, and deregulation. They are vanguards for the extractive sector, unconcerned with a need for the "uprooting of unjust political and economic structures and systems" (Barry-Shaw and Oja Jay 2012, 144).

We will return to ideas of voluntary organization and civil society later in the chapter, because they are more germane to the work of Canadian international development organizations, to their idea of themselves, and to how they interact with the Canadian government. There is, however, one more typology worth noting. A Johns Hopkins University study (Salamon and Anheier 1992) looked for a technical definition of the modern voluntary organization—regardless of whether it was involved in welfare or development or systemic change. The study argued that to qualify, an organization should make "a good showing" in each of four categories. It should be *formal*: it should be incorporated or registered in some way, have office bearers and some degree of institutional permanence. It should be *private*: separate from government even though it might receive government funding. It should be *non-profit* and self-governing, and it should have some degree of *voluntary* participation.

Canadians Working Internationally

When thinking about international development, it is important to remember that all of the typologies and almost all of the history of civil society is about organizations and people working in their own societies. The subjects of this chapter are a hybrid: they are people and organizations who aim—mainly—to do something elsewhere. It is not unusual in the history of charitable activity for rich outsiders to arrive bearing gifts: the monarch, lady bountiful, or the corporate magnate with a charitable foundation. Historically, however, most of these people worked in their own countries with their own people.

Beyond Canada, the title of oldest international NGO goes, in a sense, to St. John Ambulance. This is a foundation of the Order of St. John, a modern continuation of the medieval order of St. John of Jerusalem and the Knights Hospitaller, founded in 1099 during the First Crusade. The crusaders were militarized missionaries, and like them, church organizations have been sending teachers and doctors abroad for centuries as part of their evangelizing mission.

The modern international NGO era can be said to date from Henri Dunant and the founding of the Red Cross in the 1860s. Within a few years, Red Cross societies had sprung up across Europe, although they were limited at first to emergencies in their own countries. The Canadian Red Cross, established in 1896, sent its first medical personnel and relief supplies abroad in 1899 in aid of the sick and wounded in the Anglo-Boer War in South Africa. In line with the typologies described above, others among today's name-brand international NGOs began as a humanitarian response to war. Save the Children began in Britain at the end of the First World War. Foster Parents Plan, now known as Plan International, began as a response to the suffering of children during the Spanish Civil War of the 1930s. The Oxford Committee for Famine Relief—today's Oxfam—was a British response to the Greek Famine of 1942. CARE, originally the Cooperative for American Remittances to Europe, began at the end of the Second World War; World Vision grew out of the Korean War (1950–1953); and Médecins sans Frontières was inspired by the Biafran

War (1967–1970) in Nigeria. All started as international relief and welfare organizations and, in time, most expanded their mandate to include development.

Although none of these organizations were Canadian in origin, Canadian committees and branches of each were soon established, primarily for fundraising purposes. One of the very few pre-1960 Canadian NGOs was the Unitarian Service Committee of Canada (now USC-Canada), founded by Lotta Hitschmanova in 1945. Like CARE, it aimed to help those suffering in the aftermath of the Second World War.

By the early 1960s, many Canadians were working in developing countries, usually on assignments from Canadian churches or their international affiliates, or on contract to the United Nations. The secular, homegrown Canadian NGO scene in 1960 was, however, patchy. Although Canadians were generous in their giving to international fundraising efforts, there were few domestic organizations of note. Money raised by CARE went to New York for programming; money raised by Oxfam went to Oxford; and if a Canadian wanted to work in a developing country on something more than a student exchange she would likely have to make arrangements through a church body.

Two things happened during the 1960s to change this. The first was the creation in 1961 of Canadian University Service Overseas (CUSO). Within a few short years, CUSO had more than a thousand volunteer teachers, doctors, nurses, and engineers working abroad. (See Case Study 10.) It established offices throughout Asia, Africa, the Caribbean, and Latin America, and was frequently the only visible Canadian presence in a country. The second was the transformation of the small External Aid Office into the Canadian International Development Agency (CIDA) in 1968. (See Chapter 4.) CIDA grew rapidly in its early years and Canada was one of the first countries to establish a mechanism for government funding of development NGOs. CIDA's matching grant initiative allowed small NGOs to grow and new NGOs to germinate. Without CIDA support, for example, CUSO could never have become—as it was by 1970—Canada's largest international development NGO.

CIDA was also responsible for a transformation among the branch-plant NGOs. It told CARE, Oxfam, Plan, and others that if they wanted matching CIDA funds, they would have to demonstrate Canadian value added. In other words, CIDA wanted to see active Canadian involvement in an NGO's international programming. And it happened. Because they were no longer simply fundraisers, the Canadian content in these organizations blossomed. They and the fast-growing CIDA were populated to a large extent during these years by returning CUSO volunteers, people who had first-hand experience living and working in developing countries.

Professional Organizations

As noted above, the term "civil society" applies to a much wider range of organizations than those created solely for the purpose of delivering development and humanitarian assistance. For many years, a wide variety of Canadian professional organizations have been involved in international development work, usually with counterpart organizations in similar fields. Examples include the Canadian Bar Association, the Canadian Institute of Planners, the Canadian Public Health Association, La Fédération professionnelle des journalistes du Québec, the Native Women's Association of Canada, and many others. The Canadian Nurses Association, active internationally for almost four decades, works on global health issues worldwide and supports national nursing associations in developing countries. As with many professional organizations, its work is often a two-way street, bringing expertise, innovation, and policy change back to the Canadian organization.

Solidarity Funds

Beginning in the 1980s, a number of Canadian labour unions established "solidarity funds" to promote the rights of workers internationally and contribute funds to development projects. Sometimes these funds work through counterpart organizations in developing countries and sometimes in partnership with mainstream Canadian development organizations. Among the most active are those of the Canadian Union of Public Employees, the United Steelworkers Humanity Fund, and the Unifor Social Justice Fund. Typically, these funds are financed by small deductions negotiated in collective bargaining agreements (CBAs) between the union and the employer. Like other CSOs, the solidarity funds have been eligible for matching grants from government. The Steelworkers Humanity Fund in 2014, for example, took in $1.5 million in CBA contributions and $111,000 in government funding. It made contributions to food banks across Canada, supported counterpart workers' organizations in Latin America, and contributed $100,000 in humanitarian assistance to emergencies in Africa, Asia, and elsewhere (Steelworkers Humanity Fund Members' Report 2014).

It is worth noting that professional associations and solidarity funds are organically different from organizations created specifically for international development and humanitarian work. Professional organizations and unions have a "rootedness" in Canada that sets them apart. They have the potential to create partnerships and bridges that are based on more than projects and project funding, and on a dynamic that goes beyond the culture of "aid."

Humanitarian Action

Humanitarian assistance is not the same as development assistance, although they are related. Humanitarian assistance responds to natural and conflict-related emergencies. These may be "fast-onset" disasters, as in the case of a flood, an earthquake, or an epidemic like the Ebola crisis of 2014–2015 in West Africa. Or they may be disasters that are slower to advance: a famine, for example, may take months or even years to develop. And conflict-related emergencies such as those in the Democratic Republic of the Congo or South Sudan may ebb and flow over many years. Humanitarian activities are regulated by international humanitarian law, while development programs are regulated by national laws.

As noted above, several of today's large international NGOs and their Canadian counterparts were created in response to a particular emergency and moved later into doing development work as well. In both fast-onset and complex emergencies these organizations may already have a development presence in the region that can be converted into a humanitarian response, and they have the capacity to move into reconstruction and development again when it passes. A handful of NGOs, most notably Médecins sans Frontières, work almost exclusively in the field of humanitarian action.

In 2010, several prominent Canadian NGOs (CARE, Oxfam Canada, Oxfam Québec, Plan International, and Save the Children) formed the Humanitarian Coalition, which bands together during major emergencies for joint fundraising. Based on similar partnerships in Europe, the Humanitarian Coalition reduces competition and fundraising costs, and provides donors with clear and timely disaster and response information.

Changing Partners, Changing Roles

Until the mid-1970s, most Canadian NGOs took a hands-on approach to development. They managed and reported on projects that they designed themselves. If wells were to be dug, the Canadian organization hired the diggers and managed the process from beginning to end. If a school was to be built, the NGO designed it, bought the materials, hired the masons and carpenters, and supplied the

furniture. Some projects were small; some were very large. During the 1980s, CARE Canada, with CIDA funding and assistance from CARE USA, designed a major infrastructure initiative in Bangladesh. The Rural Maintenance Project hired destitute women to maintain important farm-to-market roads. The scope was vast: at its peak, 60,000 miles of dirt road were being maintained and new jobs for poor women were being created at the rate of 10,000 a year.

The do-it-yourself approach began to wane in the late 1970s, because in many developing countries local civil society organizations were coming into their own. (See Chapter 13.) Many formed in the same way as Northern NGOs—as community-based operations or in response to a humanitarian emergency. And many followed the evolution described by Samuel Martin, growing from small, localized efforts into organizations with national mandates. BRAC is one of the most prominent examples. BRAC, originally the Bangladesh Rural Advancement Committee, began as a Bangladeshi response to humanitarian needs following the country's liberation war of 1971 and then turned to development. Today it is one of the largest NGOs in the world, focusing primarily on education, health, and economic empowerment for women, and reaching beyond Bangladesh to several countries in Asia and Africa.

Organizations like BRAC have distinct advantages over their Northern counterparts. They know the language and culture; they understand the political context better than outsiders; and they can operate without the plane fares and expatriate salaries of their Northern counterparts. Canadian NGOs began to see that it made more sense to work with and through organizations like these than to try to do everything themselves.

Surprisingly, the idea of supporting local CSOs was a radical one at first, pioneered by Oxfam and Inter Pares. Today, however, it is the norm rather than the exception, and it underlines one of the voluntary sector's great comparative advantages over other forms of international cooperation: the ability to mobilize and involve people, to create real partnerships, and to build the social capital that de Tocqueville and Putnam found so necessary to democratic development.

The business of sending Canadians to work overseas also changed. Young, fresh-faced graduates were phased out as countries produced young, fresh-faced graduates of their own. Volunteer-sending programs focused more on mid-career professionals and short-term assignments aimed at solving specific problems. Increasingly, the learning opportunity for young Canadians came not so much from two-year work placements as through short internships and workcamp opportunities. (See Case Study 11.)

Public Engagement

Fundraising

NGO engagement with the Canadian public occurs in three ways: fundraising, advocacy, and development education. Of these, the first two are fraught with pitfalls and controversy. Early Canadian NGO fundraising was based to a very large extent on what came to be known as the pornography of poverty: images of crying, fly-blown children. Nothing tugs at heartstrings and the chequebook more than a child in distress.

By the 1970s, however, there was a backlash against this type of fundraising from other international development organizations and from their partners in developing countries. Starving-baby fundraising implied that people in developing countries were helpless and that little could be done without outside aid. It flew in the face of what NGOs knew, and it didn't reflect the reality of the places where they worked, or of the people they were working with. The Canadian Council for International Cooperation (CCIC), an umbrella organization formed during the 1960s to support and promote the work of Canadian international development organizations, created a *Code of Ethics and Operational Standards* (CCIC 2009), dealing with this issue. Member organizations agreed to "respect the dignity and rights of the individuals

portrayed" and to "portray local communities as active agents in their own development."

This code notwithstanding, the most successful fundraising tool for Canadian NGOs in the second decade of the twenty-first century remains child sponsorship, a technique developed by Foster Parents Plan during the 1930s and honed to new levels of sophistication by a dozen Canadian NGOs, notably World Vision, Plan Canada, Canadian Feed the Children, SOS Children's Villages, Compassion Canada, Christian Children's Fund of Canada, Food for the Hungry, Chalice, the Salvation Army, and the Christian Blind Mission. In 2013–2014, child sponsorship donations to World Vision Canada, at $222 million, outstripped non-sponsorship donations by a factor of almost five (World Vision Canada 2014). This was as much, if not more, than all the private donor money raised by all other Canadian NGOs combined. In contrast, Oxfam Canada, another well-known organization, but one that does not engage in child sponsorship, raised only $7.7 million in private donations the same year.

Child sponsorship works so well because it shortens the distance between the giver and the receiver. For the donor, it gives a name and a face to the recipient, humanizing both the need and the contribution. Child sponsorship is controversial, however, because it requires high overheads, and some argue it paints a simplistic picture of development and developing countries. Regardless of how good the NGO's work is in the field, the impression created in the minds of hundreds of thousands of Canadian donors is of children without parents of their own, or whose parents cannot look after them without Canadian support. (See Chapter 2.) Such imagery clashes with ideas of self-help and of local organizations taking over the hands-on role that Northern NGOs once took for granted as their own.

Development education

Some organizations have seen the importance of explaining their work and the challenges associated with development to Canadians. For some this kind of work is a primary mandate;

for others it is a sideline. Distinct from fundraising and advocacy, development education takes place in schools, churches, clubs, and the workplace, through curriculum development media presentations, conferences, and speaking tours. The work was actively supported by CIDA in the 1970s and 1980s through the creation of a dozen or more international development "learner centres" across Canada, and in hundreds of projects aimed at building greater understanding and support for international development. CIDA shut down the unit responsible for this work following the budget cuts of 1995. (See Chapter 4.)

Advocacy

The word *advocacy* is derived from the Medieval Latin *advocatia*, which means "summon, call to one's aid." According to the *Oxford English Dictionary* it means "to recommend or support by argument (a cause, policy, etc.)." This seems like a very reasonable activity for any organization that aims to end poverty or promote development. A charitable organization aiming to "save children," "feed children," or "free children" wouldn't be doing its job properly if it ignored the *rights* of children and if it did not speak up on their behalf. There have always been limits on the advocacy work of registered charities—also referred to as political activities—not least because as charities, they issue tax deductible receipts which are, in effect, contributions from government in the form of taxes forgone.

According to a 2003 Canada Revenue Agency (CRA) policy statement, "a registered charity may take part in some political activities as a way of furthering its charitable purpose(s). However, charities do not have complete freedom to support any cause they like. Special legal rules apply to charities because of their charitable and tax statuses" (Canada Revenue Agency 2014). Courts have further established that charities cannot dedicate more than 10 percent of their resources to acceptable political activities. Definitions, however, are fluid and CRA's enforcement of the rules is selective. Amnesty International, a registered charity, is almost exclusively about advocacy on behalf of the victims of human rights abuses. Research groups and think tanks with charitable status often target their work directly at policy makers. The Fraser Institute, for example, says that it has been "very successful in reaching policy makers directly. On many occasions, too frequent to be quoted here, the Institute's policy recommendations have been adopted by Canadian governments, and by foreign governments as well" (Fraser Institute 2004). Under the Conservative government of Stephen Harper (2006–2015), the CRA conducted audits of the political activities of a number of registered charities, mostly on the political centre and left. The audits ceased after the Liberals took power in 2015.

Challenges Ahead

Government funding

There is a long history of Canadian government support for international development NGOs. It can be divided into three broad types. The first and oldest is responsive funding. This began in the 1960s with matching grants from CIDA to NGOs whose projects it wished to support. The principle was simple: if Canadians were giving money to an NGO over and above the portion of their taxes that was already going to official development assistance, this should be supported. Not only could NGOs reach people and places that government could not, NGOs could build domestic support for the broader Canadian development enterprise. One-to-one funding soon grew to ratios of 3:1 and 4:1, and annual, project-by-project funding grew into multi-year program funding for seasoned NGOs during the 1980s.

Alongside responsive funding, a second, needs-based approach began to emerge in the 1980s. CIDA created special funds aimed at drawing NGOs into geographic and sectoral areas that were of interest to the Canadian government. To do this, better matching ratios, often as high as 9:1, were created. Special new funds were developed for programming in Mozambique, in the Philippines, for women in development, and later there were wholesaling operations with generous CIDA support for NGO consortia: the South Asia Partnership and Partnership Africa Canada.

In the early 1980s CIDA initiated a third funding opportunity for NGOs. This one, known as country focus, allowed NGOs to take larger proposals to CIDA's bilateral (country-to-country) divisions, where they would be judged on the basis of how well they fit with CIDA's priorities for that country or region. Within a few years, several NGOs had grown much larger on the 9:1 and even higher funding ratios available here. The upshot of all these "windows" was that many Canadian organizations developed a high level of dependence on Canadian government funding. For the chilsponsorship agencies the percentage was low, in part because CIDA would not match funds raised in this way, and in part because they had a vibrant mechanism for private donor support and did not need CIDA the way others did. As a percentage of World Vision's combined government funding and tax-receipted donations in 2011, the government portion amounted to only 5.6 percent, and for Plan Canada the proportion was only 7.2 percent (Canada Revenue Agency 2011a). For others, the numbers were higher. As a percentage of its Canadian income in 2010–2011, Save the Children received 26 percent from government; Inter Pares received over half; and CARE Canada received over 75 percent (Canada Revenue Agency 2011b).

High levels of dependence on a single donor are inherently risky, but most Canadian NGOs knew how the evolving systems worked, and as long as the mechanisms were reasonably consistent, the risk seemed low. In 2010, however, everything changed. The Harper government effectively cancelled the responsive approach and most program funding. NGOs would now be expected to bid on proposal calls issued by CIDA for countries and sectors of its choosing. For almost a year, nothing moved at CIDA, and when the calls for proposals came, they were few and far between. Some organizations that had been critical of government in their advocacy work were defunded entirely, and others found themselves engaged in costly and protracted audits by the Canada Revenue Agency, implementing a crackdown on so-called political activity.

A February 2012 report by CCIC and seven provincial umbrella organizations analyzed the first 18 months of CIDA's new system.

> The sudden and drastic reduction of funds coming from CIDA—compounded by long delays in announcing funding decisions ... has meant that dozens of Canadian organizations now have to reduce or end partnerships with local organizations in developing countries. This is occurring just a year and a half after this funding mechanism was introduced. The lack of predictability in terms of potential future funding outcomes for organizations is jeopardizing long-standing relations CIDA has had with organizations, partnerships in developing countries and essential development projects on the ground ... [This] will most likely have a knock-on effect in terms of the amount of funds that organizations can subsequently leverage from other donors: multilateral, provincial, individuals, etc. It also has an impact on the organization's credibility and on public support. (Alberta Council for Global Cooperation 2012)

Despite the problems, some organizations thrived under the new system. As a percentage of its Canadian income, CARE's government contributions went from 75 percent in 2010 to 79 percent in 2014 and Plan's grew from 7.2 percent to 21.7 percent. But others suffered, and some NGOs staggered under the cancellations, reductions, and delays in funding. The Harper government had come to view civil society very differently from the way its predecessors did. It essentially saw those willing to participate in the new regime as contractors—or, as David

Korten had described them years before, "public service contractors." The government had no problem with whatever else a CSO might want to do, but that was its own business, to be paid for with its own money.

Although the Trudeau government, elected in 2015, was much more NGO-friendly, its "Feminist Development Assistance Policy" did not appear for almost two years and, short on specifics about funding and funding mechanisms, did little to clear up continuing problems for NGOs in government predictability or consistency. There are two lessons from the Harper period and its aftermath. The first is about the fragility of NGO financing and how disruptive a major or sudden change in funding patterns can be. This is a lesson for all donors, not just government. The second has to do with the risks inherent in over-dependence on any one large donor. For international development organizations, however, the admonition to diversify the funding base—much easier said than done—recalls the suggestion attributed to Marie Antoinette about eating cake in the absence of bread.

The political economy of CSO fundraising

Many studies over the years have shown that while Canadian public support for international development is wide, it is not deep, and the level of understanding about the complexities in poverty reduction is low (Smillie 2003). As noted above, Canadians respond generously to emergency appeals and to the idea of child sponsorship, but most CSOs have learned that fundraising for long-term, sustainable development is difficult, especially given the competition from more emotive appeals. All large Canadian development organizations have two or more of the following four features: an emergency response capacity, child sponsorship, affiliation with a church or a larger international NGO, and a high dependence on Canadian government funding.

Organizations with none of the first three of these attributes tend to be small or mid-sized; very few of them have budgets over $10 million.

The only exceptions are volunteer-sending organizations such as WUSC, CECI, CUSO, and a few others, which have historically enjoyed consistently high levels of government support. The demise of the Canadian Hunger Foundation (CHF) in 2015 illustrates the problem. CHF, a respected mid-size NGO focusing on food security and sustainable livelihoods in Africa, Asia, and the Caribbean, was not a member of a larger international consortium; it rarely engaged in emergency work; and it eschewed child sponsorship as a fundraising tool. Its annual income averaged around $10 to 12 million, about 60 percent of it from government. For years, despite solid investments in public fundraising, it was rarely able to generate more than about 10 percent of its total income in donations from the general public. In fact, the cost of raising a dollar at CHF probably rose to more than 50 cents, but that was necessary in order to meet the government's matching requirement. The CIDA changes and slowdown in 2010–2011, along with internal management problems, combined to expose the inherent financial fragility of such organizations, and soon CHF was gone. The North-South Institute, a respected development think-tank, closed shop in 2014 under similar circumstances.

Some small and mid-size NGOs have survived through mergers or partial mergers. World University Service of Canada (WUSC) took two failing CSOs, Farm Radio Network and Match International, under its wing in 2004 and 2011 respectively, and they were able to regroup and return to financial health. They and others have been able to develop niche markets in terms of what they do internationally, and in the care and nurturing of a select, dedicated donor base. Their continuation and survival might be likened to the survival of independent automobile manufacturers in the 1930s or independent bookstores in the 2000s. A few can make it, but over the medium and long term, many probably will not.

Questions about the survivability of small and mid-size CSOs seem almost counter-intuitive in the face of the expansion and apparent flourishing of what might be called "micro-NGOs"—tiny mom-and-pop operations frequently started by an individual or a group, targeting a single community in a single developing country. Improved travel and communications have made such CSOs possible, although often their ambitions are limited to sending books, or musical instruments, or taking a summer trip to a place where Canadian supporters can participate in building a clinic or school. CANHAVE and Project Tembo are two Ottawa-based examples. CAN-HAVE supports HIV/AIDS orphans in Kenya, and Project Tembo supports education for girls and micro-enterprise development for women, primarily in the village of Longido in Tanzania. CANHAVE was co-founded by a Ugandan-Canadian, and Project Tembo was started by two Canadians following a climb up Mount Kilimanjaro in Tanzania. Neither has an annual budget of more than $150,000, and both are entirely dependent upon the work of volunteers for their management and fundraising.

There are probably hundreds of organizations like CANHAVE and Project Tembo in Canada. They are almost certainly the product of a genuine desire to help—and of an unwillingness to join with established organizations in doing so. Despite whatever good work they may do, such organizations illustrate an odd and widespread phenomenon: in contrast with almost any other walk of life, many Canadians think that development in poor countries can be done inexpensively, on a part-time basis, and by amateurs.

Ways of Working

Development challenges have been transformed in the half century since the developing countries gained independence from the late 1940s to the 1960s. Great poverty persists in many countries, but there is much better understanding of what can be done to end it, and of who can and should contribute. Development assistance—foreign aid in its many manifestations—can help, but it is by no means the largest or most important part of the equation. Investment, trade, and good governance are clearly part of the mix. (See Chapter 13.) Local civil society organizations can and do play a prominent role in all of this, from planning, innovating, and managing to pushing for change.

A distinct, if not odd, feature of Canada's international CSO community is that historically it has been more or less divided into three compartments: development organizations, those working on environmental issues, and those promoting human rights. This is perhaps because funding, especially government funding, has been more readily available for development work. But "development" can no longer be so easily compartmentalized and, in developing countries, CSOs frequently see no differentiation among the three.

Outsiders can help, but the nature of that help is changing. The old adage, "Give a man a fish and he can eat for a day; teach a man to fish and you feed him for a lifetime," doesn't just leave out half the population—women—it fails to recognize that many people who once fished no longer do so because of pollution, overfishing by foreign trawlers, or because of markets disrupted by external dumping, quotas, and restrictions. While feeding people or teaching them to fish may still fill gaps, the barriers to development often lie elsewhere. Canadian NGOs will almost certainly be challenged in the future to become more engaged in research and advocacy, and this may require changes to the boundaries that currently exist around the definition of charitable activity. The notion of charity itself may require change.

"Capacity building" has become a clarion call within the international development community, not least among NGOs. Often, however, this falls under the-teach-a-man-to-fish rubric, based on priorities established by outsiders. As noted above, throughout the developing world there has been a rapid growth in civil society organizations, both in size and in the quality of their work. And while they may need technical and managerial know-how as well as financial support, they also need partners who can support them in their *own* aims and objectives, and who can take on wider roles in building and preserving an enabling environment for change. This is likely to have more to do with the creation of space for civil society in a developing country than with well-drilling or school building. It may be about the regulation of the non-profit sector, the development of local philanthropy, and issues of governance, representation, and human rights. (See Chapter 11.)

It also means that Northern CSOs will have to work more with their Southern counterparts in tackling international issues that impinge on poverty reduction, issues that Northern organizations can address in ways that Southern NGOs cannot. Lowering international trade barriers—the aim of the World Trade Organization's Doha Development Agenda since 2001—is an example of where civil society could have played an important role, and could still do so. Developing country indebtedness, gender equality, land mines, and the perils of foreign direct investment are areas where NGOs have in the past had an impact. Some Canadian NGOs have taken on an advocacy role in Canada regarding problems created by Canadian

mining companies in developing countries. Often the most successful work in such areas is done in partnership with Southern civil societies.

Explaining all this to Canadians is an essential part of getting the political buy-in at home that is necessary for change internationally. An additional challenge for Canadian CSOs, therefore, is their fundraising message. To the extent that the primary focus remains on children and emergencies, on helplessness rather than systemic change, CSOs will be part of yesterday's problem rather than part of tomorrow's solution.

The challenge, as Canadian civil society confronts new and changing development issues, will be to find new ways of working together across disciplines, across the North-South divide, and across artificial barriers created by organizational ego and identity. It will require new ways of understanding what it is to "help," and it will require new ways of explaining what this means to the Canadian public, not only as a way of gaining more sophisticated and sustainable institutional support, but to supplement, complement, and push governments on questions of trade, investment, the environment, and human rights—the building blocks of genuine, sustainable, international development.

Key Terms

advocacy, p. 137

Canadian civil society, p. 142

civil society organizations
      (CSOs), p. 132

fundraising, p. 134

government funding, p. 133

humanitarian action, p. 136

Non-Governmental
      Organizations (NGOs),
      p. 132

North-South, p. 142

public engagement, p. 137

volunteers, p. 135

Suggested Readings

Banks, Nicola, David Hulme, and Michael Edwards. 2015. "NGOs, States, and Donors Revisited: Still Too Close for Comfort?" *World Development*, no. 66, 707–718.

Brodhead, Tim, and Brent Herbert-Copley. 1988. *Bridges of Hope? Canadian Voluntary Agencies and the Third World*. Ottawa: North-South Institute.

Brouwer, Ruth. 2013. *Canada's Global Villagers: CUSO in Development, 1961–86*. Vancouver: University of British Columbia Press.

Choudry, Aziz, and Dip Kapoor. 2013. *NGOization: Complicity, Contradictions and Prospects*. London: Zed Books.

Nutt, Samantha. 2012. *Damned Nations: Greed, Guns, Armies and Aid*. Toronto: McClelland & Stewart.

Smillie, Ian. 1995. *The Alms Bazaar: Altruism under Fire—Non-Profit Organizations and International Development*. London: IT Publications.

Suggested Video

Munro, Lauchlan T. (2017) "Too close for comfort, relatively speaking? Development NGOs' dependence on home government funding in comparative perspective." http://blog.gdi.manchester.ac.uk/gdi-lecture-series-development-ngos-dependence-home-government-funding-professor-lauchlan-t-munro/

Suggested Websites

Association québecoise des organismes de coopération internationale (French only): http://www.aqoci.qc.ca/

Canadian Council for International Cooperation: www.ccic.ca

Charities Directorate, Canada Revenue Agency: http://www.cra-arc.gc.ca/charities/

Global Affairs Canada, Development Section, Development Partners: http://www.international.gc.ca/development-developpement/partners-partenaires/index.aspx?lang=eng

Works Cited

Alberta Council for Global Cooperation et al. 2012. *Putting Partnership back at the Heart of Development: Canadian Civil Society Experience with CIDA's Call for Proposal Mechanism, Partnerships with Canadians Branch*. Edmonton: ACIC.

Barry-Shaw, Nikolas, and Dru Oja Jay. 2012. *Paved with Good Intentions: Canada's Development NGOs from Idealism to Imperialism*. Black Point, NS: Fernwood Publishing.

Canada Revenue Agency. 2011a. T3010 Report for Plan Canada. Ottawa: CRA.

———. 2011b. T3010 Report for World Vision Canada. Ottawa: CRA.

———. 2014. "Political Activities; Policy Statement CPS-022." Effective date September 2, 2003. http://www.cra-arc.gc.ca/chrts-gvng/chrts/plcy/cps/cps-022-eng.html#N10282, accessed Dec. 1, 2014.

Canadian Council for International Cooperation. 2009. *Code of Ethics and Operational Standards*. Ottawa: CCIC.

Fraser Institute. 2004. "The Fraser Institute at 30: A Retrospective." Vancouver: The Fraser Institute.

Korten, David. 1990. *Getting to the 21st Century: Voluntary Action and the Global Agenda*. West Hartford, CT: Kumarian.

Martin, Samuel. 1975. *Financing Humanistic Service*. Toronto: McClelland & Stewart.

Putnam, Robert D. 1993. *Making Democracy Work: Civic Traditions in Modern Italy*. Princeton: Princeton University Press.

Salamon, Lester, and Helmut Anheier. 1992. *In Search of the Non-Profit Sector I: The Question of Definitions*. Working Papers of the Johns Hopkins Comparative Nonprofit Sector Project, No. 2. Baltimore: The Johns Hopkins Institute for Policy Studies.

Smillie, Ian. 2003. "Canada." In *Public Opinion and the Fight against Poverty*, edited by Ida McDonnell, Henri-Bernard Solignac Lecomte, and Liam Wegimont. Paris: OECD.

Steelworkers Humanity Fund. 2014. *Members' Report 2014*. http://www.usw.ca/act/activism/humanity/SHF-report-14-WEB-EN.pdf, accessed Oct. 23, 2015.

World Vision Canada. 2014. *Financial Statements of World Vision Canada, 2013–14*. Mississauga: World Vision Canada.

8 Canada, Quebec, and La Francophonie

Pierre Beaudet

Key Terms

sub-Saharan Africa

Agence universitaire de la Francophonie (AUF)

Agency for Cultural and Technical Cooperation

Françafrique

Francophonie

International Organization of La Francophonie (IOF)

international cooperation

Quebec

Overview

This chapter aims to explain the involvement of Canada and Quebec in what is called La Francophonie, which is a political and cultural space that brings together francophone or partially francophone nations in the world. In the period since the Second World War, these ties have developed in line with the process of decolonization of several French-speaking countries, and along with the political development of Canada and Quebec. Over the years, these links have continued diplomatically and economically, as well as in the field of international cooperation. In this chapter, we discuss the structure and the recent evolution of these relations, with particular attention to French-speaking countries of the South.

Learning Objectives

By the end of this chapter, students will be able to:

- understand the evolution of the relationship between Canada and the other francophone countries.
- understand Canada's intervention in the institutions of La Francophonie in the context of globalization.
- understand the African perspective on La Francophonie and explore the demands and mobilizations underway.
- be able to find ways in which Canadians and Quebecers may work in solidarity with African aspirations for development and democracy.

Introduction

Why look at la Francophonie (with a small "l") and La Francophonie (with a capital "L") in a book on international development? Well, Canada has the privilege of being inhabited by a diverse population of various origins and cultures. In this diverse population base, there is a specific history, including the fact that over 22 percent of the population declare French as their mother tongue, more than seven million people, including six million who live in Quebec and constitute about 80 percent of the population of that province. Canada is officially a bilingual country given the adoption of the *Official Languages Act*, in 1969, which established the equality of status of the two languages, in Parliament, the federal government, federal Crown corporations, agencies, and laws. In Quebec, the primacy of French has been the law since 1976, although the English-speaking minority retains its rights, especially in education and public services.

These facts show that the francophone reality is part of the Canadian "imaginary," or self-image. As we will see later, this reality is what defines the bonds of cooperation and solidarity between the francophone society of Canada and other French-speaking countries of the world. Moreover, this is what also explains the importance of the International Organization of La Francophonie (IOF) to the Canadian government, particularly for policies governing development and international cooperation.

If the francophone reality is a distinctive feature of Canadian society, another factor motivating the interest is la Francophonie, or the global community of French speakers. Globally, there are over 274 million French speakers across five continents. In many of these countries, the French language is the dominant language of work and is the first language of the people. Elsewhere, there remain significant francophone minorities. About 45 percent of francophones live in Western Europe (mostly in Belgium, France, and Switzerland); 33 percent of francophones live in sub-Saharan Africa; and another 10 percent in North Africa. Only around 7 percent of francophones live in the Americas, mostly in Canada and Haiti.

Today, the majority of the la Francophonie is in the South, particularly in Africa. The IOF, of which Canada is a founding member, has 57 member states and 22 associated states or observers.

As shown in **Table 8.1**, Africa has the most states with French as their official language.

First Steps

Canada, if we remember its history, begins with a conflictual encounter between Indigenous peoples and a French colony that was established in the seventeenth century. (See Chapter 1.) At the time of the British conquest in 1760, the francophone population, which was concentrated along the banks of the St. Lawrence River, kept alive its institutions, language, culture, and religion. Starting in the nineteenth century, French-speaking Canada was a significant centre of Christian missionary activity. Thousands of young priests, brothers, and nuns left then to "save souls" in the northern regions of Canada, where Indigenous communities abound and where the Catholic Church, according to the very influential Canon Lionel Groulx, should "integrate the wild (i.e., Indigenous) people into the French nation, introduce them to European civilization and stop wandering and civilize" them (Groulx 1962).

Later, the missionary ships left francophone Canada for Latin America and the Caribbean, but also for Asia, especially China, and Africa, especially to the British colonies of Lesotho and Zambia. In the early 1950s, there were 1,500 French-Canadian missionaries in Africa, including more than 100 White Fathers in francophone Africa (Gendron 2006). The ideology behind the missions was explicitly religious, as proclaimed by Lionel Groulx: "the Canadian missionary is only the herald of the gospel. His apostolate is absolutely disinterested" (Groulx 1962). This "Christian social order" put forward by the clerical elite—which included an economic and social dimension relayed through

credit unions ("Caisses populaires") inaugurated by Alphonse Desjardins in 1900—aimed to create international links through mutual groupings associated with the Catholic Church in various countries of the world (Lévesque 2009); one of its objective was to help the poor through microcredit schemes. (See Chapter 12.)

A New World is Being Established

After the Second World War, Canada and the world entered a period of transformation. Politically, Canada no longer wanted to be seen merely as a part of the British Empire; therefore, it aimed to develop its autonomy and separate international identity. Gradually, Canadian diplomatic and economic activity developed in line with the establishment of a Western bloc, under the hegemony of the United States. Meanwhile, the struggle for hegemony moved from Europe to Asia, Africa, and Latin America,

Table 8.1

Countries Using French as an/the Official Language

Countries Using French as the Only Official Language	Countries where French is an Official Language
Benin	Belgium
Burkina Faso	Burundi
Congo, Republic of the	Cameroon
Congo, Democratic Republic of the	Canada
Côte d'Ivoire	Central African Republic
France	Chad
Gabon	Comoros
Guinea	Djibouti
Mali	Equatorial Guinea
Monaco	Haiti
Niger	Luxembourg
Senegal	Madagascar
Togo	Rwanda
	Seychelles
	Switzerland
	Vanuatu

where Western dominance was challenged by the other superpower of the time, the Soviet Union. This global struggle proved to be fertile ground for the establishment of national liberation movements that confronted the colonial powers, for example in the French colonies of Algeria, Cameroon, and Madagascar. At the time, the Canadian government took a dim view of liberation movements like the National Liberation Front of Algeria.

Faced with this development, and after crushing defeats of its colonial empire in Vietnam and Algeria, in 1958 France adopted a new policy for formal independence, provided the new states agreed to be part of a "French Community." Under pressure from France, all the newly independent African states except Guinea accepted this offer that ensured continued French influence and domination over former colonies' economic, political, and even military spheres. (See dependency theory in Chapter 2.)

Nevertheless, the new African states were also often trying to open up to the rest of the world, including the socialist states like the Soviet Union and China, which developed close ties with Guinea and Mali in particular. In the 1960s, several new African countries also established links with Canada. (See Chapter 4.) At the same time, relations grew between Canada and Haiti, where a violent dictatorship forced much of the Haitian elite into exile. Thus, special links developed between Haiti and Quebec. (See Chapter 6.)

Discovering Cooperation

In Africa, where the newly independent states were trying to build their infrastructure, France proposed new mechanisms such as the Conference of Ministers of Education of French-speaking countries (1960), the Association of Francophone Universities (1961), the Association of International French-Speaking Parliamentarians (1967), and finally, an institution

supposed to oversee cooperation between all francophone countries, the Agency for Cultural and Technical Cooperation (1971).

Meanwhile, Canadian aid workers, mostly from Quebec, began flocking to francophone African countries such as Senegal, Côte d'Ivoire, Mali, and the former Belgian colonies of Burundi, Congo, and Rwanda. Missionaries were still present as well, especially in Central Africa. In West Africa, where much of the population was Muslim, many of the Canadian aid workers worked for non-denominational organizations such as the Canadian University Service Overseas (CUSO), which specialized in sending staff to work in primary and secondary education. (See Chapter 4 and Case Study 11.)

A Quebec-Canada Dispute

This development cooperation with francophone countries overseas soon became part of the new "conflictualités" that grew up between the federal government and the provincial government of Quebec, which was experiencing a period of expansion in the wake of the Quiet Revolution of the 1960s. Quebec in effect tried to take control of its institutions, while modernizing education and the economy. Moreover, it aimed to assert its right to have an international presence. Paul Gérin-Lajoie, then Minister of Education (see **Figure 8.1**) in this effervescent Quebec, proposed a new perspective in which Quebec could and must take the lead in the international arena, including at the level of development cooperation, at least within the scope of its jurisdiction:

> When the Quebec government is aware of its responsibility for the implementation of the special destiny of Quebec society, it has no desire to abandon to the federal government the power to enforce agreements whose objects are under provincial jurisdiction. [...] Therefore, in a federation like Canada, it is now necessary that member communities

(of that federation) who wish it must become actively and personally involved in the development of those international conventions that directly affect them. [...] It is no longer acceptable, either, that the federal government exert a kind of supervision and control over the openings that Quebec may wish to pursue as part of its international relations. (in Paquin 2006)

Faced with this development, the Canadian government reacted, especially once France started to publicly reinforce Quebec's aspirations. Conflicts arose in the context of international conferences to which the Quebec government had been directly invited, such as the 1967 meeting of ministers of education of Francophone states in Libreville, Gabon. These tensions increased with the visit of French President General Charles de Gaulle (1959–1969) to Canada in 1967, when he proclaimed his support for the Quebec independence movement. This competition between Ottawa and Paris carried over into debates about the founding of La Francophonie.

The Establishment of a System

It was within this context of conflictualités between Quebec, Canada, and France, along with the emergence of dozens of newly independent Third World countries, that the Canadian government established the Canadian International Development Agency (CIDA) in 1968. (See Chapter 4.) CIDA aimed to expand Canada's development assistance generally, but particularly in francophone countries; previously, Canadian aid had overwhelmingly been directed toward former British colonies, and only 0.4 percent of Canadian aid had gone to French-speaking countries (Paquin and Chaloux 2010). Provided with deep pockets and headed by Paul Gérin-Lajoie, who had been called to Ottawa by Liberal Prime Minister Pierre Trudeau (1968–1979 and 1980–1984),

Figure 8.1
Paul Gérin-Lajoie, Quebec Minister of Education (1964–1966) and President of CIDA (1970–1977)

Source : http://www.larevolutiontranquille.ca/fr/paul-gerin-lajoie.php.

CIDA was fast becoming the backbone of Canadian development cooperation. Another change was that the Canadian government adopted a new stance, calling for solidarity rather than charity. At the UN General Assembly in 1970 when Third World countries took centre stage, Canada asserted that international aid did not constitute a "gift," but the establishment of a new partnership (Morrison 1998). As Mitchell Sharp, the Secretary of State for External Affairs (1968–1974), described it:

Canadian foreign policy goals include economic development, social justice and quality of life, as well as the international extension to promote the well-being of Canadians. [...] We cannot aspire to create a truly just society in Canada if we are not willing to play our part in creating a more just global society. (in Beaudet 2009)

Canada proceeded to start several development cooperation programs in francophone Africa, although France remained the dominant player in virtually all areas of the economy and governance, providing over a third of all aid disbursements to Africa (Jacquemot 2011). Canadian investments focused mainly on Senegal and Mali, secondarily on Burkina Faso, Niger, and Rwanda. Canadian aid flowed to several sectors: education, rural development, and infrastructure. From 1961 to 1964, Canada's aid budget for francophone Africa grew from $300,000 to more than $7.5 million (Paquin 2006)!

Meanwhile, the 1970s were a kind of "golden age" for Canadian non-governmental organizations (NGOs) (See Chapters 4 and 7 and Case Study 11). Volunteering was expanding, with the proliferation of agencies that operated via semi-volunteer aid workers, as is the case for CUSO and several other groups that appeared later, such as Oxfam-Québec, the Centre for Study and International Cooperation, and the World University Service of Canada. Several hundred volunteers were sent to francophone Africa, and after returning home, they often became unofficial ambassadors for the African cause. Many joined CIDA.

Although NGOs received financial support from CIDA, including through project co-financing, over time the NGOs became more critical of the policies and actions of the Canadian government, especially concerning human rights and the social impacts of economic development. Solidarity campaigns were put in place to criticize mega-dams on the Senegal River, which flows through four countries in West Africa. In this case, Canada and other donors invested heavily in a project whose purposes and methods were questioned by NGOs and local peasant organizations. These critics accused CIDA of not questioning production practices and the focus on the export of cash crops at the expense of food crops (Reboul 1984). Meanwhile, the Mobutu

regime in Congo (later Zaïre, then the Democratic Republic of the Congo) was the target of several NGOs that accused Ottawa of not being proactive enough in isolating this bloody regime. In the 1978 federal budget, Canadian aid allocations were reduced, which moved Canada away from the promise to devote 0.7 percent of its GNP to official development assistance.

From la Francophonie to La Francophonie

In the 1970s, as Canada and the French-speaking countries of the developing world built up important links to each other, La Francophonie itself went into another phase. In 1970, at the initiative of Senegal, the Agency for Cultural and Technical Cooperation (ACCT) was formed. There was pressure from Ottawa on Paris and African countries for Quebec not to be invited to join. Finally, a compromise allowed Quebec to be accepted not as a member but as "participating government."

In 1984, a new Progressive Conservative government was elected in Ottawa under Prime Minister Brian Mulroney (1984–1993), with a heavy contingent of Quebec MPs. Quebec's international relations were by then no longer in dispute. The first international conference of La Francophonie was held in 1985; the heads of state of francophone countries assembled and the Quebec delegation was present under the name of Canada-Quebec; New Brunswick acquired the same status. ACCT became the Intergovernmental Agency of La Francophonie (AIF). The following year was the Francophone Summit in Paris, which meets every two years. Two of these summits were held in Quebec City, in 1987 and 2008. At the 1998 Summit, the International Organization of La Francophonie (IOF) was created. The IOF also oversees four French-language cooperative bodies:

1. The Agence universitaire de la Francophonie (AUF)
2. TV5 Monde, the international French-language TV channel
3. The International Association of Francophone Mayors (IAFM)
4. The Senghor University of Alexandria

This organization has roughly 300 staff and a budget of $100 million, to which Canada is the second largest contributor, after France (figures from 2013).

The Impact of La Francophonie

All in all, La Francophonie is a modest body on the international stage. It is not in the "elite club" of the large international agencies acting in the economic realm, such as the International Monetary Fund, the World Trade Organization, or the UN's developmental agencies. On the political and diplomatic level, the influence of La Francophonie is not comparable to that of the UN or of regional organizations like the European Union. Furthermore, La Francophonie is not a forum like NATO (see Chapter 5 and Case Study 4), where important politico-military decisions are made.

In short, La Francophonie, much like the Commonwealth (whose role in recent years has been even more marginal), is an entity of variable geometry reflecting a contradictory cultural and political reality (see **Table 8.2**). The role of France in La Francophonie remains central, and is the legacy, firstly, of the time when France had a vast colonial empire and, secondly, of the special bonds that still tie its former colonies to that country. In fact, until recently France has occupied a dominant role in the economics, politics, and the military affairs of some regions, especially West Africa. The establishment of a large military presence in several former colonies has allowed France to exercise fairly direct control over that region.

In economic terms, the impact of La Francophonie is mixed. Its modest development assistance budget means that it cannot make a big difference. Africa, especially francophone Africa, remains one of the poorest regions on earth. Almost all francophone African countries are among the least developed countries. A few francophone countries have a healthier economy, for example Côte d'Ivoire and Gabon, but in recent years, these economies have been shaken by various crises. While the percentage of the population living in extreme poverty ($1.25 a day) has decreased (from 60 percent to 50 percent) in recent decades, the absolute number of extremely poor people has increased from 290 to 400 million.

Table 8.2
Objectives and Missions of La Francophonie

Objectives of La Francophonie	Missions of La Francophonie
• Establishment and development of democracy. • Prevention, management, and resolution of conflicts and support for the rule of law and human rights. • Intensification of dialogue between cultures and civilizations. • Reconciliation of peoples through mutual understanding. • Strengthening their solidarity through multilateral cooperation to promote the growth of their economies. • Promoting education and training.	• Promote the French language and cultural and linguistic diversity. • Promote peace, democracy, and human rights. • Support education, training, higher education, and research. • Develop cooperation for sustainable development

Source: International Organization of La Francophonie (IOF).

In Mali and Niger, as part of structural adjustment programs, donors imposed severe cuts in social spending and the privatization of public services such as the national railway, which was bought for a tenth of its worth by the Canadian company Canac/Getma. In Mali, growth comes almost entirely from the mining sector, where foreign interests are dominant and employment creation is minimal. Despite the increase in development assistance, the country has regressed in the international rankings. Ranked 150th in 2001 on the human development index (see Chapter 2), Mali was ranked 173rd in 2006 out of 177 countries (Canet 2008).

According to a report submitted to the National Assembly of France, "the international community and France have favoured short-term stabilization over an approach that would deal with the root causes of stability and development, though the latter alone can have a chance of successfully solving the country's problems, despite being a far more complex task" (Commission des affaires étrangères 2015). The former Minister of Foreign Affairs of France, Hubert Védrine, admitted in a report to the French president that the French sphere of influence in Africa was poorly managed compared to other regions in Africa, resulting in a disastrous situation where only 30 percent of Africans in the French sphere of influence have access to electricity and roads, irrigation, and drinking water (Védrine 2013). There are only a few exceptions to this story, for example, tiny Mauritius (population 1.1 million) whose government has attempted to diversify its economy and improve people's lives. We cannot say that the authorities of La Francophonie are very effective in changing this difficult economic situation, despite the IOF's efforts to develop an economic strategy (IOF 2014).

The Dilemma of Poor Governance

In the passage from colonial times to independence, many African countries have struggled to establish democratic systems and ensure respect for human rights. After independence, internal and external conflicts have followed rapidly, bringing many *coups d'état*, which have often been supported by France. For example, the Malian army overthrew President Modibo Keita in 1968 with support from France, which considered him too leftist and too strong a supporter of a pan-Africanism. Several other francophone African countries were taken over by dictators that France and Canada tolerated, partly because they were part of the allied Western countries' Cold War struggle against communism. The most obvious case in Africa was that of Mobutu Sese Seko, who reigned supreme in the Congo (later called Zaire) from 1965 to 1998. Mobutu enjoyed the support of the United States, Canada, France, and Belgium because he was a strong anti-Communist and supported pro-Western factions in the Angolan civil war. For decades, large-scale democratic movements tried to overthrow Mobutu, but the violence of the repression overwhelmed the demands for democratic change.

In 1990, after the end of the Cold War, however, French President François Mitterrand (1981–1995) called upon African states to open up to democracy and free elections. (See Chapter 11.) Some African countries followed this path, but several others sank into what the Moroccan opposition leader Abraham Serfaty has called "démocrature," which roughly translates as "democratorship," meaning a regime that has elements of democracy and dictatorship. In this situation, repressive systems continue to function without hindrance; the media are muzzled, civil society organizations and unions are constrained; and elections are often rigged, as in Burkina Faso, where, in 1987, a civil-military regime was put in place after the assassination of President Thomas Sankara. France and Canada supported this civil-military regime all along, until its overthrow in a popular uprising in 2014.

According to Ugandan economist Yash Tandon, too many African countries are led by kleptocrats who work in the interests of multinational corporations and international financial institutions (Tandon 2013). The opaque system of close ties between African governments and multinational corporations based in middle and big powers, especially France, has been called Françafrique. This opaque system leads the French government and major French companies such as Areva, Bolloré, and Bouygues to exploit natural resources in ways that violate international standards (Verschave 2002).

According to researcher Alaiń Deneault (2008), the situation is hardly rosy as regards Canada in Africa either. Canadian mining companies support dictators and their militias, especially in the Democratic Republic of the Congo. In Mali and Burkina Faso, they do not respect government regulations, and behave this way with the complicity of local authorities. The distribution of Deneault's book by the publishing house Écosociété was halted following an out-of-court settlement of a lawsuit brought by a Canadian mining firm, Barrick Gold, which was one of the targets of Deneault's investigation.

Dislocation and Military Interventions

Today, much of Africa, especially francophone Africa, is slipping into a spiral of conflict. Relatively wealthy countries, such as Côte d'Ivoire and Libya, long thought to be stable under the control of "effective" dictatorships, have been disrupted by violent civil wars. The armed destabilization now extends to Mali, Niger, Central African Republic, Congo, and Gabon. Popular uprisings have rocked Senegal, Burkina Faso, and Togo. These issues have been compounded by the fact the Sahelian African countries are heavily affected by the current crisis in North Africa and the Middle East. (See Case Study 10.)

This crisis produces collateral damage, such as the departure into exile of tens of thousands of young Africans trying to cross the Mediterranean in inhumane conditions.

> In Francophone Africa, France continues to act as the policeman, with more than 5,000 soldiers deployed in various countries. The French government, aware of the major issues that affect its economic interests, wants to strengthen its presence on the continent at all levels, especially in its "backyard" (pré-carré) in West, North, and Central Africa. (Védrine et al. 2013)

In some countries where crises worsen, Western countries claim to intervene on "humanitarian grounds" to defend women and children. (See Case Studies 3 and 7.) They say they want to prevent massacres like the one that occurred in Rwanda in 1994. But France had supported the Rwandan government that organized that genocide of nearly a million people, until its defeat at the hands of the Rwandan Patriotic Front. As the old regime fell, France intervened militarily, ensuring that key members of the armed forces of the old regime escaped. In the Sahelian countries, France has recently raised the threat of radicalization caused by the growth of groups proclaiming political Islam. To many observers, however, radical Islam is a consequence rather than a cause. According to the feminist Malian Aminata Traoré, Africa's population have their backs to the wall:

> We are all prisoners hostage to an unequal and unjust economic and political system that excels in the art of breaking resistance through financial blackmail. The removal of external aid has resulted this year [2012] in a budgetary shortfall of 429 billion CFA francs (roughly C$930 million). Almost all public investment is suspended. The closure of many companies has caused layoffs and unemployment for tens of thousands of workers while food prices continue to surge. (Traoré 2012)

According to the International Crisis Group (ICG), the situation in the Sahel could become a cataclysm (International Crisis Group 2015). According to ICG, European governments' decision to focus their efforts on military intervention and repression of armed groups is misguided. France's military operations in the region, including in Mali, Libya, and Chad, are inadequate to do the job, especially since they work with local armed forces who practise predation and violence against the population.

In short, the radicalization, criminalization, and militarization of significant sectors of the population cannot be controlled without reinstalling transparent and accountable governments. This process involves addressing the root causes: pervasive poverty, underdevelopment of peripheral regions, the exponential growth in the number of young people who have no prospect of employment and who have little other choice than emigration or joining armed groups. The real solution, ICG believes, lies in long-term action through the establishment of democratic governance and reconstruction of the country on the basis of sustainable development. (See Chapters 11 and 14.)

What is the Future of La Francophonie?

In these uncertain times, the future of La Francophonie, as well as la Francophonie, is not clear. A book with the provocative title *Why La Francophonie?* brought together several authors who asked that question while stating that La Francophonie needs to find a "second wind" and fight for its relevance (Beaudoin and Paquin 2008). One important obstacle is the dominant position of France, with its heavy colonial past and its claims to manage Africa. The other developed francophone countries, Canada, Switzerland, and Belgium, are more or less uncomfortable with this situation, but they are not willing to throw their weight behind a serious effort to change things.

Figure 8.2

Michaëlle Jean upon her Election as Secretary General of the IOF, 2014

Source: Global Affairs Canada.

Structured around the IOF, La Francophonie is supposed to promote peace and sustainable development but, as previously mentioned, it is questionable whether these two "missions" are progressing. For supporters of La Francophonie, however, the project still makes sense as a way to promote a multicultural and multi-linguistic world that can mitigate the effects of an all-too-intrusive economic globalization under the hegemony of the United States. Therefore, in other words, its mission is the fight for cultural diversity. As stated by Louise Beaudoin, former Quebec cabinet minister:

> The current commercial and financial globalization, intense, fast and unbridled, undermines social and cultural rights of peoples. As such, cultural and linguistic diversity appears as the front line in the struggle to delimit and humanize globalization. (Beaudoin 2004, 210)

For the former Secretary General of the IOF (2003–2014), Abdou Diouf, La Francophonie gets its "fuel" from common values such as the philosophy of "the Enlightenment, the ideals

Box 8.1

The Haïtian Case

While most of the relationships within La Francophonie occur between Canada, Europe, and Africa, a special case arises in the form of the poorest country in the Americas, Haiti. It is important to recall some of the more salient features of the Haitian case, especially since the prolonged crisis in that country is a matter of concern to various components of La Francophonie.

For decades, Haiti was run by a plutocracy headed by the Duvalier family. The United States, France, and Canada were relatively indifferent to this situation, and on some level were beneficiaries, as was the case with the massive influx of Haitian graduates from the 1960s onwards. In the 1980s and 1990s, however, a powerful popular movement arose to peacefully resist the plutocracy. With the support of the Catholic Church and some NGOs, this movement finally overthrew the second President Duvalier. In 1990, during the first free elections, a priest who was close to these popular organizations, Jean-Bertrand Aristide, was elected with 67 percent of the popular vote. In 1991, he was overthrown in a violent coup d'état that drew support from the United States and its local ally, the former head of the Tonton Macoutes militia, Emmanuel Constant. In 1994, Aristide came back with the support of the new US administration of President Bill Clinton (1993–2001). Aristide was quickly faced with hostility from the former colonial power France, from which he had demanded compensation for the destruction perpetrated against Haiti in the aftermath of independence. Other conflicts arose with the United States on opening the Haitian market to US products. Social tensions have deepened. Aid was suspended. In 2004, the country was again in crisis. The United States, Canada, and France worked together to overthrow the elected president, while various mediation attempts were underway under the auspices of the Caribbean Community. Following Aristide's exile, foreign aid was restored. The country remained stuck in poverty, however, until the terrible earthquake of 2010. Since then, Haiti has been practically under the tutelage of its major donors. (See Chapter 14.)

---

of the French Revolution, which embraces the desire for greater equality, freedom, brotherhood (and fights) for pluralism, for democracy, for freedom. La Francophonie is wary of [a world in which there is only] a single language, a single culture, a single way of thinking" (quoted in Montenay 2005).

This is the message carried forward by the new Secretary General of the IOF—the former Governor General of Canada, Michaëlle Jean (see **Figure 8.2** opposite). She was elected to this position at the XV Summit of La Francophonie in Dakar in 2014 (IOF 2014). Nevertheless, we must ask whether La Francophonie can play a constructive role in the future as the number of stumbling blocks continues to grow: "unclear objectives, endlessly growing ambitions,

increasing numbers of Member States that have nothing Francophone about them,[1] meager budget, mixed results" (Beaudoin 2004).

At the 2014 Summit in Dakar, the Canadian government made commitments totalling $38 million for the institutions of La Francophonie in 2014, in four areas:

- Promoting the French language and cultural and linguistic diversity.
- Promoting peace, democracy, and human rights.

---

1. Several countries that have no Francophone heritage have nonetheless joined La Francophonie: Albania, Armenia, Bulgaria, Cyprus, Ghana, Greece, Moldova, FYR Macedonia, Qatar, and Romania.

- Supporting education, training, higher education, and research.
- Developing programs for sustainable development and solidarity.

These commitments represent approximately 2 percent of the budget devoted by Canada to international development.

In addition to this overall support to La Francophonie, Canada also provides aid to several member countries of La Francophonie individually, with commitments totalling $1.2 billion in 2014, of which $692 million came from the development section of what was then the Department of Foreign Affairs, Trade and Development (now Global Affairs Canada). Among the priority countries identified by Canada are Senegal, Mali, and Haiti (see **Box 8.1** above). However, these aid programs take place within a context of budgetary cuts going on since 2010. According to the Canadian Council for International Cooperation, the Harper Conservative government (2006–2015) reduced its development aid by $1.4 billion after 2010, meaning that Canada's aid to GNP ratio (see Chapter 4) sank to 0.22 percent 2016. Canada thus finds itself in the company of the least generous donor nations, along with the United States and Japan.

The Answer from Below

Must we, as many say, continue with La Francophonie? Is it realistic to work for it to become what it could and should become: a space for people gathered around the sharing of the French language; a space where solidarity is not an empty word; and a space where new global dialogue, or even a new global governance, takes place (Beaudoin 2004)?

The bet is risky in these difficult times, as extractivist economic practices (see Chapter 12) continue to expand in a context of multiple conflicts. One could add to this the already perceptible effects of climate change (see Case Study 8)

> **Box 8.2**
>
> ### The Agence universitaire de la Francophonie (AUF) (Francophone University Association)
>
> - The AUF manages the exchanges and projects from around 800 French academic institutions spread across the world.
> - More than 1,200 students benefit from mobility grants, and 113 international cooperation projects are underway.
> - Nearly 9,000 teachers benefit from distance learning.
> - The AUF annual budget is about $50 million.

and these are expected to worsen, particularly in vulnerable regions such as the Sahel. The Intergovernmental Panel on Climate Change (IPCC) estimates that an additional 600 million Africans could be exposed to famine by 2080 as a result of climate change. Such scenarios are complicated by the proliferation of militias, massive population movements, ethnic conflicts, collapse of public health systems (as was seen in the Ebola crisis), and humanitarian crises of all kinds.

However, development of resistance can also be found within and around these events. For instance, the Arab Spring (see Case Study 10) has made waves in Senegal, Togo, and especially Burkina Faso, where the Blaise Compaoré regime was overthrown in 2014. In several countries, we have seen strikes in the public service and in industry, roadblocks by farmers who want to prevent land grabbing, student demonstrations, and, increasingly, mobilization of urban youth, the unemployed, and people from the informal economy. In Senegal, the movement "Y en a marre" ("We've had enough!")

sprang largely from the unemployed graduates who form a growing part of the population.

The African Social Forum, as well as other gatherings that acted on a regional, national, or continental scale, set in motion broad coalitions (now known as a "social movements") that have unfolded in several forms. These movements fight against corruption and against the Economic Partnership agreements; they fight for transparency in the extractive sector. These African networks mesh to provide the foundation for the creation of new networks with social movements around the world, including elsewhere in the francophone world.

Do You Want to Get Involved?

Several sites have information on how to better work together with people of the francophone community:

- We can support the struggle for democracy and ask our governments to punish dictators and predators. One can support the campaigns of these social movements in Africa directly, but also through various diasporas in Canada who are involved in these struggles in Senegal, Mali, Togo, Cameroon, and Burundi.
- We must push for more development assistance, and demand that financial institutions cancel illegitimate debts.
- We must oppose military adventures undertaken by the former colonial powers such as France, as well as the sale of arms and military equipment from Canada to regimes that violate human rights.
- We must closely monitor Canadian mining companies that undertake activities harmful to people and the environment, particularly in the Democratic Republic of the Congo and Mali.
- Finally, we must establish direct links with the people and their organizations through support for small projects and work placements in the field. Several Canadian and Quebec NGOs that are present in francophone Africa as well as in Haiti support and work in solidarity with local grass-roots organizations.
- We must demand that the Canadian government show a more generous policy towards asylum seekers from Africa and take more vigorous action to protect them when they leave their country of origin.

Questions for Further Learning

- Are the institutions of La Francophonie still valid and effective in achieving the goals they seek?
- What is the specific role of France in La Francophonie? Can France separate its military and economic objectives from its development cooperation policies?
- Why is Canada so invested in La Francophonie? What is its particular role?
- What is the African perspective on La Francophonie? Are Africans truly committed to La Francophonie?
- What can be done to promote links of cooperation and solidarity between Canada, Quebec, and French-speaking Africa?

Key Terms

Agence universitaire de la Francophonie (AUF), p. 158

Agency for Cultural and Technical Cooperation, p. 148

Canada, p. 146

Françafrique, p. 153

France, p. 146

Francophonie, p. 146

International Organization of La Francophonie, p. 158

international cooperation, p. 146

Quebec, p. 146

sub-Saharan Africa, p. 146

Suggested Readings

Relatively little is written in English on la/La Francophonie.

Beaudet, Pierre. 2009. *Qui aide qui? Une brève histoire de la solidarité et de la coopération internationales au Québec*. Montréal : Boréal.

Gendron, Robin. 2006. *Towards a Francophone Community*. Montreal and Kingston: McGill-Queen's University Press.

Martinez, Andrea, Pierre Beaudet, and Stephen Baranyi. 2011. *Haïti hier, Haïti aujourd'hui. Regards croisés*. Ottawa: University of Ottawa Press.

Organisation internationale de la Francophonie. 2005. *Charte de la francophonie*. Paris : OIF http://www.francophonie.org/IMG/pdf/charte_francophonie.pdf.

———. 2014. *Cadre stratégique de la Francophonie*. Adoptée à la Conférence de Dakar. http://www.international.gc.ca/franco/assets/pdfs/Cadre-strategique-Franco.pdf.

Survie. 2014. *Françafrique, la famille recomposée*. Paris: Éditions Syllepse.

Tandon, Yash. 2015. *Trade is War*. New York: OR Books.

Thomas, Dominic. 2013. *Africa and France: Postcolonial Cultures, Migration, and Racism*. Bloomington: Indiana University Press.

Suggested Websites

Agence universitaire de la francophonie (English website): https://www.auf.org/auf/en-bref/anglais/auf-brief/

Association québécoise des organismes de coopération internationale: http://www.aqoci.qc.ca/

Centre de recherche et d'information pour le développement: http://www.crid.asso.fr/

Global Affairs Canada, Francophonie Section (English website): http://www.international.gc.ca/franco/index.aspx?lang=eng

International Organization of La Francophonie (English website): http://www.francophonie.org/Welcome-to-the-International.html

Survie (Observatoire de la Françafrique): http://survie.org/

Works Cited

Beaudet, Pierre. 2009. *Qui aide qui? Une brève histoire de la solidarité et de la coopération internationales au Québec*. Montréal: Boréal.

Beaudoin, Louise. 2004. "Vue d'Afrique, à quoi sert la francophonie?" *Le Devoir*, 24 November.

Beaudoin, Louise, and Stéphane Paquin. 2008. *Pourquoi la francophonie?* Montreal: VLB Éditeur.

Canet, Raphaël. 2008. "Un développement approprié? Étude des politiques de lutte contre la pauvreté au Mali en vue de l'application du principe d'appropriation de la Déclaration de

Paris." Montréal: Association québécoise des organismes de coopération internationale.

Commission des affaires étrangères de l'Assemblée nationale de France. 2015. "Rapport de la mission d'information sur la stabilité et le développement de l'Afrique francophone." *compte-rendu*, no. 70, 15 April.

Deneault, Alain, et al. 2008. *Noir Canada: Pillage, Corruption et Criminalité en Afrique*. Montréal: Écosociété.

Gendron, Robin. 2006. *Towards a Francophone Community*. Montreal and Kingston: McGill-Queen's University Press.

Groulx, Lionel. 1962. *Le Canada français missionnaire*. Montréal: Fides.

International Crisis Group. 2015. "Central Sahel: The Perfect Sandstorm." *Africa Report* 227.

Jacquemot, Pierre. 2011. "Cinquante ans de coopération française avec l'Afrique subsaharienne. Une mise en perspective." *Afrique contemporaine* 2 (238): 43–57.

Lévesque, Benoît. 2009. "Les relations internationales de l'économie sociale du Québec (1840–2008)." *Globe, revue internationale d'études québécoises* 12 (1): 67–94.

Montenay, Yves. 2005. *La langue française face à la mondialisation*. Paris: Les Belles Lettres.

Morrison, David. 1998. *Aid and Ebb Tide: A History of CIDA and Canadian Development Assistance*. Waterloo: Wilfrid Laurier University Press.

OIF. 2014. *Quinzièm Conférence des chefs d'État et de gouvernements de pays ayant le français en partage*. Dakar, 29 November.

http://www.francophonie.org/IMG/pdf/sommet_xv_strategie_economique_2014.pdf.

Paquin, Stéphane. 2006. "La relation Québec-Paris-Ottawa et la création de l'Organisation internationale de la Francophonie (1960–2005)." *Guerres mondiales et conflits contemporains* 3 (223): 31–37.

Paquin, Stéphane, and Louise Beaudoin, eds. 2006. *Les relations internationales du Québec depuis la Doctrine Gérin-Lajoie (1965–2005)*. Québec: Presses de l'Université Laval.

Paquin, Stéphane, and Annie Chaloux. 2010. "Le Québec sur la scène internationale." *Globe : revue internationale d'études québécoises* 13 (1): 25–45.

Reboul, Claude. 1984. "Barrages contre le développement? Les grands aménagements hydrauliques de la vallée du fleuve Sénégal." *Revue Tiers Monde* 25 (100): 749–760.

Tandon, Yash. 2013. "Capitalisme kleptocrate." *Alternatives Sud*, no. 20.

Traoré, Aminata. 2012. *L'Afrique mutilée*. Paris: Éditions Taama. Extrait publié dans Médiapart, 22 January 2013.

Védrine, Hubert, et al. 2013. "Un partenariat pour l'avenir : 15 propositions pour une nouvelle dynamique économique entre l'Afrique et la France." *Rapport au ministère de l'Économie et des Finances*.

Verschave, François-Xavier. 2002. *Noir Chirac*. Paris: Les Arènes.

Notes

9 Challenging the Colonialism at the Heart of Western Development

A Decolonizing Perspective

Tracy Coates, Kathlean Fitzpatrick, Trycia Bazinet, and Rodney Nelson[1]

Key Terms

Aboriginal Peoples

development

divine right

Enlightenment

First Nations

governance

Indigenous

Indigenous social movements

relationality

traditional leadership

Western culture

Overview

From conversion to modern concepts of development, this chapter provides an introduction to some of the historical social, political, and economic processes that created and maintain unbalanced hierarchical systems of dominance and control within Western states. A discussion of various forms of development and ideology used to legitimize the West's[2] colonization of its internal populace, and of Indigenous peoples[3] worldwide, provides an introduction to how the imposition of Western social systems has functioned to undermine the self-determination and rights of the internally and externally colonized.

The intent of this chapter is to generate a critical investigation of the historically and culturally specific origins of the Western model of social organization, which includes political and economic structures. In doing so, we seek to challenge the predominant understandings of "development," which often position the Western model as universally applicable and legitimate it as an ideal framework for international development. Ideally, this process will help to create space for a multitude of critical dialogues, allowing for the possibility of a pluriversality of projects (Grosfogeul 2011, 4). From this new beginning, it may be possible for the real and existing alternatives presented by First Nations and other Indigenous as ways of knowing, being,

1. We would like to extend credit and special thanks to the Elders and First Nations, Metis/Métis, and Inuit scholars, knowledge keepers, and leaders who came before us and have shared their knowledge with us through scholarly works and personal communications. It is only on the basis of their immense contributions that we are able to put forward this small contribution towards building bridges of understanding between the Western culture and First Nations/Indigenous cultures. We would also like to give specific thanks to Elder Pauline Shirt, Carolyn Laude, Nadia Abu-Zahra, and Diana El Richani for their efforts and contributions, without which this work would not have been possible.

and doing (as seen in Indigenous forms of social and economic organization) to be seen and heard by the dominant discourse of mainstream development theory.

Implicit in this approach is the belief that we need to give serious consideration to the assumed superiority and universal applicability of the Western model of development, and its position as the dominant form of international development, prior to imposing it on Indigenous communities and others. A starting place for this reflection may be found in an examination of why Indigenous peoples have been resisting Western models of governance and socio-economic assimilation for over 500 years, and continue to do so today. Our hope is that this chapter will also play a small part in a longer process that sees current development students freeing the field from its historical and pervasive belief in Western superiority—a belief that has impeded the ability of past generations to see the violence, oppression, and negative consequences of imposing the Western model of social organization on other cultures at the expense of their own models. In doing so, practitioners and students can open a larger space for more collaborative and egalitarian development theories and practices that embody the spirit of reconciliation and renewal.

We use the colonization of Turtle Island (North America) as an example of how governance and social structures in settler-colonial states replicate the Eurocentric empire-style model from which they originated. Grounded in the subordination of both Indigenous and non-Indigenous peoples, this hierarchical model perpetuates social inequality and exploitation in the modern nation-state, benefiting an elite few at the expense of the majority. With the exception of the final section of this chapter, the elements of colonialism discussed are not unique to Turtle Island (Stewart-Harawira 2005). We hope this chapter will help readers better understand both the historical and present context of Indigenous/non-Western societies around much of the world, from Australia to the Middle East, Africa to the Arctic, and beyond. (See Case Studies 2, 9, and 10.)

---

2. The terms Western, Western-European, Europe, and the West are used interchangeably throughout this chapter and the next in discussions of pre-twentieth-century history to refer to the nations found in western Europe, including the Netherlands, France, Spain, Portugal, and the United Kingdom. In discussions about contemporary post-twentieth-century topics, the term "Western culture" is used to denote the culture inherited from these European colonial nations, which is now found in settler-colonial nations, such as the United States and Canada, as well as elsewhere around the world. Various authors have expounded on defining "Western culture" in colonial contexts using terms such as "Eurocentric fundamentalism" (Grosfoguel 2011, 1).

3. The term "Indigenous" is used throughout this chapter and the next to denote "a particular subset of humanity that represents a certain common set of experiences rooted in historical subjugation by colonialism, or something like colonialism ... Indigenous peoples are identified, and identify themselves as such, by reference to identities that predate historical encroachments by other groups and the ensuing histories that have wrought, and continue to bring, oppression against their cultural survival and self-determination as distinct peoples" (Anaya 2004, 5). At times, the terms Indigenous and First Nations are used interchangeably to refer to the pre-contact Indigenous inhabitants of Turtle Island (North America).

Learning Objectives

By the end of this chapter, students will be able to:

- critically deconstruct the Western model of social organization by discussing its relevant underlying ideologies as they have emerged and changed over time.
- explain how the Western development model is informed by, and perpetuates, hierarchical structures and forms of domination and oppression.
- identify the main goals of the colonial development mandate.
- discuss the impacts the colonial development mandate has had on First Nations in Canada.
- extrapolate and assess some of the impacts that the social and economic imbalance between the elite and the majority has had on the body politic of Western nations.
- compare differences between key elements of the Western model of social and economic organization and certain First Nations models.
- determine where First Nations, Métis, and Inuit (FNMI) peoples and non-FNMI Canadians are situated in broader social movements, both domestically and internationally.

Introduction

International development is generally rooted in Western paradigms that make a series of assumptions that need to be investigated. (See Chapter 2.) An investigation of Western paradigms underlying mainstream development theories is an important strategy for decolonial thinking. Such an investigation questions the very foundational and axiomatic concepts that are assumed to be "common sense" but which are in fact hidden and/or protected from critiques that aim to reveal their historical and culturally specific origins. Within the context of development, ideas about the nature and structure of governance, progress, and cultural evolution generally presume that the Western model is the standard to which others should be held. This assumed superiority of the Western model of development goes beyond being a "best practice" in that it has historically been imposed as a universal ideal type. (See Chapter 2, especially modernization theory.) The model

is not universal, however, as it is grounded in—and specific to—the European social and historical context. Based on a linear understanding of history, Western states produced a social model of organization that emerged, and is reproduced, by containing political opposition at home through domination, control, and the export of the Western model, for example, through colonialism. Contemporary Western development theories and practices are embedded in this legacy and unconsciously replicate it to the detriment of Indigenous and non-Western peoples. In particular, these development practices marginalize Indigenous social structures and forms of self-determination by imposing foreign models of socio-economic governance that engender the unequal distribution of power, control, and wealth.

To broadly understand the implications of contemporary development requires the critical deconstruction of the evolution of European (Western) political, economic, and social systems of domination that concentrate power and control in the hands of an elite few. The replicating nature of these systems is explored in this chapter through an historical examination of three models of Western social organization: the traditional model (divine right/ feudalism), the Enlightenment model, and the modern liberal democratic state. This discussion gives an overview of how these models have, first, functioned to internally control and/ or colonize the body of common people across Western nations, and second, supported the external colonization of Indigenous peoples in the Americas and elsewhere. Understanding the historical foundations of the Western model of development, along with how the myth of inherent superiority supports it, is key to understanding and critically assessing contemporary development theories and practices.

We begin with an examination of the myth of Western superiority, which has been a common thread throughout the history of Western civilization. A genealogical study of how the three models of social organization developed then provides a foundation for understanding the role that contemporary development theory and practice play in maintaining a long-established pattern of reproducing Western development models, which may not take into account the best interests of the majority of those they purport to assist. This is followed by a discussion of specific elements of certain First Nations approaches to social organization to illustrate examples of viable and differentiated models. We conclude with a commentary on potential avenues for social change, transformation, and collaborative learning through an exploration of differences and commonalities in contemporary Western and Indigenous social movements. It is hoped that the insights and critical distance provided by this analysis will serve as the basis for engaging in a much-needed conversation about the value and inappropriateness of imposing Western development systems on non-Western communities. Students may also use this material as an opportunity for self-reflection on the burdens the Western model imposes on the majority of the populace where the Western model of social organization exists.

Deconstructing the Western Development Model: The Myth of Western Superiority

The historical notion that Western people, cultures, and models of social organization and development are superior is a myth that serves to produce, maintain, and legitimize social distinctions and hierarchical power relations. Settler colonial theory explores how settler superiority is grounded in the unfounded belief that certain individuals and groups are inherently superior to others (Fanon 1961; Coulthard 2014). Within Western society, this myth has maintained the power of governing elites, who are viewed as superior to the populace, whether as a result of divine right or some form of constructed secular merit. Supported by Christian dogma, the myth has also perpetuated a patriarchal hierarchy that privileges men over women, and Europeans over other races (Gage 1893; de las Casas 1971; Badcock 1976).

According to social dominance theory, dominant elite groups in society use ideological instruments, such as legitimizing myths, to control subordinate groups by "controlling what is and what is not considered legitimate discourse, and promoting the idea that the rule of elites is moral, just, necessary, inevitable, and fair" (Sidanius and Pratto 2012). Within Western society, dominant groups have historically benefited from a disproportionate share of power and "the good things in life," while subordinate groups have been deprived of access to resources and have received a disproportionately greater share of "the bad things in life" (ibid.). This disproportionate allocation of power and wealth helps to perpetuate the cultural hegemony of the elites by providing the ruling classes with the ongoing capacity to control subordinate groups. This control often comes about through the manipulation of the beliefs, perceptions, and worldviews that are the basis of Western culture (Lears 1985; Grosfoguel 2011, 9–13).

Historically, the myth of superiority has functioned to reinforce social hierarchies and power relations based on arbitrary group distinctions and socially constructed categories such as race, religion, lineage, nationality, ethnicity, social class, and economic status (Sidanius and Pratto 2012, 419). In ancient Greece and Rome, politics was constructed around the natural superiority of masters over slaves and of the civilized over the barbarian. Medieval Europe was similarly structured on the superiority of the nobility over the peasants and the Christians over the heathens. (See the traditional model discussed below.) The early modern period (seventeenth century CE) was organized under dynastic monarchs ruling over subjects and European nations seeking to colonize societies they termed Oriental or savage, inferior, or worse. After the Enlightenment (eighteenth century), modernity created its own version of superiority grounded in science, technology, linear progress, property ownership, and liberal individualism. The racial categorization of different peoples as either civilized or savage has been used to legitimate the conquest and assimilation of "inferior" societies through colonization.

The myth that the Western model is superior, neutral, and universally applicable is supported and legitimized within Western society by the historic belief that other systems are particularistic (i.e., geared to advancing the interests of a specific group), along with a series of unreliable characterizations of non-Western peoples:

We went from the sixteenth-century characterization of "people without writing" to the eighteenth- and nineteenth-century characterization of "people without history," to the twentieth-century characterization of "people without development" and more recently, to the early twenty-first-century

characterization of "people without democracy." (Grosfoguel 2011, 7)

Externally, the myth of superiority has served as both the driving force and the redemptive narrative for the colonization of Indigenous and other peoples worldwide (Blaut 1993). This Western worldview legitimized—in the colonizers' view—the forced assimilation of the Indigenous occupants of both foreign lands (e.g., Africa) and newly "discovered" lands (e.g., North and South America). It also legitimized acts of genocide and enslavement. Such acts were justified by the Western elite as reasonable and even necessary methods for achieving the West's benevolent mission and were thus divorced from moral or ethical consequences. The result was that, in order to "save the savages," the "superior" Europeans subjected them to a process of colonization that systematically denied, devalued, and destroyed their pre-existing governance, economic, and cultural systems.

The Traditional Model of Divine Right and Feudalism

The first stage in this short history of the development of the Western model of social organization begins with the traditional model of divine right and feudalism. The traditional model of Western social organization (pre-seventeenth century) was based on the classical and Christian belief in the strict division between rulers and ruled. The division was justified by divine right and the belief in the inherent superiority of the noble classes. This hierarchical worldview flowed from top to bottom beginning with God, the Pope, and the king at the top as the rulers and commanders, followed by archangels, bishops, and nobles in the middle, who enacted and enforced the rules on the ruled, which were the commoners, slaves, women, and non-Christians (Lovejoy 1936).

The basic hierarchical tenets of the ideological

and political structures of the traditional model, which evolved over time, were conceived at the Christian Church's Council of Nicaea in 325 CE. As well as deciding important elements of theological doctrine, the Church council also ruled on concerns such as marriage, property, and inheritance rights, the just rules of war, and the classification of crimes punishable by excommunication (Coleman 2000). Excommunication was important because it meant that contracts, debts, and oaths made to someone who was excommunicated no longer had to be honoured. Through the act of clarifying and codifying the sacred texts, the Papal Curia provided a "universal" structure for combining and mutually reinforcing the ideological and political forces of Church and State in a manner that came to define the Middle Ages.

Throughout this era, Church and State worked together to support each other's power and control over the population by maintaining a hierarchical model that punished and excluded those who disobeyed the status quo. This model omitted Christianity's more egalitarian teachings, allowing the ruling classes to develop a version of Christianity that legitimated their own social dominance. Grounded in the Christian belief in a transcendent, unquestionable, and omnipotent God, the social order itself became unquestionable, because it was put forward as embodying the order that God had established (Gilson 2002). St. Augustine's interpretation of the concept of original sin also served to reinforce obedience to the established social order. Augustine's doctrine was used to condemn human nature as inherently evil and human beings as incapable of rational or moral action without God's saving grace, which could only be dispensed by the Church (Augustine 1961). In so doing, it further legitimated the dominance of the privileged elite who claimed to be in service to God.

From an Augustinian perspective, conflict was seen as a natural by-product of social interaction, which could only be controlled by the government and religious authorities (Augustine 1994). This ideology of inherent conflict among men gave rise to a presumed political need to maintain law and order *over*, rather than *with*, the populace. It was also a dramatic change from the classical foundations of Roman law, which saw man and nature as parts within the whole of a good and rational cosmos (Cicero 1999). Augustine's doctrine provided the ruling classes with the theoretical foundations for a socially constructed need to control the populace. This foundation served to justify the combining of forces between the church and state elites, giving them greater power to control and discipline the population. It also served to reinforce and maintain the power of the dominant groups and shape European interpretations of divine, natural, and positive (human-made) law. The Church's and States' "universal" approach was also fundamental to Western expansion by the Roman Empire. It later helped to legitimize the efforts of crusaders and missionaries tasked with spreading Christian "civilization" to other nations that were self-servingly characterized by Western nations as infidels and savages in need of salvation (Wright 2001).

Social and Economic Domination and the Western Model of Social Organization

In addition to holding ideological and political power, the traditional model allowed European nobility to exercise unchallenged social and economic authority as resident landlords on their feudal estates. The nobility were able to live the good life of leisure, "honour," and military virtue, supported by an extensive system of state taxes, church tithes, and fines levied on the populace (Peters 1983). Work of any kind, particularly manual labour, was considered vulgar and degrading by the elite and was left to the lower classes. Social mobility under the traditional model was limited by economic and social policies that were justified by a complex system of constructed ideologies and myths related to superiority, gender, class, lineage, and race (Doyle 1992). Law tied serfs and peasants to the villages of their birth and forced them to work in support of the ruling noble class. Under the Poor Laws, the unemployed were legally forbidden to leave their local community in search of employment or relief (Hill 1976). In both rural and urban settings, the poor and working classes had very little access to local authority.

The lower orders were often left with little more than moral and ethical appeals that were easily dismissed by the nobles. This meant that they had to rely on the charity of their local parish to support them in their poverty (Hill 1976). Life in the towns was only slightly better for commoners, women, and slaves. Townsmen had the benefit of urban "liberties" not found in the rural feudal order of things. Artisans, traders, and merchants were legally "free men" and as a result of this independence were marginally better off economically (Poggi 1978). This economic liberty did not translate into political power or mobility until much later; common men were still excluded from voting or holding positions of power within the government (Mann 1986). The parliaments, King's councils, and courts were reserved to the clergy and land-owning nobility, this being another avenue for using divine, natural, and state (positive) law in combination to reinforce the status quo by limiting social mobility.

Opportunities for mobility did sometimes come about for wealthy commoners through noble families seeking advantageous alliances. By the later part of the early modern period it became possible for a limited number of extremely wealthy commoners to move up the social ladder by purchasing lands and titles (Doyle 1992). Kings seeking to subordinate their rivals increasingly sought financial support from wealthy commoners, which was one way these opportunities for social mobility were created (Mann 1986). Eventually, this began to shift the balance of power from the church and nobility to wealthy merchants and financiers. The result was a uniquely Western

form of social organization that concentrated and centralized political, social, and economic power in a narrow elite that completely dominated and marginalized the vast majority of the population (Mann 1986). This internal subordination and colonization of the European populace provided the groundwork and worldview that would drive concentrated efforts by European nations to externally colonize nations and peoples. In particular, feudal relations of land and labour based on direct forms of political domination were replicated in sixteenth- and seventeenth-century colonial practices in eastern North America, which were then transformed into more successful modern practices of capitalist agriculture in the eighteenth and nineteenth centuries (Graham 2011; Dunbar-Ortiz 2014).

In the seventeenth century, the evolution of "royal absolutism" as a form of government further centralized power, limited upward mobility, and reinforced the structures of internal colonization. Within this system, the King became supreme ruler over the lesser feudal lords within his territory, with their lands and titles being his to bestow, rather than as traditionally familial fiefdoms held independently by custom (Bonney 1991). In the Middle Ages power was more decentralized and the King was the first among equals, often being elected from among the nobility to serve as their leader (Gierke 1993). The European war system, however, had resulted in the subordination of the nobility as well, as large numbers became subservient to, and dependent on, royal power institutionalized in the state bureaucracy (Giddens 1985). The King's law and power took precedence over local authority within what had become an imperial dominion. Within this "dominion," the monarchy literally dominated everything, including local laws, customs, and traditions, all of which were abolished and replaced with the state's "universal" authority (Mann 1986). Noble families found themselves challenged and diminished by the king's court-appointed administrators, whose positions and power were directly dependent on the King. Previously independent towns found their economic liberties and freedoms withdrawn and rewritten to benefit the monarchy (Poggi 1978). As this model of imperial monarchy expanded across Europe, it created a system of independent sovereign states that competed for supremacy in Europe and beyond.

The nobility, frustrated by the centralization of power by the crown, their own loss of power and prestige, socio-economic issues, a transitioning economy, and the rise of a new bourgeoisie, began to stir with notions of revolt (Calder 1998). Charges of tyranny against Kings, their inner Councils, and their bureaucrats increased (Locke 1995). As an effective strategy for releasing internal tensions that were building towards the centre of European power, Kings began to send nobles to the frontiers of their empires on great expeditions of conquest, conversion, and colonization (Giddens 1985). On the northern and western edges of empire, barbarian and Celtic "tribes" were forcibly incorporated as subordinate vassals and protectorate kingdoms (Canny 2001). To the south and east, Crusaders exiled entire Jewish communities and invaded and confiscated Muslim lands, properties, and titles (Wright 2001). Eurocentric concepts of divine right and natural law gave the European conquerors confidence that they had full sovereignty and authority over the peoples and lands they conquered. Defeated enemies could only retain their traditional lands, titles, and properties by converting to Christianity and submitting to imperial authority (Canny 2001). The Imperial Monarch was then free to redistribute the war gains back to the leaders of the formerly independent nations that were now under the King's control.

Despite efforts to quell rebellion, over time Europe underwent a massive social revolution due to the growing distance between the elite and the majority of the population and the continued exclusion of the nobility and wealthy classes from power. The resistance movements found support in theories about the right of resistance to tyrants developed by theorists such as John Locke and Jean-Jacques Rousseau. Writing about the natural rights of man, these modern liberal political theorists challenged the traditional model's ideological foundations and practical applications. As the popularity and acceptance of these philosophies grew, notions of divine right and pedigree as the basis for established social hierarchies were no longer accepted as valid.

These new philosophical ideas were instrumental to the advent of the Enlightenment, the seventeenth- and eighteenth-century intellectual revolution that moved Europe from the traditional model of divine right and feudalism to the scientific era and modern liberal state. The old feudal order simply could not withstand the onslaught of bourgeois competitive capitalism and its ideology of individualism, economic liberty, and infinite progress. This set in motion what social historian Karl Polanyi describes as the "Great Transformation" in which modern industrial capitalism replaced pre-modern feudal systems of village subsistence agriculture and small-scale artisan production (Polanyi 1944). While this series of shifts radically reshaped who was at the top of the social order in Western European society, it did little to change the structures of inequality and domination, which continued to concentrate power and control in the hands of the new elite. In the Great Transformation, social protection by the state was eroded in favour of market dominance, as the economic came to dominate the social and political rather than the social and political controlling the economic. With this, the land and human labour were transformed and reified as commodities and objects of production (Polanyi 1944).

The Enlightenment Model and the Modern Liberal State

While the Enlightenment brought a certain degree of political and social emancipation to the bourgeois class (wealthy commoners) in Europe, it did not actually change the existing state structures or the basic elements of social organization. It simply changed who was in power. The same coercive bureaucracies that were developed under the crown remained, only now they were deployed by an elite capitalist ruling class, which controlled the majority of wealth and means of production (Sayer 1991). Uniquely Western concepts of absolute and unlimited sovereign authority and prerogative powers continued to be enforced, but now through institutionalized "public powers" such as national legislatures and parliaments (Rousseau 1984). Meanwhile, the gap in power and wealth between the dominant elite and the majority of the population remained unchanged, as did the elites' dependence on the populace as their primary source of production.

The social contract, developed by Thomas Hobbes (1558–1679), became the new prevailing ideology by which the political power and authority of the new elite was justified. Essentially an updated version of original sin, the ideology engendered by the theory of the social contract replaced the traditional notion of divine right while maintaining the hierarchical social structure. Within this modern ideology, "man" was no longer evil, but merely self-interested; man was no longer a communal being, but an abstract individual. The social contract theory asserts that the "original condition" of man was a pre-social and amoral "state of nature" outside of culture and history. To escape this, every human being is automatically party to a social contract through a voluntary act of "free will" that occurs by virtue of one's birth. From this social contract governments emerge to provide the social control needed for society to exist, for Hobbes advocated that without a powerful sovereign to ensure peace,

security, and order—through the creation and enforcement of laws—life would be "nasty, brutish and short" (Hobbes 1994).

Of course, this new ideology did little to help the lower classes, as the bourgeois class merely inserted itself into the well-worn and established systems of class, gender, and racial oppression that had supported their predecessors. In the eighteenth century, only substantial men of considerable property were eligible to participate in the political system; all others (women, slaves, the poor, and the working class) were deemed too irrational and/or dependent to exercise mature political judgment (Kant 1991). The new liberal social and economic order replicated the old hierarchies of masters and slaves, husbands and wives. However, this was done without any of the moral boundaries and constraints that kept these unequal social relations from being explicitly exploitative under the traditional divine right model. Indeed, social contract theory was fundamentally divorced from notions of morality, as the new ideology saw morality as an irrational construct, good and evil as constructed products of civil society, and men as naturally self-interested (Hobbes 1994).

Power remained concentrated within an elite class of white male property owners, but the concept of property now extended beyond land to include commercial and industrial property. Existing religious and legal systems of dynastic monarchy that had secured property were simply transformed by the new capitalist order. This was in order to justify elite domination through individual effort rather than noble birth (Macpherson 1975). In the new liberal order, material success was a sign of salvation, while the pursuit of wealth, rather than being vulgar, was understood as an outward sign of moral superiority (Weber 1997). In a society that valued individual effort and responsibility, those at the bottom of the social order (the working classes and the poor) were now condemned as indigent, idle, and immoral, regardless of their level of productivity and effort.

Hobbes's vision of natural man and natural

rights also came to form the theoretical basis for the development of nineteenth-century positivist social science, economics, and history. In place of the traditional model's ethical standards of human well-being and ecological balance, ideologies of unlimited power, control, and progress came to dominate all fields of human knowledge, including both the natural and social sciences (Marcuse 1972). The separation of Church and State was a central aspect of this modernizing process, as both politics and economics lost their internal ethical limits and religious sanction. The "attributes of God" and Universal Truth were transferred to "(Western) Man" as the bearer of a universal, ego-centric, and transcendent point of view (Grosfoguel 2011, 6). The result was a divorce of the physical and metaphysical: as politics and economics lost their internal ethical limits, and holistic approaches to knowledge were no longer seen as legitimate and were subjected to radical doubt (Descartes 2003). Moral and spiritual concerns were relegated to the (private) world of individual conscience and belief, and excluded from (public) rational scientific and capitalist thought and debate. The result of this split between the physical and metaphysical was that modern European culture came to understand nature, and human nature, merely as raw material awaiting rational appropriation and use (Heidegger 1982). Previously held European ideas of divine order and providence were rewritten to become secular national histories based upon stages of development measured in terms of technological progress and productivity (see **Box 9.1** opposite).

The modern scientific model rendered everything, including people and nature, as objects with predictable patterns of behaviour that needed to be observable, quantifiable and rational (Arendt 1989). Attempts to bring "rationality" to human behaviour and social organization resulted in hard science becoming the model for the social sciences (Arendt 1989). The loss of morality in the shift from a religious to a scientific model meant that

European thought came to view the natural world as a wasteland, its only potential value being in humanity's (the elite's) ability to put it into productive use as efficiently and seamlessly as possible (Graham 2011). Human beings, in turn, were no longer defined as social and political by nature, but as self-interested individuals who related to the world through the purely utilitarian calculation of ends and means, costs and benefits, pleasures and pains (Bentham 2001). Western culture came to radically alienate its subjects from both nature and human nature as they were forever torn from the holistic and interconnected web of beings, related and interrelated, within the great mystery of creation. It is this process of alienation, along with the commodification of land and people and the institution of a pervasive hierarchy that continually privileges a powerful elite at the expense of the labour, degradation, abuse, marginalization, and liberty of the vast majority of the populace, that we refer to here as internal colonization.

Modern science also gave the West a self-proclaimed mandate of absolute authority over all other peoples by delegitimizing their forms of knowledge. (See Chapter 1.) Traditional understandings of the distinctions between the material and the spiritual collapsed as all of creation was reduced to a strict materialism. All forms of knowledge based in custom, tradition, religion, and spirituality that governed political, social, and economic relations were considered erroneous, irrational superstitions that needed to be replaced with modernity and the new capitalist order (Marx 1978). Traditional knowledge and understandings of the natural world were also rejected, unless they could be proven using the scientific method. The meaning, truth, and substance of traditional knowledge relied on by the populace in Western nations, by Indigenous nations, and by other foreign nations was discredited and dismissed. In order for Indigenous and foreign nations to become "developed" they would have to give up their traditional ways of knowing, as well as their forms of social

Box 9.1

Human Capital

In speaking with the capitalist and the colonizer: "You ... forget your part in the whole setup, that bureaucracy is one of your inventions, ... and [that] all the laws that you know mysteriously favour you. Do you know why people like me are shy about being capitalists? Well, it's because we, for as long as we have known you, *were* capital, like bales of cotton and sacks of sugar, and you were the commanding, cruel capitalists, and the memory of this is so strong, the experience so recent, that we can't quite bring ourselves to embrace this idea that you think so much of. As for what we were like before we met you, I no longer care ... . [N]o documentation of complex civilizations is any comfort to me. Even if I really came from people who were living like monkeys in trees, it was better to be that than what happened to me, what I became after I met you."

—Jamaica Kincaid, *A Small Place*

organization, and be assimilated by the modern hierarchical model of the west.

The traditional model's legacy of coercive state power and its dynamic of internal and external colonialism found renewed strength and vigour in the ideologies that defined modernity. The oppression, domination, and exploitation of the working class and poor did not change; the new elite merely adopted legitimating ideologies, such as the social contract, that saw inequality as natural and inevitable (Macpherson 1975). Inequality had previously been a product of the idea of divine right, but within the enlightened capitalist ideology it was now justified as the result of a lack of merit. Divorced from notions of morality, the new ideology was at liberty to position the poor as an entirely expendable surplus population. The most extreme example of this was Thomas Malthus's *Essay on the Principle of Population*, first published in 1798 (Malthus 2015), which provided the ideological framework for the state, supported by churches and their charitable organizations, to erect poorhouses, workhouses, and prisons to instruct the lower orders in the virtues of obedience, hard work, and self-control (Hill 1976). For those who proved themselves incapable of improvement at home, there was always the option of deportation abroad, where the criminal and dispossessed classes of Europe could make themselves useful as the indentured servants and foot soldiers of the empire (Kiernan 1978).

Modern Progress and Development: Colonization at Home and Abroad

Internal and external colonial policies and practices served to reinforce and reproduce hierarchies of power and privilege both inside and outside of Europe. The imposition of the modern Western model on other peoples and nations worldwide through colonization and conquest brought massive disenfranchisement, underdevelopment, oppression, and poverty to Indigenous and foreign nations that became subject to the West's exploitative and dictatorial model of social organization (Arendt 1976). Science and capitalism produced new instruments of power and knowledge that were ruthlessly deployed in these imperial efforts. European colonialism differed considerably under the Spanish, French, Dutch, English, and other European nations, but every nation maintained the same common and unquestioned justification for their actions of Western superiority and divine destiny (Pagden 1995).

However, with the shift from traditional to modern models for legitimizing the Western model of social organization, the need arose for a new justification for colonization and the oppression of other nations and territories by European nations. To this end, the traditional justifications of conversion and conquest used by Romans and Christians were replaced in the "modern" era with positivist international law and its theories of treaty and effective occupation (Williams 1990; Slattery 1992). The foundational legal premise for colonial expansion was the Doctrine of Discovery, which justified the appropriation of lands not occupied by a Christian monarch (Dunbar-Ortiz 2014). The Doctrine essentially made the absurd assertion that only European Christians could claim land. The result was that if a European Christian from one side of the world "discovered" land on the other side of the world, that person assumed rights to the land that precluded, denied, and erased the sovereignty and rights of the Indigenous nations and peoples to their own traditional territories (Badcock 1976). This gave rise to settler colonialism, which unlike other forms of colonialism, imagined the land as being empty and open for settlement (Forman and Kedar 2004). The fact that Indigenous peoples, nations, and advanced societies previously existed on the land was easily addressed by systematically denying and erasing any evidence to this effect.

The self-proclaimed right of European Christians to claim the lands and rights of Indigenous peoples, and to impose on them Western models of social organization, has left an important mark on European settler societies. It justified using alleged European superiority to design colonial policies, practices, laws, and all other elements of colonial societies. In 1823, for example, US Chief Justice John Marshall embedded both the Doctrine of Discovery and the myth of European superiority into North American law as a legitimate basis for undermining Indigenous rights and sovereignty:

On the discovery of this immense continent, the great nations of Europe were eager to appropriate to themselves so much of it as

they could respectively acquire... *the character and religion of its inhabitants* afforded an apology for considering them as people over whom the *superior genius of Europe* might claim an ascendancy ... But it was necessary to establish a principle which all [colonial nations] should acknowledge as the law by which the right of acquisition, which they all asserted, should be regulated as *between themselves*. This principle was that *discovery* gave [them] title. (Johnson v. McIntosh 1823; emphasis added)

The emphasis placed by the Doctrine of Discovery on the falsely characterized societies of Indigenous peoples in North America also illustrates how modern Eurocentric "standards of civilization" had become the basis for recognition of other peoples as civilized.

As a result of their own experience in transforming from a traditional model to a modern liberal capitalist model, the West came to believe that this type of transition was a necessary step in the development of all societies (Rostow 1960). This need to transform other societies from their traditional structures to modern Western structures in turn became central to contemporary development theories and practices. The challenge today is to be clear about future choices and future directions. Contemporary neoliberal globalization (see Chapter 3), far from being a departure from and a dismantling of Empire, is merely the transformation and restructuring of the modern model to meet the demands of yet another technological revolution. Moreover, the contemporary model does not restore the balance needed between the physical and metaphysical that was lost during the creation of the Western model of social organization and its foundational beliefs. This balance is necessary to address the Western power dynamics, sense of superiority and privilege, and colonial practices that serve to perpetuate the ongoing disparity and inequality seen at the intersections of class, race, ethnic, and gender oppressions around the world.

Inspiration for how to approach this may be found by reflecting on different Indigenous people's ways of knowing, being, and doing, and how these have been incorporated into their traditional economic and social models of organization.

A Contrasting Approach: The Underlying Tenets of Certain First Nations' Models of Social Organization

[T]he most notable fact connected with women's participation in governmental affairs among the Iroquois is the statement of Hon. George Bancroft that the form of government of the United States was borrowed from that of the Six Nations. Thus to the Matriarchate or Mother-rule [of the Iroquois] is the modern world indebted for its first conception of inherent rights, natural equality of condition, and the establishment of a civilized government ….(Gage 1893)

The notion of Western European superiority espoused by colonial governments and settlers left them ill-equipped to understand the depth and value of the worldviews, societal structures, and knowledge systems of the First Nations that they encountered on Turtle Island. First Nations systems were and are often fundamentally different from the Western model described above. Where the Western model was and is divorced from the metaphysical and emphasizes social hierarchies, capitalist accumulation, and materialism, First Nations models are generally more egalitarian and focused on the interconnections within and between individuals and the natural world. Where the Western elite had to construct and enforce legitimating ideologies to justify their power and domination, this did not happen in First Nations societies, where traditional leadership models are based on community relations, merit, morality, reciprocation, and consensus.

Balance, Responsibility, and Respect: Cooperation, not Conflict

Unlike in the Western societies discussed above, many First Nations societies do not see conflict as a necessary product of society or human interaction (Monture-Okanee 1994). This is a defining differentiation, as without this assumption there is no need to imbue a dominant elite with the power and rights to impose coercive enforcement on the general populace. In contrast, in many First Nations societies, social norms are based on a community ethic and a relational worldview that gives rise to a self-reinforcing model of internalized social control that traditionally holds individuals, collectives, and leadership to account (Monture-Okanee 1994). Such norms and ethics include a socially embedded recognition of the reciprocal relationship between individual and communal responsibilities, the importance of respecting individual rights, and adherence to principles of truth and honesty by all individuals in the society, especially leaders (Monture-Okanee 1994). Truth is commonly understood among First Nations to be multidimensional and complex, due to its multifaceted and dynamic nature, the interplay between elements such as perspective, experience, and relation, and the ways in which truth manifests (Truth and Reconciliation Commission of Canada 2015; L. Shirt 2015). Underestimating the power of truth or allowing oneself to be alienated from it is known to have significant physical and metaphysical consequences. It was commonly understood, for example, that when an individual lies they create a new reality that, if not corrected, can have significant impacts, including forcing them to live an unnatural path in life. The result of this approach was that traditionally truth, honesty, and responsibility were lived practices in the daily life of individuals in these First Nations. This gave rise to social norms that required and expected individuals to take responsibility for their actions in a forthright manner; to do otherwise being an offence to the notion of justice (Monture-Okanee 1994).

Historically, this framework provided these First Nations societies with a successful formula for resolving interpersonal and inter-nation conflicts and maintaining communal harmony, without giving coercive powers to a dominating elite. Essentially, balance, peace, and social order was self-maintained through respectful and reciprocal relationships among individuals.

Within many First Nations cultures, such as the Anishinabeg and Haudenosaunee, balanced relations between men and women are essential to achieving this level of community well-being. The egalitarian models developed by these nations reflect the codependent nature of the relationship between men and women. Within many of these frameworks men are generally respected for their physical and spiritual strength, while women are respected for their mental and spiritual strength. Historically, the voices of women have been correspondingly held in high regard in many First Nations societies. In Anishinabeg nations, for example, it is said that the women are the "heart of the nation" (Compton 2012). Mother Earth and women have traditionally been honoured in these nations for the responsibility and authority they must carry as both the source and caretakers of life, and for their roles as the keepers of essential resources like the waters and knowledge (L. Shirt 2015; Jacobs 2000; Simpson 2011). In Haudenosaunee Confederacy nations, prior to assimilation efforts by Europeans, women— not men—possessed the right to vote for leaders and had the power to remove leaders for failing to carry out their responsibilities (Porter 2008, 115; Native North American Travelling College 1984). Within First Nations worldviews, respectful relations and relative power between women and men are often a reflection of the balance between the spiritual and physical. When an individual, community, or culture loses this balance, it is manifested in the harsh and unjust treatment of women and Mother Earth (the environment), which generally extends to children and other living things. When this occurs, conflict is a natural by-product that can

only be addressed by regaining balance in relationships between men and women. In considering the value of these Indigenous approaches, it is important to ask whether the beliefs that allowed for the historic lack of gender balance in Western society also contributed to the "chaos" that St. Augustine, Hobbes, and other Europeans observed in their own nations.

The importance of relationships forms the basis for the worldviews of many Indigenous peoples. This includes: the relationships of individuals to each other; the relationship of individuals with the earth; the relationship of individuals with the spiritual and the metaphysical. This concept of **relationality** is central to the Lakota concept of Mitakuye Oyasin and the Anishinabe concept of Nii-ka-nii-ga-naa, or "all my relations." It is also articulated in the words, actions, daily activities, and protocols of numerous First Nations. The Ohén:ton Karihwatéhkwen, or Opening Address of the Mohawk nation, which translates as "what we say before we do anything important" (Porter 2008, 5, 9) serves as an example of how relationality is incorporated into the daily activities of Mohawk people. The Opening Address is literally something that is said before anything important is done. It speaks to and acknowledges the "essence of ... our existence" through its recognition of and thanksgiving for all of the relationships we have to each other (men and women, family, village, community, nation), to the earth, the waters, the sun and moon, the sacred winds and sacred beings, and to all of creation from the smallest insect, bird, and plant to the largest and beyond (Porter 2008, 8–26). It also emphasizes the importance of kindness and gratitude and the respect that is essential to maintaining good relations and well-being within and between all people. It is a "skeleton key to the world we live in ... [it] opens up all things for us," not just for Indigenous peoples but all the peoples of the world (Porter 2008, 26). It is the "universal truth" that survival and well-being are grounded in all of our relationships; something all peoples once knew and to which we all must return if we are to live in balance and prosperity (ibid.).

The emphasis that Indigenous peoples place on relationality is important for understanding Indigenous social and economic organization, ontology, and ways of knowing, being, and doing. To ensure that it will remain a living piece of knowledge, it is passed down through stories, illustrated in symbolic expressions, and practiced through traditional methodologies and societal structures. Here, too, it is important to reflect on the differences between Indigenous and Western models. Where Western traditions dictate that knowledge should be referenced to an individual or small group of immediate authors, Indigenous ways of knowing, being, and doing often see knowledge as being the product of an intergenerational collective. This perspective is actualized by a constant recognition of and respect for all those who came before us to create the knowledge we hold today, and an ongoing mindfulness of how we will bring that knowledge to the next generation. This model centres a person within the universe and humbles them as being only a small part of a larger world, with responsibilities that extend back into the past, forward into the future, and laterally to all those who currently share the world with us.

Reciprocal Political and Economic Relations: Inclusive Decision-Making

Traditional leadership models common among First Nations are generally based on moral leadership and merit. The role of leaders in Haudenosaunee nations is to act as an advisor to the people working to achieve their goals (Native North American Travelling College 1984, 30). Mutual respect between leaders and the community is not only expected, but demanded (Alfred 1999, 91). The active participation of the community in determining the society's goals means that consent is essential prior to political action. This approach necessitates open and honest communication, as leaders are held accountable for "maintaining an unbroken chain of answerability and inclusion in decision-making" (ibid.). Within this model, social esteem, as opposed to control and coercion, provides the primary means for moving the community forward towards a common goal. As noted by Mohawk author Taiaiake Alfred, "in a culture deeply respectful of individual autonomy, the only real political power consists in the ability to persuade" (1999, xix).

Within Anishinabe leadership traditions, there existed a system of leadership where specific individuals would have certain responsibilities relating to and granted by their community. If a specific leader ever acted outside of the expected roles of truth, honesty, and responsibility, the community would no longer follow that individual and another leader would be selected to take their place, based on their merit and wisdom. From a macro-governance level, when decisions affecting the entire nation were needed, several leaders would come together to form a sacred fire circle where they would discuss the relevant issues and make decisions based on the best interests of the whole nation, even if that decision was not in the best interests of the individual leaders.

In many First Nations, traditional leadership-based governance finds legitimacy in decision-making that comes from a place of consensus rather than supremacy. Consensus in a traditional sense may not mean that everyone agrees, but rather that everyone has spoken his or her concerns and opinions and they agree to move forward together despite differences in viewpoints. This is often done in a circle format, which structurally reaffirms that all participants are equal. All those involved have the responsibility to look after the needs of all of the people and reflect the will of all the people. Consensus allows everyone to have a voice in discussions and debate. In the end, participants only leave when they are satisfied with what has been said. At that point all must follow the decision, even if some still disagree. In this context, the role of leadership is not to make the decision on behalf of all; it is to make sure everyone's voice is heard, to mitigate conflicts, and to negotiate a decision that is in the best interest of the entire community or, in the case of a sacred fire circle, in the best interest of the entire nation. Given these requirements on leadership, it is essential that leaders possess specific qualities and abilities to be effective. As a result, both the nature and abilities of those selected as leaders is often embedded in societal norms, leadership structures, selection processes, or the constitutions of the various Confederacies and individual First Nations.

Unfortunately, the result of the intersection of European notions of superiority and the relational approach of First Nations to knowledge, economics, politics, power, and social organization, was the emergence of a large body of Eurocentric myths, disinformation, and false conceptions about First Nations and other Indigenous peoples. Within Western society, this body of misinformation served to further justify the legitimating ideologies of the European colonialists and their self-imposed mandate to develop and civilize Indigenous peoples (Barsh 1986, 181). The end result was a pervasive and self-reinforcing monologue within European and settler communities in Canada and elsewhere that devalued and infantilized the cultures and societies of First Nations, as well as the Inuit, Métis, and other Indigenous peoples. This monologue also reinforced a paternalistic approach to relations with First Nations by succeeding colonial governments, up to and including the current Canadian government. This includes the imposition of policies, processes, and development projects that have not been in the best interests of the First Nations, Métis, Inuit, or other Indigenous peoples that they purport to assist. This body of myths also allowed settler-nations like Canada and the United States to dismiss the social, political, economic, and technological benefits that they acquired through interactions with Indigenous peoples, which include the acquisition of advanced feats of technology and engineering, the structures that are the basis of the United States' model of government, as well as the inspiration for the Women's Rights Movement and Socialism (Sage 1893; Grinde 1991; Coates 2015; Wagner 2001).

Finally, the historic and ongoing use of European languages as the primary means of learning about First Nations' ways of life is also fundamentally problematic, as European languages were developed to give voice to the European worldview, including its model of social organization and legitimating ideologies. European languages, including English, have historically lacked the words and concepts needed to understand First Nation's social and economic models of organization, ontology, and ways of knowing, being, and doing. Today, efforts to move beyond these barriers to understanding in order to correct the historical record and create space for First Nations, Métis, Inuit, and other Indigenous models are essential to reconciliation between Indigenous peoples and settlers within Canada and worldwide. While neoliberalism claims to allow space for traditionalism, there is a long way to go in order to see traditional ways of knowing as equal to mainstream knowledge. A new discursive space is required to decolonize not only the systems in place but also the minds of settlers and their leaders. This will provide a basis for moving away from notions that traditional ways of knowing are quaint or colloquial and allow for a true understanding of the value these models offer for improving and benefiting from the relationship individuals and societies have to each other, their communities, and the environment.

Within Canada there is a growing consciousness of the country's past and ongoing injustices and abuses against First Nations, Métis, and Inuit people. This collective awareness is supported by the results of public inquires, such as the Truth and Reconciliation Commission (TRC 2015) and the Royal Commission on Aboriginal Peoples, and a growing number of social movements by Indigenous and non-Indigenous peoples. There is a need to understand the relational shift that is happening both within and between the nation and at the grass-roots level.

Resistance to the Western Model of Social Organization and Development: Contemporary Social Movements and Decolonization

As one might start to notice, history seems to repeat itself in slightly different ways. The genealogy of early colonialism presented above demonstrates how systems of domination have been repeated under new guises within the development of Western nations. Even in the aftermath of social revolutions and political institutional change, the familiar systems and patterns of domination, such as the centralization of wealth and power, remain stubbornly in place. This does not mean that such movements are useless or ineffective. Rather, identifying the shortcomings of social and political movements for change can help us in designing more effective and transformative ones.

A recurrent problem with many movements is that they are not intersectional. This means that they do not consider the interconnected and overlapping aspects of oppression and how those aspects reinforce inclusion and exclusion between and across social groups. In addition to the familiar sociological variables for social exclusion, such as race, class, and gender, there are some often ignored or marginalized variables: Eurocentrism, heterosexism, ableism, and ageism. Without accounting for how these variables intersect, progressive social movements can contain and perpetuate different forms of oppressions—often because they seek one narrow end goal. Having a narrow end goal becomes problematic when it leads to a hierarchy of priorities that require time, money, and social resources, the acquisition of which reproduces the very inequality the movement is resisting.

Knowledge and action are both invariably tied to interest, and an academic division between expertise and advocacy based upon strategic and short-term decision making, that replicates the kind of fragmented and partial thinking that is at the root of this problem. As a consequence, some individuals within a movement may feel left out. There are countless examples of this, such as Marxist movements that did not account for a feminist analysis. (See Chapter 1.) Many feminist movements themselves have also been explicitly racist by limiting their scope to the human rights of white middle-class women. Anti-racist movements have also often failed to take into account the voices of women of colour, or again to acknowledge the inherent rights of Indigenous peoples, including Indigenous claims to sovereignty and self-determination on the lands where these different social movements engage in their multiple and often competing struggles.

Indigenous Resistance, Resurgence, and Reconciliation

Resistance movements by Indigenous peoples are generally aimed towards or embody decolonization. To decolonize, as we define it, requires a deconstruction of a given Western model, a collective and genuine acceptance of the validity of that deconstruction, and a willingness to name, engage with, and change present colonial practices. Importantly, decolonization is linked to land justice, which is not a simple equivalent of the goals of Western social movements (Alfred 2015). Land justice means the return of stolen and disenfranchised land, as well as compensation and restitution for its loss and the loss of natural resources that have been and continue to be removed due to colonization. Decolonization is—among other things—a complex social and political movement grounded in the goals of Indigenous self-determination and land return (Tuck and Yang 2012). It involves addressing the impacts of colonization and creating equal space for

Indigenous peoples, their laws and institutions, their economic systems, and their cultural and spiritual knowledge, as well as their approaches to social organization and power, as explored earlier in this chapter.

Decolonization enables Indigenization and, in turn, Indigenization is crucial to reconciliation. Indigenization is the process of Indigenous peoples self-determining how the spaces created through decolonization are to be used. The use of those spaces may include, for example, how lands that were stolen and returned will be used or even how to Indigenize the academy. The process of Indigenization is grounded in existing Indigenous ways of knowing, being, and doing that can potentially radically challenge and restructure the dominant society, including some of its most basic and fundamental beliefs such as its own sense of superiority and what counts as "civilization."[2] At the same time, the purpose of Indigenization must not simply be the improvement, development, or progress of Western societies, but the emancipation of the power and creative energies of Indigenous peoples in and for their own communities. Indigenous nations and peoples are resisting colonization and Western models of social organization in order to exercise their international right to national self-determination and to be free of oppression and occupation on their own lands.

The goal of Indigenous peoples' movements is generally to reassert or maintain their existing coherent, powerful, and functioning social and economic structures and established societies. These existing solutions and structures are important elements lacking in many Western social movements, which are by definition institutionally fluid and prone to change. While flexibility can be an asset, lack of solidity, permanence, and a strategic plan for moving society forward can also be an organizational problem, as commitment and enthusiasm is often voluntary and informal, while resources are insecure and unreliable. Having established social structures and sound options for addressing the social issues that are at the centre of a social movement are important assets for creating and sustaining change in the long term.

For example, while the Occupy Movement enjoyed a level of popularity and managed to mobilize large masses of protesters for limited and specific actions; its long-term viability was called into question by its lack of organization, its inability to equitably acquire and distribute resources, and its lack of sound and collectively supported structures that can be implemented in order to realize the desired change.

---

2. To illustrate the difference between decolonizing and Indigenizing, imagine a standard Western university classroom where the seats are stationary and face the front. This configuration implies a hierarchy between the professor and the students. In an Indigenized classroom, the chairs would likely be set up in a circle, implying egalitarianism between the teacher and students, a perception reinforced by First Nations pedagogies/Indigegogies that highlight student participation and respect, and the inherent value of all participants and their knowledge, without precluding recognition of the immediate relevance of the knowledge of some participants, such as the professor. This Indigenized classroom, however, is still required to adhere to the rules of the Western university paradigm, unless the whole university and pedagogical paradigm have been decolonized. So the course itself is not decolonized, as the professor must still provide assignments, grade papers, and so on, in accordance with the Western model. In contrast, a fully decolonized and/or Indigenized course would also employ different methods of student assessment, a different conception of class time, and in all other ways be constructed using Indigenous pedagogical knowledge, principles, and methods.

Differences and Similarities between Indigenous and Non-Indigenous Movements

With the above reflections in mind, we can take a look at contemporary movements for change, such as the Occupy (the "99 percent" Movement) and Indigenous movements like "Idle No More," to explore the challenges and opportunities posed by intersectionality. The Occupy Movement started with Occupy Wall Street in New York in 2011. It was inspired by the Arab Spring. (See Case Study 10.) The aim of the Occupy movement is straightforward: equal rights and access to resources and wealth for everyone. The Idle No More movement is an example of an Indigenous resistance movement that was initiated in Canada by Indigenous women (Nina Wilson, Sylvia McAdam, Jessica Gordon, Sheelah McLean) and extended internationally, drawing broad support from Indigenous and non-Indigenous peoples. It continues to work towards a peaceful resistance that honours Indigenous sovereignty and protects the land and the waters.

Resistance to wealth inequality and the concentration of power in an elite few is an important goal of Occupy, but definitely not a new one. The masses of Western civilization have, throughout history, had problems with domination by an elite. The concern is that the Occupy movement will fail, as other social revolutions in the past have failed, because it has chosen to focus narrowly on the wealth gap and economic inequality. In order to help resolve this issue, something new is required: a greater and more holistic critical engagement with power and the overlapping structures of oppression. To get at such an analysis, not only the institutional structures of Western society, but also the ideological foundations of domination itself as central to the Western model of social organization and development, must be addressed.

Sometimes, in order to better understand the hegemonic power of the dominant culture, a critical encounter with difference and other ways of knowing and being is required. At the same time, such an engagement must be grounded in dialogue, equality, and respect; otherwise, cultural appropriation will simply become yet another form of objectification and exploitation. Those constructed as "non-Westerners," including Indigenous peoples and their philosophies, are alive and well, and not some frozen relics of a traditional and/or authentic past, ready to be used and abused for the benefit of privileged people, especially academics.

The Idle no More Movement and the Occupy Movement share a common concern with inequality and social solidarity. However, while there are certainly similarities between the Idle No More and the Occupy movements, there are also many differences. Internal systems of domination exist within progressive social movements. For instance, many of them do not challenge the "persistent and pervasive" invasion (Barker 2012, 328, 329) that is settler colonialism. The persistent and pervasive invasion means that most social movements do not take into account how most parts of society are invested and interested in the future and continuation of the settler-colonial status quo in North America. In certain respects, this is also the case with the Occupy movement, because Indigenous peoples are a super minority within it (Tuck and Yang 2012, 23).

And where the Occupy movement lacks a defined and tried solution, many Indigenous nations have long-standing methods for redistributing wealth that are embedded in political, social, and economic systems and are often not considered a separate field of social action. The potlatch system practiced by the Southern Kwakiutl, Sliammon, and other First Nations are examples of this type of structure, which are premised on the central principle of wealth redistribution as a source of social power and prestige; such an institutionalized practice ensures that political and economic power remain balanced and relational (Washington 2004; Ringel 1979).

Indigenous resistance and resurgence are thus often more than social movements, as they come with established approaches to creating change that include addressing social issues created through colonization. While many have grouped Indigenous resurgence and resistance movements into the category of "new social movements," they are perhaps more accurately described as communities organizing for autonomy and to preserve their own political cultural space. By their very existence and their inherent rights to land and self-determination, Indigenous movements also present a deeper challenge to neoliberalism than other movements

(Hall 2008a, 1880). It thus makes sense for social movements to reflect on and learn from Indigenous models, while ensuring that Indigenous cultural knowledge is not misappropriated.

Indigenous self-determination (as defined in the UN Declaration on the Rights of Indigenous Peoples [UNDRIP]) (United Nations 2007) has considerable potential to influence the unrelenting drive towards globalization and capitalist expansion, which relies on access to land for exploitation and extraction of natural resources. Among other reasons, Indigenous self-determination would mean that the final decision-making power about natural resources—a right coveted by transnational capitalist corporations—could be returned to the traditional holders of the land. Since Indigenous peoples often hold very different perspectives on the land, they may not allow forms of extractive development that are unsustainable or run contrary to their worldviews. This is especially true of communities where the implementation of the decision-making right alleviates some of the impacts of dispossession and the conditions of dependency created by colonization.

Because of the obstacles that may be posed by Indigenous resistance and resurgence, and the various forms of decolonization that may come with it, Indigenous movements are often harshly opposed. Alternatively, they may be severely compromised, such that they lose core values and potential, by being made to fit into Western institutions and worldviews. An example would be using the language of decolonization and Indigenization to give the appearance of change on the surface without actually engaging with and changing underlying structures. At other times, Indigenous movements are dismissed altogether as something unnecessary or already achieved; for instance, the belief that Canada is in a post-colonial era.

Therefore, while neoliberal states may give the appearance of encouraging and welcoming cultural differences on the surface, they simultaneously implement macroeconomic policies that are destructive of Indigenous economic and socio-political systems (Sieder 2011, 247; Coulthard 2014, 7). For example, we will openly hear ideas of inclusion and multiculturalism as long as the authority of Canada in accessing stolen land and its resources is not seriously threatened. The imperative of development and of global neoliberal economics continues to displace Indigenous peoples, and exploit their lands and natural resources, largely for the benefit of an elite few, thereby replicating colonial practices and relations of power. In North America, Indigenous peoples continue to oppose these colonial practices through the courts, but also through a variety of direct actions including anti-pipeline, anti-fracking, and anti-mining protests, like for example those held in Tsleil-Waututh's Burnaby Mountain, the Unitst'ot'en's Wet'suwet'en camp, the Standing Rock Sioux Nation, and in the Lakota Black Hills. The great numbers of conflicts and resistances occurring demonstrate how "colonial domination continues to be structurally committed to maintain, through force, fraud, or negotiations, ongoing state access to the land and resources" of Indigenous peoples (Coulthard 2014, 7). It is crucial for any social movements to centre and support decolonization if they do not want to replicate or be part of these larger structures of dispossession. For this reason, the Occupy movement may be seen as problematic, because it has assumed that the riches obtained through pre-existing and continuing colonial occupation rightfully belong to the settler masses.

Still, there are many complex, intersectional, and progressive avenues for solidarity between Indigenous-led movements and other social movements. Globalization has also made possible the establishment of many of these connections, both domestically and internationally. The internationalization of the Idle No More movement and its extensive support by non-Indigenous people is an excellent example of this. Thus, in certain contexts, spaces are created for Indigenous communities to strategically form alliances with non-Indigenous movements that may have struggles in common (Blaser 2004, 35–36). Creating such lines of solidarity can lead to the combining of resources, knowledge, and capacity to achieve greater impacts.

Decolonization: Creating a Paradigm Change

Each revolution necessitates a rising of the masses, or the majority. Of course, it is normal that some diversity in opinion and tactics will exist within such huge movements. However, it becomes particularly problematic when power relations are sidelined under the pretext that a main goal of the movement is the most important right now. In the case of Occupy, the ideal of ending wealth inequality is indeed an attractive one for the regular citizen. So what is the moral of the story? How can we achieve a change that takes everyone into account, and the intersections of the experiences of certain groups? Can liberations be achieved together, since our oppressions are bound together in complicated ways that we are just starting to understand? Perhaps what is required is a plan and a structure for what is meant to be achieved by the social movement rather than just the ideal. Unfortunately, even though many social movements seeking change may result in new discussions and slight change on the ground, they are also very likely to be absorbed and/or involved in the setting up of slightly changed systems of domination. Perhaps decolonization can provide a different paradigm. Decolonization can point to an emerging but tangible paradigm in which to live differently. In practice, it can mean a world where more is expected from our leaders and one where reciprocity in all relationships is necessary and conflict is not.

Conclusion

This chapter has sought to explain the interplay between the social, economic, and political conditions under which colonialism and "modernized" forms of development were constructed. It then explained how these systems of domination were employed to subordinate and/or internally colonize the populace of Western nations. This was followed by an outline of how colonization was exported to foreign and Indigenous nations, and the processes through which both internal and external colonization continues to be maintained and replicated today. It then offered a window into Indigenous worldviews and social structures as a point of comparison and contrast. Through this process, it is hoped that the habitual superiority complex of Eurocentric theory and history will be challenged, or at least questioned, by being brought into full and self-conscious view. The argument is made that First Nations, Métis, and Inuit peoples have intact social, political, and economic systems that have served them well in the past and that are still vital and alive in the contemporary context. As Indigenous people have survived and continue to survive colonialism on their lands, it is time for the settler society to begin to make the internal, critical changes that are necessary to rebuild relations. Contemporary social movements by Indigenous peoples and Western peoples are one means of resisting the perpetuation of the colonial mandate, which seeks to funnel the labour, resources, and energy, both physical and spiritual, of the majority of humankind to the benefit of an elite few ("the 1 percent"). Such a concentration of wealth and power is both unsustainable and unconscionable; social movements of resistance, including Indigenous movements like Idle No More, need to continue to grow and have a global impact if change is to be achieved.

We have reviewed in a very short space how the continuing processes of oppression, exploitation, and dispossession of the majority, whether Indigenous or non-Indigenous, have been rationalized and normalized within the Western model of social organization. In the broader context of Indigenous peoples and Western nations worldwide, the organized violence of state power and the exploitative relations of neoliberal capitalism, colonial development, and globalization can all be viewed as the latest incarnation of an imposed hierarchical Western imperial order. This is a consequence of the emphasis on progress as a linear understanding of development, and the ongoing assertion of the superiority of Western technological prowess over and against all "others" it encounters. This concept is grounded in the idea that the goals of development—which in this context are limited to the adoption of Western models—impose a universal approach to progress founded on Western norms, classical science, the politics of control, and the economics of accumulation. It manifests in the contemporary commitment of modern development to transform all Indigenous or "traditional" societies into liberal capitalist societies. Viewed in this light, globalization and development can be seen as a mutating process that enables the continuation of the hierarchical conditions imposed by Western colonization, both internally and externally. Consequently, contemporary neoliberal theories of development are imbued, though not necessarily intentionally, with colonial constructs that continue to replicate Western cultural imperialism. Decolonization and Indigenization remain the challenge of our time; a challenge we have the responsibility and the power to meet with both heart and mind.

Questions for Further Learning

- Explain "development colonialism" in your own words. Identify examples within Canada.
- Discuss the Western myth of superiority and how it is replicated in development practices today. Is the term development inherently colonial? What alternatives exist?
- How does Western development reproduce internal colonialism?
- What does it mean to divide social development between traditional and modern forms?
- How is the concentration of social, economic, and political power in an elite problematic?
- What is settler colonialism and how does it support Western cultural dominance?
- What kinds of insights can be gained through learning about Indigenous social structures?
- What are frequent problems recurring in social movements, and how can they be addressed?
- Discuss your understanding of the differences between decolonization and social movements, and how they can intersect.

Key Terms

Aboriginal Peoples, p. 176	First Nations, p. 164	relationality, p. 174
development, p. 163	governance, p. 163	traditional leadership, p. 173
divine right, p. 164	Indigenous, p. 163	Western culture, p. 165
Enlightenment, p. 164	Indigenous social movements, p. 164	

Suggested Readings

Abu-Zahra, Nadia, and Adah Kay. 2013. *Unfree in Palestine: Registration, Documentation and Movement Restriction*. London: Zed Books.

Alfred, Gerald Taiaiake. 2009. "Colonialism and state dependency." *Journal of Aboriginal Health*. November.

Benton-Banai, Edward. 1988. *The Mishomis Book: The Voice of the Ojibway*. Minneapolis, MN: University of Minnesota Press, and Hayward, WI: Indian Country Communications.

Corntassel, Jeff. 2008. "Toward Sustainable Self-Determination: Rethinking the Contemporary Indigenous-Rights Discourse." *Alternatives: Global, Local, Political* 33 (1): 105–132.

Coulthard, Glen. 2007. "Subjects of Empire: Indigenous Peoples and the 'Politics of Recognition' in Canada." *Contemporary Political Theory* 6 (4): 437.

Gehl, Lynn. 2004. "The Rebuilding of a Nation: A Grassroots Analysis of the Nation-Building Process in Canada." *Canadian Journal of Native Studies* 23 (1): 57–82.

———. 2005. "'Oh Canada! Your Home is Native Land': The Algonquin land claim process." *Atlantis* 29 (2): 148–150.

Langdon, Jonathan. 2013. "Decolonising Development Studies: Reflections on Critical Pedagogies in Action." *Canadian Journal of Development Studies* 34 (3): 384–399.

Lee, Erica Violet. 2015. *That Deadly Academic Silence: Outspoken Indigenous Students & Unsettling the Canadian University*. Online at: moontimewarriorblogspot.com.

McCoy, Kate, Eve Tuck, and Marcia McKenzie, eds. 2016. *Land Education: Rethinking Pedagogies of Place from Indigenous, Postcolonial, and Decolonizing Perspectives*. New York: Routledge.

Rynard, Paul. 2001. "Ally or Colonizer? The Federal State, the Cree Nation and the James Bay Agreement." (Abstract). *Journal of Canadian Studies* 36 (2): 8.

Sidanius, Jim, and Felicia Pratto. 2012. "Social Dominance Theory." In *Handbook of Theories of Social Psychology*, edited by Paul Van Lange, Arie Kruglanski, and E. Tory Higgins. London: Sage Publications.

Tuck, Eve, and K. Wayne Yang. 2012. "Decolonization is Not a Metaphor." *Decolonization: Indigeneity, Education & Society* 1 (1), 1–40.

Suggested Videos

Faith Spotted Eagle, Confronting settler colonialism. https://vimeo.com/198902656

Gord Downie, The Secret Path https://www.youtube.com/watch?v=yGd764YU9yc

Poor Us: An animated history of poverty—Why poverty? fod.infobase.com/PortalPlaylists.aspx?wID=99232&xtid=55240.

The Storytellers Documentary, http://www.firstnationsfilms.com/

Suggested Websites

Assembly of First Nations: http://www.afn.ca/index.php/en

Decolonial Atlas: https://decolonialatlas.wordpress.com/

Global Social Theory: http://globalsocialtheory.org/topics/decoloniality/

Inuit Tapiriit Kanatami: https://www.itk.ca/

Métis Nation: http://www.metisnation.ca/

Native Solidarity: https://nativesolidarity.org/

The Hence Forward: http://www.thehenceforward.com/

The Onaman Collective: http://onamancollective.com/

Unsettling America: https://unsettlingamerica.wordpress.com/

Works Cited

Alfred, Taiaiake. 1999. *Peace, Power, Righteousness: An Indigenous Manifesto.* Don Mills, ON: Oxford University Press.

Anaya, James. 2004. *Indigenous Peoples in International Law.* Oxford: Oxford University Press.

Arendt, Hannah. 1976. *The Origins of Totalitarianism.* New York: Harcourt Brace.

———. 1989. *On the Human Condition.* Chicago: University of Chicago Press.

Augustine. 1961. *Confessions.* London: Penguin Classics.

———. 1994. *Political Writings.* Indianapolis: Hackett Publishing Company.

Ayers, Lewis. 2006. *Nicaea and Its Legacy.* New York: Oxford University Press.

Badcock, William. 1976. *Who Owns Canada?: Aboriginal Title and Canadian Courts.* Ottawa: Canadian Association in Support of the Native Peoples.

Barker, Adam. 2012. *Already Occupied: Indigenous Peoples, Settler Colonialism and the Occupy Movements in North America.* Social Movement Studies 11 (3-4): Occupy!

Barsh, Russel. 1986. "The Nature and Spirit of North American Political Systems." *American Indian Quarterly* (Spring), 181–198.

Bentham, Jeremy. 2001. *On Utilitarianism and Government.* Hertfordshire: Wordsworth Edition Ltd.

Blaser, Mario, Harvey Feit, and Glenn McRae. 2004. *In the Way of Development: Indigenous Peoples, Life Projects and Globalization.* London: Zed Books, in association with International Development Research Centre, Ottawa.

Blaut, James. 1993. *The Colonizer's Model of the World: Geographical Diffusionism and Eurocentric History.* London: The Guilford Press.

Bonney, Richard. 1991. *The European Dynastic States 1494–1660.* Oxford: Oxford University Press.

Calder, Angus. 1998. *Revolutionary Empire.* London: Pimlico.

Canny, Nicholas. 2001. "England's New World and Old 1480s–1630s." In *The Oxford History of British Empire, Vol. 1: The Origins of Empire*, edited by Nicholas Canny. Oxford: Oxford University Press.

Cicero. 1999. *On the Commonwealth and on the Laws.* Cambridge: Cambridge University Press.

Coates, Tracy. 2015. "Indigenous dispute resolution and leadership models: A platform for cooperative governance in the Arctic." *Border Crossings: Indigenous Dialogues and Diplomacy from Around the World.* Special Issue of *Diplomat Magazine* 1 (5).

Coleman, Janet. 2000. *A History of Political Thought: From Ancient Greece to Early Christianity.* Oxford: Blackwell Publishers.

Coulthard, Glen. 2014. *Red Skin, White Masks: Rejecting the Colonial Politics of Recognition.* Minneapolis: University of Minnesota Press.

de las Casas, Bartolomé. 1971. *History of the Indies.* New York: Harper and Row.

Descartes, René. 2003. *Discourse on Method and Meditations on First Philosophy.* New Haven: Yale University Press.

Doyle, William. 1992. *The Short Oxford History of the Modern World: The Old European Order (1660–1800).* 2nd ed. Oxford: Oxford University Press.

Dunbar-Ortiz, Roxanne. 2014. *An Indigenous Peoples' History of the United States*. Boston: Beacon Press.

Fanon, Frantz. 1961. *The Wretched of the Earth*. New York: Grove Weidenfeld.

Forman, Geremy, and Alexandre Kedar. 2004. "From Arab Land to 'Israeli Lands': The Legal Dispossession of the Palestinians Displaced by Israel in the Wake of 1948." *Environment and Planning D: Society and Space* 22: 809–830.

Gage, Matilda Joslyn. 1893. *Woman, Church and State*. New York: The Truth Seeker Company. Available at http://www.sacred-texts.com/wmn/wcs/index.htm.

Giddens, Anthony. 1985. *The Nation-State and Violence*. Cambridge: Polity Press.

Gierke, Otto von. 1993. *Political Theories of the Middle Ages*. Cambridge: Cambridge University Press.

Gilson, Étienne. 2002. *God and Philosophy*. 2nd ed. New Haven: Yale University Press.

Graham, Nicole. 2011. *Lawscape: Property, Environment, Law*. Abingdon, UK: Routledge.

Grinde, Donald A., Jr., and Bruce E. Johansen. 1991. *Exemplar of Liberty: Native America and the Evolution of Democracy*. Los Angeles: University of California Press.

Grosfoguel, Ramón. 2011. "Decolonizing Post-Colonial Studies and Paradigms of Political Economy: Transmodernity, Decolonial Thinking, and Global Coloniality." *Transmodernity: Journal of Peripheral Cultural Production of the Luso-Hispanic World* 1 (1).

Hall, Thomas, and James Fenelon. 2008a. "Revitalization and Indigenous Resistance to Globalization and Neoliberalism." *American Behavioral Scientist* 51 (12), 1867–1901.

———. 2008b. "Indigenous Movements and Globalization: What Is Different? What Is the Same?" *Globalizations* 5 (1).

Heidegger, Martin. 1982. *The Question Concerning Technology and Other Essays*. New York: Harper Collins.

Hill, Christopher. 1976. *Reform and Industrial Revolution. Vol. 2*. New York: Penguin.

Hobbes, Thomas. 1994. *Leviathan*. Indiana: Hackett.

Jackson Lears, T.J. 1985. "The Concept of Cultural Hegemony: Problems and Possibilities." *American Historical Review* 90 (3): 567–593.

Jacobs, Beverley. 2000. "International Law/The Great Law of Peace." LL.M. thesis, Saskatoon, University of Saskatchewan.

Johnson v. McIntosh. 1823. 8 Wheaton 543 (US Supreme Court).

Kant, Immanuel. 1991. *Political Writings*. 2nd ed. Cambridge: Cambridge University Press.

Kiernan, Victor. 1978. *America: the New Imperialism: From White Settlement to World Hegemony*. London: Zed Books.

Kincaid, Jamaica. 1988. *A Small Place*. MacMillan.

Locke, John. 1995. *Treatise of Civil Government and A Letter Concerning Toleration*. New York: Irvington Publishers.

Lovejoy, Arthur. 1936. *The Great Chain of Being*. Cambridge, MA: Harvard University Press.

Macpherson, Crawford. 1975. *The Political Theory of Possessive Individualism: Hobbes to Locke*. Oxford: Oxford University Press.

Malthus, Thomas. 2015. *An Essay on the Principle of Population*. London: Penguin Classics.

Mann, Michael. 1986. *The Sources of Social Power, Vol 1: A History of Power from the Beginning to A.D. 1769*. Cambridge: Cambridge University Press.

Marcuse, Herbert. 1972. *One Dimensional Man*. London: Abacus.

Marx, Karl. 1978. "The Communist Manifesto." In *The Marx-Engel Reader*, 2nd ed., edited by Robert Tucker. New York: W.W. Norton.

Monture-Okanee, Patricia. 1994. "Alternative Dispute Resolution: A Bridge to Aboriginal Experience?" In *Qualification For Dispute Resolution: Perspectives on the Debate*, edited by C. Morris, and A. Pirie, 217), . Victoria, BC: University of Victoria Institute for Dispute Resolution.

Muldoon, James. 1998. *Canon Law, the Expansion of Europe, and World Order*. Brookfield: Ashgate.

Native North American Travelling College. 1984. *Traditional Teachings*. Cornwall Island, ON: Native North American Travelling College.

Pagden, Anthony. 1995. *Lords of All the World: Ideologies of Empire in Spain, Britain and France c. 1800*. New Haven: Yale University Press.

Peters, Edward. 1983. *Europe and the Middle Ages*. New Jersey: Prentice Hall Inc.

Poggi, Gianfranco. 1978. *The Development of the Modern State*. London: Hutchinson.

Polanyi, K. 1944. *The Great Transformation*. Boston: Beacon Press.

Porter, Tom. 2008. *And Grandma said … Iroquois Teachings as Passed Down through the Oral Tradition*. Philadelphia, PA: Xlibris Corporation.

Ringel, Gail. 1979. "The Kwakiutl Potlatch: History, Economics, and Symbols." *Ethnohistory* 26 (4).

Rostow, Walt W. 1960. *Stages of Economic Growth: A Non-Communist Manifesto*. Cambridge: Cambridge University Press.

Rousseau, Jean-Jacques. 1984. *A Discourse on Inequality*. London: Penguin Books.

Salée, Daniel. 2006. "Quality of Life of Aboriginal People in Canada: An Analysis of Current Research." *IRPP Choices* 12 (6).

Sayer, Derek. 1991. *Capitalism and Modernity: An Excursus on Marx and Weber*. London: Routledge.

Shirt, Pauline. 2015. Elder, Saddle Lake First Nation, Interview. (Tracy Coates, Interviewer).

Sidanius, Jim, and Felicia Pratto. 2012. "Social Dominance Theory." In *Handbook of Theories of Social Psychology*, edited by Paul Van Lange, Arie Kruglanski, and E. Tory Higgins, 418–439. London: Sage Publications.

Sieder, Rachel. 2011. "'Emancipation' or 'Regulation'? Law, Globalization and Indigenous People's Rights in Post-war Guatemala." *Economy and Society* 40 (2), 239–265.

Simpson, Leanne. 2011. *Dancing on Our Turtle's Back, Stories of Nishnaabeg Recreation, Resurgence and a New Emergence*. Winnipeg: Arbeiter Ring Publishers.

Slattery, Brian. 1992. "Aboriginal Sovereignty and Imperial Claims." In *Co-Existence? Studies in Ontario – First Nations Relations*, edited by Bruce W. Hodgins, Shawn Heard, and John S. Milloy. Peterborough, ON: Trent University, Frost Centre for Canadian Heritage and Development Studies.

Stewart-Harawira, Makere. 2005. *The Indigenous New Responses to Imperial Globalization Order*. London: Zed Books.

Truth and Reconciliation Commission. 2015. *Honouring the Truth, Reconciling for the Future: Summary of the Final Report of the Truth and Reconciliation Commission of Canada*. Ottawa: Truth and Reconciliation Commission of Canada.

Tuck, Eve, and K. Wayne Yang. 2012. "Decolonization is Not a Metaphor." *Decolonization: Indigeneity, Education & Society* 1 (1), 1–40.

United Nations. 2007. *United Nations Declaration on the Rights of Indigenous Peoples (UNDRIP)*. (A/61/I.67 and Add. 1). New York: United Nations.

Venne, Sharon. 1998. *Our Elders Understand our Rights: Evolving International Law Regarding Indigenous Peoples*. Penticton, BC: Theytus Books.

Wagner, Sally. 2001. *Sisters In Spirit: Haudenosaunee (Iroquois) Influence on Early American Feminists*. Summertown: Native Voices.

Washington, Siemthlut Michelle. 2004. "Bringing Traditional Teachings to Leadership." *American Indian Quarterly*. 28(3/4).

Weber, Max. 1997. *From Max Weber: Essays in Sociology*. London: Routledge.

Williams , Robert, Jr. 1990. *The American Indian in Western Legal Thought: The Discourses of Conquest*. New York: Oxford University Press.

Wright, Shelley. 2001. *International Human Rights, Decolonization and Globalization: Becoming Human*. London: Routledge.

Notes

10 Development Colonialism in a Canadian Context

Tracy Coates, Rodney Nelson, and Kathlean Fitzpatrick

Key Terms

Aboriginal

Anishinabe

Bimaadiziwin

Cree

development colonialism

epistemology

First Nations

Haudenosaunee

Indian Act

Inuit

Nunavut

Métis

relational worldview

self-determination

seven generations philosophy

Yukon

Overview

This chapter explores a few of the ideologies, social structures, and worldviews shared by certain First Nations, as well as the Métis and Inuit (FNMI).[1] Successful present-day Indigenous[2] businesses that have sought to incorporate a more traditionally balanced approach to development are presented to illustrate how opportunities for self-determined development[3] can result in greater economic stability and community well-being. These concepts are presented in such a way as to illustrate for the reader how imposed—as opposed to self-determined— development strategies may operate at the expense of those they purport to assist. Tools to help ensure that new development projects promote self-determination and preserve traditional principles and models of social organization and economic development are provided.

Learning Objectives

By the end of this chapter, students will be able to:

- discuss examples of some First Nations approaches to social organization and economic systems that existed in North America prior to the discovery of colonial settlers on Indigenous territories.
- understand some of the common attributes of First Nations epistemology and how these inform their approaches to social organization and economic systems.
- explain the concept of development colonialism with examples related to First Nations in Canada.
- describe examples of successful First Nations businesses that are sustainable and grounded in traditional approaches to development and community well-being.

1. We would like to extend credit and special thanks to the Elders and First Nation, Metis/Métis, and Inuit scholars, knowledge keepers, and leaders who came before us and have shared their knowledge with us through scholarly works and personal communications. It is only on the basis of their immense contributions that we are able to put forward this small contribution towards building bridges of understanding between Western culture and First Nations/Indigenous cultures. In acknowledgement of the limits of the experience and knowledge of the authors, and being mindful of the diversity among First Nations, Métis, Inuit, and other Indigenous peoples, this paper only deals with commonalities in the worldviews and experience of First Nations. The Indigenous or FNMI population in what is now known as Canada comprises the Metis/Métis and Inuit as well as over 70 distinct First Nations, including the Haida, Blackfoot, Cree, Secwepemc, Gwich'in, Innu, Mi'kmaq, Seneca, Onondaga, and Mohawk. It must be clearly understood, though, that each First Nation is a separate and distinct nation, with its own unique body of national knowledge, socio-political systems, and societal frameworks. Thus, while there may be common features among First Nations, there is also wide diversity. Where commonalities exist, variation may still be seen in the implementation methods of a given Nation. As such, it should not be assumed that the concepts explained here apply uniformly to any given First Nation. Given the diversity of First Nation histories, circumstances, and interests, this analysis strives to avoid a false homogenization when describing socio-political and ideological structures by, wherever possible, providing examples attributed to specific First Nations. We would also like to give specific thanks to Elder Pauline Shirt, Carolyn Laude, Leona Shirt, Nadia Abu-Zahra, Diana El Richani, Kiera Kaia'tano:ron Brant, George Halfe, and Sandy Jackson for their efforts and contributions, without which this work would not have been possible.
2. The term Indigenous is used to encompass both the international scope of the literature and the national context of Aboriginal peoples as defined in the Constitution of Canada. The terms First Nations and Aboriginal are used when referring to specific organizations or when referring to contexts specific to Canada.
3. A good example of self-determined development, specific to the field of social work and family services, is discussed in Blackstock, Cross, George, Brown, and Formsma (2006).

Introduction

If one thinks about the large cities that existed prior to contact with European colonialists, one might not think of cities of Indigenous nations on Turtle Island (North America). Yet, one of the largest pre-contact cities in the world was a city called Cahokia, located along the Mississippi River near what is now St. Louis, Missouri (Nabokov 1991, 136). The capital of the Mississippian nation, Cahokia had a five-square-mile "downtown" area and, in 1250 CE, was larger than the city of London, England (Cahokia Mounds State Historic Site 2008; Mann 2005; Nabokov 1991, 138). This sophisticated society had an "effective economic structure" based primarily on the production of artistic works and on agricultural sciences, in particular the cultivation of different types of maize (Nabokov 1991, 136; Rasmussen 2000, 341). As would be expected in a large nation-state, the Mississippian society had a highly developed and established system of laws, justice, and governance (Nabokov 1991, 135–138). Major Mississippian towns, such as Cahokia, Moundville, and Angel, were fortified and offered a centralized location where individuals from countryside hamlets could congregate for social and spiritual activities, seek recourse from arbiters for dispute resolution, and obtain protection during times of war (Nabokov 1991, 137).

Cahokia is only one example of the many large communities and cities that Indigenous societies built across Turtle Island before contact with European nations. How could historical Indigenous nations and societies have existed, like that of the Mississippians, without most people having any knowledge of their existence and significance? The answer lies in the deliberate exclusion of accurate information about Indigenous peoples' societies, economies, cultures and models of social organization from historical records and education systems in Canada, the United States, and worldwide. One reason for this is that the reality of pre-contact Indigenous societies and nation-states challenges the validity of the legal principles and legitimizing ideologies upon which the colonial meta-narrative—used to justify the colonization of Indigenous nations and peoples—is historically premised (Moreton-Robinson 2011). In Canada and elsewhere, these principles and ideologies include the Doctrine of Discovery (Reid 2010), the myth of European superiority, and the belief that the European colonial nations, and subsequent settler states, were engaged in a benevolent mission to save Indigenous peoples from their supposed "savagery." (See Chapter 9.)

One method by which European colonial nations, and settlers, legitimized colonization was through the creation of a large body of myths, disinformation, and false conceptions about Indigenous peoples that dehumanized them and devalued their societies and knowledge systems. By rendering Indigenous peoples to a state of savagery, colonialists were able to justify their "development" so that they could benefit from the supposedly superior model of economic and social organization established by European nations. Unfortunately, the belief in the benevolent intent of colonization contrasted significantly with the actual practice of colonization, which involved concerted attempts to destroy the cultures, societies, and economic and social structures of Indigenous peoples.

In Canada, the United States, and elsewhere, this was accompanied by the often-illegal appropriation of Indigenous lands and resources and the enslavement and/or forced assimilation of Indigenous peoples, in order to support the development of settler-societies on Turtle Island. Eventually, through a systematic process of domination, dispossession, denationalization, dehumanization, and assimilation, the Indigenous peoples of Turtle Island were rendered subject to, and dependent upon, the American and Canadian settler-states (Borrows 1999). Despite this history, Indigenous peoples on Turtle Island today —referred to variously as

the Native Americans, First Nations, Inuit, and Métis, continue to fight for recognition of their inherent rights to self-government, to the benefits of their traditional lands and resources, and to economic independence. There needs to be a decolonizing of colonial development to ensure that Indigenous self-determined development has a chance to prosper.

This chapter provides a series of short introductions to historical and contemporary issues that illustrate concerns about development in the context of Indigenous peoples from an Indigenous perspective along with allied settler viewpoints. It is not "post-colonial," as we are still in a state of colonization, but rather a pragmatic decolonizing view of certain perceptions and systems that prevent self-determined development within Indigenous communities. It begins with a condensed discussion of First Nations societies pre-contact, and introduces the relational worldview that informs the economic and social systems of many Indigenous peoples.

The intent of this brief exploration is to convey the logic and benefits of First Nations epistemology and to illustrate the inherent value of Indigenous social and economic structures, structures that continue to be dismissed and silenced by most modern development theories. This is followed by a succinct overview of some of the barriers to economic success for First Nations that have resulted in a state of dependency in the Canadian context. These include development initiatives by the Canadian government like the reserve system, residential schools, and imposed *Indian Act* governments. We then introduce the concept of development colonialism, which is a systematic approach to disintegrate Indigenous economies and replace them with market economies favouring the colonial system. We then provide a checklist of wise practices for creating partnership-based development programs with Indigenous communities. The chapter ends with two case studies of successful First Nations economic endeavours that are grounded in, and informed by, their traditional worldview and practices. It is hoped that these brief examinations will stimulate curiosity in the reader such that they will seek out more in-depth discussions of each topic in order to critically reflect on the implications and validity of imposing Western development models on Indigenous peoples in a contemporary context, particularly when it comes at the expense of their own structures.

It is also important to understand Indigenous cosmologies and how they are reflected in today's developmental discussions. There has always been tension between Indigenous ways of knowing and Western knowledge, with the latter being privileged. There is a need for more understanding of Indigenous communities and philosophies, such as collective rights, generational sharing, and environmental stewardship (Watts 2016; Nelson 2016). By developing an understanding of First Nations/Indigenous worldviews, knowledge, economies, governance, and forms of social organization, barriers to self-determined change (development) can be overcome.

First Nations Worldviews and Societies: A Brief Introduction

The original Indigenous people of Turtle Island are the First Nations/Native Americans and Inuit. The estimated pre-contact population of Indigenous peoples living on Turtle Island ranges from approximately 50 million to 100 million (Borah 1962; Chansonneuve 2005, 11). In comparison, the estimated pre-contact population in Europe ranges from 50 million to 90 million. Prior to contact, First Nations lived throughout the continent and came to be known as Indians, due to Columbus's mistaken belief about his geographical location. Today, the term First Nation is used to refer to the "Indians" who live in the colonial settler-state known as Canada; while similarly, the term Native American is generally used to refer to those living in the United States. The Inuit people are a

separate group that have historically lived, and continue to live, in the northern regions of Canada, Alaska, Russia, and Greenland. The Métis people, another group of Indigenous peoples who live in Canada, emerged as a nation after contact with Europeans and have a dual heritage, yet a distinct identity (MNC 2015). For the sake of simplicity, the term First Nations is used in this chapter to refer to First Nations and Native American peoples collectively; the terms Inuit and Métis are used where the discussion specifically touches on these groups, or the term Aboriginal may be used to refer to First Nations, Métis, and Inuit groups collectively from a legal perspective. The term Indigenous is more commonly used to reflect all the traditional peoples of Turtle Island.

When First Nations on Turtle Island first discovered European colonialists on their territories, they encountered social structures and worldviews that were very different from their own. The European model of social organization, grounded in reductionism, individuality, and determinism, centralizes wealth and power among an elite few who use legitimizing ideologies to maintain the status quo and dominate subordinate groups. This contrasts distinctly with the holistic, participatory, and egalitarian frameworks of many First Nations societies, which emphasize relationships, individual responsibility, and collective harmony (Monture-Okanee 1994; Borrows 2010, 60–106). The capitalist economy of European nations also differs substantially from the traditional economic systems of First Nations. The European model, is based on a linear worldview (Cross 1997), that allows nature and people to be reduced to commodities and resources so they can be exploited for the benefit of infinite progress and the individual accumulation and retention of wealth. In comparison, the traditional economic systems of First Nations are commonly based on a relational worldview that supports communal ownership of resources, the redistribution of wealth, and a deep respect for the relationship between human beings and the natural world (Cross

1997; Blackstock 2011; Borrows 2010, 78; Usher 1993, 38–44; Daugherty 1991, 65; Kidwell 1991, 396; Coulthard 2014; Nelson 2016, 32–33). (See Chapter 9.)

Despite the differences in their worldviews and cultures, commonalities also existed between European and First Nations societies. Like Europeans, pre-contact First Nations had developed complex bodies of knowledge that spanned a variety of disciplines, including education, commerce, agriculture, engineering, science, metaphysics, physics, law, philosophy, and leadership/governance (Battiste 2002). First Nations had also developed distinct cultures, languages, economies, and models of social organization that gave expression to the bodies of knowledge they had accumulated. First Nations, as well as European nations, had developed robust education systems in accordance with their own worldviews and ways of knowing, being, and doing. As between the various nations found across Europe, there were, and continue to be, striking differences between the various First Nations societies on Turtle Island, differences that must not be ignored in favour of a false homogeneity. For example, some First Nations were matrilineal, while others were patrilineal; some First Nations had strict hierarchies, while others did not; some First Nations practised slavery, although most did not; and some First Nations had elected leadership systems, while others had hereditary systems or some combination of both (Trovato and Romaniuk 2014; Goldmann and Delic 2014.)

The relational worldview and First Nations economic and social systems

As discussed in Chapter 9, First Nations societies generally shared—and continue to share— a "relational worldview" that sees life as a network of harmonious relationships, and individual and communal well-being as a product of maintaining balance between the many interrelating factors that affect these relationships (Cross 1997; Blackstock 2011). The relational worldview stems in part from different ways of

knowing, being, and doing that are grounded in a balanced understanding of the interplay between the spiritual/metaphysical world and the physical/material world. Relationality gives rise to, and stems from, knowledge and principles commonly shared and understood by many First Nations and other Indigenous peoples. One example of this is that all things are alive and have a spirit of their own and as such must be respected (Deloria 1999). Others include respect for different ways of knowing; a high regard for the expertise and experience of Elders and Knowledge Keepers (Simpson 2008, 82; Venne 1998); "radical" egalitarian participation in the development of social structures (Borrows 2010, 44); the extension of "generous and liberal" personal liberties (ibid.); and, the importance of individual responsibility, individual rights, and collective harmony (Borrows 2010; Monture-Okanee 1994; Monture-Angus 1995).

The relational worldview is given effect through social structures that maintain and reproduce practices that embed and manifest the principles and knowledge, often an oral and symbolic system, that informs the worldview (Cornellius 1999, 44–46; Battiste 2002: 2–3). This complex cycle is guided by the understanding that for a worldview to be actualized, the knowledge it is based upon must be understood and lived at an individual and collective level (Alfred 1999). It is not enough for individuals or institutions to just go through the motions (P. Shirt 2015). The principles and knowledge derived from and informing this worldview must be embedded in day-to-day concepts and actions in order to benefit the well-being of individuals and communities (P. Shirt 2015; Alfred 1999). This includes intrinsically embedding them into the societies' norms, ethics, culture, organizational structures, activities, language, protocols, practices, and other processes and systems. The results are evident in First Nations social, economic, and political structures that seek to preserve and revitalize respectful, balanced relationships between human beings, as well as between human beings and the natural world. Examples include economic systems based on a conservation ethic and respect for nature, and social structures that promote egalitarianism and respect for individual and collective rights by according voting rights to women and using consensus-based decision making.

Traditional stories are another example of how the relational worldview is embedded into social practices, informs the development of social and economic structures, and is transferred from one generation to the next (Cornelius 1999, 45). Traditional stories serve these purposes in many ways. Many traditional stories explain the interdependent relationship of humans with each other and with nature, and ways that individuals and cultures can respectfully adapt "old ways to ... newer realities" (Cornelius 1999, 46). They generally provide some combination of philosophical, scientific, technological, methodological, sociological, economic, and psychological knowledge, and collectively convey an understanding of how these spheres of knowledge are interrelated, interdependent, and grounded in nature. They serve as repositories and reminders of the principles and practices that individuals and societies need to embody to maintain balanced relationships and individual and collective well-being. They also provide a means of instilling relational values into new generations, such as peace, humility, honesty, respect, harmony, wisdom, flexibility, and respect for the inherent value of all creation. Taken together, traditional stories provide an important medium for communicating and understanding the relational worldview. The principles of well-being emphasized in traditional stories also provide a coherent and comprehensive moral and ethical system that actively informs the social organization and structures of First Nations societies (Alfred 1999, 45).

Haudenosaunee stories of Sky Woman and the Three Sisters illustrate the breadth of relational knowledge that is contained in and transmitted through traditional stories and how they inform the development of First Nations economic and social structures (Horn-Miller 2009). Near the beginning of the story, Sky Woman falls to earth through a hole in Sky World. On the way down she grabs seeds (strawberries, corn, squash, and beans) and tobacco leaves in her hands (Porter 2008; Mann 2000; Horn-Miller 2009). Though there are different variations of the Sky Woman story (Fenton 1998, 35; Horn-Miller 2009), each version tends to incorporate teachings about biology, physics, agriculture, and ethics. They also provide insight into the agriculture-based economies and the means of production and distribution practiced by Haudenosaunee confederacy nations (Horn-Miller 2009; Hall 2008, 149–152; Mann 2000); for example, the prominence of corn, squash, and beans in Haudenosaunee agriculture (Cornellius 1999; Hall 2008; Nabokov 1991).

In addition to the Haudenosaunee, agriculture was an important source of economic resources for many First Nations communities, such as the Pawnee, the Navajos, and the Abenakis (Iverson 1991, 89, 110–117; Nabokov 1991, 119–127). Pre-contact, First Nations in the eastern part of Turtle Island had a long history of farming. These First Nations societies had refined two main horticultural techniques, swidden and flood plain farming (Nabokov 1991, 124–126). By 1492, Mississippian communities, for example, had been using flood plain farming to cultivate crops of maize, beans, and squash for over six centuries (Nabokov 1991, 125). Among many farming societies, like the Mahicans and Pocumtucks, hunting and gathering served to subsidize their farm productions (Nabokov 1991, 124–126). Other First Nations societies, such as those in northern and woodland areas, like the Algonquians, used a mixture of fishing, hunting, foraging, and vegetable and maple syrup production to develop an economy that was more suited to the environment where they lived (Nabokov 1991, 124–126).

Extensive trade networks between First Nations cities and communities provided access to economic goods that could not be satisfied through domestic production. Some trade networks, such as those between British Columbia and the plains, have been dated to as early as 3,300 years ago (Furniss 2002). Trade networks also connected Indigenous nations across North America to Central and South American markets. Some of the goods traded along these networks included furs, red ochre, quahog shells, pottery, and tools, the remnants of which have been found throughout Turtle Island (Rich 1960). Trade networks also provided avenues for the exchange of knowledge and technology, the development of inter-nation alliances, and economic and political partnerships, all of which have a long history in First Nations and Inuit societies that predate the arrival of Europeans (Furniss 2002; Keyser 2001).

From a relational perspective, many First Nations changed (developed) over time through what we will refer to here as a system of collective emergent participatory growth. This model emphasizes individual participation in collectively determining the evolution of society and its structures as a result of interactions and relationships between self, others, and the world around them. It is multifaceted and evolving, and is seen in methods that provide for culturally appropriate economic renewal (Hall 2008, 154). Although it can be classified as a form of development, this approach differs from prescribed methods of development that arise as a result of a limited-participation or non-participatory hierarchical system disconnected from the natural world. It also differs from systems imposed by an external force, such as colonialism or development programs and policies that are not community-based (Coulthard 2014). An important element of collective emergent participatory growth is that it is based on First Nations theories of land, space, and time (Blackstock 2011), and as such is not linear, nor does it depend on the temporal idea of progress to attain something better, this idea being a Western construct based on the myth of modernity (Dussel 1993). This Indigenized understanding of development coincides more with relational principles such as harmony, balance, and adaptation, as opposed to European/ Western notions of modernity, linear progress, materialism, and individualism.

This approach to change, and the influence of the relational worldview, can also be seen in First Nations systems that balance communal ownership of resources with exclusive rights, that provide for the consumption needs of the society while maintaining a conservation ethic and a deep respect and understanding of the natural world (Borrows 2010, 78; Usher 1993, 38–44; Daugherty 1991, 65; Kidwell 1991, 396). It can also be seen in egalitarian distribution systems, including systems of individual wealth balanced with complex redistribution structures. This model is often evidenced in the traditional view shared by many First Nations that the individual accumulation of wealth is a means to an end and not an end in itself (Monture-Okanee 1994; Monture-Angus 1995). In this context, relational principles that emphasize collective harmony and maintaining a balance between the physical and metaphysical meant that knowledge, prestige, and other forms of non-material wealth were more highly prized than money and goods. Examples include First Nations societies that practiced the potlatch ceremony, wherein the accumulation of individual material wealth provided a means of gaining prestige when that wealth was ceremonially redistributed to other members of society or to other communities that were in need (Borrows 2010; Washington 2004; Ringel 1979; Piddocke 1965; Clutesi 1969). This gave rise to social stigmas where people were seen as being very poor if all they had was money (Monture-Okanee 1994; Monture-Angus 1995).

Barriers to First Nations Economic Development in Canada

Perhaps one of the most important issues in Canada today is the continued colonial, neoliberal body politic's marginalization of Indigenous people and the consequent cycle of First Nations dependency on the settler-state (Helin 2009). Indigenous peoples in Canada are commonly misrepresented as unilaterally anti-development and/or as passive victims of development. In reality, many Indigenous communities are actively developing economic plans and engaging in partnerships with external businesses and governments. These communities are looking towards self-government as a way to exercise self-determination, as defined by the communities themselves, and overcoming the cycle of poverty and dependency that has resulted from colonization (Nelson 2015; Loxley 2010). Self-government is having the structures of governance put in place by the people it rules. Self-determination is how those structures are created and how they are managed. The Harvard Project on American Indian Economic Development indicates that First Nations self-government is the key to economic self-sufficiency (Cornell 2010). First Nations community leaders are increasingly turning to self-government to promote economic development, entrepreneurial growth, and business partnerships to increase wealth and generate local economies in their communities (Loxley 2010; Nelson and Sisco 2008). Unfortunately, development barriers continue to exist, in the form of Canadian laws, policies, and approaches that continue to impede the economic resurgence of First Nations, forcing their communities to remain in a perpetual struggle for self-actualization. This includes government policies, from colonial times to the present, through which Canada has sought to forcibly assimilate First Nations peoples into the Western model of development as a matter of official policy (Gordon 2010, 66–133; Venne 1998). There is also an ongoing commodification and privatization of land that

dispossesses Indigenous populations and suppresses alternative forms of Indigenous economies (Harvey 2004, 74).

The 1876 *Indian Act*, which was unilaterally developed and implemented by the Canadian government, is one of the main tools that the Canadian government has used to destroy First Nations economies, governments, and social structures. Canadian government legislation and policy has supported various crimes against humanity and acts of genocide against First Nations, Métis, and Inuit peoples, including mass killings (Woolford 2009), forced sterilization designed to limit births (Pegoraro 2015), cultural genocide through the forcible removal of children to residential schools, the destruction of social and political structures, forced removal from traditional lands, and the deliberate infliction of conditions designed to destroy First Nations, Métis, and Inuit peoples' way of life (TRC 2015, 1). Amendments to the *Indian Act* in the 1920s also stripped First Nations of their civil and human rights by making it illegal for First Nations people to gather in groups, hire a lawyer to represent their rights, or engage in the cultural and spiritual practices that defined them as peoples. The *Indian Act*, along with other government policies and programs, has also served as a tool for restricting and setting up barriers to the economic success of First Nations.

Three of the most damaging barriers to First Nations' economic development resulting from Canadian policies and legislation have been the dismantling of traditional leadership/governance systems, the implementation of the reserve system, and the residential school system. The *Indian Act* provides the Canadian government with the authority to impose a patriarchal quasi-democratic system of government at the community level that has been used to destroy and devalue traditional forms of First Nations governance. When First Nations fought against it, it was sometimes imposed by force through the incarceration of traditional leaders, and the withholding of food, goods, and access to their children. Under the *Indian Act*, First Nations governments, including inter-nation governments such as the Haudenosaunee confederacy, Three Fires confederacy, and the Abenaki confederacy, were not recognized as legitimate systems. On the Canadian west coast, the banning of the potlatch and the systematic dismantling of the hereditary Chief system prevented development among the Haida, Tsimshian, and Gitxsan. Voting restrictions and the imposition of a two-year electoral system in the *Indian Act* (1985) meant that First Nations' governments did not serve long enough to create or implement any long-term development strategies (Nelson 2015). At the same time, the supposedly democratic election system the *Indian Act* imposed was undermined by the fact that the ability of elected Chiefs to serve was and remains subject to approval by the Canadian Minister responsible for Indigenous Affairs.

The reserve system, originally accepted by many First Nations desperate to protect their few remaining lands, has been used by the Canadian government as a way to segregate and control First Nations and limit their economic capacity. Historically, it limited land use that was traditionally used for subsistence and trading economies by confining people within a reserve boundary. The "pass system," which is no longer in effect, was used for decades to prevent First Nations people from leaving the reserve without the express permission of the Indian Agent (Brewer 1980; Smith 2014; Williams 2015). Implemented without legal sanction (Smith 2014; Williams 2015), the pass system restricted the mobility of First Nations, allowing the government to impede First Nations from accessing trade networks, commercial alliances, means of production and resources on their traditional territories, or participating in actions to protect their rights and interests (Williams 2015). The restriction of mobility facilitated colonial expropriation of land and resources from First Nations ownership, use, and control—in Canada (Harvey 2003; 2004).

Through the *Indian Act*, the Canadian government also granted itself the authority to hold reserve lands in trust for First Nations and to make determinations about how their lands could be used (*Indian Act*, s. 18). Under this regime, First Nations "Bands" can only administer their lands with the approval of, and within the confines established by, the Canadian government, a system that continues today. First Nations businesses on reserves are also prevented from accessing capital through collateral or by leveraging their assets (*Indian Act*, s. 89).

Over time, these government policies increasingly forced First Nations into a state of dependency on the Canadian government for the revenue needed for basic survival (Helin 2009). First Nations economies, which had flourished across Turtle Island during the pre-contact and early post-contact periods, began to disappear as First Nations were impeded from accessing resources and developing new economic initiatives. The result was that First Nations, as well as Métis and Inuit peoples who experienced similar restrictions, have generally been excluded from Canada's economic and social prosperity, despite their inherent Indigenous and/or Treaty rights to the lands and resources that have been, and continue to be, used to support the economic development of Canada and non-Indigenous Canadians (Calder v. British Columbia 1973; *Constitution Act* 1982, s. 35; McNeil 2007). According to the Institute for Research on Public Policy, the "persistence of significant gaps between the living conditions of Canada's Aboriginal and non-Aboriginal populations (particularly those of European descent) remains a stark, undeniable reality, an unflattering blemish on Canada's purportedly enviable record of social justice" (Salée 2006). This disparity is a direct result of Canadian policies meant to "develop" First Nations and is something that reflects poorly on the Canadian government and Canadian society (Treasury Board of Canada Secretariat 2004).

Development Colonialism:
A Global Legacy

Today Indigenous peoples living in Canada are left with the legacy of colonial rule that continues to haunt development. Colonialism systematically disintegrated Indigenous societies and replaced their economic systems with a market economy (Harvey 2003). It also created a mass migration into settler-cities, as this was often the only source of work and food. The result of this assimilative process has been that in some places traditional knowledge of ecological management, communal reciprocity, and alternative justice systems has become less significant, as the ability to support them has been lost. In Canada and worldwide, development programs have made only limited attempts to restore traditional territories, pre-colonial traditional cultures, or traditional governments, and have often impeded the efforts of Indigenous peoples to do so (Goldsmith 1997), as to do so conflicts with the ongoing, yet flawed, view that Westernization is the apex of social, economic, and political ideologies. This leaves limited space for Indigenous worldviews and creates a context in which Indigenous communities are often pressured into conforming to Western forms of development in order to survive.

The power of the Western development model is a historically enforced and perpetuated belief in its claim to universal applicability that denies its own origin in a particular social/historical context. The ability of the colonial development model to leap out from its own shadow and impose what it claims is a transcendent, objective, and disinterested program of "modernization" and "progress" virtually ensures that all possibility of respectful relations and inter-cultural dialogue is closed off from the beginning. Modern development theory is not very far removed from this basic fundamental assumption, which can be seen in its explicit attempt to dismiss and delegitimize non-European societies as backward, traditional, and primitive, unless and until they take part in the dominant culture's social, economic, and political systems. This approach is reinforced by the sustained belief in the superiority of Western civilization, knowledge, and economic and political systems. It is this notion of inherent superiority that remains the justification for past and current development projects in Indigenous communities that do not centrally position the interests, goals, and worldviews of Indigenous peoples.

Any type of development initiative, whether social, human, industrial, or otherwise, is an ongoing form of colonialism

1. insofar as it seeks to impose Western concepts of progress, modernity, governance or economics on Indigenous peoples, without being invited to and/or at the expense of their own traditional models; and

2. when the core of the undertaking does not reflect the interests, goals, worldviews, and short- and long-term interests of the Indigenous people or community it purports to assist.

A development paradigm is also inherently colonial when it starts with the assumption that Indigenous peoples need to assimilate to the dominant culture rather than respecting their inherent right to self-determination (UNDRIP 2007). Development colonialism thus occurs when a project is conceived for, or about, Indigenous peoples without their full involvement in the design and implementation of both the development model and any given development initiatives, the result being the denial of voice and agency to the Indigenous peoples whom the development paradigm claims to be helping. One of the many results of this approach is the infringement of their inherent, legal, and treaty rights to lands, resources, and an equitable standard of living.

The lack of First Nations, Métis, and Inuit voices within national development dialogue has been an ongoing constitutional issue in Canada. Supreme Court rulings have stated that if there is a real or perceived threat to Aboriginal title from a development project, then there is a duty of meaningful consultation that must take place with affected communities. This is known as the duty to consult and accommodate. Unfortunately, this is often a powerless process, as it does not accord FNMI communities with a veto power and does not set specific standards for consultation or accommodation. As a result, industry and government can consult and offer accommodations on a development project according to their own self-determined standards and then proceed with the project whether the community wants the development on their territory or not, with the primary recourse for the affected and disenfranchised FNMI communities being lengthy and costly court proceedings.

Inherent rights are self-determined rights and are not created by treaties but are acknowledged by them (Schulte-Tenckhoff 2000). Therefore, Indigenous people do not have to prove title or right, but rather those that are infringing on inherent rights have to consult with them in a meaningful way. Yet the constant undermining of inherent rights over national interest continues to undermine FNMI self-determination. Some examples of this include the *Northwest Territories Devolution Act*, which set time limits for environmental assessments and extended ministerial control. The *Act* also established "sweeping and deep" changes to the terms of resource development that significantly impacted the inherent rights, territorial title, and pre-existing agreements with First Nations. Further, the *Act* was passed by the Canadian government despite legal concerns raised by the First Nations most impacted by the legislation.

Another example is the *Yukon and Nunavut Regulatory Improvement Act* (S.C. 2015, c. 19) which amended the *Yukon Environmental and Socio-economic Assessment Act (YESAA)* (2003) and the *Nunavut Waters and Nunavut Surface Rights Tribunal Act* (NWNSRTA) (2002).

The Bill was opposed by Yukon First Nations because it was being imposed without appropriate consultation and accommodation, it infringed on their Treaty Rights, and it contradicted some First Nations self-government agreements (Gagnon 2015). It also infringed on the Umbrella Final Agreement (UFA), a comprehensive political agreement that setting out the framework for land claim settlements agreements that was finally reached in 1988 after a long process of negotiations between the Council of Yukon First Nations, Canada, and the Yukon (UFA 1990; Gagnon 2015). The changes to the NWNSRTA also impact the Inuit, as it directly infringes on the Nunavut Land Claims Agreement (2013), which was signed by Canada and grants the territory authority over regulation, use, and management of waters in the Nunavut Settlement Area. The result is that the *Act* could directly undermine Inuit governance and self-determination in the north. Clouthard (2014, 2) refers to this as the "politics of recognition," in that the current colonial system reproduces the very configurations of colonialist, racist, and patriarchal state power that Indigenous people have historically sought to rise above. From a land-use perspective, there is only tacit acknowledgement of self-determination and title, yet from a nationalistic perspective it is still relative to the Crown ownership of all lands and title.

The influx of policies and initiatives to increase development in the North has pressured many First Nations, Inuit, and Métis to react. Concerns over land claim infringements, traditional ways of life, and environmental impacts are an ongoing threat to self-determination. Extractive industries are constantly trying to engage with First Nations and Inuit communities to gain access to their lands and resources for development projects. Deep pockets and lobby groups make it next to impossible for many communities to handle ongoing and continual requests for consultation, partnerships, and research, which generally have financial, social, or environmental implications that need to be assessed. Communities often feel overwhelmed with requests that are unmanageable due to a lack of financial resources and the internal capacity required to respond. This is not to say that many communities do not want some form of development or the opportunity to engage in financial partnerships, but they need to be able to do so on their own terms, in their own time, and with the necessary financial supports.

Wise Practices for Decolonizing Development

Indigenous development is defined as the growth or progress of an Indigenous community in their originality or within the context of their ethnic identity in a holistic way (Permanent Forum on Indigenous Issues 2010). So how can development programs assist First Nations, Métis, Inuit, and other Indigenous peoples to preserve and maintain Indigenous models of development and construct respectful and co-operative relations with Indigenous societies?

A first step is to create a new paradigm for development that is rooted in values consistent with and supportive of the Indigenous community's or nation's values. This can be accomplished by supporting, and learning from, traditional Indigenous models of emergent participatory growth. This includes developing an understanding of:

a. Oral history
b. Customary laws and governance
c. Traditional and hybrid models of social organization
d. Decision-making processes
e. Concepts around gender equality
f. Values and cultural traditions
g. Traditional knowledges; ways of knowing, being, and doing; and differing worldviews.

Development initiatives also need to undertake a responsibility to support the maintenance of Indigenous peoples' knowledge systems and models of social organization and prevent the breakdown of traditional legal systems and governance and social structures (ibid.).

This approach can be supported by the development of a set of wise practices (Wesley-Esquimaux 2010; Voyageur 2015) for engaging in development projects with Indigenous peoples. Wise practices are those that are by nature idiosyncratic, contextual, and textured, and may often be inconsistent (Davis 1997). In comparison, best practices are often standardized, impersonal, and formulaic (Wesley-Esquimaux 2010). Wise practices engender relationality with a given community and the formation of mutual respect between proponents and the individuals and community as a whole. They are a method for developing appropriate actions with a given community, so as to contribute to the overall well-being of that community, by coming to understand what they know their needs are and what they know are appropriate solutions for their community. This participatory action based[1] approach ensures the relationship is one of respect and good intentions. A wise practices and community participation approach coincides with the Ojibway concept of Bimaadiziwin, which loosely translates to living a good life; it is a philosophy of living with a good heart, a good head, and a good spirit.

Wise practices for decolonizing and Indigenizing development should have as a baseline:

1. a respectful understanding of Indigenous knowledge systems and societal structures, from the perspective of the Indigenous peoples who developed them, and
2. a concerted effort to listen to Indigenous peoples about what their goals for

---

1. Originating with the work of Kurt Lewin, Participatory Action Based Research is based on a community-centric approach to working with communities. This includes working with communities on projects and research they see as important rather than what the researchers see as important. It also implies action or advocacy for the community.

development are, in a given context, prior to initiating a development project.

The following checklist provides a list of considerations for working with an Indigenous community, whether on a development project or a research, social, health, or other initiative. These are not intended to provide a universal approach or exhaustive list, but are rather wise practices to be considered and used as appropriate.

Wise practices to consider in order to decolonize and Indigenize development initiatives:

- Initiative is community-based (e.g., goals, project plan, and outcomes are developed by/with the community) and supports community-led economic development grounded in the Indigenous community's principles, values, and concepts of wealth management.
- Utilizes a partnership model that incorporates methods of joint decision-making, is reciprocal, and provides the community with actual authority over the direction and methodology of the initiative.
- Initiative is sustainable and supports the creation of lasting benefits for all stakeholders, especially the Indigenous community.
- Community involvement is promoted through the establishment of a trusting relationship with proponents.
- The initiative prioritizes the goals of the Indigenous community, particularly if the undertaking will have long-term effects on the community, its lands, resources, and economy, or results in considerable opportunity costs that are not in the short- or long-term (national) interests of the Indigenous community/nation.
- The Indigenous community as a whole (including, as applicable, the political leadership, traditional leadership, Elders, and community members in general) has a genuine sense of ownership over the project.

- All stakeholders recognize that the Indigenous community, and project proponent, have a necessary and legitimate role to play in achieving the initiative's goals.
- The consultation process is determined in conjunction with the community and preliminary and ongoing community consultations are incorporated into all stages of the initiative, including the initial planning stages.
- Empowers the community, and increases its independence, by improving individual and collective capacity through the acquisition of skills and knowledge predetermined and desired by the community itself.
- Has ethical research methods that recognize that the ownership of traditional knowledge, community knowledge, individual knowledge, and Indigenous knowledges generally remains solely the property of the Indigenous peoples who created and shared it.
- The Indigenous community's right to free, prior, and informed consent (as set out in the United Nations Declaration on the Rights of Indigenous Peoples or UNDRIP) is respected, including the right to deny consent to a development initiative on their territory if the initiative is not in the best short- or long-term interests of the Indigenous community.
- All aspects of the initiative, including the planning process, accords the Indigenous community, and its leadership, the same type of respect and treatment you (as an individual) would want to receive if someone (a big company, organization, or government) decided they wanted to undertake this initiative on your property.

Both prior to and since colonization, the bodies of metaphysical and material knowledge acquired by First Nations have continued to evolve. Today they exist as living contemporary systems, grounded in the inherent value of the physical, spiritual, and scholarly knowledge acquired and accumulated by their ancestors, and up to the present day (Coates 2015). This inheritance has provided First Nations with proven survival and adaptation strategies that are internationally competitive and compelling in an era increasingly subjected to neoliberal global institutions. Contemporary development initiatives can use several strategies to support First Nation, Métis, Inuit, and other Indigenous peoples in overcoming the socio-economic disadvantages created by the settler colonial system and the imposition of Western development models. One effective approach is to support the creation of sustainable Indigenous business enterprises that are community-based and stimulate skills development and sustainable economic initiatives with long-term benefits for Indigenous communities. Indigenous peoples want self-determination, to create stable economies, and to develop well-being in their families and communities. Business opportunities and partnerships created in conjunction with, on the terms of, and along timelines set by Indigenous communities would help support these goals.

First Nations Development Today: Two Case Studies

First Nations peoples continue to work hard to overcome the limitations placed on their social, political, and inherent rights, and the undermining of their traditional economic systems. In many cases, they are developing successful businesses founded on their traditional values and participatory models of leadership and decision-making. The following case studies highlight two strategies for economic development that have been successfully undertaken by First Nations communities. The first of these approaches illustrates an economic initiative that might emerge when an industrial resource development is on or near the traditional territory of an Indigenous community, and the

community undertakes a lateral enterprise, on their own terms, to alleviate poverty, regain independence, or otherwise benefit from, or adapt to, the imposed development project. The second is an economic enterprise initiated based entirely on the terms, principles, interests, goals, and traditional ways of the First Nation. It highlights how initiatives undertaken independently may be supported through partners and self-government agreements.

1) Community Case Study:
Whitefish Lake First Nation, Alberta

Whitefish Lake First Nation (WFLFN) #128, located in northeastern Alberta, provides an example of an economic development enterprise undertaken as a means of adapting to the impacts of colonization and benefiting from the external exploitation of the natural resources on their traditional territory (Nelson 2016). In 1978, the First Nation developed Goodfish Lake Development Corporation (GFLDC) through a community-based approach that illustrates the process of collective emergent participatory growth. Emerging in response to the community's circumstances, the mandate of GFLDC promotes their traditional principles, community participation, and the flow of benefits to the community for their collective well-being.

As early as the 1870s, the people who came to be known as Whitefish Lake First Nation were suffering from starvation and increasing poverty due to colonization and the loss of their lands to settlers, both of which were decimating their traditional economy and way of life (Houle 2014; WFLFN 2015). Having refused to accept the colonial government's authority and settle on an insufficient plot of reserve lands chosen for them, they were denied access to rations and other supplies they needed for their survival (WFLFN 2015).

The Elders and community members supported their leader, Chief Pakan (James Seenum), in seeking a way to restore their economic self-sufficiency and end the cycle of poverty and dependency resulting from colonization (Jackson 2010; L. Shirt 2015; Nelson 2016). It was self-evident to the community that preserving the land was the most important thing for future generations (Nelson and Sisco 2008; L. Shirt 2015; Nelson 2016). They decided to enter into treaty with the Canadian government to regain more of their lands, as it was not possible for them to survive on the small area they had been pushed onto by the settlers (L. Shirt 2015). First Nations had been entering into, and respectfully upholding, treaties with each other since before contact, some of which have lasted for centuries. On this basis, entering into treaties with Canada was a logical long-term way for the community to preserve their lands and restore their independence and well-being. In 1876, Chief Pakan became one of the principal signatories of Treaty 6 (WFLFN 2015). He, like other First Nations leaders across Canada, likely could not foresee that the colonial mindset would inevitably allow the Canadian government to breach their contractual obligations by refusing to uphold the terms of the treaty.

Three decades later, in 1908, the Canadian government finally established the reserve for the WFLFN community. As with many First Nations, the land the community acquired fell short of meeting their socio-economic needs and was thousands of acres smaller than what they were legally entitled to and were promised. The suffering they had sought to alleviate by signing the Treaty continued to increase. Despite the terms of the Treaty, government policies denied them access to the resources on their traditional lands and prevented them from engaging in their spiritual and cultural practices. These policies were devastating to their economic and social well-being and traditional way of life. With this sustained privation and loss of culture came a decline in pride in their traditional beliefs, way of life, and themselves—emotions that were reinforced by the denigration and suppression of their culture and traditions in residential school (L. Shirt, P. 2015; TRC 2015).

Despite their history of hardships and inequities, the community continued to sustain a strong vision for independence, individual success, and community-based economic initiatives (Nelson and Sisco 2008; P. Shirt 2015; Nelson 2016). At that time, the First Nation was mainly dependent on cattle ranching and fishing. These pursuits were not sufficient to sustain everyone, however. At the same time, oil development in the region had become more intense and new opportunities in the oil industry offered possibilities for employment for some men in the community (Norris 2009). Not all who sought employment with the oil industry were successful, though, due to the poor level of education provided in the residential schools (L. Shirt 2015). Those who were successful either left the community entirely or started extended work leaves. This loss of community members created more suffering for the family members who were left behind (Halfe 2012). Recognizing the need to address this issue, members of the community, along with then-Chief Sam Bull and his wife, Linda Bull, began to look at ways to create community-based employment (Halfe 2012; Nelson 2016).

In collaboration with the women in the community, the idea emerged that the First Nation could gain revenue by doing repairs on the garments of the people working in the oil sands, something the women's circle already did for community members working there (Halfe 2012; Nelson 2016). The community approached two of the oil companies about doing repairs to the garments. The companies were interested in this idea, and asked if the community would consider providing cleaning services as well. At that time the oil companies were shipping the oil-soaked overalls to the United States for cleaning, which was time-consuming and expensive (Halfe 2012). The community quickly founded the GFLDC and, by 2005, it was employing 82 people, 88 percent being Indigenous (AANDC 2005). It remains 100 percent owned and operated by the First Nation and now has three divisions, including Canada's largest industrial dry-cleaning company. The WFLFN also owns a number of businesses, including a busing company, an oil well servicing company, and a bakery (WFLFN 2015).

Elders, community members, and leadership developed GFLDC's mandate and values, collectively drawing on the traditional beliefs of the First Nation (Nelson and Sisco 2008). The result was a mandate that promotes community and culture, prioritizes the inherent value of the land and the community's responsibilities as caretakers, and captures the Elders' and community's desire that their business ventures refrain from damaging the earth (Halfe 2010). Having seen firsthand the damage caused to the environment by the oil sands, the community did not want their reserve lands to suffer the same fate. Unfortunately, upholding these principles was difficult due to the limited number of economic options available to them as they sought their economic independence. Over time, the harsh chemicals used in the cleaning process began to negatively impact the health of many of the women working for GFLDC (L. Shirt 2015). The chemical effluent from the cleaning process also began to pollute Goodfish Lake, adversely impacting the viability of the community's traditional fishing economy. Today, GFLDC has addressed these issues by inventing new methods of preventing chemical contamination and collecting the chemicals for recycling. GFLDC is now recognized as a leader in environmental sustainability, being the first Indigenous business in Canada to attain the ISO 14001-2004 (environmental) standard, and has been recognized as an outstanding Aboriginal Business by Cando and the Canadian Council of Aboriginal Business.

The WFLFN is now beginning to overcome the bitter effects of colonialism, though poverty and many other intergenerational impacts remain. The development of businesses opportunities and community-based employment has provided the First Nation community with the capacity to regain some independence and economic self-sufficiency. The education level

has improved and recently the culture has begun to be reclaimed, as many see restoring the Cree culture and language as essential to fostering community solidarity and individual and collective well-being and pride (L. Shirt 2015). Thanks to the community's adherence to their traditional values, and their collective resilience and ingenuity, members continue to embody and reimagine their ancestors' vision for renewed self-sufficiency and well-being.

2) Community Case Study: Carcross/Tagish First Nation, Yukon

Carcross/Tagish First Nation (CTFN) provides an example of a development project based on the terms, principles, interests, goals, and traditional models of the First Nation. The CTFN is one of a limited number of First Nations in Canada that has a settled land claim and self-government agreement. This means that they are no longer subject to the *Indian Act* (1985) and that the Canadian and Yukon governments recognize their jurisdiction over their territory and affairs, such as business development projects (UFA 1990). When the CTFN achieved self-government, they quickly set out a plan for land management, infrastructure, and businesses based on tourism (O'Neil 2015). Community gatherings were held, and ideas and concerns were identified; what emerged from this community-based approach was a community vision that respected their people, traditions, culture, and the environment, and was "suited to the strength of the people and the region" (Carcross 2015). At the forefront of this plan was a unique economic initiative: a network of world-class mountain bike trails (ibid.) developed through a system of collective emergent participatory growth.

The idea for the mountain bike trails also provided the CTFN community with a plan and a way to redirect their youth to a healthy way of life by reconnecting them with their culture, heritage, and lands (O'Neil 2015). To accomplish this goal, the development of the mountain bike trails was led by youth with the help of

Elders and traditional knowledge keepers. The project started with 15 youth, ages 14 and up, carving trails, while Elders and others taught them about "how to plan and build trails, identify plants, protect heritage sites, use traditional place names, and appreciate nature" (ibid.). The project also revived the community's long history of making trails for trade, a disappearing practice that was only remembered by a few Elders (Carcross Wordpress 2013). The project restored pride to the youth and community, and today people from all over the world come to use the bike trails, further demonstrating the success of the project.

The CTFN has since expanded its tourism industry with the development of a retail village, including a museum, arts and gift shop, carving centre, tour companies, and food establishments (O'Neil 2015). It now enjoys a growing level of economic self-sufficiency and independence. In addition to the economic benefits, their tourism has also provided the community with a way to preserve and protect their culture, language, traditional knowledge, and ways of life (ibid.).

A Resurgence of First Nations, Métis, and Inuit Independence and Economic Self-sufficiency

Whitefish Lake First Nation and Carcross/ Tagish First Nation are not unique instances of successful community-based FNMI businesses founded on traditional cultural principles. Many other examples exist, such as the Osoyoos Indian Band in British Columbia, which owns vineyards and an environmentally sustainable industrial park through the Osoyoos Indian Bank Development Corporation; Atuqtuarvik Corporation in Nunavut, an Inuit-owned investment company that aids the development of other Inuit businesses; and Membertou First Nation in Nova Scotia, which owns a number of businesses, including a trade centre and renewable resource company.

Across Canada, a growing number of projects between Indigenous communities and non-Indigenous partners can also be found that are based on a decolonized and Indigenized model of development. One example is the G'Wiigwaamnaaniin (Our Homes) project between the Atikameksheng Anishnawbek First Nation and the Holmes Group. Designed to reflect the rights, traditions, and interests of the First Nation, this project built safe, healthy, and durable homes and infrastructures in the community, and taught building and trade skills to community members. Emerging out of the crisis in FNMI housing across Canada, it provided long-term and sustainable benefits for the community, and incorporated community-based decision-making and participation throughout the initiatives planning and implementation phases.

As these examples show, the ingenuity of FNMI community-based initiatives, founded on traditional practices, values, and knowledge, is providing successful outcomes for FNMI communities and leading to their renewed independence. This is despite having to function in a system that is not conducive to supporting FNMI prosperity, and has intentionally impeded FNMI communities from accessing the resources on their traditional lands, in many cases by according the right to benefit from those resources to non-FNMI industries. This context has often been a catalyst for conflict between FNMI communities and government and/or the corporations that seek to exploit the natural resources on Indigenous peoples' traditional territories, reserves, or unceded lands. Conflict also commonly arises where proposed industrial development projects would have demonstrably negative effects on the environment and/or the lives or national/community interests of the Indigenous peoples living near or downstream from the project. This has created a series of diverse resistance movements across Canada that at times have coincided with the social-justice-oriented struggles of non-Indigenous groups, which are briefly explored in the next section.

Rethinking Indigenous Economic Development within a Capitalist System

Economic development depends on an economic system. Yet, historically, Indigenous economic systems have been dismissed, destroyed, and marginalized. A new discursive space must be created for dialogue about the value of alternative economies. This dialogue must include a discussion of how alternative economies can thrive within the broader capitalist economy and whether the capitalist system needs to change to be more inclusive of alternative economies and their underlying values and worldviews. Community-based economic development can create opportunities for jobs, wealth, and greater well-being in communities, including through revitalization of language and culture (Anderson 1999; Cornell 2010; Nelson 2015). However, the Western development model has a history of forced relocations, segregation, establishing welfare economies, preventing competitiveness within global markets, and imposing the imperative of resource exploitation and environmental degradation for short-term profits, all of which have contributed to the cycle of poverty and dependency of many Indigenous communities (Helin 2009; Loxley 2010). Max-Neef (1992) argues against capitalist notions of perpetual growth in favour of recognition that the economy depends on the ecosystem on which it is based. This argues for a shift in economic development models from focusing on perpetual growth to a relational model and conservation ethic, and even on generational sustainability.

The seven generations philosophy is a philosophy that transcends one culture, but has been attributed to the Haudenosaunee, Anishinabe, Cree, and West Coast nations. The seventh generation is one we will never meet. They are our grandchildren seven generations into the future. We are seven generations from those who came before us. Even those living today are ancestors to those that will come after us, so we must live our lives in a good way in order to protect their future. The Anishinabemowin word Bimaadiziwin embodies this teaching. The direct translation of the word Bimaadiziwin in English is "the good life"; however, it means we must live the teachings of Bimaadiziwin, or the good life, in a good way, with a good mind, a good heart, and a good spirit. According to Anishinabe teachings, this means we must consider how the decisions of today will impact the future generations that will follow us seven generations into the future.

Taking into consideration the seven generations philosophy, imagine a corporation today based on this philosophy. Immediate profits and gains for shareholders would be replaced by decisions based on an intergenerational decision-making process. The philosophy would recognize the importance of true sustainability for generations to come. This is not a popular model for corporations today, yet may be the future of capitalism. Corporations today see social responsibility as an important part of their business (see Chapter 12); yet they still have much to learn to truly grasp the concept of long-term sustainability from an Indigenous perspective.

Conclusion

Indigenous communities across the world have rich, diverse, and advanced cultures, and social and knowledge systems that have been discredited and deliberately dismantled through colonization. Many Indigenous peoples are looking towards development as a means to gain self-governance, self-determination, and economic self-sufficiency. However, as shown, there are many issues and barriers to attaining meaningful development. Embracing capitalism leads to loss of culture, identity, traditional ways of knowing, being, and doing, and a disconnection from the natural world. Development in an Indigenous community must occur on their own terms and support their cultural ways of life and worldview. From a state perspective, development cannot become a means of assimilation nor be invoked in the name of national interest, for risk of cultural genocide. Following the Canadian Truth and Reconciliation Commission's (TRC 2015) recommendations for reconciliation, equal partnership must be the focus of national and international dialogue on development.

Unfortunately, the power dynamics and practices of colonialism are currently being replicated in development projects locally and abroad. This is the case in development colonialism, which (subtly or not) assumes that Indigenous peoples must assimilate and follow the values of the dominant culture, an assumption that is contemporarily hidden under pretexts of economic growth and human development. Development colonialism can be given different names or rationalized differently by the dominant system, but it inevitably conflicts with the inherent rights of Indigenous peoples to self-determination and free, prior, and informed consent. To address these issues requires a critical examination, deconstruction, and analysis of past and current development practices and the acceptance that the design of Western institutions, including development models, were conceived in a very different belief system to achieve very different objectives from those of the Indigenous peoples with whom they are employed.

Understanding the impacts of colonization on Indigenous peoples, the complex and multifaceted past of Indigenous communities, and their interactions with colonial government policies and tools is essential in a development context, as this history affects how they, and you, will see and act in the present (Smith 2014). It is also important to employ a critical lens when reviewing contemporary research, judicial decisions, and policies regarding Indigenous peoples. These are likely to be founded, at least in part, on the research, judicial decisions, and writings of past generations of colonists/settlers, which in turn have likely been influenced by, or written through, the lens of the European colonial mindset. In some instances, such as the Doctrine of Discovery and the legislation and policies stemming from it, there may even be a misguided attempt to legitimize colonial actions or the colonial development mandate. By critically assessing the information that informs contemporary actions, you will be better equipped to understand the communities you are working with and engage in an intelligent and informed dialogue with them. This will increase the likelihood of discovering innovative approaches to your development projects and support the creation of ethical relationships of reciprocity, respect, and understanding that will contribute to the initiatives' overall success.

Questions for Further Learning

- What are the main differences between Indigenous and Western models of governance and leadership?
- Explain development colonialism in your own words. Are there any recent examples within Canada?
- Is the term development inherently colonial? What alternatives exist?
- What are some common features found in the examples given of Indigenous-led development projects in Canada? (Tagish/Carcross First Nation and Whitefish Lake First Nation)
- What is the importance of land in any discussion of development, given the history of colonization?

Key Terms

Aboriginal, p. 192

Anishinabe, p. 206

Bimaadiziwin, p. 200

Cree, p. 204

development, p. 191

development colonialism, p. 191

epistemology, p. 191

First Nations, p. 191

governance, p. 190

Haudenosaunee, p. 194

Indian Act, p. 191

Inuit, p. 191

Nunavut, p. 205

Métis, p. 191

relational worldview, p. 191

self-determination, p. 196

seven generations philosophy, p. 206

Yukon, p. 204

Suggested Readings

Benton-Banai, Edward. 1988. *The Mishomis Book: The Voice of the Ojibway*. Minneapolis, MN: University of Minnesota Press and Hayward, WI: Indian Country Communications.

Blackstock, Cindy. 2009. "Why Addressing the Over-Representation of First Nations Children in Care Requires New Theoretical Approaches Based on First Nations Ontology." *Journal of Social Work Values and Ethics* 6 (3): 1-18.

———. 2011. "The Emergence of the Breath of Life Theory." *Journal of Social Work Values and Ethics* 8 (1).

Cornelius, Carol. 1999. *Iroquois Corn in a Culture-Based Curriculum: A Framework for Respectfully Teaching about Cultures*. Albany: State University of New York Press.

Coulthard, Glen. 2014. *Red Skin, White Masks: Rejecting the Colonial Politics of Recognition*. Minneapolis: University of Minnesota Press.

Gehl, Lynn. 2004. "The Rebuilding of a Nation: A Grassroots Analysis of the Nation-Building Process in Canada." *Canadian Journal of Native Studies* 23 (1): 57–82.

Hall, L. 2008. "The Environment of Indigenous Economies: Honouring the Three Sisters and Recentring Haudenosaunee Ways of Life." In *Lighting the Eighth Fire: The Liberation, Resurgence, and Protection of Indigenous Nations*, edited by Leanne Simpson. Winnipeg: Arbeiter Ring Publishers.

Helin, Calvin. 2009. *Dances With Dependency*. Woodland Hill: Raven Crest Publishing.

Langdon, Jonathon. 2013. "Decolonising Development Studies: Reflections on Critical Pedagogies in Action." *Canadian Journal of Development Studies* 34 (3): 384–399.

Mann, Barbara. 2000. "Iroquoian Women: The Gantowisas." *American Indian Studies*, Vol. 4. New York: Peter Lang.

Nelson, Rodney, and Ashley Sisco. 2008. *From Vision to Venture: An Account of Five Successful Aboriginal Businesses*. Ottawa: The Conference Board of Canada.

Truth and Reconciliation Commission (TRC). 2015. *Honouring the Truth, Reconciling for the Future Summary of the Final Report of the Truth and Reconciliation Commission of Canada*. Ottawa: Truth and Reconciliation Commission.

Suggested Videos

I'm not the Indian You had in Mind. http://www.nsi-canada.ca/2012/03/im-not-the-indian-you-had-in-mind/

"Canada is a Pretend Nation" REDx Talks—Leroy Little Bear. https://vimeo.com/172822409

Cree Documentary: Together We Stand Firm. https://www.youtube.com/watch?v=HoxJ9zwCIhA .

Ecological Footprint: William Rees. http://fod.infobase.com/p_ViewVideo.aspx?xtid=58262

Indigenous ways of knowing. http://fod.infobase.com/p_ViewVideo.aspx?xtid=93990

Native Ecology: Gregory Cajete. http://fod.infobase.com/portalplaylists.aspx?wid=99232&xtid=56718.

The Other Side of the Ledger: An Indian View of the Hudson's Bay Company. www.nfb.ca/film/other_side_of_the_ledger.

Suggested Websites

Assembly of First Nations: http://www.afn.ca/index.php/en

Decolonial Atlas: https://decolonialatlas.wordpress.com/

First Nation Films: http://www.firstnationsfilms.com/

Inuit Tapiriit Kanatami: https://www.itk.ca/

Métis Nation: http://www.metisnation.ca/

Native Solidarity: https://nativesolidarity.org/

The Onaman Collective: http://onamancollective.com/

Unsettling America: https://unsettlingamerica.wordpress.com/

Works Cited

Aboriginal Affairs and Northern Development Canada. 2005. *Annual Report*.

Alfred, Taiaiake. 1999. *Peace, Power, Righteousness: An Indigenous Manifesto*. Don Mills, ON: Oxford University Press.

Anderson, Robert. 1999. *Economic Development among the Aboriginal peoples in Canada: The Hope for the Future*. Concord, ON: Captus Press.

Battiste, Marie. 2002. *Indigenous Knowledge and Pedagogy in First Nations Education: A Literature Review with Recommendations*. Prepared for the National Working Group on Education and the Minister of Indian Affairs Indian and Northern Affairs Canada (INAC). Ottawa: Indian and Northern Affairs Canada.

Blackstock, Cindy. 2009. "Why Addressing the Over-Representation of First Nations Children in Care Requires New Theoretical Approaches Based on First Nations Ontology." *The Journal of Social Work Values and Ethics* 6 (3): 1–18.

———. 2011. "The Emergence of the Breath of Life Theory." *Journal of Social Work Values and Ethics* 8 (1).

Blackstock, Cindy, Terry Cross, John George, Ivan Brown, and Jocelyn Formsma. 2006. *Reconciliation in Child Welfare: Touchstones of Hope for Indigenous Children, Youth, and Families*. Ottawa: First Nations Child and Family Caring Society of Canada.

Blaser, Mario, Harvey Fiet, and Glenn McRae. 2004. *In the Way of Development: Indigenous Peoples, Life Projects and Globalization*. New York: Zed Books.

Blaut, James. 1993. *The Colonizer's Model of the World: Geographical Diffusionism and Eurocentric History*. London: The Guilford Press.

Borah, Woodrow. 1962. "America as Model: The Demographic Impact of European Expansion upon the Non-European World." *Actas y Memorias XXXV Congreso Internacional de Americanistas*. Mexico.

Borrows, John. 1999. "Sovereignty's Alchemy: An Analysis of Delgamuukw v. British Columbia." *Osgoode Hall Law Journal* 37 (3): 537–596.

———. 2010. *Canada's Indigenous Constitution*. Toronto: University of Toronto Press.

Brewer, Anthony. 1980. *Marxist Theories of Imperialism: A Critical Survey*. London: Routledge & Kegan Paul.

Cahokia Mounds State Historic Site. 2008. Cahokia. http://cahokiamounds.org/

Calder v. British Columbia (AG). 1973. S.C.R. 313.

Carcross First Nation. 2013. https://carcross.wordpress.com/2013/01/.

———. 2015. "Invest Carcross: Boundless Opportunity—About. Website." http://www.investcarcross.ca/about/about_us.html

Chansonneuve, Deborah. 2005. *Reclaiming Connections: Understanding Residential School Trauma among Aboriginal People*. Ottawa: Aboriginal Healing Foundation.

Clutesi, George. 1969. *Potlatch*. Sidney: Gray's Publishing Ltd.

Coates, Tracy. "Indigenous Dispute Resolution and Leadership Models: A Platform for Cooperative Governance in the Arctic." *Border Crossings: Indigenous Dialogues and Diplomacy from Around the World*. Special Issue of *Diplomat Magazine* 1 (5).

Constitution Act, 1982, being Schedule B to the *Canada Act 1982* (UK), 1982, c. 11.

Cornelius, Carol. 1999. *Iroquois Corn in a Culture-based Curriculum: A Framework for Respectfully Teaching about Cultures*. Albany: State University of New York Press.

Cornell, Stephen, and Joseph Kalt. 2010. The Harvard Project on American Indian Economic Development. http://hpaied.org/

Cross, Terry. 1997. "Understanding the Relational Worldview in Indian families." *Pathways Practice Digest* 12 (4).

Coulthard, Glen. 2014. *Red Skin, White Masks: Rejecting the Colonial Politics of Recognition*. Minneapolis, MN: University of Minnesota Press.

Daugherty, Richard. 1991. "People of the Salmon." In *America in 1492: The World of the Indian Peoples Before the Arrival of Columbus*, edited by Alvin Josephy and Frederick Hoxie, 49–84. New York: Vintage Books.

Davis Jr., O. L. (1997). "Beyond 'best practice' toward wise practices. *Journal of Curriculum and Supervision*. 1s (1), 1-5.

Deloria, Vine, and James Treat. 1999. *For This Land: Writings on Religion in America*. New York: Routledge.

Dussel, Enrique. 1993. "Eurocentrism and modernity." *Boundary 2* 20 (3): 65–76.

Fenton, William. 1998. *The Great Law and the Longhouse*. Norman: University of Oklahoma Press.

Foot, Richard. 2014. "An economic transformation." *Canadian Lawyer Magazine*, 7 April. http://www.canadianlawyermag.com/5082/An-economic-transformation.html.

Furniss, Elizabeth. 2002. *The Burden of History: Colonialism and the Frontier Myth in a Rural Community*. Vancouver: University of British Columbia Press.

Gagnon, Alain-G. 2015. " Introduction" in *Understanding Federalism and Federation*, edited by Alain-G. Gagnon, Soeren Keil, and Sean Mueller. Farnham: Ashgate.

Goldmann, Gustave, and Senada Delic. 2014. *Aboriginal Populations: Social, Demographic, and Epidemiological Perspectives*. Edmonton: University of Alberta Press.

Goldsmith, Edward. 1997. "Development as Colonialism." http://www.edwardgoldsmith.org/751/development-as-colonialism/

Halfe, George. 2010, 2012, 2014. Interview with G. Halfe, CEO, Goodfish Lake Development Corporation. (Rodney Nelson, Interviewer).

Hall, L. 2008. "The Environment of Indigenous Economies: Honouring the Three Sisters and Re-Centering Haudenosaunee Ways of Life." In *Lighting the Eighth Fire: The Liberation, Resurgence, and Protection of Indigenous Nations*, edited by Leanne Simpson. Winnipeg: Arbeiter Ring Publishing.

Harvey, David. 2003. *The New Imperialism*. New York: Oxford University Press.

———. 2004. "The 'New' Imperialism: Accumulation by Dispossession." *Socialist Register*, no. 40, 63–87.

Helin, Calvin. 2009. *Dances with Dependency*. Woodland Hill: Raven Crest Publishing.

Horn-Miller, Kahente. 2009. *Sky Woman's Great Granddaughters: A Narrative Inquiry into Kanienkehaka Women's Identity*. Ph.D. thesis, Montreal, Concordia University.

Houle, Jody. 2014. Chief Pakan History as told by Jody Houle by her Grandfather, late Albert Houle. http://www.wfl128.ca/chief_history.html

Indian Act. 1985. Government of Canada., R.S., 1985, c. I-5. http://laws.justice.gc.ca/en/I-5/

Iverson, Peter. 1991. "Taking care of the earth and sky." In *America in 1492: The World of the Indian Peoples before the Arrival of Columbus*, edited by Alvin Josephy and Frederick Hoxie. New York: Vintage Books.

Jackson, Sandy. 2010, 2014. Interview with Sandy Jackson, Councillor, Whitefish Lake First Nation. (Rodney Nelson, Interviewer).

Keyser, James, and Klassen, Michael. 2001. *Plains Indian Rock Art*. Vancouver: University of British Columbia Press.

Kidwell, Clara Sue. 1991. "Systems of Knowledge." In *America in 1492: The World of the Indian Peoples before the Arrival of Columbus*, edited by Alvin Josephy and Frederick Hoxie. New York: Vintage Books.

Loxley, John. 2010. *Aboriginal, Northern, and Community Economic Development Papers and Retrospectives*. Winnipeg: Arbeiter Ring Publishing.

Mann, Barbara. 2000. "Iroquoian Women: The Gantowisas." *Reference and Research Book News* 15 (4). http://search.proquest.com/docview/199536588?accountid=14701.

Mann, Charles. 2005. *1491: New Revelations of the Americas before Columbus*. New York: Knopf Publishing.

Max-Neef, Manfred. 1992. *From the Outside Looking In: Experiences in Barefoot Economics*. London: Zed Books.

McNeil, Kent. 2007. *The Jurisdiction of Inherent Right Aboriginal Governments*. National Centre for First Nations Governance.

Métis National Council. 2015. http://www.metisnation.ca/

Monture-Angus, Patricia, and Brenda Conroy. 1995. *Thunder in my Soul: A Mohawk Woman Speaks*. Halifax: Fernwood.

Monture-Okanee, Patricia. 1994. "Alternative Dispute Resolution: A Bridge to Aboriginal experience?" In Catherine Morris and Andrew Pirie, *Qualifications for Dispute Resolution: Perspectives on the Debate*. Victoria, BC: UVic Institute for Dispute Resolution.

Moreton-Robinson, Aileen. 2011. "The White Man's Burden: Patriarchal White Epistemic Violence and Aboriginal Women's Knowledges within the Academy." *Australian Feminist Studies* 26 (70), 413–431.

Nabokov, Peter, and Dean Snow. 1991. "Farmers of the Woodlands." In *America in 1492: The World of the Indian Peoples before the Arrival of Columbus*, edited by Alvin Josephy and Frederick Hoxie, 119–146. New York: Vintage Books.

Nelson, Rodney, and Ashley Sisco. 2008. *From Vision to Venture: An Account of Five Successful Aboriginal Businesses*. Ottawa: Conference Board of Canada.

Nelson, Rodney. 2015. "Corporate Social Responsibility and Partnership Development with First Nations." *Journal of Aboriginal Management*.

———. 2016. *Rethinking Economic Strategies for First Nations in Canada: Incorporating Traditional Knowledge into Governance Practices*. Ph.D. thesis, Ottawa: Carleton University.

Norris, L. 2009. "Goodfish Takes the Bait." *Alberta Venture*, May. http://albertaventure.com/2009/05/goodfish-takes-the-bait/.

Nunavut Tunngavik Inc. and the Minister of Indian Affairs and Northern Development and Federal Interlocutor for Métis and Non-Status Indians. 2010. *Nunavut Land Claims Agreement: an Agreement between The Inuit of the Nunavut Settlement Area as represented by the Tungavik Federation of Nunavut and Her Majesty The Queen in Right of Canada.* Ottawa.

Nunavut Waters and Nunavut Surface Rights Tribunal Act. 2002. S.C. 2002, c. 1.

O'Neil, Beverly, Peter Williams, Krista Morten, Roslyn Kunin, Lee Gan, and Brian Payer. 2015. *National Aboriginal Tourism Research Project 2015: Economic Impact of Aboriginal Tourism in Canada.* Aboriginal Tourism Association of Canada.

Permanent Forum on Indigenous Issues. 2010. *Report on the ninth session.* (19–30 April 2010). Economic and Social Council Official Records.

Pegoraro, Leonardo. 2015. "Second-rate Victims: The Forced Sterilization of Indigenous Peoples in the USA and Canada." *Settler Colonial Studies* 5 (2): 161–173.

Piddocke, Stuart. 1965. "The Potlatch System of the Southern Kwakiutl: A New Perspective." *Southwestern Journal of Anthropology* 21 (3): 244–264.

Porter, Tom. 2008. *And Grandma said ... Iroquois Teachings as Passed Down through the Oral Tradition.* Philadelphia, PA: Xlibris Corporation.

Rasmussen, R. Kent. 2000. *The American Indian Tribes: Culture Areas, Tribes and Traditions, Abenaki, Missouri.* Volume 1. Pasadena, CA: Salem Press.

Reid, Jennifer. 2010. "The Doctrine of Discovery and Canadian law." *The Canadian Journal of Native Studies*, vol. 2: 335–359.

Rich, E.E. 1960. "Trade Habits and Economic Motivation among the Indians of North America." *Canadian Journal of Economics and Political Science* 26 (1): 35–53.

Ringel, Gail. 1979. "The Kwakiutl Potlatch: History, Economics, and Symbols." *Ethnohistory* 26 (4).

Salée, Daniel. 2006. "Quality of Life of Aboriginal People in Canada: An Analysis of Current Research." *IRPP Choices* 12 (6): 1–38.

Shirt, Leona. 2015. Interview with Former Economic Development Officer for Whitefish Lake and Other Communities, Indian and Northern Affairs Canada. (Tracy Coates, Interviewer).

Shirt, Pauline. 2015. Interview with Elder Pauline Shirt, Saddle Lake First Nation. (Tracy Coates, Interviewer).

Schulte-Tenckhoff, Isabelle. 2000. "A Brief Note on Treaties, Real and Fictitious." *Indigenous Law Bulletin*, no. 12.

Simpson, Leanne. 2008. "Our Elder Brothers: The Lifeblood of Resurgence." In *Lighting the Eighth Fire: The Liberation, Resurgence, and Protection of Indigenous Nations,* edited by L. Simpson. Winnipeg: Arbeiter Ring Publishing.

Smith, Keith, ed. 2014. *Strange Visitors: Documents in the History of Indigenous-Settler Relations in Canada from 1876.* Toronto: University of Toronto Press.

Tobias, John. 1983. "Protection, Civilization, Assimilation: An Outline History of Canada's Indian Policy." In *As Long as the Sun Shines and Water Flows: A Reader in Canadian Native Studies,* edited by Ian Getty and Antoine Lussier. Vancouver: University of British Columbia Press.

Treasury Board of Canada Secretariat. 2004. *Government of Canada, Aboriginal Peoples: Canada's Performance.* Ottawa. http://www.tbs-sct.gc.ca/report/govrev/04/cp-rc5_e.asp.

Trovato, Frank, and Anatole Romaniuk. 2014. "Introduction." In *Aboriginal populations: Social, Demographic, and Epidemiological Perspectives,* edited by Frank Trovato and Anatole Romaniuk, xxiii–xxxvi. Edmonton, AB: University of Alberta Press.

Truth and Reconciliation Commission of Canada (TRC). 2015. *Honouring the Truth, Reconciling for the Future: Summary of the Final Report of the Truth and Reconciliation Commission of Canada.*

Umbrella Final Agreement between the Government of Canada, the Council of Yukon Indians and the Government of the Yukon (UFA). 1990. http://cyfn.ca/wp-content/uploads/2013/08/umbrella-final-agreement.pdf.

Usher, Peter. 1993. "Northern Development, Impact Assessment, and Social Change" in *Anthropology, Public Policy and Native Peoples in Canada*, edited by Noel Dyck and James B. Waldram. McGill-Queen's University Press, Montreal.

Venne, Sharon. 1998. *Our Elders Understand Our Rights: Evolving International Law Regarding Indigenous Peoples*. Penticton, BC: Theytus Books.

Voyageur, Cora, Laura Brearley, and Brian Calliou. 2015. *Restorying Indigenous Leadership: Wise Practices in Community Development*. Banff, AB: The Banff Centre.

Washington, Siemthlut Michelle. 2004. "Bringing Traditional Teachings to Leadership." *American Indian Quarterly* 28 (3/4): 583–603.

Watts, Vanessa Amanda. 2016. *Re-meaning the Sacred: Colonial Damage and Indigenous Cosmologies*. Ph.D. thesis. Kingston, ON: Queen's University.

Westwood, Rosemary. 2013. "A First Nations Fix: How a Small Group of Reserves Plans to Borrow a Page from Big Government to Fuel Economic Growth." *Maclean's Magazine*, 4 March. http://www.macleans.ca/economy/business/a-first-nations-fix-2/.

Wesley-Esquimaux, Cynthia, and Brian Calliou. 2010. *Best Practices in Aboriginal Community Development: A Literature Review and Wise Practices Approach*. Banff, AB: The Banff Centre.

WFLFN. 2015. Whitefish Lake History [online]. http://www.wfl128.ca.

Williams, Alex. (Director). 2015. *The Pass System* [Documentary]. Canada: Tamarack Productions.

Woolford, Andrew. 2009. "Ontological Destruction: Genocide and Canadian Aboriginal Peoples." *Genocide Studies and Prevention* 4 (1): 81–97.

Yukon Environmental and Socio-economic Assessment Act. 2003. S.C. 2003, c. 7. http://laws-lois.justice.gc.ca/eng/acts/Y-2.2/index.html.

Part III

Current Issues

11 A Canadian Way to Promote Democracy Abroad?

Lessons from an Abortive Experiment

Gerd Schönwälder[1]

Key Terms

authoritarianism

democracy

democracy promotion

democratization

policy impact

values-based foreign policy

state preferences

Overview

This chapter reviews the efforts by Canadian policymakers and civil society groups to support democratization processes abroad over the past two and a half decades. The first section looks at the motivations that drive democratic countries like Canada to support democratization beyond their own borders—or not do so. Considered "natural" and self-evident by some, this turns out to be a complex proposition. The second section reviews the specific mix of policies and institutional frameworks that have emerged in the Canadian case, arguing that while distinctive in certain respects, these have never amounted to a truly alternative model to the dominant American and European approaches. The third and final section asks what impact these policies have had, based on an assessment of the two principal phases of Canadian democracy support, dominated in turn by competing Liberal and Conservative visions. While earlier Liberal policies were justly criticized for being unfocused and poorly coordinated, the turn towards a more muscular and sometimes punitive approach under the recent Conservative government has not brought the hoped-for gains in direction and effectiveness.

1. This article reflects the personal views of the author, for which he takes full responsibility. It does not reflect the official opinion of the European Union, where the author now works, or of the Centre for International Policy Studies at the University of Ottawa, where he carried out the research on which the article is based.

By the end of this chapter, students will be able to:

- describe how Canadian foreign policy over the last two decades has sought to support democratization in other countries, and to distinguish the different approaches and motivations behind different Canadian policies of democracy promotion.

- discuss in an informed manner the specific contribution Canada could bring to the democracy promotion field.

- understand and describe the specific challenges of assessing results and impacts of value-based foreign policies, including but also going beyond quantitative measures.

Introduction

Canada was not the first country to promote democracy abroad; when it did so it followed in the footsteps of others, chiefly the United States and some European countries. The principal goal of these policies, in Canada and elsewhere, was to accelerate the transition from authoritarian to more transparent and accountable systems of government, by providing external support to pro-democratic actors, institutions, and processes.[2] Following on the heels of the return to democratic rule in most of Latin America during the 1980s and 1990s, these policies received a further boost with the end of the Cold War in 1989–1990 and the ensuing "third wave" of democracy (Huntington 1991) that was sweeping across Eastern Europe, Africa, and Asia. Democracy promotion, previously shunned by many as interference in the domestic politics and even the sovereignty of other nations, was now more broadly accepted, in light of what some considered an inexorable move towards political systems based on representative democracy and free markets (Fukuyama 1992).[3] A sometimes hesitant newcomer to the field—prior support for better governance and more gender equality notwithstanding—Canada was keen to establish a specific "Canadian way" of supporting democratization processes abroad. Such differences in approach—the "how" of democracy promotion, in other words, and what distinguishes the main democracy promoters from one another—have long been a focus of the relevant literature (Perlin 2003). The second main section of this chapter reviews the specific mix of policies, as well as institutional frameworks that emerged in the Canadian case, arguing that while distinctive in certain respects, this never amounted to a truly alternative model to the dominant American and European approaches.

Before and after, in its first and third sections, the chapter turns to two big questions that underlie the debates on means and

---

2. Since the term "democracy promotion" is sometimes taken to include the imposition of democracy by force, some prefer to speak instead of "democracy support" or avoid mentioning the term "democracy" altogether. Given that the exact meaning of these terms remains contested, they will be used interchangeably here, and generally without any reference to the use of force. See Burnell (2007, 1ff.) for an attempt to arrive at more precise definitions.

3. The enthusiasm for this version of modernization theory (see Chapters 1 and 2) has long evaporated. Today, the main challenge is to prevent more countries from sliding back into authoritarianism, or from remaining stuck in a grey zone between democracy and authoritarian rule. See below.

methods. The first one—concerning the "why?" of democracy promotion—is addressed in the following section just below. It revolves around the motivations that drive democratic countries to support democratization beyond their own borders—or not do so. Considered "natural" and self-evident by some—why *wouldn't* democratic states like Canada want to spread the norms and values they are built on?—this is actually a more complex proposition, in which interests, identities, and the specific ways in which they are formulated all play a crucial role.

The second meta-question revolves around the "so what?" of democracy promotion, that is, the results and impact of the policy. It is addressed in the final section just before the conclusion. Based on an assessment of the two principal phases of Canadian democracy support—dominated by competing Liberal and Conservative visions in turn—the section also offers some general thoughts on the challenges and dilemmas inherent in determining the outcomes of any values-based foreign policy, of which democracy promotion is just one expression.

Why Promote Democracy Elsewhere? A Look at Values, Interests, and Preferences

Why would Canada—or other democratic states—want to support democracy elsewhere? Why would they want to use their precious resources to influence the political dynamics of autocratic states, instead of marginalizing or simply ignoring them? Most times, the answer to this question it is based on a version of the theory of the democratic peace (Rosato 2003; Doyle 2005). This theory holds that democratic nations do not wage war on one another because their rulers are accountable to the people, who are generally averse to war. In addition, democratic nations favour market economies and encourage the economic activities of their citizens, which tends to raise the

level of mutual trade and has a beneficial effect on overall prosperity. And since democratic nations have a general proclivity to seek peaceful solutions to their differences, they will also be more open to finding collaborative solutions in areas other than security or economic welfare.

Given these benefits, it is plausible that democratic states would want to coexist with others that have comparable goals and visions, in an environment that allows for negotiation and compromise, rather than in hostile surroundings. But in reality, democratic states sometimes behave quite differently, supporting autocratic regimes or ignoring their abuses, often hesitating to back democratic reform movements and sometimes actively discouraging them. They do so *not* simply because they are democracies in name only, an accusation often levelled at the Western states, particularly the US, although their political systems are of course far from flawless. Even for committed democracies, there are some good arguments *against* promoting democracy abroad.

In part, these arguments are rooted in the nature of democracy itself. Democratization requires a long-term, strategic commitment to succeed, making its benefits tenuous and uncertain, while the risks and costs are direct and immediate. For example, regimes in the process of democratizing tend to be less politically stable than stable and established autocracies (Mansfield and Snyder 1995), and the repercussions of such instability, even in faraway places, may well be felt at home. Recall, for example, the impact of instability in Afghanistan on the rest of the world through the 9/11 attacks. (See Case Study 4.) Furthermore, the benefits of trading with authoritarian states, especially big ones such as China and Russia, may appear to outweigh the benefits of any improvements in their governance and human rights practices, tempting democracies like Canada to turn a blind eye to abuses that take place abroad. More generally, democratic states may fear losing influence in the international arena if they lean too much on authoritarian states and their clients, and so democracies often tone down their criticisms instead.

Clearly, then, there are two different logics at play, one working in favour of supporting democracy elsewhere, and another against it. The first logic emphasizes states' long-term, strategic interests—peace, prosperity, greater collaboration to solve shared problems. The other one points to the more immediate risks—greater instability and more violence in the short and medium term, and the potential of damaging external trade, security, or strategic position.

Faced with these competing logics, democratic states have different options. One is not to promote democracy at all, or perhaps just via passive demonstration and diffusion effects, relying on the power of one's own example. Samuel Huntington (1991) and others (Gleditsch and Ward 2006) have shown that such external influences were indeed instrumental in bringing about the "third wave" of democracy

in the late twentieth century. But since demonstration and diffusion requires proximity, such a strategy would not be very effective in Canada's case, since the non-democratic states it may wish to influence are simply too far away.

To make matters worse, a strategy based on demonstration and diffusion does not seem to prevent the re-emergence of autocratic regimes, or the emergence of hybrid regimes that are neither truly democratic nor fully authoritarian. The fact that countries can remain "stuck" somewhere in a grey zone between authoritarianism and democracy (Carothers 2002; Diamond 2002), and sometimes even go backwards, remains one of the greatest challenges in the democracy promotion field today (Freedom House 2016). A democracy-promotion strategy that doesn't face up to this central challenge is of little practical use (see **Figure 11.1**).

A second option, therefore, is to support external democratization processes more proactively, but still cautiously and selectively, trying

Figure 11.1
Freedom in the World, 2016

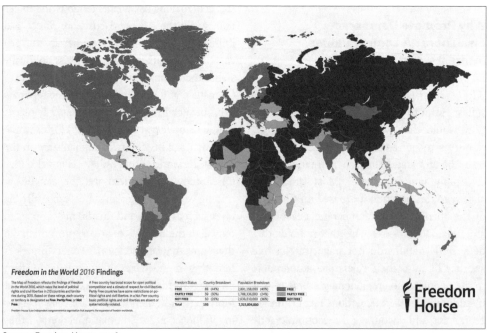

Freedom in the World 2016 Findings

Source: Freedom House, 2016

to control and if possible eliminate the inherent risks. Arguably, Canada did so at times when "embedding" its democracy support in other, less offensive-sounding policies, such as its governance support or its broader international development assistance (although even this may still be too sensitive for many authoritarian regimes!). Another good example comes from the democratic emerging powers, such as India, Brazil, South Africa, or Indonesia, which have begun to provide democracy assistance to others but studiously avoid describing their support in such terms (Schönwälder 2014a). Typically, such a cautious strategy would be responsive and demand-driven, privileging relatively uncontroversial activities such as capacity building and training to run elections over more contentious ones like funding civil society organizations to foster democratic values.

A third option is to support democracy abroad openly and forcefully, *despite* the associated risks. Again, why would democratic states chose to do so? One reason is that their civil societies, and public opinion more generally, push them to pursue a normatively driven foreign policy, grounded in values such as human rights, gender equality, and the rule of law. In Canada, most civil society organizations have consistently expressed such views, and public opinion has been strongly in favour of an activist role for the Canadian government in foreign affairs (Paris 2014).

But pressures from civil society alone cannot fully explain states' differing foreign policy stances. More accurately, such postures should be seen as the result of shifting "state preferences" (Moravcsik 2008; 2010). Importantly, such preferences are derived not just from social values and identities, but also from economic interests as expressed by firms, asset owners, and workers, as well as structures of representation and power that determine which social groups or coalitions are able to "capture" the state and impose their views. Depending on these parameters, states can come to "decide" that promoting democracy is not only "the right thing to do" but also, crucially, in their own best interests, given the long-term strategic benefits of the democratic peace or, in other words, the "utilitarian value" of democratic rule.

State preferences, then, are the result of domestic societal processes of identity formation, as well as interest formulation and political articulation, which in turn determine state or "national" interests and therefore the stances that states take in the international arena. They are not static and immutable, as both realists and institutionalists in international relations theory would have it, but vary according to domestic societal preferences (Moravcsik 2008; 2010). At the same time, since states themselves are embedded not only in domestic but also in transnational society, their actions are framed and conditioned by regional and global contexts as well. Canada, as we will see below, has always framed its democracy support in the context of broader narratives, describing its role in the international arena as a good global citizen and champion of multilateralism (past and present Liberal governments), or a lone but stalwart defender of "what is right" (the Conservative government of 2006–2015).

Canadian Democracy Support in Practice

Canadian democracy support, which began in earnest after the end of the Cold War (1946–1989), can be divided into three broad phases. The first one began in the mid-1980s, marked by the establishment of the International Centre for Human Rights and Democratic Development (ICHRDD) in 1988, the formulation of the first Canadian policy framework for the promotion of "human rights, democratization, and good governance" in 1996 (CIDA 1996), and the proliferation of Canadian non-governmental organizations (NGOs) and other civil society groups engaged in pro-democracy and human rights work.

The second phase started in 2004 when

Thomas Axworthy, Leslie Campbell, and David Donovan published their blueprint for a Canadian Democracy Institute (Axworthy, Campbell, and Donovan 2005). Meant to unite the country's wide-ranging but dispersed pro-democracy activities, and at the same time put a distinctive Canadian stamp on them, the proposal spawned successive parliamentary reports and the growth of a new institutional infrastructure in the following years.

The third phase got underway after the Conservative Party won a majority in the federal elections of 2011. Characterized by a more hard-headed and arguably more ideological approach to the country's foreign affairs, it led to a reversal of previous policies, the dismantling of both government departments and arm's-length agencies previously involved in democracy support (notably ICHRDD), and crippling cutbacks in government support for pro-democracy NGOs and civil society groups. At the time of writing (mid-2017), it remains to be seen if the Trudeau Liberal government will embark on a fourth phase of Canadian support to democracy abroad.

Each phase differed with regard to its underlying drivers and motivations, the institutional framework as well as the civil society networks it fostered and created, and the particular mix of policies it produced. The first phase had its origins in the political debates that led to the foundation of ICHRDD in 1988, themselves an outgrowth of the adoption of Canada's Charter of Rights and Freedoms in the 1982 Constitution and the following reorientation of Canada's foreign policy (Miller 1989; Schmitz 2004). In establishing ICHRDD as an arm's-length Crown corporation modelled on the older and much larger International Development Research Centre (see Chapter 4 and Case Study 6), Canada's Parliament pursued a double-pronged strategy. On the one hand, they kept ICHRDD's budget fairly small and insisted that ICHRDD's mandate did not extend to meddling in another nation's internal affairs, much less "exporting" Canadian norms and values. But on the other hand, they went beyond the traditional human rights agenda built around the notions of protection and redress, to endorse a much wider interpretation that also allowed for institution building and democratic human rights development.

Over the years, ICHRDD, or "Rights and Democracy" as it liked to be called, was respected for its international work on both human rights and democratic development, typically carried out in close cooperation with human rights defenders and non-governmental groups from the countries concerned. But it continued to be constrained by its small budget, which it spread thinly to cover a wide territory, and a resulting lack of visibility, certainly when compared to the bigger donors in the field, such as the US National Endowment for Democracy (NED) or the German political party foundations. And while it may have acted as a spur for other, bigger, federal government departments and agencies to become themselves more engaged in the promotion of human rights and democratic development, Rights and Democracy always seemed to occupy a space separate from "official Ottawa," which never made full use of its many resources and sometimes seemed curiously unaware of its very existence.[4] ICHRDD's tendency to point to shortcomings in Canadian foreign policy making and side with critics of the government did not help, although doing so was not only fully in line with its mandate, but one of the very reasons why Parliament had established it as an arm's-length Crown corporation, and not a government department.

Being part of the Canadian government, the Canadian International Development Agency (CIDA—see Chapter 4) naturally took a more cautious line than Rights and Democracy, but it also responded to different influences. Perhaps

---

4. For example, the debates around 2004–2009 concerning the possibility of establishing a Canadian Democracy Institute or similarly named new entity seemed at times to ignore the fact that any such new agency would have a mandate that overlapped with Rights and Democracy's already existing legislative mandate.

the most important one was the growing attention paid to "good governance" in international development circles, including the OECD Development Assistance Committee (OECD-DAC—see Chapter 4) and international financial institutions such as the World Bank or the International Monetary Fund (IMF). In a notable departure from the structural adjustment policies of previous years, which had been predicated on the neoliberal notion of a minimalist state and tight controls on public spending, good governance—alongside health and education—now came to be regarded as a key ingredient for successful development outcomes (World Bank 2015, 3).

CIDA responded to these influences not only by increasing its spending in the relevant areas, but also by devising a new, overarching policy framework, titled "Government of Canada Policy for CIDA on Human Rights, Democratization and Good Governance" (CIDA 1996). Comprehensive and well-intentioned as it was, the framework remained conceptually vague and failed to provide concrete guidance for the design of more specific policies and programs. It did not help things that some of the Policy's key concepts, notably "governance" itself, carried—and continue to carry—a number of very different meanings. When it did become more specific, for example, in defining governance as the "exercise of power by governments," the framework downplayed equally important dimensions such as political participation or the role of citizens in holding governments accountable. In fact, the political—and indeed democratic—dimension of governance tended to be overshadowed by more practical considerations, revealing a strong bias within CIDA in favour of technical forms of assistance and an equally strong reluctance to engage in forms of support that could be construed as partisan, or worse, as interference in another country's affairs (Schmitz 2004).

A considerable part of CIDA's new programming was delivered via NGOs and civil society groups, whose number and operating budgets grew rapidly, thanks to the increasing resources invested in them. Many of these groups did take sides, but generally not in favour of political movements, parties, or programs—sharing CIDA's reluctance to do so—but rather focusing on specific populations in the developing world they considered marginalized or disadvantaged (e.g., women, ethnic minorities, or simply "the poor"). While providing practical empowerment and moral backing, this kind of support, just like CIDA's technical assistance, did not lend itself easily to political campaigning or day-to-day struggles over political appointments or the design and mandate of political institutions. In fact, the most *political* kind of support that Canada provided during this period was probably via Elections Canada, in the form of training for election officials or hands-on advice and assistance in the running of elections. Despite being obviously political, such work had to be scrupulously non-partisan almost by definition.

By the beginning of the new millennium, Canada's pro-democracy support had grown to encompass a wide range of (sometimes quite distinct) activities, which were delivered by an equally broad assortment of actors, including government departments, arm's-length Crown corporations, and a variety of NGOs and civil society groups. Considered a plus by some, this richness and diversity prompted others to reflect on how to carve out a more distinctively Canadian space for the support of *political* democracy abroad, distinguishing it from human rights work designed to empower and protect the rights of disadvantaged people, or efforts to improve the governance of public institutions in developing and emerging countries and the quality of the services they delivered.

In what marked the start of the second phase in Canada's external democracy support, these reflections culminated in a proposal for a new Canada Democracy Institute in 2004 (Axworthy, Campbell, and Donovan 2005). Essentially a new arm's-length organization that would have bundled all the relevant activities under one roof, the proposed new entity was modelled on the American NED, but also meant to put a distinctly Canadian stamp on the country's support for democracy abroad.[5]

Canada's democracy-support community—especially outside government—reacted cautiously, although the Liberal minority government under Prime Minister Paul Martin (2003–2006) did establish a "Canada Corps" under the auspices of CIDA and later a "Democracy Council" under its 2005 International Policy Statement, to "guide good governance policy making" (DFAIT 2005). Both were allowed to die by later governments.

Subsequent Conservative governments were more enthusiastic, at least initially. The first Conservative minority government under Stephen Harper (2006–2008) set up a Democracy Unit at the Department of Foreign Affairs and International Trade (DFAIT) in 2006 and morphed CIDA's Canada Corps into the Office of Democratic Governance. The next Conservative minority government (2008–2011) went a step further and endorsed the idea of a "new, non-partisan democracy promotion agency" in the 2008 Speech from the Throne, in line with an earlier report by a parliamentary committee (SCFAID 2007). Following the announcement, it turned to Thomas Axworthy, a member of the Liberal Party and one of the co-authors of the original proposal, to chair an independent advisory panel that would make practical recommendations as to how to put the idea into practice.

Curiously though, once the panel had done so in November 2009, the government first remained silent and then, without explaining itself publicly, changed course. In what signalled the beginning of a third phase in Canada's external democracy support, CIDA's Office of Democratic Governance was re-absorbed into the agency's other services, DFAIT's Democracy Unit folded into the department's Democracy

and Francophonie division, and the Democracy Council allowed to die of atrophy. Only after winning a majority in the 2011 federal elections did the Conservatives explain that democracy support would now be part of a new, more "principled" foreign policy.

In a series of speeches and media interviews, government ministers insisted that Canada would no longer "go along" just to "get along," that it would stand by its friends (notably Israel), and that it would punish those that violated the principles it cherished, through boycotts, sanctions, even military action.[6] In essence, this meant that all foreign policy instruments, including formerly arm's-length bodies explicitly set up to provide independent policy advice to the government, would now be marshalled in support not only of Canada's values, but also its interests, including commercial ones.[7] Leaving little room for ambiguity, the government also served notice to Canada's democracy-support community, and civil society at large, that unless they were prepared to toe the government's line, they should not expect to be treated with kid gloves.

The closure of Rights and Democracy in 2012, and cutbacks to NGOs such as KAIROS (an interchurch development coalition), the Canadian Council for International Development, and the North-South Institute, only confirmed the impression of a government no longer interested in pluralism or a variety of views. (See Chapter 7.) These actions also added to the dismantling of Canada's democracy-support infrastructure, both in government and civil society. In fact, the

---

5. Some of the principal proponents had worked—or were still working—for the National Democratic Institute (NDI), one of the "core grantees" of the NED, but felt that the distinctive features of Canada's democratic system would be better reflected in a Canadian democracy promotion agency.

6. Breaking with past practice, the Conservative government never published a formal foreign policy or aid policy review or held a major debate in Parliament on its new foreign policy orientations. (See Chapter 4.) Instead, the Conservatives relied on press releases, social media, and speeches by Foreign Minister Baird and Prime Minister Harper (Baird 2011 and 2013; Harper 2014) to convey their policy orientation.

7. Canada's trade promotion strategy (DFATD 2013) promised to harness "all Government of Canada diplomatic assets to ... support the pursuit of commercial success by Canadian companies and investors." However, the strategy is silent on the social, environmental, and indeed political implications this approach might have.

only new institution created by the Conservatives to promote its pro-democracy agenda was the Office of Religious Freedom, part of the then Department of Foreign Affairs and International Trade. Announced in 2011 and given an annual budget of just $5 million, the Office struggled for several years to become operational, issuing its first call for proposals only in August 2014. More importantly perhaps, the new Office was immediately attacked for its perceived failure to treat all religions equally, and for distracting from the larger challenge of promoting *all* democratic freedoms, not just religious ones.

With the relevant government departments and public agencies brought to heel or closed down, and many pro-democracy NGOs and CSOs (civil society organizations) facing, or already experiencing, drastic cuts (see Chapter 7), it is no surprise that the overall volume of Canada's external democracy support diminished as well. According to figures derived

from the yearly statistical reports on international assistance prepared by CIDA (CIDA 2009–2013), funding for democracy-related activities rose from $193.39 million in fiscal year 2005/2006 to a peak of $238.45 million in 2008/2009, and then declined to only $121.7 million in 2014/2015.[8]

Even at these much-reduced levels, Canada's external democracy support remained significant. Yet, based on the available evidence, it is hard to establish in what way and to what extent this support actually contributed to the new foreign policy agenda of the Conservative government, and how much of it represented

---

8. These yearly totals are the result of adding the respective amounts under the sub-categories Democratic Participation and Civil Society, Elections, Legislatures and Political Parties, Media and Free Flow of Information, Human Rights, and Women's Equality Organizations, all of which appear under the general heading Government and Civil Society. Figures from before fiscal year 2005/2006 are not usable since they are not broken down into sub-categories.

Table 11.1
Canada's Support to Democracy Abroad

Category Title**	Expenses by Fiscal Year (in CAD $ millions)									
	2005-06	2006-07	2007-08	2008-09	2009-10	2010-11	2011-12	2012-13	2013-14	2014-15
Democratic participation and civil society (**)	107.1	120.53	144.55	121.59	103.83	94.90	80.30	58.64	49.92	47.77
Elections	46.33	37.92	16.17	46.16	17.47	33.85	9.60	24.38	15.48	19.39
Legislatures and political parties (**)	N.A.	N.A.	1.04	3.49	6.15	6.61	4.38	2.89	2.78	3.92
Media and free flow of information (**)	6.28	8.28	5.89	5.25	6.42	6.70	4.75	4.98	3.45	3.23
Human rights	33.66	50.13	48.29	54.92	50.98	52.39	51.46	43.37	44.44	42.31
Women's equality organizations and institutions	N.A.	4.78	7.48	7.04	8.88	5.51	4.96	5.78	5.19	5.08
Total democracy support by fiscal year	193.4	216.86	223.42	238.45	193.73	199.96	155.45	140.04	121.26	121.7
(**) Titles or categories may differ before FY 2007–2008.										

Source: CIDA (2006–20) Statistical Reports on International Assistance.

simply a continuation of programming lines established long before the Conservatives took power. In part, this is because the relevant data is much too general to be useful, given the level of aggregation. In addition, many of the labels used, such as electoral assistance, institutional or civil society support, media assistance, and so forth, resemble or are identical to those used by previous governments. The following third section will take a closer look at these issues, in assessing the outcomes of Canadian democracy promotion policies not just by the recent Conservative government but also its Liberal predecessors. As we will see, there are reasons beyond the quality of the available data that make it difficult to establish the "results" and "impacts" of external democracy promotion policies, largely because these go beyond counting dollars and cents (see **Table 11.1** on previous page).

The Bottom Line

Assessing the outcomes of external democracy promotion policies presents specific difficulties (Burnell 2007; 2011). One such difficulty is that these outcomes are hard to quantify. As opposed to specific results or "outputs," which are easy to count and to express in aid dollars spent (e.g., how many election monitors were trained?), more general—and more important—impacts or "outcomes" need to be expressed using qualitative criteria (e.g., were the resulting elections free and fair?). Asking even more general questions (e.g., "based on the last, or the last several elections, has country X become more or less democratic?") results in even more complex challenges.

These issues are compounded by the fact that the concepts used (e.g., "quality" of democracy, or "democratic legitimacy," or even "democracy" as such) are themselves contentious. Furthermore, the perspectives of those providing democracy support can differ substantially from those receiving it. Moreover, since no democracy in the world is perfect, there is always room for disagreements over whether what has been achieved is "truly" democratic or "democratic enough."

Given that democracy promotion tends to take place in complex circumstances, there is a further challenge, which can be termed the "aggregation problem." Even the big democracy promoters with large resources intervene in settings where many factors and variables are effectively beyond their control (e.g., the "Arab Spring"). As a result, it is often difficult or even impossible to establish clear causal linkages between specific interventions and concrete developments on the ground. The fact that there are often several external actors present, pursuing similar goals and supporting similar actors or activities, adds to the difficulty of pinpointing just who had an impact on whom or what.

In the face of these challenges, and given the dearth of comprehensive and systematic evaluations (see CIDA 2008 and SCFAID 2007), any assessment of Canada's external democracy support policies in the last two and a half decades will be open to debate. Nonetheless, it is still possible to offer some observations on what these policies have, or have not, achieved. The focus here is on three specific questions, relating to the overall motivations for Canada's move into the democracy promotion field (discussed in the first section of this chapter), the purpose and objectives behind specific programs or initiatives, and the effectiveness of the means and mechanisms for delivering them. Specifically, I ask to what extent Canada's external democracy support policies have helped to:

- advance democracy in autocratic countries, if not at the system level then at least in some specific respects, while avoiding to do harm;
- develop a distinctive Canadian approach to supporting democratization abroad, and to build an effective institutional framework as well as civil society capacity around it; and
- promote Canada's foreign policy goals and enhance Canada's standing in world.

The most significant outcome of the first phase of Canada's external democracy support, which resulted from a shift in Canada's foreign policy outlook, was the emergence of a an institutional and societal infrastructure dedicated to the strengthening of human rights and the promotion of democratic development abroad. What began with the establishment of Rights and Democracy as an arm's-length Crown corporation in 1988, over time led to changes within the federal bureaucracy itself, notably at CIDA, where programming lines related to human rights, democratization, and good governance were strengthened and expanded, or created from scratch. In parallel, government support to relevant quasi-public agencies such as the Parliamentary Centre or the Federation of Canadian Municipalities was stepped up, while funding from CIDA helped nurture a growing web of Canadian NGOs that worked with local counterparts to advance human rights and democracy in the developing world.

All this work helped project an image of a compassionate and caring nation to the outside world, arguably helping Canada to advance its global standing as a champion of peaceful democratic development and a middle power "punching above its weight." It also helped build capacities within Canada's democracy support community, and often those of local partners. But it is debatable whether these activities amounted to a distinctly Canadian approach to democracy building, notwithstanding some pockets of specific expertise in, say, the strengthening of legislatures or electoral support. Indeed, the very breadth and richness of Canada's democracy support concealed a glaring lack of coordination and collaboration, which made it difficult to discern strategic directions, pinpoint synergies or disconnects, and indeed determine the impact of Canada's significant investments in building democracy abroad.

The 2007 report by the House of Commons Standing Committee on Foreign Affairs and International Development (SCFAID 2007)

turned a spotlight on these issues, calling for deep reforms of the existing structures, while reconfirming the underlying broad conception of democracy support with its emphasis also on governance and human rights.[9] It was building on the earlier blueprint for a Democracy Canada Institute (Axworthy et al. 2005), which in 2004 had inaugurated the second main phase in Canada's democracy support abroad, and was itself followed by an advisory panel report again recommending the creation of an umbrella institution to unite the many strands of Canada's activities in this area, this time called the "Canadian Democracy Promotion Agency" (Axworthy et al. 2009).

The Conservative foreign policy U-turn from 2009 onwards aborted all talk about such a new agency, but the preceding debates and the resulting proposals still had a lasting impact. If nothing else, they suggested concrete remedies for some persistent shortcomings in the way Canada's external democracy support was structured and delivered, and they helped to better delineate Canada's potential role in an already fairly crowded international democracy-support environment (Perlin 2003). These are crucial building blocks for future policymakers, if they decide to use them.

A less benign impact was the beginning of dismantling Canada's democracy support infrastructure, which signalled the beginning of the third main phase in Canada's external democracy support. As mentioned, this trend accelerated with the Conservative election victory in 2011, resulting in the retrenchment of most of Canada's remaining democracy support within DFAIT and CIDA (both of which merged in 2013 to become the Department of Foreign Affairs, Trade and Development, or DFATD).

9. Unbeknownst to SCFAID, an internal CIDA evaluation was coming to similar conclusions regarding the agency's governance programming (including democracy and human rights), eventually calling its management and delivery "ineffective" and noting "an enormous gap between policy and implementation" (CIDA 2008; see also Schmitz 2013).

But contrary to what some may have expected, the drastic reduction in Canada's external democracy support abroad, both in terms of the overall funding and the number of actors involved, did not result in any appreciable gains in focus, effectiveness, and efficiency, based on the available evidence. A glance at DFATD's International Development Project Browser, under the sector heading "democratic governance," revealed a bewildering assortment of activities, including project titles such as "Catastrophe Risk Insurance Facility" and "Energy Sector Capacity Building." In the face of such diversity, distilling meaningful results and impacts at aggregate levels remained very difficult.

To some, these shortcomings are more than compensated for by the Conservative government's forceful defence of "democratic principles" in the international arena, expressed in its strong opposition against those seen to violate them—Russia, Sri Lanka, Iran—and even stronger support for likeminded friends (mainly Israel). But it is at least debatable whether Canada's foreign policy under the Harper government resulted in greater respect for the values purportedly driving it, and whether Canada's role in defending these values gave it greater clout in world affairs. Arguably, Canada's actions often failed to produce the intended results, while its rejectionism, combined with an evident lack of hard power resources and a perceived lack of impartiality and even-handedness in its approach, put it firmly on the sidelines in key international processes (Schönwälder 2014b). In terms of real impact and results, and not forceful rhetoric, Canada did little to advance the cause of democracy, while its actions eroded Canada's status as a moral leader on the world stage.

Conclusion

In the last twenty-five years or so, Canada's external democracy support has evolved through three distinct phases. Initially, inspired by a long tradition of Canadian liberal internationalism (see Chapter 2 and Case Study 1), it produced a growing if dispersed policy framework that included not only democratic development but also human rights and good governance. Subsequently, Canada's democracy-support policies moved closer to US and European approaches, with their clearer institutional structures and more explicit goals and objectives, but without ever resulting in a distinctly Canadian model. In the third phase, overall funding levels and the institutional infrastructure, as well as civil society networks linked to Canada's democracy support policies, went into reverse, as policymakers increasingly turned to strong rhetoric and punitive action as a substitute for the long and painstaking work of helping to build democracy from the ground up.

In a sense, therefore, Canadian democracy support is an unfinished, or if you will, an abortive exercise, but that doesn't mean that it has been pointless. For one thing, the sheer variety and extent of Canada's democracy support policies over the years not only proves that there is a role for countries with longer democratic traditions to help those with shorter or non-existent track records build their own. In principle, it also reinforces the case for a specific Canadian perspective and approach to supporting democracy elsewhere, although the added value of Canada's experience and expertise needs to be demonstrated in each specific case.[10] At the same time, it is clear that such a project can only succeed if there is a much clearer sense of strategic goals and directions than there has been so far, independently of what institutional framework is chosen in the end. Canada's experience shows that neither a very broad policy framework without specific objectives nor the embedding of democracy support in other unrelated actions will yield much by way of concrete results, and therefore cannot replace a more targeted approach.

At the same time, it is clear that "targeted" doesn't mean "directive." It remains up to democratizing nations themselves to determine what route they want to travel and which models they want to use as inspiration. All that outsiders can do is help facilitate these processes, and to work with and strengthen those actors most likely to advance the cause of democracy in their countries, both within and outside political institutions. As others have found out before Canada did, such an approach by necessity implies disagreements as well as setbacks: these are part of the democratic process itself. Attempts to correct them from the outside almost inevitably backfire, sometimes, as seen recently in the Middle East, doing great damage to the very idea of democracy itself, and to its underlying norms and principles. Even-handedness and equanimity are therefore essential, but of course democracy supporters may themselves decide to disengage from certain settings if they conclude that they cannot make a difference there. This should remain the exception rather than the norm: arguably, democratization works best, and its mutual benefits are only realized, when it is based on true partnerships between local pro-democracy actors and external democracy supporters, both playing to their respective strengths.

---

10. All democratic nations have such a contribution to make, based on their individual histories and circumstances, including the democratic emerging democratic powers (Schönwälder 2014a).

Questions for Further Learning

- What motives drive democratic states to promote democracy elsewhere? Are they justified in doing so? How can they distinguish their actions from interfering in the sovereign affairs of other nations?

- What could constitute a distinctive Canadian approach to democracy promotion? What could Canada bring to the field that other democratic states cannot?

- What are the advantages and disadvantages of the three approaches to promoting democracy discussed in the text, respectively: (1) to embed democracy promotion in other, less offensive-sounding policies, (2) to promote democracy openly, by way of a focused, targeted approach, and (3) to couple democracy support with strong sanctions against violators of democratic principles?

- What is the best way to overcome the inherent challenges of assessing the results and impact of value-based foreign policies, such as the promotion of democracy abroad?

Key Terms

authoritarianism, p. 220
democracy, p. 218
democracy promotion, p. 218

democratization, p. 218
policy impact, p. 219

values-based
 foreign policy, p. 219
state preferences, p. 221

Suggested Readings

Axworthy, Thomas, Pamela Wallin, Leslie Camp-
bell, and Eric Duhaime. 2009. *Advisory Panel
Report on the Creation of a Canadian Democracy
Promotion Agency*. Ottawa.

Mansfield, Edward, and Jack Snyder. 1995. "Democratization and the Danger of War." *International Security* 20 (1): 5–38.

Schmitz, Gerald. 2013. *Canada and International
Democracy Assistance: What Direction for the
Harper Government's Foreign Policy?* Occasional
Papers Series 67. Kingston, ON: Centre for Inter-
national and Defence Policy, Queen's University.

Suggested Videos

Democracy Promotion: America's New Regime-
Change Formula, (12:02 minutes), http://www.
dailymotion.com/video/x2w55ra.

EU democracy promotion, (6:41 minutes), https://
www.youtube.com/watch?v=3fSLUDO9nJc.
Short statements on the EU's democracy support and how it could be improved.

Head to Head: Is democracy wrong for China?,
(47:29 minutes), http://video.aljazeera.com/
channels/eng/videos/head-to-head---is
-democracy-wrong-for-china%3F/3953151888001.
An eminent Chinese scholar argues that liberal
democracy is not right for his country.

Michael Walzer on Democracy Promotion,
(3:06 minutes), https://www.youtube.com/
watch?v=9ruaDrxgBY8. Brief mainstream
view on why the US should promote liberal
democracy.

President Barack Obama: Democracy vs. Authoritarianism, (7:35 minutes), https://www.youtube
.com/watch?v=2JYi4kxLHuc. A more eloquent
version of the US mainstream view: why
democracy is better than authoritarianism.

TEDxHayward - Ben Rowswell - Open Source Democracy Promotion, (17:58 minutes), https://www.
youtube.com/watch?v=I-zWJaXhHpI.
A Canadian view of democracy promotion,
focusing on the Middle East and Central Asia.

Suggested Websites

Carnegie Endowment for International Peace /
Democracy and Rule of Law Program: http://
carnegieendowment.org/programs/democracy/
Centre for the Study of Democracy and Diversity,
Queen's University: http://www.queensu.ca/csd/
External Democracy Promotion: http://
external-democracy-promotion.eu/?lang=en
International Institute for Democracy and Electoral
Assistance: http://www.idea.int/
National Democratic Institute: https://www.ndi.org/
Westminster Foundation for Democracy:
www.wfd.org/

Works Cited

Axworthy, Thomas, Leslie Campbell, and David
Donovan. 2005. *The Democracy Canada
Institute: A Blueprint*. Montreal: Institute for
Research on Public Policy.

Axworthy, Thomas, Pamela Wallin, Leslie Campbell, and Eric Duhaime. 2009. *Advisory Panel*

Report on the Creation of a Canadian Democracy Promotion Agency. Ottawa.

Baird, John. 2011. *Address by the Honourable John Baird, Minister of Foreign Affairs, to the United Nations General Assembly*. New York City, 26 September 2011, http://www.international.gc.ca/media/aff/speeches-discours/2011/2011-030.aspx?lang=eng, accessed 25 February 2015.

———. 2013. *Address by Minister Baird to the 68th Session of the United Nations General Assembly*. New York, 30 September 2013, http://www.international.gc.ca/media/aff/speeches-discours/2013/09/30a.aspx?lang=eng, accessed 25 February 2015.

Burnell, Peter. 2007. *Does International Democracy Promotion Work?* Discussion Paper 17/2007. Bonn: German Development Institute.

———. 2011. *Promoting Democracy Abroad: Policy and Performance*. New Brunswick, NJ: Transaction Publishers.

Carothers, Thomas. 2002. "The End of the Transition Paradigm." *Journal of Democracy* 13 (1): 5–21.

CIDA. 1996. *Government of Canada Policy for CIDA on Human Rights, Democratization and Good Governance*. Hull, QC: Canadian International Development Agency (CIDA).

———. 2008. *Review of Governance Programming in CIDA, Synthesis Report*. Hull, QC: Canadian International Development Agency (CIDA).

———. 2006–2013. Statistical Reports on International Assistance. Hull, QC: Canadian International Development Agency (CIDA). http://www.international.gc.ca/development-developpement/dev-results-resultats/reports-rapports/sria-rsai-2012-13.aspx?lang=eng, accessed 1 March 2015.

DFAIT. 2005. *Canada's International Policy Statement: A Role of Pride and Influence in the World, Overview*. Ottawa: Department of Foreign Relations and International Trade.

DFATD. 2013. *Global Markets Action Plan*. Ottawa: Department of Foreign Affairs, Trade and Development.

Diamond, Larry. 2002. "Thinking about Hybrid Regimes." *Journal of Democracy* 13 (2): 21–35.

Doyle, Michael. 2005. "Three Pillars of the Liberal Peace." *American Political Science Review* 99 (3): 463–466.

Freedom House. 2016. *Freedom in the World 2016*. Washington, D.C.: Freedom House.

Fukuyama, Francis. 1992. *The End of History and the Last Man*. New York: Free Press.

Gleditsch, Kristian, and Michael Ward. 2006. "Diffusion and the International Context of Democratization." *International Organization* 60 (4): 911–933.

Harper, Stephen. 2014. *Speech to the Israeli Parliament*. Jerusalem, 20 January. http://www.theglobeandmail.com/news/politics/read-the-full-text-of-harpers-historic-speech-to-israels-knesset/article16406371/, accessed 25 February 2015.

Huntington, Samuel. 1991. *The Third Wave: Democratization in the Late Twentieth Century*. Norman, OK: University of Oklahoma Press.

Mansfield, Edward, and Jack Snyder. 1995. "Democratization and the Danger of War." *International Security* 20 (1): 5–38.

Miller, Robert. 1989. "The International Centre for Human Rights and Democratic Development: Notes on Its Mission." In *Human Rights, Development and Foreign Policy: Canadian Perspectives*, edited by Irving Brecher. Halifax, NS: The Institute for Research on Public Policy.

Moravcsik, Andrew. 2008. "The New Liberalism." In *The Oxford Handbook of International Relations*, edited by Christian Reus-Smit and Duncan Snidal. Oxford: Oxford University Press.

———. 2010. "Liberal Theories of International Relations: A Primer." Princeton, NJ: Princeton University. Available at http://www.princeton.edu/~amoravcs/library/primer.doc, accessed 7 Nov. 2013.

Paris, Roland. 2014. "Are Canadians Still Liberal Internationalists? Foreign Policy and Public Opinion in the Harper Era." *International Journal* 69 (3): 274–307.

Perlin, George. 2003. *International Assistance to Democratic Development: A Review*. IRPP Working Paper Series no. 2003–04. Montreal: Institute for Research on Public Policy.

Rosato, Sebastian. 2003. "The Flawed Logic of Democratic Peace Theory." *American Political Science Review* 97 (4): 585–602.

SCFAID. 2007. *Advancing Canada's Role in International Support for Democratic Development.* Ottawa: House of Commons Standing Committee for Foreign Affairs and International Development (SCFAID).

Schmitz, Gerald. 2004. "The Role of International Democracy Promotion in Canada's Foreign Policy." In *IRPP Policy Matters* 5 (10). Montreal: Institute for Research on Public Policy.

———. 2013. *Canada and International Democracy Assistance: What Direction for the Harper Government's Foreign Policy?* Occasional Paper Series 67. Kingston, ON: Centre for International and Defence Policy, Queen's University.

Schönwälder, Gerd. 2014a. *Promoting Democracy: What Role for the Democratic Emerging Powers?* Discussion Paper 2/2014. Bonn: German Development Institute.

———. 2014b. *Principles and Prejudice: Foreign Policy under the Harper Government.* Policy Brief. Ottawa: Centre for International Policy Studies, University of Ottawa.

Snyder, Jack. 2004. "One World, Rival Theories." *Foreign Policy*, no. 145, 52–62.

World Bank. 2015. *World Development Report 2015, Overview: Human Decision Making and Development Policy.* Washington, D.C.: World Bank.

Notes

12 Canada's Aid Program and the Private Sector

Shannon Kindornay and Fraser Reilly-King

Overview

This chapter examines the increasing focus on partnerships with the private sector to achieve sustainable development outcomes, both internationally and within Canada. The chapter situates current trends in their historical context and provides an overview of the key mechanisms by which bilateral donors, including Canada, are engaging the private sector to achieve sustainable development internationally. This discussion is followed by an examination of the key opportunities and challenges that arise from private sector engagement, including ensuring that private sector partnerships enhance sustainable development outcomes, leverage core business practices, and align with international principles for effective international cooperation.

Learning Objectives

By the end of this chapter, students will be able to:

- understand the historical and current trends related to the role the private sector plays in sustainable development, including the motivating factors behind such trends.
- situate Canadian trends within the broader international context.
- articulate how the Canadian government and other donors are promoting and partnering with different types of private sector actors.
- identify some of the challenges and opportunities for engaging the private sector in sustainable development and how policy makers and practitioners can ensure that private sector partners contribute meaningfully to sustainable development outcomes.

Introduction: What Is the Issue?

Development practitioners and theorists have long recognized the important role of the private sector in contributing to sustainable development outcomes—as an employer, taxpayer, service provider, financier, and innovator. Throughout the 1980s and 1990s, neoliberal policies (see Chapters 1 and 2) promoted economic growth through deregulation, privatization of national services, trade, and financial liberalization. The 1990s and 2000s saw a strong focus on enhancing financial services for the poor—microcredit and microfinance for individual entrepreneurs and small business. In their efforts to promote pro-poor local economic development in developing countries, aid agencies and governments also focused on building the business skills and financial literacy of individuals and organizations, including cooperatives, smallholder farmers, and social enterprises. Since the 2008 global financial crisis, development partners have focused on the role of the state to selectively intervene in the market and correct market failures, raise domestic resources, address agricultural productivity and food price volatility, and create a minimum floor of social protection, with developing country governments and donors playing a more active role on all fronts.

More recently, the international development community has become concerned with the role of the private sector as a partner for achieving sustainable development outcomes. Large private foundations, such as the Bill & Melinda Gates Foundation, are contributing billions of dollars to combat global sustainable development challenges. This has also earned them a spot at the table in identifying and promoting policy solutions and large-scale development initiatives. Multinational companies, such as Unilever, PepsiCo, and others, are also contributing through commitments to improve positive sustainable development outcomes along their supply chains. Bilateral donors, multilateral institutions, such as the World Bank and United Nations (UN) agencies, and many civil society organizations (CSOs) are excited by the possibilities presented through increased engagement with the private sector, including leveraging limited aid dollars, supporting the creation of more development-friendly business models, and harnessing innovative private sector inspired solutions to global development challenges. The private sector is now expected to play a key role in realizing the UN's Sustainable Development Goals (SDGs—see Chapter 2) agreed to by all governments in 2015. Agenda 2030 and its 17 SDGs set out a global plan of action until 2030.

Canada is no stranger to current trends. Since the mid-2000s, the Canadian government has taken a number of measures to increase its engagement with the private sector, including through partnerships with Canadian mining companies and CSOs to deliver development programming in Latin America and Africa, and through support for innovative financing mechanisms that aim to incentivize private sector actors to develop solutions to development challenges, such as the creation of new vaccines, research to improve agricultural productivity, and the adoption of new business models for providing finance to small and medium-sized enterprises (SMEs).

While there is no question that the private sector has an important contribution to make to development, partnerships with the private sector—which aim to serve both commercial and development objectives—present both opportunities and challenges. This chapter unpacks historical trends and assumptions related to the role of the private sector in development. It provides an overview of partnership mechanisms with a special focus on the Canadian context. It concludes by raising five opportunities and challenges to ensuring the private sector makes a meaningful and long-term contribution to sustainable development.

The Role of the Private Sector in Development

International trends

While there has been an increasing emphasis on the role of the private sector as a partner for development, interest in how the private sector can contribute to development outcomes is not new. Indeed, the 1980s and 1990s saw neoliberal Structural Adjustment Programs in many developing countries (see Chapter 2), which aimed to promote economic growth through deregulation, privatization of national services, trade liberalization, and financial openness. In this context, it was argued that market liberalization would pave the way for private investment, leading to much-needed economic growth. Following the failures of structural adjustment in many countries (see Chapter 2), a broader approach to development was enshrined in the Millennium Declaration in 2000. While these goals brought greater attention to poverty reduction, health, education, gender equality, food security, and environmental sustainability, among other things, development outcomes continued to be pursued within a broad neoliberal framework (Soederberg 2004); in fact, the state was not necessarily encouraged to play a

more proactive or interventionist role in promoting economic growth, but rather to expect that the market would play this role.

Since the global financial crisis in 2008, donors and multilateral institutions have increasingly recognized a role for the state to selectively intervene in the functioning of markets and correct market failures implicated in poverty and social exclusion. At the same time, the important role of the private sector in promoting economic growth through job creation and investment, but also in serving as a key partner in achieving development outcomes, has been noted across international fora, including at the United Nations (DCED 2010; UNGC 2013), the Organisation for Economic Co-operation and Development (OECD) (HLF4 2011a; 2011b; OECD 2011), and other international fora (EC 2011; G20 2010) (for an overview, see Kindornay and Reilly-King 2013; Pingeot 2014). Governments are seeking to harness and leverage the potential of the private sector to deliver on development outcomes as an investor, funder, employer, service provider, innovator, and development partner. Donors see the private sector as an engine of growth, but also an important development partner to harness in addressing broader development challenges in areas such as health and education (see **Box 12.1** overleaf).

The increasing focus on the private sector is the result of a number of push and pull factors. Following the financial crisis in 2008, donors pursued private sector partnerships as a means to leverage declining official development assistance (ODA) budgets. While ODA budgets rebounded in 2013, donors continue to emphasize approaches they see as demonstrating "cost effectiveness," "value for money," and even "return on investment" to taxpayers, with private sector partnerships touted as an expedient way to harness limited resources in achieving development outcomes. Donors are taking measures to leverage aid budgets by using aid as the "capital base" to catalyze additional resources from the private sector and

Box 12.1

Who Is the Private Sector?

The private sector ranges from individual entrepreneurs to large multinational corporations.

The private sector includes organizations whose mission focuses on profit-seeking activities, whether by production of goods, provision of services, or commercialization. It includes financial institutions and intermediaries; micro, small, and medium-sized enterprises (MSMEs); individual entrepreneurs; farmers; cooperatives; social enterprises; large corporations; and multinational companies. Within the private sector, organizations focus on social and environmental dimensions as part of their mission to varying degrees. For example, cooperatives often channel profits back into their organization or to their members to promote positive social outcomes as part of their mission; multinationals and large corporations may channel a portion of their profits into corporate social responsibility (CSR) initiatives; other companies may have no social and environmental objectives.

Source: Adapted from Kindornay and Reilly-King 2013, and Klassen and Reilly-King, 2014.

private foundations, and to engage private sector actors in identifying innovative solutions to development challenges.

As part of this trend, the OECD's Development Assistance Committee (DAC) has agreed to better reflect donor efforts to promote and leverage greater aid dollars through the use of private sector instruments in the figures they release on official development assistance (see Chapter 4) (OECD-DAC 2016). The OECD-DAC will now report data on amounts mobilised from the private sector as part of its regular data collection. The OECD's work on a new measure of total official support for sustainable development will also reflect the amounts DAC members leverage from the private sector (Oxfam 2016).

The emphasis on partnership also coincides with concerns over the competitiveness of Northern economies and increasing questions regarding the provision of aid in the aftermath of the financial crises; partnership with the private sector, particularly companies domiciled in the North, offers a way to promote donors' own private sector abroad and maintain current levels of competitiveness (Kindornay, Heidrich, and Blundell 2013; ITUC 2013; Heinrich 2013). Indeed, developing countries are recognized as key markets or investment sites for donor countries' firms and investors. (See Chapter 13.) Partnership offers a means by which donors can promote their own commercial interests alongside development objectives, though donors vary in terms of the extent to which they see the promotion of their own commercial interests as an overt goal of private sector engagement (Byiers and Rosengren 2012, 6; Kindornay and Reilly-King 2013, 15).

In addition, donors also suggest that working with the private sector will serve as a kind of "game-changer" that will enable the realization of internationally agreed development goals, including the SDGs (ITUC 2013, 2). They emphasize the role of the private sector in contributing to job creation, tax revenues, and technology transfers in developing countries, which raises government's and citizens' incomes, enabling developing country governments to provide essential services and, ultimately, contribute to growth and development (Kindornay and Reilly-King 2013; OECD 2016). Donors highlight the role of the private sector in meeting financing gaps to address development challenges, such as infrastructure, climate change, and the provision of essential services (ITUC 2013, 16; OECD 2016). Many donors are seeking to harness the private sector to deliver goods and services to poorer populations (Kindornay and Reilly-King 2013, 15).

Another important motivator for donors is that the private sector is interested in engaging with the development sector (Byiers and Rosengren 2012, 6; UNGC 2013) to improve their public image and brands (Kindornay, Higgins, and Olender 2013; ITUC 2013, 17). Beyond image, companies are interested in opportunities for enhanced market access and the role donors can play in absorbing risks and helping the private sector face competition from emerging markets (Byiers and Rosengren 2012). On the financing side, companies see engagement as beneficial for accessing funding for initiatives that "do not have an adequate business case upfront or that they cannot afford but can be of strategic relevance in the exploration of new markets and products" (Heinrich 2013, 5). Working with donors also provides access to developing country governments (ITUC 2013), existing development structures and networks, and donor expertise (Heinrich 2013; OECD 2016).

The Canadian context

Canada's approach to the role of the private sector in development has evolved over the past two decades. In the 1990s and early 2000s, Canada took a progressive, nuanced approach to understanding private sector contributions to development. The Canadian International Development Agency's (CIDA) 1996 *Policy on Poverty Reduction* and 2003 policy *Expanding Opportunities through Private Sector Development* articulated a vision for private sector development that focused on empowering people as political, social, and economic actors within their own communities in developing countries. The policies of the Liberal government of Jean Chrétien (1993–2003) were progressive in comparison to international trends. CIDA's work on private sector development was to encourage the growth of domestic businesses, including SMEs in developing countries, and

job creation with programs aimed at benefiting "more poor than non-poor people" and combating the sources of poverty, including "the lack of human, physical and financial capital needed to sustain livelihoods, and inequities in access to, control of, and benefits from political, social or economic resources" (CIDA 1996, 2 and 6; CIDA 2003, 2). CIDA recognized that there "is no automatic link between economic growth and poverty reduction" and that the empowerment of people living in poverty is key to ensuring that economic growth promotes development (CIDA 1996, 8).

In 2010, the Conservative government released its *Sustainable Economic Growth Strategy*, which marked a divergence from previous policies. While it included many of the same private sector development programs of previous policies, the assumptions behind CIDA's approach had changed. Previous policies were explicit that the link between growth and poverty reduction is not automatic. The 2010 strategy assumed that sustained economic growth would automatically result in poverty reduction and benefit the poor—by targeting the conditions that would lead to growth rather than specific initiatives that ensured people would benefit from growth. The strategy stated that growing the economy was the best first step to helping people lift themselves permanently out of poverty, and focused on the establishment of the right opportunities through growth and matching individuals with the right skills to take advantage of these opportunities (CIDA 2010). The challenges that people face were linked to a lack of opportunities and appropriate skills. There was no recognition that structural barriers and ongoing inequalities stifled people's opportunities to contribute to, and benefit from, growth. (See Chapter 2.)

In 2015, Canada saw a change of government. In 2016, the new Liberal government launched an International Assistance Review. This review included an examination of how Canada could be more effective in its development cooperation, including with respect to supporting innovation and partnerships with Canadians, the private sector included. Not surprisingly, "Clean economic growth and climate change" was among one of the five thematic priorities identified in a discussion paper for the consultation. While the priority maintained a strong focus on growth as a means of reducing poverty by generating jobs for individuals, building their skills and knowledge, and generating revenue for governments, it made a rhetorical departure from the *Sustainable Economic Growth Strategy* in various ways. It recognized private-sector-led growth was not a panacea and that current patterns of growth were not sustainable. It also noted that "growth that is environmentally and socially sustainable requires adequate public policies, institutions and rule of law" and, that in the light of growing global inequality, not all people were benefiting from growth nor had access to opportunities and resources (Global Affairs Canada 2016, 15–16). With this, the priority signalled a shift towards clean energy and technology, sustainable consumption, natural resource management, climate mitigation and adaptation, infrastructure and public transportation, the rule of law and governance, and corporate accountability, while maintaining a strong focus on education, skills development and training, women's economic empowerment, and financial inclusion.

In the past, Canada's private sector programming did not specifically target the private sector—Canadian or other—as an implementation partner, though the private sector was recognized as one partner among many (Douglas and Kindornay 2013). In recent years, and coinciding with international trends, the Canadian government has taken a more proactive approach to private sector engagement. The official approach has focused on leveraging investments for development—harnessing private sector finance; establishing partnerships that achieve both commercial and development objectives; and supporting private sector innovations for development, such as the creation of new technologies or approaches

to address development challenges (DFATD 2013a). This approach led to measures aimed at promoting Canadian commercial interests, in particular, improving the image of Canadian mining companies operating abroad through support to CSR initiatives, as well as contributing to innovative financing mechanisms (discussed in more detail below). Under the 2006–2015 Conservative government, official support for Canadian commercial interests became a guiding vision for Canadian foreign policy, through the use of aid, trade, and diplomatic resources. This was best illustrated in 2013 by the merger of the former CIDA into the Department of Foreign Affairs, Trade and Development (DFATD) and the government's launch of its Global Markets Action Plan (see DFATD 2013b). The latter promised to marshal "all Government of Canada diplomatic assets ... to support the pursuit of commercial success by Canadian companies and investors," including "leverage[ing] development programming to advance Canada's trade interests" and "the development of an extractive sector strategy to further the interests of Canadian companies abroad" (DFATD 2013c). It is not yet clear how salient a feature this will be of the new Liberal government's policies.

How Are Donors Engaging the Private Sector?

Overview

In their assessment of traditional donors' approaches to the private sector, Kindornay and Reilly-King (2013) argue that donors both *promote* private sector development in developing countries and *partner* with domestic and foreign private sectors to address broader development challenges in developing countries. In other words, they take steps to *build* the private sector in developing countries and *leverage* private sector contributions (ActionAid 2014).

In promoting private sector development, donors often see the link between growth and poverty in developing countries as a direct one: a thriving private sector contributes to growth, which in turn contributes to poverty reduction. This approach aligns with Canada's 2010 *Sustainable Economic Growth Strategy*. Supporting the private sector is valuable in its own right, because it facilitates growth and/or helps integrate developing countries' private sector actors into the global economy, which in turn benefits the poor.

Private sector engagement occurs in all sectors, through a range of mechanisms, as shown in **Table 12.1** (overleaf). As implementing partners, donors seek to harness the skills, expertise, innovation, and finances of the private sector through, *inter alia*, traditional public-private partnerships (PPPs), advanced market commitments (AMCs), the provision of goods and services to poorer populations, research, innovation or challenge funds, concessional financing windows, innovative financing tools, and support for CSR. PPPs are arrangements between one or more governments (the public sector) and one or more private sector companies; they are typically long-term contracts wherein governments get the private sector to invest in and possibly manage a project in exchange for a low-risk, long-term stream of income. Many infrastructure projects such as toll roads are PPPs. In an advance market commitment (AMC), a government may promise to buy a given quantity of a new product at a given price, provided that the private sector firm can invent that product. AMCs are often used, for example, to encourage pharmaceutical companies to invest in research to develop drugs or vaccines for diseases that mostly affect poor people; since poor people cannot afford expensive new treatments, private for-profit companies would not invest in the research and development costs without such a government guarantee.

A number of donors, including Sweden, the United Kingdom, and the United States, combine the logic of partnership with the private sector with the logic of promotion of the private sector. In this context, donors seek to create business relationships between their domestic private sector actors and companies from developing countries through initiatives such as challenge or innovation funds. Here donors are essentially *partnering* with the private sector to *promote* private sector development in recipient countries by partially supporting or subsidizing their own companies to establish new business ventures or particular products and services in developing countries.

Table 12.1 provides an overview of modalities of private sector engagement by donors. **Box 12.2** (overleaf) outlines the roles played by the private sector.

The Canadian context

CIDA partnered with the private sector through its Industrial Cooperation Program (CIDA-INC) from 1978 until 2012. CIDA-INC was designed to meet Canada's commercial objectives and development goals through the provision of concessional loans and professional services to Canadian firms for the establishment of "long-term business relations with developing countries in order to promote and support sustainable socio-economic development and poverty reduction" (CIDA 2007, 2). However, difficulties existed in fulfilling CIDA-INC's objectives and CIDA's broader priorities. For example, the bulk of CIDA-INC finance went to rapidly developing countries, mostly in Asia. (See Chapter 13.) The program did not align with CIDA's focus on countries in Africa and the Middle East that had more acute development financing needs. CIDA-INC's attempt to meet development goals by supporting commercial interests was also often ineffective, with "[n]either agenda ... served" (CIDA 2002, 14). Between 2002 and 2009, direct partnerships through CIDA-INC declined. An evaluation showed that businesses found the program to be overly bureaucratic and found it was often difficult to reconcile CIDA's development objectives and countries of focus with the investment priorities of businesses (CIDA 2007). In 2012, the

Table 12.1

Private Sector Engagement by Donors: Modalities, Objectives, Mechanisms, Roles, and Risk.

Modality	Objectives
Knowledge and information sharing	• Advance solutions by sharing new methods, tools, and innovative approaches to addressing development challenges
Policy dialogue	• Develop policy agendas and frameworks at international, national, and local levels that reflect all parties' interests • Change behaviour, such as through improvements in corporate practices and industry standard-setting
Technical assistance	• Enable private sector actors to effectively engage in development cooperation, such as through support for project design • Improve private sector actors' operational capacities and effectiveness
Capacity development	• Improve capacities of private sector actors to contribute to development results • Change or modify business operations
Finance	• Leverage or raise private sector finance and investment promotion • Test innovation and scale success • Monetize development results (e.g., output-based mechanisms) • Support expansion of more and better business, including through the promotion of business-to-business partnerships, inclusive business, responsible business conduct, and corporate social responsibility • Harness private sector expertise and market-based solutions to tackle development challenges

Source: Modified from OECD, 2016

program was suspended following a review that revealed financial irregularities.

Although the Canadian government has no publicly announced private sector strategy *per se*, Canada's current approach to private sector engagement tends to focus on leveraging the private sector to address broader development challenges rather than partnering with the private sector to promote private sector development in developing countries. Canada began leveraging private sector finance and expertise in addressing broader development challenges in the mid-2000s. For example, Prime Minister Stephen Harper announced in 2006 that Canada would support an advance market commitment to create a vaccine for the pneumococcal virus with a US$100 million contribution. In 2010, Canada supported the SME Finance Challenge Fund, an initiative of the Group of Twenty (G20) which engages the private sector to find innovative ways to finance SMEs. More recently, Canada has worked to position itself as a leader on blended finance (initiatives that combine public and private finance), notably in 2015 through the role of Canada's Minister of International Development and La Francophonie as chair of the Redesigning Development Finance Initiative Steering Committee that was set up by the World Economic Forum and the OECD to create global mechanisms for blended finance.

Perhaps most importantly, both past and current Canadian governments have included the extractive sector (mining, oil, and gas) as a big part of their private sector engagement, including offering indirect support for corporate social responsibility (CSR) initiatives that

Mechanisms	Roles of the Private Sector	Level of Financial Risk
• Multi-stakeholder networks • Learning platforms • Conferences, seminars, workshops, and other events • Funding for research (specifically on private sector engagement in development cooperation)	• Beneficiary • Participant • Resource provider	• Low
• Multi-stakeholder networks and platforms • Cross-sector roundtables • Specialized hubs or institutions • Institutionalized dialogues	• Beneficiary • Participant • Target	• Low
• Business advisory services • Feasibility studies	• Beneficiary	• Moderate • Private sector beneficiaries typically contribute to costs
• Training activities and other forms of capacity development programming • Professional exchanges and secondments	• Beneficiary • Reformer • Target	• Low
• Private sector instruments including grants, debt instruments, mezzanine finance instruments, equity and shares in collective investment vehicles, guarantees, and other unfunded liabilities • Includes the range of instruments captured under innovative finance	• Beneficiary • Implementer • Reformer • Resource provider • Participant	• Moderate to high

Box 12.2

The Role of the Private Sector in Development Cooperation

Vaes and Huyse (2015) suggest that the private sector plays six main roles in development cooperation. It functions as a *beneficiary* when it benefits from development cooperation activities, such as through financial support, capacity development, technical assistance, knowledge sharing, and improved business environments. Private partners are *implementers* when they introduce new business models to realize better social, economic, and environmental outcomes, and *reformers* when they adapt existing business models to realize similar ends. They serve as *resource providers* when they invest financial, expertise, or other strategic resources into projects and initiatives. As *participants*, private sector partners participate in development-related initiatives such as policy dialogue, knowledge sharing, and multi-stakeholder initiatives. Finally, the private sector can be a *target* of government, multilateral organizations, civil society, and other private sector stakeholders to change its business practices.

aim to address local development challenges in developing countries. CSR activities are undertaken by private sector firms either out of genuine concern or in an attempt to improve their public reputation, or both. CSR activities may include mitigating the effects of the company's own commercial activities beyond what the law requires or promoting some broader public good, like sponsoring charity events.

In 2014, the government released an extractive sector strategy and updated its 2009 CSR strategy for the Canadian international extractive sector (DFATD 2014).[1] In its development work, the government has supported the Extractive Industries Transparency Initiative in developing countries, requiring mining, oil, and gas companies to fully disclose all payments to foreign governments, and for governments to fully disclose the revenues received. The *Extractive Sector Transparency Measures Act* requires a commensurate measure by all mining, oil, and gas firms listed in Canada. This measure is deemed necessary because some companies in the extractive industries have been accused of paying bribes to officials in some developing countries in order to obtain contracts; some companies have even been accused of complicity in human rights abuses overseas. Canada has also established the Canadian International Resources and Development Institute to support and build natural resource management capacity in developing countries and has set up four pilot projects between Canadian CSOs and Canadian mining companies operating in Africa and Latin America.

However, many in civil society feel that these efforts fall short. For over a decade, organizations led by the Canadian Network on Corporate Accountability have sought to get legislation passed through the Canadian Parliament to give more teeth to these measures in the form of an independent human rights ombudsperson for the international extractive sector and access to justice in Canadian courts for the foreign victims of corporate abuse by Canadian companies. How the new Liberal government will deal with these issues is not yet clear as of mid-2017.

Looking Ahead: Opportunities and Challenges for Working with the Private Sector

In order to achieve the SDGs, it will be important to continue to engage all development actors, including the private sector, to ensure that they make a positive contribution towards the economic, social, and environmental pillars of sustainable development. Nevertheless, the primary mandate of the private sector remains the maximization of profit. Accordingly, many CSOs and communities remain skeptical about the role that the private sector can play in sustainable development, beyond token and voluntary measures like CSR, pointing to countless examples of the damage and devastation that companies have brought on communities and the environment.

The push for private sector engagement does not effectively address broader challenges related to the effect of companies' regular business operations on development outcomes. Rather it continues to focus on the potential of a few companies or isolated initiatives to "do good" rather than addressing regulatory challenges or balancing "do good" initiatives with real efforts to make sure companies also "do no harm." How to reconcile these two elements? This section looks at a number of broader changes—both opportunities and challenges—that need to occur in Canada and globally to shift the current context, and ensure that the potential benefits to sustainable development by a broader set of private sector actors can be maximized, and the negative impacts minimized.

---

1. These measures are important, since over half of the world's publicly traded mining companies are based in Canada.

New solution or old problem?

The push for private-sector partnerships has not introduced meaningful policy and regulatory reforms that draw on past experience, remedy social and environmental wrongs, and offer recourse for redress. As donors push the private sector to deliver basic social services (for example via PPPs), critics point to the liberalization and privatization era of the 1980s and 1990s and the disastrous effects of privatization on the poor and marginalized, with no means of recourse for these failures. As donors talk about using aid to leverage finance or rely on financial intermediaries (like banks) to channel money towards development, critics point to the total mismanagement by a broad array of financial institutions that catalyzed the financial crisis of 2008, all within the context of weak legislative oversight and little substantive change since. As donors look to open new markets for their companies and push for large infrastructure projects to facilitate the enabling environment for these businesses, critics point to the race to the bottom in social and environmental standards that is occurring in many developing countries, and foreign investment protection agreements that freeze further legislative changes to protect the environment and communities. As donors dismiss the importance of ODA relative to foreign direct investment, critics point to the hundreds of billions of dollars that leave developing countries, including through tax evasion and avoidance. They also note that calls for legislation to address these issues are usually met with new voluntary standards by governments and CSR initiatives by companies.

Canada is a good case in point of this approach. The government's strong focus on promoting extractive industries both domestically and internationally has been accompanied by a set of clear CSR guidelines and voluntary initiatives. Furthermore, the well-documented evidence of the negative social and environmental impacts that countless Canadian mining companies have had around the world and domestically (see Chapter 8), has led Canadian CSOs to call since 2005 for "mandatory, not voluntary" measures. Yet on at least two occasions, legislation has been defeated in Parliament that would have introduced legal redress for mining-affected communities overseas and would have created an independent ombudsman with clear powers to sanction companies for harmful activities. As legal cases continue to make their way to national and regional courts, looking ahead, the Canadian government needs to get the balance right between "do good" (partnership) and "do no harm" (regulation).

Core business: The missing link?

If part of the rationale of partnering with the private sector is to leverage their financial resources and expertise to address global development challenges and improve the outcomes for people living in poverty, then the concept of tapping into core business practices offers some insight into how this might work. For many critics, maximizing profit is the inexorable priority of "for-profit" companies, and any efforts to address social or environmental concerns will amount to nothing more than "greenwashing," that is, portraying actual corporate practices as "greener" or more eco-friendly than they really are. But there is a growing sentiment in the business community that "the leading companies of the future will be those that do business in a way that addresses the major development challenges," challenging the notion that sustainable development and poverty reduction are necessarily mutually exclusive from profit-making (WBCSD et al. 2010, 1). Instead, inclusive core business models can "harness the core competencies of business to respond directly to the needs of poor consumers or to build productive beneficial linkages with poor producers" (ibid.).

While definitions vary, such core businesses look at "products and services from a sustainability perspective and a whole of life cycle approach" (Davies 2011, 8), putting issues of development and environmental sustainability at the heart of the business model. By doing so, donor, NGO, and company-led or hybrid partnerships can contribute to sustainable development and poverty reduction in a number of ways: by integrating local producers, service providers, and workers into company value and supply chains; by investing in these products and communities to generate more predictable, higher quality, consistent, niche, sustainable, or responsible sourcing of products for a company's supply chain; by supplying products to low-income households as consumers and clients that meet their basic needs; and by developing innovative models to provide access to energy, communications technologies, and finance for these communities (WBCSD et al. 2010; Di Bella et al. 2013). In an assessment of 30 trade-related private sector development partnerships, Kindornay and Higgins (2013, 9) note three types of contributions from these partnerships: "Economic development including improving productive capacity, incomes and livelihood opportunities; social development including support for community initiatives, education, health care and gender equality; and environmental protection including reduced use of agricultural inputs (fertilizer, pesticides, water) and conservation efforts." Proponents point to the transformative potential of such partnerships, particularly when they are linked to national, regional, or global supply and value chains. Critics reject the instrumental side of the initiatives, and point to the fundamentally flawed nature of a market-obsessed financial and economic system that maintains inequitable structures of power and wealth. (See Chapter 1.)

The former Conservative government's policies assumed that when it comes to growth, development, and poverty reduction, a rising tide raises all boats. Thus, promoting Canadian commercial interests and key Canadian sectors in strategic emerging markets will bring shared prosperity to developing countries and their populations, while also growing the Canadian economy. Consequently, this approach assumes that the key to poverty reduction lies in improving legal and regulatory frameworks and creating enabling conditions for business that will in turn generate growth and create jobs. While growth is important, in the end, our objective should be not be to create the conditions for the private sector to develop but to create the conditions for the private sector to contribute to development. The Canadian government needs to create space and incentives for more business models that genuinely put sustainability at the heart of their approach.

"It's none of your business": self-interest versus country ownership

Attempts by donor countries, including Canada, to promote their own private sector interests (or thematic priorities) through development partnerships stands in direct contrast to international commitments and frameworks aimed at promoting effective aid and development cooperation. (See OECD 2016.) Through various fora, donors have committed to supporting developing countries' "ownership" over the development agenda. This commitment, which applies to all aid programming, recognizes that "partnerships for development can only succeed if they are led by developing countries, implementing approaches that are tailored to country-specific situations and needs" (HLF4 2011b, 3). In order to support developing countries, donors have agreed to align their efforts behind developing country priorities and plans, and to deliver assistance through country systems as the default option (HLF4 2011b).

However, donor policies related to the private sector still do not promote space for developing countries to establish strong national ownership over the growth and private sector agenda. Donor approaches, alongside the impact of decades of neoliberal policies, continue to diminish the policy space for developing countries to establish socio-economic models specific to their national (and regional) contexts that take into account the views of their citizens. A 2011 consultative study on the private sector and aid effectiveness, based on approximately 50 interviews with donors, developing-country governments, civil society partners, and business leaders, found that the majority of respondents stressed the importance of supporting country ownership in relation to private sector development at the country level (Davies 2011). This means supporting country-led initiatives that build progressive taxation systems with provisions to address capital flight, establish industrial policies, strengthen social and environmental policies, ensure citizen engagement, and establish safeguards and safety nets for the poor and marginalized. Donors can play a role in encouraging developing countries to initiate truly multi-stakeholder processes that shape domestic development plans which engage CSOs, business associations, trade unions, and other actors, in addition to private-sector stakeholders.

Since 2012, aid effectiveness as a principle seems to have slipped from the Canadian government's agenda. From 2009 to 2012, CIDA had an Aid Effectiveness Action Plan. When the plan expired in 2012, it was never renewed. And based on the lack of reference to aid and development effectiveness principles in the *International Assistance Review* (IAR) paper in 2016, it does not seem to be any more of a priority for the present Liberal government. Similarly, noting that current initiatives for the private sector were increasingly promoting Canada's national economic interests and Canada's domestic private sector, the 2012 OECD-DAC Peer Review noted that Canada should ensure that development objectives and partner country ownership were paramount in the activities and programs Canada supported. "There should be no confusion between development objectives and the promotion of commercial interests" (OECD 2012, 11). Any private sector strategy should provide a clear rationale for Canada's engagement, including "well-defined aims, strategic objectives and transparent procedures for partnerships with private sector enterprises" (ibid.).

Transparency, results, and accountability

An important assumption behind partnerships with the private sector is that they will automatically generate better and more positive outcomes for development and that without donor support, such programs wouldn't have taken place. Yet there is little evidence to back up this assertion that such partnerships can guarantee either development or financial additionality, that is, new financial resources that would not otherwise have been forthcoming (Streck 2010). In terms of development additionality—a demonstration that the investment will have clear development and poverty reduction outcomes—Kindornay and Reilly-King (2013) note that many donors do not have transparent monitoring and evaluation mechanisms in place to assess the results from their private sector programs, and that where they do, strong variations exist between programs. Ellmers, Molina, and Tuominen (2010) and Heinrich (2013) note that, in the absence of clear parameters, assessing financial additionality may often be left to a judgement call by program officers in a donor agency. Furthermore, as Kwakkenbos (2012) points out, assessing the additional finance that public investments may leverage from the private sector assumes that any private sector money on offer is new. In practice, a number of sectors favoured by public finance often already have substantial private investment, and seldom need additional public funding, whereas credit-constrained SMEs in developing countries often lose out. In the absence of more rigorous expectations for *public* results and evaluations that focus on development outcomes, it is difficult to assess the extent to which donors are ensuring financial and development additionality in their work with the private sector.

Canada is no exception. While the levels of transparency at Global Affairs Canada have improved in recent years, the government has no publicly available private sector strategy, nor has it publicly articulated how it will assess the financial and development additionality of partnerships with the private sector.

Conclusion

Clearly the private sector has an important role to play in global development and in development cooperation. Donors are engaging different private sectors—their own domestic companies, multinationals, and developing country businesses—at different levels, through a range of different means, and to different ends. Accordingly, donors like Canada need a broader range of approaches for working with the private sector— depending on the role that the different private sectors play, the company's origin (Canadian, multinational, or developing country), and whether it is partnering with or promoting private sector development—matching different modalities of engagement with appropriate objectives and commensurate mechanisms for realizing these object- ives, all the while putting poverty reduction front and centre.

An approach that envisages the private sector as the magic bullet for development fails to situate its role and responsibilities within the broader development landscape. No single actor can do everything. Governments have an essential role to play in realizing the human rights obligations of their citizens. CSOs have a role to play in delivering services, holding governments to account, and researching and advocating for change. Elected officials, local government, media, and citizens all have key roles to play.

The broad push by donors on the private sector side ignores the broader context that requires the private sector to contribute meaningfully and sustainably to development. To be sustainable, as we have argued here, private sector development will require a bal- ance of the carrot and the stick, a shift towards more truly sustainable core business models, genuine country ownership and policy frameworks that articulate the role of the private sector in development, demonstrable and transparent impacts and accountabil- ity for results, and institutionalized multi-stakeholder dialogue.

The ability of countries like Canada to deliver on this agenda will make the real differ- ence in delivering a truly sustainable development agenda for people and the planet.

Questions for Further Learning

- Given the opportunities and challenges, what can practitioners and policy makers do to make sure that the private sector better contributes to economic, social, and environmental development? What would be the role for civil society and different private sectors?
- Are making profit and reducing poverty mutually exclusive? What are the opportunities and solutions for bringing the two together?
- What key policy areas need to be addressed in order to improve the contribution of the (Canadian, multinational, developing country) for-profit private sector to development? How can they be addressed?

Key Terms

corporate social
   responsibility (CSR),
   p. 242

development additionality,
   p. 247
financial additionality, p. 247
private sector, p. 236

private sector development,
   p. 239
public-private partnership
   (PPP), p. 241

Suggested Readings

CSO Partnership for Development Effectiveness. 2014. *CPDE Background Paper on Private Sector Engagement in Development*. Manila: CPDE.

Douglas, Graeme, and Shannon Kindornay. 2013. *Development and the Private Sector: Canada's Approach*. Ottawa: North-South Institute. Available at: http://www.nsi-ins.ca/publications/the-business-of-development-canadian-aid-and-the-private-sector/.

European Parliament, Directorate-General for External Policies, Policy Department. 2014. *Financing for Development Post-2015: Improving the Contribution of Private Finance*. EXPO/B/DEVE/2013/36. Brussels: European Parliament.

Heinrich, Melina. 2013. *Donor Partnerships with Business for Private Sector Development: What can we Learn from Experience*. DCED Working Paper. Cambridge, UK: Donor Committee for Enterprise Development.

Klassen, Jared, and Fraser Reilly-King. 2014. *Leveraging the Private Sector? An Overview and Analysis of How Canadian International Development Organizations Are Engaging the Private Sector through Advocacy, Dialogue, Promotion and Partnership*. Ottawa: Canadian Council for International Co-operation.

Olivié, Iliana, and Aitor Pérez. 2013. *Public Aid as a Driver for Private Investment: Preparing for the 2014 Development Cooperation Forum*. New York: United Nations, Development Cooperation Policy Branch, Department of Economic and Social Affairs.

Suggested Videos

Private Sector Development: a Blessing or a Curse? https://www.youtube.com/watch?v=8ljr9Q-EwFE

UNDP: The Role of Private Sector in Sustainable Development Goals: https://www.youtube.com/watch?v=YblLkcr7sUw

Suggested Websites

Business and Human Rights Resource Centre: http://business-humanrights.org

Canadian Network on Corporate Accountability: http://www.cnca-rcrce.ca

Donor Committee for Enterprise Development: http://www.enterprise-development.org

Global Affairs Canada: Private Sector as Partners in Development: http://www.international.gc.ca/development-developpement/partners-partenaires/ps-sp.aspx?lang=eng&_ga=2.231990812.2045834396.1495573463-22107759.1495573462

OECD Peer Learning on Working with and through the Private Sector in Development: http://www.oecd.org/dac/peer-reviews/private-sector-engagement-for-sustainable-development-lessons-from-the-dac.htm#MAINREPORT

The Practitioner Hub for Inclusive Business: http://www.inclusivebusinesshub.org/

United Nations Global Compact: https://www.unglobalcompact.org

World Business Council for Social Development: http://www.wbcsd.org/home.aspx

Works Cited

ActionAid. 2014. *Aid To, With, and Through the Private Sector: Emerging Trends and Ways Forward*. ActionAid Discussion Paper. London: ActionAid UK.

Bhushan, Aniket, and James Clark. 2016. *Canada's Development Finance Initiative: Making it Happen, Getting the Details Right*. Ottawa: Norman Paterson School of International Affairs.

Byiers, Bruce, and Anna Rosengren. 2012. *Common or Conflicting Interests? Reflections on the Private Sector (for) Development Agenda*. Discussion Paper No. 131. Maastricht: European Centre for Development Policy Management.

CIDA (Canadian International Development Agency). 1996. *CIDA's Policy on Poverty Reduction*. Gatineau: CIDA.

———. 2002. *Private Sector Development: Synthesis Report*. Gatineau: CIDA.

———. 2003. *Expanding Opportunities through Private Sector Development*. Gatineau: CIDA.

———. 2007. *Executive Report on the Evaluation of the CIDA Industrial Cooperation (CIDA-INC) Program*. Gatineau: CIDA.

———. 2010. *Stimulating Sustainable Economic Growth: CIDA's Sustainable Economic Growth Strategy*. Gatineau: CIDA

DCED (Donor Committee for Enterprise Development). 2010. *Bilateral Donors' Statement in Support of Private Sector Partnerships for Development*. Cambridge, UK: DCED.

DFATD (Foreign Affairs, Trade and Development Canada). 2013a. *Private Sector and Development*. Gatineau: DFATD.

———. 2013b. *Global Markets Action Plan*. Available at: http://international.gc.ca/global-markets-marches-mondiaux/plan.aspx?lang=eng

———. 2013c. *Today, the Honourable Julian Fantino, Minister of International Cooperation Issued a Statement Following the Release of Economic Action Plan 2013*. Gatineau: DFATD. 21 March.

———. 2014. *Doing Business the Canadian Way: A Strategy to Advance Corporate Social Responsibility in Canada's Extractive Sector Abroad*. Available at: http://www.international.gc.ca/trade-agreements-accords-commerciaux/assets/pdfs/Enhanced_CS_Strategy_ENG.pdf.

Di Bella, José, et al. 2013. *Mapping Private Sector Engagements in Development Cooperation*. Ottawa: The North-South Institute. Available at: http://www.nsi-ins.ca/wp-content/uploads/2013/09/Mapping-PS-Engagment-in-Development-Cooperation-Final.pdf.

Douglas, Graeme, and Shannon Kindornay. 2013. *Development and the Private Sector: Canada's Approach*. Ottawa: The North-South Institute. Available at: http://www.nsi-ins.ca/publications/the-business-of-development-canadian-aid-and-the-private-sector/.

Davies, Penny. 2011. "The Role of the Private Sector in the Context of Aid Effectiveness: Consultative Findings Document." Paris: OECD. Available at: http://www.oecd.org/development/aideffectiveness/47088121.pdf.

EC (European Commission). 2011. *Increasing the Impact of EU Development Policy: An Agenda for Change*. 13.10.2011 COM (2011) 637 final. Brussels: European Commission.

Ellmers, Bodo, Nuria Molina, and Visa Tuominen. 2010. *Development Diverted: How the International Finance Corporation Fails to Reach the Poor*. Brussels: Eurodad.

Ellmers, Bodo. 2011. *How to Spend It: Smart Procurement for More Effective Aid*. Brussels: Eurodad.

G20 (Group of Twenty). 2010. *Seoul Development Consensus for Shared Growth*. Available at: http://www.g8.utoronto.ca/g20/2010/g20seoul-consensus.pdf.

Global Affairs Canada. 2016. *International Assistance Review*. Discussion Paper. Available at: http://www.international.gc.ca/world-monde/assets/pdfs/iar-consultations-eai-eng.pdf.

Heinrich, Melina. 2013. *Donor Partnerships with Business for Private Sector Development: What Can we Learn from Experience*. DCED Working Paper, March 2013. Available at: http://www.enterprise-development.org/page/download?id=2147.

HLF4 (Fourth High Level Forum on Aid Effectiveness). 2011a. *Expanding and Enhancing Public and Private Co-operation for Broad-Based, Inclusive and Sustainable Growth*. November 11. Available at: http://www.oecd.org/development/aideffectiveness/49211825.pdf.

_____. 2011b. *Busan Partnership for Effective Development Co-operation*. December 1. Available at: http://www.aideffectiveness.org/busanhlf4/images/stories/hlf4/OUTCOME_DOCUMENT_-_FINAL_EN.pdf.

ITUC (International Trade Union Confederation). 2013. *The Private Sector and its Role in Development—a trade union perspective*. Geneva: ITUC. Available at: https://www.ituc-csi.org/IMG/pdf/private_sector-8.pdf.

Kindornay, Shannon, and Fraser Reilly-King. 2013. *Investing in the Business of Development: Bilateral Donor Approaches to Engaging the Private Sector*. Ottawa: The North-South Institute and the Canadian Council for International Co-operation. Available at: http://www.ccic.ca/_files/en/what_we_do/2013-01-11_The%20Business_of_Development.pdf.

Kindornay, Shannon, and Kate Higgins, with Michael Olender. 2013. *Models for Trade-Related Private Sector Partnerships for Development*. Ottawa: The North-South Institute. Available at: http://www.nsi-ins.ca/wp-content/uploads/2012/11/2012-Models-for-Trade-Related-Private-Sector-Partnerships-for-Development1.pdf.

Kindornay, Shannon, Pablo Heidrich, and Mathew Blundell. 2013. *Economic Relations between Canada and Latin America and the Caribbean*. Ottawa: The North-South Institute. Available at: http://www.nsi-ins.ca/publications/economic-relations-canada-latin-america-caribbean/.

Klassen, Jared, and Fraser Reilly-King. 2014. *Leveraging the Private Sector? An Overview and Analysis of How Canadian International Development Organizations Are Engaging the Private Sector Through Advocacy, Dialogue, Promotion and Partnership*. Ottawa: Canadian Council for International Co-operation. Available at: http://www.ccic.ca/_files/en/what_we_do/2014_03_26_PSE_Report_of_Findings.pdf.

Kwakkenbos, Jeroen. 2012. *Private Profit for Public Good? Can Investing in Private Companies Deliver for the Poor?* Brussels: Eurodad. Available at: http://eurodad.org/files/pdf/1543000-private-profit-for-public-good-can-investing-in-private-companies-deliver-for-the-poor-.pdf.

OECD (Organisation for Economic Co-operation and Development). 2011. *The Role of the Private Sector in the Context of Aid Effectiveness: Supporting More Effective Partnership for Development in Busan* (updated version of draft strategy endorsed in May 2010, published June 2011). Available at: http://www.oecd.org/dataoecd/39/35/48156055.pdf.

_____. 2012. *Canada: Development Assistance Committee (DAC) Peer Review 2012*. Paris: OECD.

_____. 2016. *Private Sector Engagement for Sustainable Development: Lessons from the DAC*. Paris: OECD Publishing. Available at: http://www.oecd.org/publications/private-sector-engagement-for-sustainable-development-9789264266889-en.htm.

OECD-DAC (Development Assistance Committee). 2016. *DAC High Level Meeting Communiqué*. Paris, OECD. Available at: https://www.oecd.org/dac/DAC-HLM-Communique-2016.pdf.

Oxfam. 2016. *Recommendations on the Development Assistance Committee's Approach to Incorporating Private Sector Instruments in ODA*. Available at: https://www.oxfam.org/sites/www.oxfam.org/files/file_attachments/draft_cso_recommendations_-_psi_reform_29062016.pdf.

Pingeot, Lou. 2014. *Corporate Influence in the Post-2015 Process.* Aachen/Berlin/Bonn/New York: Brot für die Welt/Global Policy Forum/Misereor. Available at: http://www.globalpolicy .org/images/pdfs/GPFEurope/Corporate _influence_in_the_Post-2015_process_web.pdf.

Soederberg, Susanne. 2004. "American Empire and 'Excluded States': The Millennium Challenge Account and the Shift To Pre-Emptive Development." *Third World Quarterly* 25 (2): 279–302.

Streck, Charlotte. 2010. "The Concept of Additionality under the UNFCCC and the Kyoto Protocol: Implications for Environmental Integrity and Equity." Paper presented at the conference "Climate Change Governance after Copenhagen." Hong Kong: University of Hong Kong.

UNGC (United Nations Global Compact). 2013. *Architects of a Better World: Building the Post-2015 Business Engagement Architecture.* New York: United Nations Global Compact.

UNIDO (United Nations Industrial Development Organization). 2015. *What is CSR?* Vienna: UNIDO.

Vaes, Sarah, and Huib Huyse. 2015. *Mobilising Private Resources for Development: Agendas, Actors and Instruments.* BeFinD Working Paper No. 2. Leuven, Belgium: HIVA-KU Leuven.

World Bank. 2015. *What are Public Private Partnerships?* Washington, D.C.: World Bank. Available at: http://ppp.worldbank. org/public-private-partnership/overview/ what-are-public-private-partnerships.

WBCSD (World Business Council for Sustainable Development), International Business Leaders' Forum et al. 2010. *Accelerating Progress towards the Millennium Development Goals through Inclusive Business Models.* New York: United Nations.

Notes

13 Canada and the "Emerging Economies"

Not Aid, But Not Just Trade

Syed Sajjadur Rahman

Key Terms

emerging economies

emerging markets

Human Development Index (HDI)

middle-income trap

Overview

International trade and investment liberalization, combined with technological innovations in transportation and communications, have integrated global markets and brought countries closer together than ever before. Some developing countries have taken advantage of this open international environment and have achieved rates of economic growth much greater than those of more developed economies. The result has been a dramatic reduction in poverty in these countries. These countries are called "emerging economies." Emerging economies represent both opportunities and threats for Canada. Their increasing prosperity opens up new markets for Canadian goods and services and investments. At the same time, these economies may compete with Canada in international markets. The emerging economies still face a number of development challenges. Addressing the remaining challenges will require new forms of development partnerships that will include enhanced trade and investment links as well as specific knowledge-based development assistance programs.

Learning Objectives

By the end of this chapter, students will be able to:

- understand how some developing economies experienced much faster economic growth than others and became "emerging economies."
- analyze what development challenges these economies will have to solve to reach a developed economy status.
- understand how countries like Canada can form new development partnerships with the emerging economies to help them reach this status.

Introduction: What Is an "Emerging Economy"?

The concept of an emerging economy is a dynamic one. Typically, an emerging economy or market can be a low- to middle-income country. Low-income countries have gross national income per capita of less than US$1,025, and middle-income countries have between US$1,025 and US$12,475 per capita per annum as of 2015, using the World Bank's Atlas Method. Emerging economies are usually considered to be in a transitional phase heading towards a developed market status. (See modernization theory, Chapters 1 and 2.)

Emerging economies are sometimes defined as

a society transitioning from a dictatorship to a free-market-oriented-economy, with increasing economic freedom, gradual integration with the Global Marketplace and with other members of the GEM (Global Emerging Market), an expanding middle class, improving standards of living, social stability and tolerance, as well as an increase in cooperation with multilateral institutions. (Kvint 2009)

Some scholars argue that in emerging markets, financial imperatives have become much more significant; they have developed the idea of "emerging finance capitalism"—an era wherein the collective interests of financial capital are the main shapers of the logical options and choices of government and state elites, over and above those of labour and the popular classes (Marois 2012).

Who are the emerging economies?

It is difficult to make a definitive list of emerging economies or markets. From an economic market perspective, the best guides tend to be financial investment institutions like Morgan Stanley Capital International (MSCI), who are always looking for new investment opportunities around the world. In 2016, the MSCI Emerging Market Index listed 24 countries, based on their

Table 13.1
Emerging Economies Index as of June 2016

Africa and Middle East	Americas	Asia	Europe
Egypt	Brazil	China	Czech Republic
Qatar	Chile	India	Greece
South Africa	Colombia	Indonesia	Hungary
United Arab Emirates	Mexico	Korea	Poland
	Peru	Malaysia	Romania
		Philippines	Russia
		Taiwan	Turkey
		Thailand	

Source: MSCI. https://www.msci.com/market-classification

potential as investment destinations. See **Table 13.1** opposite. More than half of the world's population lives in these emerging economies.

We shall consider the countries in Table 13.1 as examples of emerging economies, with the caveat that the list remains fluid and can change rapidly over time. Some of these economies have per capita incomes above US$12,475, the World Bank's cut-off point for defining high-income economies, and we will omit these economies from our sample in the following analysis in order to illustrate the important elements in considering Canada's relationships with developing emerging economies.

What factors led them to become emerging economies?

The most important factor in becoming an emerging economy was sustained economic growth over many years, leading to what is now considered middle-income status. There were several reasons for the sustained economic growth in these countries.

Perhaps the most important reason was the transformation of these economies from inward-looking closed economies to open market economies integrated with the growing global market. This opening up allowed them to produce goods and services for which they had comparative advantages (meaning they could produce them relatively cheaper than other countries) for a much larger global market. At the beginning, these products were labour-intensive in nature, like garments, but over time they have evolved into more sophisticated capital- and knowledge-intensive products like televisions, computers, and cars. In this, the economies were aided by a relatively literate and educated labour force, and supportive rules and regulations—factors not present in some other developing countries.

Emerging markets often had younger populations. Large, low-cost, educated labour pools gave these markets a tremendous competitive advantage in production. In addition, the use of information technology made possible the innovative and efficient utilization of labour.

From import substitution to export orientation

In the immediate post-colonial period (roughly 1940s to 1970s), most developing countries followed an import substitution industrialization (ISI) policy. In part, this was meant to avoid any type of external "exploitative" economic relationships and to become, to the extent possible, self-sufficient. At the very least, this policy was intended to provide the developing country control over the "commanding height" industries like steel, cement, and oil that had the greatest vertical and horizontal linkages with the other sectors of the economy. Another factor that argued for ISI was the decline in the terms of trade for resources and primary commodities observed during the 1950s and 1960s. (See Chapter 2 on Prebisch and Dependency Theory.) This decline caused a reduction in income for the developing economies who were the main producers of these types of products and whose export earnings depended heavily on them. It was argued that it was necessary to set up domestic manufacturing industries to offset the loss in income and to generate alternative export earning possibilities. The policy instruments used to pursue ISI policies were tariffs and non-tariff barriers (e.g., import quotas) to protect infant manufacturing industries, as well as subsidies to these industries.

However successful these policies were in the short run, ISI proved to be ineffective in promoting economic growth over the longer term, especially in smaller developing economies. There were several reasons:

- Maintaining import substitution policies became unsustainable over time, with high economic and social costs. The high economic costs were due to the subsidies needed to maintain the import-substituting industries. The comfort of state ownership and protection created economically inefficient enterprises that often lost money, despite the protection they received.

- There was also an exhaustion of ISI possibilities and scope for expansion, given limited market size within a given country. Even large economies like Pakistan and Mexico offered limited scope for industrial expansion.
- Corruption became endemic, given that many of the ISI policy tools (e.g., import licences, government permits) created rent-seeking opportunities for corrupt officials seeking bribes.
- Agriculture was neglected in favour of industry, weakening food security.

But for very large economies like China and India, ISI policies often helped promote new and efficient industries. The reason was that the large consumer markets in these countries created economies of scale and competition in these industries and made them efficient. However, the other inefficiencies still remained and hampered the growth of these economies.

The failure (or, at least, the limitations) of ISI policies led governments to consider export-oriented industrialization (EOI) as an alternative means of promoting economic growth, especially given the liberalizing global markets. The EOI countries could take advantage of the growth potential offered by free trade and competition, producing for larger international markets and avoiding the distorting effects of protectionism.

International trade liberalization

The post-1945 era was marked by massive trade liberalization achieved through nine rounds of international negotiations, first under the auspices of the General Agreement on Tariff and Trade (GATT) and, after 1994, through its successor, the World Trade Organization (WTO). This wave of trade liberalization was a reaction against the anti-trade policies of the 1930s, which had worsened the Great Depression

and contributed to the rise of fascism; building institutions to promote greater international cooperation was a keystone of the post–Second World War order. (See Case Studies 1 and 5.) These trade liberalization rounds resulted in enhanced global market access for goods, services, and investment for developing countries. In addition, international agreements constrained their member countries from introducing new trade barriers and fostered trade transparency and convergence in expectations, standards, and policy instruments. There have also been an increasing number of bilateral or regional trading agreements. Canada participates in several of these, notably the North American Free Trade Agreement with the United States and Mexico.

Policies Supporting the Export Orientation

Many developing countries took advantage of the international trade liberalization by pursuing a deliberate policy of EOI. In these economies, the production and composition of exports was not simply left to market forces but was supplemented by deliberately planned interventions by the governments. Fiscal and monetary instruments like explicit export subsidies, liberal tax regimes, and preferential exchange rates attempted to pick winners and helped move the selected industries up the comparative advantages ladder towards more advanced products generating higher value added and employing more highly skilled labour and higher technology. This mix of government policies and private initiatives (and not just freeing the market, as is often suggested) accounted for the spectacular export performance of the East Asian countries like South Korea, Singapore, Hong Kong, and the two Chinas—Taiwan and mainland China.

This type of state-led planning process is often called a model of a "developmental state," or state development capitalism. These types of states are characterized by a strong state guiding the developmental process through judicious use of incentives, rules, and regulations. In some cases, the state model was one of an authoritarian state, as in the case of South Korea, Singapore, and the People's Republic of China, but there were other models as well. Chalmers Johnson, in his book, *MITI and the Japanese Miracle* (1982), characterized the developmental state as a state that is deliberately focused on economic development. According to Johnson, guidance and planning provided by Japanese government officials, particularly at the Ministry of International Trade and Industry (MITI), was responsible for much of Japan's early economic successes in the post–Second World War era.

However, there is much controversy over the role played by EOI policies. A major element of the debate relates to the sequence of domestic vs. external policy reforms and whether, in fact, urgent domestic action needed to address poverty was neglected. The difference between the Southeast Asian and the Mexican and Brazilian experiences is one example of this, where in the latter cases the economic growth resulting from the expansion in trade and investment was accompanied by a rise in poverty. Some East Asian governments made special efforts to bring companies together with public officials to explore possible new comparative advantages. In Latin America, by contrast, there was little consultation between governments and the private sector. The lack of serious coordination produced many projects with no foreseeable comparative advantage. At the same time, though, the state initiated the production of strategic intermediate goods (such as steel in Brazil) that the private sector would have avoided, given the large initial capital layouts and long gestation periods.

Increasing maturity of the private sector [1]

Virtually all theories about emerging economies give a central role to investments in capital stock through financial flows. Financial flows comprise foreign direct investment, bank loans, and portfolios flows (short-term flows) and are, in general, influenced by global economic trends. For example, there was a steady expansion of all of these flows leading up to 2007, before the global financial crisis period. In the acute crisis period of 2008–2009, foreign direct investment remained steady, but bank lending and portfolio flows declined. In the post-crisis period, after 2010, there was strong growth in portfolio flows, especially as interest rates plummeted in the developed economies. Total financial flows reached over $800 billion annually during 2010–2013, with foreign direct investment accounting for about half of the total. Developing Asia received the majority of funds. Over 95 percent of all post-crisis flows went to the middle-income emerging economies, and three countries—China, Brazil, and India—received 34 percent of all flows during this period.

The large and rapid inflows of funds had a positive effect on economic growth in the Asian countries from the 1970s onwards, an effect often termed "the Asian miracle." Theories explaining the impact of these flows fall into two groups (Page 1994):

- The accumulation theories stress the role of capital investments in moving these economies along in their production functions. If a nation makes the investments and marshals the resources, development will follow. Funds are required to increase investments. For the Southeast Asian economies, these funds came from both domestic sources, through very high savings rates, and direct foreign investment. For example, annual foreign

---

1. The statistics for this section are taken from various editions of the IMF's *World Economic Outlook*.

investment flows to China amounted to about $30 billion for more than a decade.

- The assimilation theories place importance on the entrepreneurship, innovation, and learning that was already present in these economies before they undertook outward-oriented and export-oriented policies. These enabling factors allowed them to easily assimilate and adapt new technologies from more advanced industrial nations and then to use these technologies to produce more and better goods for export.

Over all, four elements emerge as important for economic growth in the emerging economies: smart entrepreneurial decision-making enabled by a supportive developmental state, adaptation and innovation of technology, a well-educated and healthy work force, and an increase in exports.

Development Indicators in Emerging Economies

Increases in economic growth and per capita income

There is no question that the outward-oriented policies generated faster economic growth. However, the growth path exhibits distinct regional patterns, as **Table 13.2** shows.

Asia has had some of the fastest growing economies in the world, with China leading the way over the last two and half decades. China is now the second-largest economy in the world. Malaysia has become one of the strongest and stablest economies in the world. In general, Southeast Asian economies are showing signs of becoming relatively mature economies. In contrast, India's annual GDP growth rate is now the highest in the region and it looks poised for a significant takeoff.

In contrast, the Latin American economies grew at a lower rate in the last two decades. Mexico has benefited substantially from NAFTA.

Table 13.2
GDP Growth Rates in Emerging Economies

Region/Country	1990–2000	2000–2014	2015
Africa			
Egypt	4.4	4.5	4.2
South Africa	2.1	3.3	1.3
Americas			
Brazil	2.8	3.7	- 3.8
Colombia	2.8	4.6	3.1
Mexico	3.3	2.3	2.5
Peru	4.5	6.0	3.3
Asia			
China	10.6	10.3	6.9
India	6.0	7.5	7.6
Indonesia	4.2	5.5	4.8
Malaysia	7.0	4.9	5.0
Philippines	3.3	5.1	5.8
Thailand	4.1	4.1	2.8
Europe			
Russian Federation	-4.7	4.0	-3.7
Turkey	4.1	3.98	3.79

Source: The World Bank. http://data.worldbank.org/data-catalog/world-development-indicators

Brazil, given its size and resources, seems destined to become one of the global economic powers if it can overcome its current political crisis. Colombia has achieved good growth rates, but would probably have performed better had it not been for domestic political turbulence and conflict. Overall, growth in Latin American emerging economies has been higher in the 2000s as a result of high commodity prices and remittances from their citizens living overseas.

Emerging from decades of relatively autarkic socialistic statehood, the Russian Federation is now part of the globalized marketplace and therefore susceptible to the fluctuations in these markets. In general, Eastern European economies have grown significantly since the 1990s, based on their actions related to the privatization of their state-owned industries, reforms in the labour market, and an educated population. These economies have succeeded in attracting capital and foreign direct investment to drive productivity improvements and per capita GDP growth.

The increase in economic growth has resulted in an increase in per capita incomes across the emerging economies. Over the last two decades, China's per capita income has been multiplied by thirteen. Brazil, Mexico, Malaysia, the Russian Federation, and Turkey are fast approaching high-income levels. In relative terms, India's per capita income remains low, but it has still grown more than four-fold in recent decades. (See **Table 13.3**.)

Increases in the Human Development Index

The past three decades have also seen a gradual convergence of human development, as shown by the Human Development Index (HDI), a composite measure of indicators along three dimensions: life expectancy, educational attainment, and per capita income. (See Chapter 2.) All groups and regions have seen notable improvement in all HDI components in recent decades, with faster progress in low- and medium-HDI countries. (See **Table 13.4**. overleaf)

The emerging economies have performed particularly well in what the United Nations *Human Development Report 2013* (UNDP 2013) calls the "rise of the South." Some of the largest countries have made the most rapid advances,

Table 13.3
Per Capita Income in Emerging Economies (in Current US$)

Region/Country	Population 2015 (in millions)	Classification by income (2017)	1995	2000	2010	2015
Africa						
Egypt	91.5	Low MIC	920	1,420	2,390	3,340
South Africa	55.0	High MIC	3,863	3,020	7,176	6,050
Americas						
Brazil	207.8	High MIC	4,750	3,694	10,978	9,850
Colombia	48.2	High MIC	2,529	2,504	6,180	7,130
Mexico	127.0	High MIC	3,604	6,582	8,921	9,710
Peru	31.4	High MIC	2,132	1,949	5,075	6,200
Asia						
China	1371.2	High MIC	604	949	4,433	7,820
India	1,311.1	Low MIC	384	457	1,417	1,590
Indonesia	257.6	Low MIC	1,041	790	2,947	3,440
Malaysia	30.3	High MIC	4,286	4,005	8,754	10,570
Philippines	100.7	Low MIC	1,065	1,043	2,136	3,540
Thailand	68.0	High MIC	2,849	1,969	4,803	5,620
Europe						
Russian Federation	144.1	High MIC	2,640	1,710	9,980	11,400
Turkey	78.7	High MIC	2,896	4,220	10,316	9,950

Note: MIC = Middle-income countries. Per capita income is represented by per capita gross national income.
Source: World Bank. World Development Indicators. http://data.worldbank.org/data-catalog/world-development-indicators

Table 13.4

**Human Development Index Levels
in Emerging Economies**

Region/Country	1980	1990	2000	2014
Africa				
Egypt	.453	.546	.622	.690
South Africa	-	.621	.632	.666
Americas				
Brazil	.547	.608	.683	.755
Colombia	.557	.596	.654	.720
Mexico	.601	.648	.699	.756
Peru	.577	.613	.677	.734
Asia				
China	.430	.501	.588	.728
India	.362	.428	.496	.609
Indonesia	.474	.531	.606	.684
Malaysia	.569	.641	.723	.779
Philippines	.557	.586	.623	.668
Thailand	.502	.572	.684	.726
Europe				
Russian Federation	-	.729	.717	.798
Turkey	.492	.576	.653	.761

Note: An HDI value between .800 and 1.0 denotes very high human development; .700–.799 indicates high human development, and .500–.669 suggests medium human development.
Source: United Nations Development Program. http://hdr.undp.org/en/data

notably Brazil, China, India, Indonesia, South Africa, and Turkey. Most of these countries have reached the high human development level. But there has also been substantial progress in smaller economies, such as Bangladesh, Chile, Ghana, Mauritius, Rwanda, and Tunisia.

As the UNHDR 2013 suggests, the developmental paths of Brazil, China, and India, as well as less well-recognized success stories such as Bangladesh, Mauritius, and Turkey, are reshaping ideas about how to attain human development. While there is no single "right path," key drivers and principles of development have begun to emerge from the diversity of development paths. These include deepening the developmental role of states, emphasis on human development and social welfare, and openness to trade and innovation.

Poverty reduction

Between them, Brazil, China, and India account for half of the world's poorest people, and an even bigger share of those who have escaped poverty. In 1981, 84 percent of China's population was below the poverty line of $1.25 a day (in 2005 prices); in 2005 the share was just 16 percent. This amounted to a 6.6 percent annual rate of poverty reduction.

No other country did as well as China. Brazil's share of those in poverty fell by half, from 17 percent to 8 percent, an annual reduction of 3.2 percent. India did the least well, cutting the share below the poverty line from 60 percent to 42 percent between 1981 and 2005. This implies an annual reduction of 1.5 percent a year. These figures do not mirror growth rates. Brazil cut poverty by more than India despite much lower growth, just over 1 percent a year in 1993–2005, compared with India's 5 percent.

Development Challenges in the Emerging Economies

Avoiding the middle-income trap

The rapid growth in the emerging countries based on exports of relatively labour-intensive products created a higher demand for labour that often led to an increase in wages in emerging economies. This rise in wages lead to an increase in production costs, meaning that the manufacturers in these countries sometimes found themselves unable to compete with lower-cost producers elsewhere. At the same time, they were not yet technologically advanced enough to produce higher value products. The solution was a rise in labour productivity. However, some of the emerging economies have faced challenges in moving to a growth path based on higher productivity of labour. This conundrum is often called the middle-income trap, because unless the countries can raise productivity, they are "doomed" to stay at the middle-income level.

This is not an unsolvable problem. Earlier "emerging economies" like Hong Kong, Singapore, South Korea, and Taiwan have successfully transitioned from middle-income status to high-income status. They did so by deliberately emphasizing a process of technological innovations that increased productivity. For example, South Korea and Taiwan moved from being assemblers of existing technologies to being innovators in the assembly processes, and then to being inventors of new technologies; these countries are now leaders in the television and computer industries, among others. At the same time, these countries continued to remain open and allowed market forces to determine production. Strong protection of intellectual property rights (e.g., patents, copyrights, trademarks) was also a major factor in elevating total factor productivity (Watson 2014). Avoiding rigidities in the labour market and avoiding high inflation also helped maintain their competitiveness.

Shifting nature of poverty

According to the World Bank, in 1990, 93 percent of the world's poor people lived in low-income countries (LICs). Now, 73 percent of the poor live in MICs. China and India account for half of the world's poor people, despite the great progress that they have made in poverty reduction and human development. The reason why most poor people live in MICs is simple: having spent the past few decades growing fast, these countries have an average income that places them in the middle-income country category, but high levels of income inequality mean that middle-income countries still have lots of poor people, that is, people who live well below the average income.

Thus, the rise in per capita incomes seen in Table 13.3 above has not resulted in an equitable distribution of income. Dealing with inequality is thus a key part of poverty reduction in the MICs/emerging economies (UNDP 2013). Appropriate policies will have to be developed. While inequality has risen in recent decades in China and India, it has fallen in some other countries, notably Brazil. Government policy can play a big role in reducing inequality. For example, Brazil's main cash transfer program, called Bolsa Familia, provides help to 11 million families, or 60 percent of all those in the poorest 10 percent of the poor. In contrast, social security in China is still provided largely through the private sector. Government policies to fight poverty and inequality can also fail, and miserably. In India, people in the poorest fifth of the population are the least likely to have any kind of food ration cards to access subsidized food, whereas the richest fifth are the most likely to have such cards and get cheap food.

Sustainability: balancing economic growth and environmental sustainability

Developed countries and major emerging economy nations lead the world in carbon dioxide emissions. Developed nations typically have high carbon dioxide emissions per capita, but the emerging nations are fast catching up as they too industrialize and consume more manufactured goods, especially automobiles. Some emerging economies like China lead in the growth rate of carbon dioxide emissions. The emerging developing economies among the top 20 carbon-emitting countries are: China, India, Russia, South Africa, Indonesia, Brazil, Mexico, and Turkey.

The impact of these emissions is globally felt and hurts poor countries and poor communities most. Climate change is already exacerbating chronic environmental threats, and ecosystem losses are constraining livelihood opportunities, especially for poor people. (See Case Studies 8 and 9.) Although low-income countries contribute the least to global climate change, they are likely to suffer the greatest loss in annual rainfall and the sharpest increase in its variability, with dire implications for agricultural production and livelihoods. To ensure sustainable economies and societies, new policies and structural changes are needed that align development and climate-change goals. Adoption of low-emission climate-resilient strategies funded by public-private partnerships (see Chapter 12) are examples of these types of strategies. And these changes are most needed in the developed and the larger emerging economies.

Implications for the Global Economy

The *Human Development Report 2013* (UNDP 2013) reported that, for the first time in 150 years, the combined output of the developing world's three leading emerging economies, Brazil, China, and India, became about equal to the combined GDP of the principal economies of the North—Canada, France, Germany, Italy, the United Kingdom, and the United States. In 1950, Brazil, China, and India together accounted for only 10 percent of the world economy, while the six traditional economic leaders of the North accounted for roughly half. According to projections in this Report, by 2050 Brazil, China, and India will together account for 40 percent of global output, far surpassing the projected combined production of today's G7 group of countries.

There are now more middle-income countries (104 in 2015) than low-income countries (31). Not only that, the Asia-Pacific Region will host about two-thirds of the world's middle class by 2030, Central and South America about 10 percent, and sub-Saharan Africa 2 percent. Within Asia, China and India will account for more than 75 percent of the middle class, as well as its share of total consumption. Another estimate is that by 2025, annual consumption in emerging market economies will rise to $30 trillion, from $12 trillion in 2010.

This "rise of the rest" (Amsden 2001) is a transformative shift in the distribution of global power. (See Case Study 1.) Companies based in these economies are already challenging multinationals based in the developed world, and

not only in their home markets. China-based Lenovo's purchase of IBM's personal computer business in 2004 and the acquisition of Jaguar and Land Rover by India's Tata Motors in 2008 are only two examples of the increasing global mergers and acquisitions activity by companies based in emerging markets. Some observers see the financial crisis of 2008–2009 as an inflection point, accelerating the emergence of these markets as dominant players in the global economy (Khanna and Palepu 2010).

But the consequences of such dramatic expansion can be dire unless substantive action is undertaken, especially in promoting global sustainable development. The global environmental debate encapsulates the tension between "globalizing" and "deglobalizing" tendencies—that is, we should either promote globalization as the best way of protecting the environment or dismantle the global economy and allow localities to control their own resources. (See Chapter 1 and Case Study 9.) It is highly unlikely the latter option will be feasible. As Kofi Annan once said, "Arguing against globalization is like arguing against the laws of gravity." The developed as well as the emerging economies must take action to mitigate the environmental impact of their actions. The cost of inaction will be high.

Canada and the Emerging Economies

The global economy is changing dramatically. Canada is not keeping pace. The Chinese, Indian, Brazilian, Colombian, Mexican, Korean, Turkish, Vietnamese, Indonesian, and South African economies are expanding at more than twice the rate of Canada's more traditional markets. By the middle of this decade, emerging economies are expected to account for more than half of the world's production and consumption of goods and services ... The rise of emerging economies signals a profound shift in the global economy. They have become integral to the success of new production strategies focused on global value chains, as well as important markets in their own right. The postwar trade and investment architecture is inadequate to deal with these new challenges. We will see more volatility going forward as fast-developing countries exercise newfound power. The quasi-market nature of these newer global players poses unique challenges and requires innovative approaches and different negotiating, trade, and investment strategies from those Canada is now pursuing (Burney et al. 2012).

The above quote, taken from the conclusions of a national advisory council of eminent

Table 13.5

Canadian Trade with and Investment in Emerging Economies, 2015 (in $ Millions)

Region/ Country		Merchandise	Services	FDI Stocks			
		Exports	Imports	Exports	Imports	Outward	Inward
Africa							
Egypt	2015	428.0	741.2	97.0	59.0	-27	NA
South Africa	2015	621.2	880.1	209	331	3,202	1,228
	2003	316.5	503.1	187	86	112	266
Americas							
Brazil	2015	2,250.6	3,742.8	624	297	12,620	19,696
	2003	890.1	1,994.8	165	519	5,778	1,097
Colombia	2015	782.8	829	215	89	2,522	NA
	2003	307.6	373.9	37	94	270	NA
Mexico	2015	6,595.1	31,197	1,131	2,938	14,816	1,422
	2003	2,211.7	12,190.4	700	1015.0	3047	214
Peru	2015	858.3	3,260.1	NA	NA	9947	NA
	2003	133.9	262.6	CONF	CONF	1942	CONF
Asia							
China	2015	20,172.4	65,653.4	2,648.1	2,427	12,410	20,581
	2003	4,809.4	18,582.5	836	599	838	21.6
India	2015	4,317.2	3,935.3	793	1,365	934	3,100
	2003	763.5	1,423.5	253	242	204	59
Indonesia	2015	1,815.5	1,671.6	251	160	4127	NA
	2003	455.4	928	161	71	343.6	NA
Malaysia	2015	788.8	2,638.5	481	324	666	10
	2003	484	2,278	174	140	435	119.0
Philippines	2015	731.7	1,419.3	171	345	1,427	48
	2003	377.6	976.9	128	239	1,170	1.0
Thailand	2015	889.8	3,112.9	140	207	233	7
	2003	460	1,864.8	146	239	534	2.0
Europe							
Russian Federation	2015	1,240.5	1,038.2	368	690	2,261	NA
	2003	330	810	238	347	200	NA
Turkey	2015	1,126.7	1,293.6	110	165	553	-5
	2003	273.3	466.6	64	83	673	NA

Source: Global Affairs Canada. http://www.international.gc.ca/economist-economiste/statistics-statistiques/index.aspx?lang=eng

Canadians, illustrates why Canada urgently needs to re-evaluate its approach towards the emerging economies. Not only are the emerging economies now becoming important economic destinations and sources, but they will remain important from a development perspective and in achieving global development goals, including poverty reduction and sustainable development. Canada's interaction with these economies will thus need to find a balance between commercial and development objectives.

Table 13.6

Canadian Aid to Emerging Economies (in $ millions)

Region/ Country	Classification by income (2017)	2000– 2001	2014– 2015
Africa			
Egypt	Low MIC	22.11	14.72
South Africa	High MIC	19.4	6.22
Americas			
Brazil	High MIC	22.9	1.46
Colombia	High MIC	10.3	39.5
Mexico	High MIC	6.3	1.82
Peru	High MIC	19.2	29.98
Asia			
China	High MIC	67.6	6.25
India	Low MIC	77.9	8.08
Indonesia	Low MIC	38.4	29.09
Malaysia	High MIC	4.4	-
Philippines	Low MIC	27.2	21.68
Thailand	High MIC	5.6	1.15
Europe			
Russian Federation	High MIC	36.3	0.06
Turkey	High MIC	0.2	9.35

Source: Canadian International Development Platform. http://cidpnsi.ca/canadas-foreign-aid-2012/. Global Affairs Canada, *Statistical Report on International Assistance 2014–2015.* http://international.gc.ca/development -developpement/dev-results-resultats/reports-rapports/ sria-rsai-2014-15.aspx?lang=eng

Important trade and investment partners

Canada's trade and investment with the emerging economies has grown at a rapid pace, as Table 13.5 (previous page) shows. A number of these emerging economies are among the top export destinations, import sources, investment destinations, and sources for Canada. For example, China is now the second-largest export destination and the second-largest import source for Canada. Mexico and India rank among the top ten export destinations. As the US launches its request to renegotiate the North American Free Trade Agreement, many believe that Canada should start diversifying its international economic ties to rely less on the US and more on the emerging economies, which in any case are growing faster than the US or Europe.

Development assistance

Despite the spectacular growth and development of these emerging economies over the last three decades, many Canadians still think that foreign aid, or development assistance, is the main economic tie between Canada and the developing world. Canada's aid program is still important, around $4 billion a year in 2017, but our trade and investment ties with the emerging economies are much bigger, as Table 13.5 shows. Still, because these emerging countries still have large numbers of poor people, Canada also maintains an aid program with many of these countries.

Table 13.6 reports on total Canadian aid provided to the emerging economies over time.

The figures in this table include all channels of Canadian government aid, including what is provided through the development arm of Global Affairs Canada (bilateral (country-to-country), partnership (non-governmental organizations), and multilateral (e.g., UN)); through the Department of Finance; and through other Canadian government departments, Crown corporations, and provincial and municipal governments.

From 2002 to 2016, Canada identified two types of countries to which it provides development assistance; the first type is countries of focus, where it provides most of its bilateral aid, and the second type is development partners. Four of the emerging economies identified in this chapter were part of the 25 focus countries earmarked to receive the major proportion of Canadian bilateral aid by the Harper government. They are Colombia, Peru, Indonesia, and the Philippines. These countries were chosen based on their needs, their capacity to benefit from Canadian aid, and their role in meeting Canadian foreign policy priorities. A major development assistance priority for Canada in these countries is to promote economic growth by helping to build economic foundations and investing in improving people's skills. In the case of Colombia, a salient point is the support to the peace process. The development partner countries include (from our list) Egypt and South Africa. The choice of development partners reflects more importance being given to Canada's strategic political and economic interests than in the case of the countries of focus.

For other emerging economies, the Canadian aid presence has been reduced in recent years. For example, Canadian development assistance to Brazil has fallen from almost $23 million in 2000/01 to less than $1.5 million in 2014/15; similarly, Canadian aid to India fell from $78 million to $8 million in the same period. In these and other cases, direct bilateral assistance to these countries is no longer provided, although Canadian non-governmental organizations are still active in these countries, often with funding from the Government of Canada. The major portion of Canadian development assistance to Brazil, India, and other emerging economies now flows through multilateral institutions like the UN and the World Bank, based on imputed share of our funding to these institutions of which Canada is a shareholder or contributor.

This decline in aid to the emerging economies, both absolutely and in relation to trade, investment, and remittances, indicates that economic and strategic political considerations

have become much more important ways for Canada to interact with these emerging economies. This is only natural, as Brazil and India are on their way to becoming major global and regional economic and political powers on their own.

These interests are reflected in Canada's regional development assistance strategies for the Americas and Asia. For example, the Americas strategy identifies three objectives: increasing Canadian and hemispheric economic opportunity; addressing insecurity and advancing freedom, democracy, human rights and the rule of law; and fostering lasting relationships. For Asia, the three main Canadian strategic objectives are building partnerships, development assistance, and economic and commercial engagement.

Future partnerships between Canada and the emerging economies

Canada's future relationships with the emerging economies will have to be multifaceted, encompassing diplomacy, economic relations, and targeted development partnerships.

As befitting the increasing importance of these economies as destinations for Canadian exports and sources of Canadian imports, Canada has continued to intensify its trading relationship with these countries. In the absence of a global agreement on trade, given the failure of the Doha Round to reach satisfactory conclusions for both the developing and the developed countries, Canada's emphasis has been on reaching bilateral free trade agreements with many of the emerging economies.

As Table 13.5 illustrates, the emerging economies have also become important destinations for Canada's direct foreign investments, as well as important sources of funds for Canada. In recognition of this, the government has been negotiating foreign investment protection agreements with many of these economies in order to safeguard and protect Canadian investments, and vice versa, including agreements on repatriation of profits. These free trade agreements and foreign investment protection agreements are important elements of Canada's Global Markets Action Plan. (See Chapter 12.) Emerging economies are specifically targeted in that plan.

New development partnerships

As we saw above, the emerging economies still face important developmental challenges like poverty, inequality, environmental unsustainability, and the middle-income trap. The good news is that the emerging economies are gradually acquiring the ability to address these challenges, sometimes with Canadian help. (See Case Study 6.)

The middle-income trap: A favourable international climate, and intensifying trade and investment relationships, accompanied by rapid global integration can result in productivity enhancements if accompanied by appropriate and encouraging domestic policies that promote technological progress and innovations following the examples of the earlier "emerging economies." Countries like Canada can help by contributing to capacity development such as enhancing skills and encouraging innovative thinking. (See Case Study 6.)

Urban poverty and inequality: Donors like Canada should *not* engage in targeted poverty reduction efforts in the emerging economies or try to offset the impact of inequality. This is because, as emerging economies with strong current and potential economic growth, these countries ought to be able to address the issue of poverty in their own countries. Where development assistance may play a useful role is in transferring knowledge and know-how as to how to prepare and implement appropriate fiscal redistribution mechanisms, such as progressive taxes and social welfare schemes. Donors may also have a role in helping to strengthen public accountability mechanisms such as Parliament and the Auditor General's office. (See Chapter 11.) These offices will play an important role in monitoring and reporting that the growth process does not result in inappropriate distribution patterns and unsustainable practices. At another level, aid could also be useful in piloting small, civil society–led innovative poverty reduction schemes. The latter role may become important with the re-emergence of local philanthropies in many emerging economies. However, if these pilots prove to be good and successful ideas, scaling them up to address country-wide poverty or inequality should be the responsibility of the national governments and not the donors.

Sustainable development: The 2015 Paris Accord provides concrete direction as to how the world plans to reduce global greenhouse-gas emissions and to mitigate global warming. Sustainable development is a global issue to be handled together by changes in behaviour by all people. For emerging economies, the problem is even more urgent, as they, with the developed economies, are now the largest polluters in the world. The establishment of the $100 billion Global Climate Change Fund (to which Canada is a contributor) in 2011 in Durban to be spent by 2020 is a declaration of intention to address the adaptation issues faced in many of these countries at the local level. However, the utilization of this fund will not necessarily result in mitigation or a reduction in greenhouse gas emissions unless there is a radical change in consumption patterns in developed and emerging economies. (See Case Study 8.) From a development assistance perspective, sustainable development should be considered as a global public good—a result in which there is a shared and common interest. Canada should continue to contribute to the Global Climate Change Fund and should actively participate in global efforts to achieve this goal.

Conclusion

The emerging economies have gained significantly from the liberalization of international trade and capital flows facilitated by globalization. However, the continuation of this growth is not automatic, but will require the continuation of an open international environment and successful avoidance of the middle-income trap. Internally, the governments in these countries will need to provide the institutional architecture needed to implement successful, pro-growth, and technologically innovative industrial policies. But the appropriate distribution of the gains from this growth remains a challenge. A new pattern of poverty is emerging, and the adoption of sustainable development practices is becoming increasingly urgent, not only for emerging economies but for the entire world.

The approach to development taken by and with the emerging economies in the coming years will differ significantly from what was done the past. Aid is no longer the driver of these economies, or of Canada's relations with these countries. In the future, Canada's relations with these countries will encompass trade, investment, and development partnerships. As increasingly economically powerful countries, these emerging economies will guide not only their own destinies but that of our planet as well. Canada can assist, but not by using the traditional policy instrument of aid alone. Development partnerships will now be as much in terms of trade, investment, and diplomatic relationships as in terms of specific development assistance.

Questions for Further Learning

- What factors were responsible for economic growth in the emerging economies?
- What can other developing countries learn from their experience?
- What should be the role of larger emerging economies like Brazil, China, and India in promoting sustainable development practices?

Key Terms

emerging economies, p. 256   Human Development Index   middle-income trap, p. 263

emerging markets, p. 256   (HDI), p. 261

Suggested Readings

Amsden, Alice. 2001. *The Rise of "The Rest":
Challenges to the West from Late-Industrializing
Economies*. Oxford: Oxford University Press.

United Nations Development Program. 2013.
*Human Development Report 2013: The Rise of the
South: Human Progress in a Diverse World*. New
York: UNDP.

Wade, Robert. 2003. *Governing the Market:
Economic Theory and the Role of Government
in East Asian Industrialization*. Princeton, NJ:
Princeton University Press.

World Bank. 1993. *The East Asian Miracle*.
Washington, D.C.: World Bank. http://
documents.worldbank.org/curated/
en/975081468244550798/Main-report.

Suggested Videos

Size Matters: BRICs Economies Catching Up to US. https://www.youtube.com/watch?v=degNJPnyUsc

What are the BRICs Countries? https://www.youtube.com/watch?v=F03yzqR4gYI

What are emerging economies? https://www.youtube.com/watch?v=iyCPqyHRqbo

Suggested Websites

Canada's State of Trade: Trade and Investment Performance: http://www.international.gc.ca/economist-economiste/performance/index.aspx?lang=eng.

Winning in a Changing World—Gowlings: www.gowlings.com/.../20120626_Winning-in-a-Changing-World-EN.p...

Global Affairs Canada: http://www.international.gc.ca/international/index.aspx.

World Bank: World dataBank http://data.worldbank.org/.

Works Cited

Amsden, Alice. 2001. *The Rise of "The Rest": Challenges to the West from Late-Industrializing Economies*. Oxford: Oxford University Press.

Burney, Derek, Thomas d'Aquino, Leonard Edwards, and Fen Osler Hampson. 2012. *Winning in a Changing World: Executive Summary, Securing Canada's Global Economic Future: Canada's Strategy for Emerging Markets*. Report of a Round Table at the Norman Paterson School of International Affairs. Ottawa: Carleton University.

Global Affairs Canada. 2017. http://www.international.gc.ca/development-developpement/index.aspx?lang=eng

Ghosh, Palash. 2010. "What Exactly Is an Emerging Economy Anyway?" *International Business Times*, 15 December.

IMF. Various years. *World Economic Outlook*. Washington, D.C.: International Monetary Fund.

Johnson, Chalmers A. 1982. *MITI and the Japanese Miracle*. Redwood City, CA: Stanford University Press.

Khanna, Tarun, and Krishna G. Palepu. 2010. "How to Define Emerging Markets." *Forbes Online*, 27 May.

Kvint, Vladimir. 2009. *The Global Emerging Market: Strategic Management and Economics*. London: Routledge.

Leftwitch, Adrian. 1995. "Bringing Politics Back In: Towards a Model of the Developmental State." *Journal of Development Studies* 31 (3): 400–427.

Marois, Thomas. 2012. *States, Banks and Crisis: Emerging Finance Capitalism in Mexico and Turkey*. Cheltenham, UK: Edward Elgar.

Page, John. 1994. "The East Asian Miracle: Four Lessons for Development Policy." In *NBER Macroeconomics Annual 1994*, Vol. 9. Washington, D.C.: National Bureau of Economic Research.

United Nation Development Program (UNDP). 2013. *Human Development Report 2013: The Rise of the South: Human Progress in a Diverse World*. Oxford: Oxford University Press.

Watson, William T. 2014. "Beating the Middle-Income Trap in Southeast Asia" Special Report #156 on the Economy, 27 August, 2014. Washington, D.C.: The Heritage Foundation.

Notes

14 Canada and the Security-development Nexus in Fragile and Conflict-affected States/Situations

Stephen Baranyi

Key Terms

fragile and conflict-affected states/situations (FCAS)

peacebuilding

peacekeeping

securitization

security-development nexus

whole-of-government (WOG) approaches

Overview

Proponents of Canada's "whole-of-government" approach to engagement in Afghanistan have presented that strategy as being entirely new, yet its roots can be traced back to the strategies adopted to combat communist/nationalist insurgencies after the Second World War. Since then, Canadian approaches have evolved greatly: from the coordination of humanitarian assistance with US-led counter-insurgency strategy during the Vietnam War, to the coordination of aid with United Nations–led peacekeeping in contexts like Central America during the 1990s, to the integration of military, diplomatic, and aid instruments in Afghanistan from 2007 to 2012. This chapter summarizes the evolution of Canada's approach to the "security-development nexus" in "fragile and conflict-affected states/situations." It defines key terms and reviews the debates sparked by those experiences. The chapter reflects on the crossroads that Canada and its allies find themselves at today, as they grapple with the dilemmas of the "new wars" of Iraq, Syria, and elsewhere.

Learning Objectives

By the end of this chapter, students will be able to:

- understand how Canada's approach to combining security and development instruments, in its international interventions, has evolved since the Second World War.
- understand current Canadian policies, instruments, and debates with regard to engagement in fragile and conflict-affected states/situations.
- situate Canada's experiences in the context of wider international trends and debates.

Introduction

As Canada was pulling its combat forces out of Kandahar, Afghanistan, in 2012, several views of that intervention competed for public attention. Prime Minister Stephen Harper (2006–2015) and his officials claimed that Canada's whole-of-government approach had been bold, innovative, and fairly successful (GOC 2012). According to that perspective, Canada helped consolidate the Afghanistan government's presence and legitimacy in Kandahar, despite ongoing attacks by Taliban insurgents. It contributed to the expansion of women's and girls' access to education, the refurbishment of the Dahla Dam, and the revitalisation of irrigated agriculture in the Arghandab River basin. Ottawa was passing the torch to its US-led allies and ultimately back to the Afghan state. A peer review by the Development Assistance Committee of the Organisation of Economic Cooperation and Development (OECD) (see Chapter 4) largely accepted that positive assessment (OECD 2012).

On the other side of rather polarized debates, opposition parties, activists, and scholarly critics argued that Canada's decade-long foray into Afghanistan had ended in failure. Despite enormous whole-of-government (WOG) investments, Ottawa's securitized strategy (which more closely merged security and development concerns, and promoted cooperation between the aid and military arms of the state) was unable to stem the expansion of the Taliban insurgency and did little to consolidate public services, women's rights, or economic growth in the country. Some analysts (e.g., McAskie 2010) saw failure in Afghanistan as symptomatic of broader Canadian and Western misjudgements about appropriate responses to security-development nexus challenges in fragile and conflict-affected states/situations (FCAS).

Which assessment seems most accurate: the official narrative or the critique? To what extent can we generalize from Canada's experience in Afghanistan? How and why did Ottawa shift from an emphasis on peacekeeping and peacebuilding in the 1990s to WOG approaches in FCAS after the Al-Qaeda attacks on September 11, 2001 (known as "9/11")? How did the promotion of gender equality emerge and change during those eras? What do acronyms such as WOG and concepts like "security-development nexus" actually signify? What lies ahead for Canada and others in this complex and fluid domain?

This chapter offers introductory answers to those questions—looking at what Canada did, why, and the results. In the next section, we look briefly at historical precursors to Canada's current policies; for example, during the Vietnam War in the 1970s. Then we return to the heyday of WOG approaches in FCAS, during the decade following 9/11, by examining Canada's involvement in several FCAS. The chapter ends with reflections on the critical juncture where Canada finds itself in 2017, in its evolving approach to the security-development nexus; in other words, the complex interaction of security and development issues with each other. Throughout the chapter, we touch on some theoretical perspectives that illuminate positions taken in debates on Canada's involvement in FCAS.

Historical Precursors

During the heyday of Canada's whole-of-government engagement in Afghanistan, some enthusiasts believed that they were building something entirely new by merging security and development assistance, notably through the Provincial Reconstruction Team in Kandahar. Yet it is important to understand how Canada's approach was informed by experiences in earlier times.

Historians have documented how European colonialism had contradictory effects on the colonized peoples of the South and East (Rist 2008). Occupations disrupted the forms of development, governance, and security that had been built by Indigenous societies (and earlier conquerors) throughout the Americas, Africa, and Asia. Slavery deeply destabilized individuals, families, communities, and states. New colonial formations were designed to expand territory, control subjugated peoples, and extract resources—mostly for the benefit of metropolitan centres in Europe. When uprisings occurred, colonial states often responded with a combination of repression and concessions. Yet colonial experiences also integrated territories into emerging global markets and generated dependent forms of development and security for settler communities.

For example, when Cuban nationalists rebelled against the Spanish Crown in the 1880s, Spain responded with a counter-insurgency campaign followed by concessions for limited self-rule and economic development (Dossal 2006). Colonial and post-colonial administrations in British North America behaved similarly at that time, notably in their treatment of First Nations and Métis under the guise of bringing "peace, order, and good government" to the prairies in the late 1800s (Morton 1985). Japan's colonization of Asian territories during the early twentieth century also combined economic and security interventions. The Taiwanese film *Warriors of the Rainbow* (Te-Sheng 2011) depicts how the imperial regime used force and investment to extract resources, crush resistance, and win supporters for its colonial projects. It also movingly represents local communities' resistance to the Japanese occupations.

Such linkages between security and development continued to evolve after the Second World War (1939–1945) and during the Cold War (1946–1989). Initially, the focus was on the development and security of liberated territories: the United States led the reconstruction of Western Europe and Japan based on capitalist and liberal democratic practices, while the Soviet Union led the reconstruction of Eastern Europe based on state socialism. Yet the triumph of Mao Zedong and the Communist Party of China (CPC) in 1949 transformed the scope of the conflict. During that revolutionary struggle, Mao pursued a strategy combining the limited use of force with a multidimensional effort to "win the hearts and minds" of the Chinese people. In power, and initially with Soviet assistance, the CPC re-engineered institutions to promote broader economic and social development, as well as building up the new state's capacity to defend the revolution from internal or external threats (Chen 2009). The Chinese doctrine of a "people's revolution" inspired anti-colonial struggles across the South.

US President Harry Truman began his second term shortly before the People's Republic of China was born. In Point IV of his inaugural address, Truman announced a plan to eliminate "under-development" and "economic conditions predisposing to ... instability and war" (Truman 1949). Building on the Marshall Plan in Europe, he promised to increase military and development assistance to vulnerable US allies in Asia—notably to Taiwan, South Korea, and Iran. The idea was to use public and private funds to assist those countries' efforts to modernize their economies and institutions, including their security agencies, enabling them to neutralize Communist insurgents and their external backers. (See Chapter 2.) France increased its military and civilian assistance to stem anti-colonial insurgencies in Algeria and

Vietnam. The UK and its Commonwealth allies followed suit by launching the Colombo Plan in 1950. Under that initiative Britain, Canada, and Australia created foreign assistance programs to promote economic and social development and prevent the emergence of communist regimes in vulnerable countries such as Malaysia. (See Chapter 4.)

Starting in 1956, Canada also played a key role in enabling the United Nations (UN) to develop a mandate and capacity for international peacekeeping. The idea underlying first-generation UN peacekeeping was that the interposition of unarmed or lightly-armed neutral observers could help defuse, or at least contain, local conflicts that could otherwise escalate into global conflagrations in a nuclear age. That was seen as particularly useful to prevent the escalation of conflicts during the wave of decolonization in the South, from the 1940s to the 1970s. UN peacekeeping was also seen as providing a safe space for the provision of neutral humanitarian assistance to both sides in interstate or civil conflicts—such as the situation in Israel and the Palestinian territories. Canada played key roles in designing, commanding, or staffing all of the UN's peacekeeping missions during the Cold War. (See Chapter 5.)

In that context, Canada scaled up its international engagement beyond Europe through humanitarian aid, UN peacekeeping, and development assistance. Those were the pillars of Canada's self-image as a "helpful fixer," an image that was promoted by both Liberal and Conservative governments from the mid-1950s to the late 1990s. The promotion of equality between men and women was not a priority of Canadian and wider international involvement in war-affected societies during that era. Moreover, as we can see in **Box 14.1** on Canada and the Vietnam War, despite its carefully cultivated reputation for even-handed internationalism, in some Cold War conflicts Canada used aid and peacekeeping to advance its own geopolitical interests.

After the Cold War

The coordination of security and development assistance in Vietnam and elsewhere—notably in Latin America and the Caribbean under the US-led Alliance for Progress—fuelled considerable criticism in the US and internationally. The controversial results of that strategy, and its contribution to the spread of authoritarian regimes and human rights violations in countries like Guatemala and Zaïre, prompted a push for a clearer separation of development and security agendas. Thus, with support from US President Jimmy Carter (1977–1981), the OECD Development Assistance Committee (see Chapter 4) passed new rules to block the use of official development assistance for military and security operations.

With the exception of Vietnam, Canada generally adhered to those norms during the first decades after the Canadian International Development Agency (CIDA) was created in 1968. Yet in the late 1980s, Ottawa began experimenting with new ways of combining development assistance with peace efforts. For example, in Central America, Canada helped design and establish the UN peacekeeping missions that eventually verified the implementation of peace accords in that region. Under pressure from well-organized civil society coalitions, Ottawa also provided humanitarian, peacebuilding, democracy, and development assistance to countries (and movements) on different sides of the region's conflicts. This was also the era when CIDA adopted its guidelines on Women and Development, reflecting trends among donors.

In the 1990s, the collapse of the Soviet Union and the election of more pragmatic administrations in the US opened spaces for UN activism and the negotiated end to many conflicts in the South. Canada contributed to second-generation UN peacekeeping and peacebuilding efforts through the deployment of peacekeepers and the increased provision of aid for humanitarian purposes and peacebuilding, despite overall cuts to the aid budget. Peacebuilding involved activities

Box 14.1

Canada in the Vietnam War, 1954–1975

Context

Following the military defeat of the French colonial forces by Vietnamese nationalists in 1954, the Geneva Accords separated Vietnam into two territories and established an International Control Commission (ICC) to monitor a ceasefire between the North and South. Communist nationalists ran North Vietnam, while a Western-backed regime ruled South Vietnam. Backed by Communist China and the USSR, North Vietnam reluctantly accepted the agreement; it supported the Communist guerrilla movement in the South and eventually launched its own military operations across the border.

In response, the United States became deeply involved in South Vietnam through diplomatic, military, and development assistance. The Kennedy Administration's (1961–1963) strategic innovation was to integrate those instruments in a counter-insurgency (COIN) strategy based on an inversion of Mao's doctrine that "winning hearts and minds" was the key to victory. America invested enormous resources to reform the South Vietnamese state and promote wider development. The US called that process "nation-building," a direct forerunner to the concept of "state-building" that Western agencies used widely after 9/11. Indeed, many contemporary international development practices—notably integrated rural development, civil-military cooperation (CIMIC), and even results-based management—have their roots in the security-development nexus that the US crafted in Vietnam (Picard and Buss 2009).

Canada's roles

As one of four ICC members, Canada claimed to maintain a neutral and impartial position in Vietnam. As the war escalated, Ottawa increased what it claimed was neutral humanitarian assistance to the South. Yet Canada's role was more complicated (Levant 1986). On the ICC, Canadian officials downplayed violations of the Geneva accords by the South Vietnamese government and its US ally. Ottawa transmitted confidential ICC information to US intelligence services. It played a similar role on the International Commission of Control and Supervision that replaced the ICC in 1973. (See Chapter 5.)

Canada increased the provision of aid to South Vietnam. Yet that assistance was provided only to South Vietnam, rather than to the two sides in the conflict as per international humanitarian law (IHL). Canadian-financed hospitals were integrated into US COIN operations in the border area. When the North reunified the country by force in 1975, Canada immediately cut off civilian assistance, despite IHL and the acute need for humanitarian aid in the aftermath of the war.

To put that in context, it is important to remember that, unlike in Afghanistan after 9/11, Canada did not contribute to the US-led war effort by deploying combat troops or CIMIC teams on the ground. Ottawa sought to maintain the appearance of providing neutral security verification and humanitarian aid. Yet, like some other members of the international commissions and aid providers, it used its security and aid instruments to help one side in that Cold War conflict.

ranging from the disarmament, demobilisation, and reintegration of ex-combatants (DDR) to the organisation and observation of democratic elections; and to support for the reactivation of economic activity and social services. This was the golden age of what came to be known as "liberal peacebuilding," based on the belief that capitalist development and liberal democracy would bring peace (Paris 1997). Under the leadership of Liberal Foreign Minister Lloyd Axworthy

(1996–2000), Ottawa established new mechanisms to coordinate multidimensional Canadian state and non-governmental engagement across the relief-to-development continuum. (See Chapters 4 and 5.) After its announcement in 1996, the Canadian Peacebuilding Initiative provided a framework to coordinate Canadian contributions to peacebuilding and other issues linked to the emerging human security agenda. It informed funding decisions by the Department of Foreign Affairs and International Trade's (DFAIT) $10 million/year Human Security Program, CIDA's $10 million/year Peacebuilding Program, and interdepartmental programs such as the Canadian Police Arrangement, managed by the RCMP. It was also the basis for loose coordination with Crown corporations such as the International Development Research Centre (see Case Study 6), Rights and Democracy (see Chapter 11), and an array of non-governmental organizations, through the Canadian Peacebuilding Coordinating Committee and the Canadian Council for International Cooperation.

Despite the optimism of the early post–Cold War years, UN failures to prevent grave violence in Rwanda and the Balkans (see Chapter 5) led to the broadening of agendas beyond liberal peacebuilding. Minister Axworthy and his officials used their human security agenda to craft a more systemic approach to conflict transformation—through campaigns to ban landmines, to protect children and women in conflict, and to establish the International Criminal Court to prosecute war crimes. (See Case Studies 5 and 7.) The combination of inter-state and civil society efforts became a hallmark of the "new diplomacy" during that period. This was also when CIDA adopted its Policy on Gender Equality and its commitment to integrate gender equality as a cross-cutting priority in all ODA programming. That normative advance and Canada's active support for the adoption of UN Security Council Resolution 1325 on Women, Peace, and Security in 2000, reflected the emergence of gender equality as a key component of the security-development nexus by the late 1990s.

Ottawa also contributed to the shift towards more robust, third-generation UN peace enforcement operations. Where such operations seemed to require more military power, Ottawa actively supported the extension of NATO's mandate—first to Bosnia and Serbia, and then to Kosovo. (See Chapter 5.) In 1999, Ottawa justified its participation in NATO air strikes against Serbia on the grounds that it was necessary to stop massive human rights violations in Kosovo. Ottawa then sponsored the International Commission on Intervention and State Sovereignty, which reformulated that principle as the "Responsibility to Protect" (R2P) doctrine (ICISS 2001; see Case Study 3). That doctrine exemplified the integration of state, intergovernmental, and civil society advocacy efforts around the Liberal version of the security-development nexus before 9/11. It also reflected Ottawa's support for the integration of security and development instruments pioneered by Labour governments in the UK after 1997. Each of those shifts was debated by academics and policy analysts, as explained in **Box 14.2**.

Canada's Engagement in Fragile States after 2001

Al-Qaeda's high-profile destruction of American targets on September 11, 2001, greatly affected Ottawa's international policies and practices. As explained in Case Study 4, Canada immediately joined the military intervention to remove the Taliban regime from power in Afghanistan and to corner Al-Qaeda in eastern Afghanistan. Ottawa then deployed 1,900 troops to the NATO-led International Security and Assistance Force and made a multi-year aid pledge to help rebuild Afghanistan. Despite the departure of Minister Axworthy in 2000, insiders who believed in peacebuilding and human security kept their programs alive by adapting their language and mechanisms to the new forms of civil-military cooperation that emerged after 9/11,

Box 14.2

Theoretical Debates

Here are some of the theoretical lenses that scholars have used to analyse Canada's and other actors' approaches to the security-development nexus since the Second World War. See Chapter 1 for a definition of "theory" in social science.

The Cold War

During the early Cold War years, the main school of thought in Canadian foreign policy analysis was **liberal internationalism**. Heavily influenced by the worldview of former senior officials, it suggested that Ottawa's "middle power" approach was rooted in Canada's democratic values, anchored in international law, and closely bound to multilateral institutions, particularly the UN (Holmes 1979). **Political realists** countered that Ottawa's approach to the South actually reflected the federal state's limited ability (i.e., power) to promote Canada's distinct interests while aligning itself with the United States in the war against communism (Nossal 1985). In contrast, **dependency theorists** (see Chapters 1 and 2) explained Canada's approach (e.g., in the Vietnam War) as reflecting Canada's position as a capitalist political economy increasingly integrated with the United States and particularly with its military-industrial complex (Levant 1986).

The 1990s

The inheritors of **liberal internationalism** explained Ottawa's embrace of peacebuilding and human security in the mid-1990s, and its advocacy for more robust peace enforcement later, as reflecting a search for better ways of advancing human rights in the context of post–Cold War multi-polarity and new wars (McCrae and Hubert 2001). **New realist scholars** were more critical, arguing that liberal peacebuilding aggravated instability and that human security was little more than "hot air" (Paris 2001). Michael Ignatieff (2004) argued that liberal approaches were out of touch with realpolitik in the Balkans, Africa, and Asia; he advocated a "humanitarian realism" based on more robust strategies to deal with new wars.

Since 9/11

Post-colonial theory (see Chapter 1) stresses the continuity of "Western domination" and "biopolitical control" since the colonial era (Ashcroft, Griffiths, and Tiffin 2007). Inspired by that view, some critics suggest that peace enforcement and the new humanitarianism were steps towards failed international interventions in Afghanistan, Iraq, and Haiti after 2001 (Duffield 2007). Their Canadian colleagues argued that Ottawa participated in the securitized integration of coercion and aid after 9/11 driven by its alliances, interests, and worldview (Engler 2012). **Other critical analysts** have suggested that despite such tendencies, Canadian and other Western approaches vary considerably and have left space for the relative autonomy of some fragile and conflict-affected states (Baranyi and Paducel 2012; Baranyi 2014).

including the contested promotion of women's rights in Afghanistan (Baranyi 2005).

Canada refused to join the divisive US-led military intervention in Iraq in 2003, but Liberal Prime Minister Jean Chrétien (1993–2003) offered civilian assistance to rebuild Iraq. Shortly after he replaced Chrétien as prime minister in 2003, Paul Martin authorized Canada's participation in the US-led intervention in Haiti. Those engagements also required multi-departmental task forces to coordinate increasingly complex security and development operations in volatile environments. In 2004, Martin also launched an initiative to rethink

Canada's international policy. "Failed states," "3D" (diplomacy, defence, and development), and other concepts travelled from Washington and London to Ottawa. When the Liberals' International Policy Statement (IPS) was tabled in late 2005, it framed fragile states as threatening international and Canadian security. To meet those challenges, the government needed more capacity to coordinate interventions, restore security, reform institutions, and promote development. In the Department of Foreign Affairs, it established the Stabilization and Reconstruction Taskforce (START), and a Global Peace and Security Fund with a budget of $500 million over five years, to coordinate responses to international crises. START was mandated to work with more mobile Canadian Forces and a more focused CIDA. The IPS noted that, "We are already applying this new, integrated approach in Haiti ... " (GOC 2005, 13)

When the Conservative government of Prime Minister Stephen Harper took power in 2006, it embraced START and Canada's involvement in fragile states. Harper's government greatly expanded the "whole-of-government" engagement in Haiti, humanitarian action in Darfur, and Canadian support for the Comprehensive Peace Agreement in South Sudan. It also expanded a humanitarian-security-development program in the West Bank and Gaza, and launched Canadian airstrikes and provided limited civilian reconstruction assistance in Libya in 2011.

As noted in Box 14.2, the approaches of Canada and other international actors to fragile and conflict-affected states have generated lively debates. At the height of the WOG approach in Afghanistan, some practitioners and realist analysts believed that Canada was operating at the cutting edge of innovation by integrating security and development assistance (Stein and Lang 2007). In contrast, the inheritors of liberal internationalism argued that Canada's military-based approach was inconsistent with Ottawa's formal commitment to aid effectiveness and other multilateral principles (McAskie

2010). Post-colonial critics went further, arguing that Canada's post-9/11 WOG approaches were "securitized" and symptomatic of strategies of "biopolitical control" in the South (Brown 2008). Post-colonial feminists suggested that the drift toward securitized aid was complemented by a shift from promoting gender equality to a more paternalistic approach of framing women and girls in the South as victims needing Canada's aid and protection, notably in Afghanistan (Turenne-Sjolander and Trevenen 2010; Tiessen and Baranyi 2017).

Based on a comparison of the evidence, others have suggested that the militarized type of security-development integration that Canada pursued in Afghanistan differed significantly from the more balanced and somewhat more effective approaches in Haiti and elsewhere (e.g., Baranyi and Paducel 2012). By comparing Case Study 4 on Canada's role in Afghanistan to the overview of Canada–Haiti relations in **Box 14.3**, readers will get a sense of how those strands of critical analysis help us understand variations in forms of post-9/11 international engagement across the security-development spectrum. (See also Chapter 8.)

Future Canadian Engagement in FCAS?

In the 1990s, new American and Western doctrine defined "failed" or "fragile states" as governments whose authority, legitimacy, and capacity to provide core public services had decayed or disappeared. Later, the concept was extended to include "conflict-affected" states and situations, hence the current acronym, FCAS. There is a tension between the "security first" and the more "liberal" or "development oriented" approaches to engagement in FCAS. A decade after 9/11, it appeared as if the former were in retreat and the latter might be making a comeback. By 2010, the lacklustre results of interventions in Afghanistan and Iraq were leading the Obama administration (2009–2017) in the United States and other

Box 14.3

Canada and Haiti 2004–2015

Context

Western governments largely supported the democratic transition that gathered force in Haiti after the departure of the dictator Jean-Claude Duvalier in 1986. They opposed new military-led governments and supported the US-led restoration of President Aristide in 1994. Aristide and his allies instituted important reforms after their return, but by 2003 their increasingly repressive form of governance had polarized Haitian society once again. Negotiations failed to generate a framework for a peaceful transition. (See Chapter 8.)

In February 2004, the United States, France, Canada, and Chile conducted a controversial military intervention that ousted President Aristide and installed a Government of Transition. In June 2004, their Multinational Intervention Force (MIF) was replaced by a more broadly based UN Mission for Stabilization in Haiti (MINUSTAH). Violence endured until elections brought the more legitimate government of President Préval to office in 2006. With considerable international assistance, the Préval government (2006–2011) stabilized the economy, reduced political and criminal violence, and opened the door to other important reforms, notably of the National Police.

In January 2010, an earthquake caused approximately 300,000 deaths and destroyed many cities in the south and west of the island, including the capital of Port-au-Prince. The international community responded generously with humanitarian and reconstruction assistance, jointly coordinated by a greatly-weakened Haitian state and the UN. Controversial elections were held in that context, leading President Michel Martelly to office in early 2011. His mandate was marked by certain reforms but also by discord between his administration, both chambers of parliament, and many other Haitian stakeholders. Despite highly contested initial elections in 2015, the electoral cycle was completed

and a new president, parliament, and a large number of local representatives took office in February–March 2017.

Canadian involvement and outcomes

During the turbulent 2004–2005 period, Ottawa joined the MIF, but withdrew its military after Latin America-led MINUSTAH forces were deployed. Canada delivered a two-year aid program to assist in the implementation of an Interim Cooperation Framework, including its provisions for police reform. After supporting the conduct of relatively fair elections in 2005–2006, Ottawa committed $500 million in aid to support Préval's plans—mainly in the areas of education, health, economic growth, and agriculture. With funding from START, Canada also increased its support to reform the police, corrections, and border services; it also provided additional humanitarian aid after the 2008 hurricanes and floods.

After the 2010 earthquake, Canada responded with $400 million in relief and development aid. It deployed over 1,000 troops to provide emergency aid, but soon brought its forces home, instead supporting security system reforms and other development priorities coordinated by the Interim Reconstruction Commission. More controversially, it also supported US-led activities that led to President Martelly's election and his dubious governance record in office.

Frustrated by President Martelly's performance and the lack of visible results from Canada's assistance, Ottawa publicly criticized the Haitian government in January 2013 and delayed approving a new cooperation strategy. Still, some projects were extended and new projects were approved. With plans for fresh elections under way, a new cooperation strategy was announced in 2015. Other initiatives, such as Canada's support

(Box 14.3 continued on next page)

Box 14.3 (continued)

for a Policy and an Action Plan for Equality between Women and Men, were also quietly unveiled in 2015.

An official evaluation of Canada–Haiti cooperation (DFATD 2015a) suggests that Ottawa's emergency assistance was timely and fairly effective, as was its longer-term cooperation in the areas of education, health, and governance. The security elements of Canada–Haiti cooperation remain to be officially assessed. Yet despite post-colonial critics' conclusion that Canadian aid to Haiti has been largely "securitized" (Walby and Monaghan 2011), a more recent analysis of the historical record suggests that development and security outcomes have been more complex and somewhat more positive, at least since 2006 (Baranyi 2014).

Western governments to rethink their approach, particularly given the fiscal constraints generated by the economic recession of 2009. FCAS governments were also questioning prevailing priorities and calling for new approaches. Their calls were informed by surveys, coordinated by the OECD Development Assistance Committee (see Chapter 4), on the implementation of the Paris Declaration and the Principles for International Engagement in Fragile States. Those surveys showed that Western donors were not meeting their commitments on issues like donor alignment on national priorities, or on linking rapid action with long-term engagement, despite significant advances in some FCAS (OECD 2010).

One outcome of that call for change was the "New Deal" (International Dialogue 2011), signed by Northern donors grouped in the International Network on Conflict and Fragility (INCAF) and the new g7+ grouping of 19 FCAS. The New Deal renewed both sides' commitment to goals such as putting national ownership (by governments and citizens of FCAS) at the centre of their cooperation. It underscored the need for a better balance between post-9/11 goals, such as state security, and wider goals, such as legitimate politics, peoples' security, and inclusive employment. It offered new instruments for working together in FCAS, such as the negotiation of tripartite (host state + donors + civil society) national compacts. Earlier that year, the World Bank (2011) focused

its World Development Report specifically on conflict, development, and security. It anticipated the New Deal and recommended ways that INCAF, the g7+, and other actors, such as emerging donors, could contribute to its realization. Meanwhile, the United Nations called for greater investment in the Peacebuilding Commission—a mechanism that was working in tripartite fashion and supporting a balanced approach to peace, state building, and development in countries like Burundi and Sierra Leone. In 2015, those shifts were embedded in the Sustainable Development Goals (see Chapter 2) and the priority they gave to working with FCAS to ensure their implementation in those extremely difficult contexts.

Those international shifts also opened space for rethinking in Canada, leading notably to Ottawa's military withdrawal from Afghanistan between 2012 and 2014. The Harper government's reluctance to get militarily involved in the Malian crisis in 2012–2013, the freezing of cooperation with Haiti, and Ottawa's initial caution about military involvement in Syria were all also motivated by its sober private assessment of WOG in FCAS. For a brief moment in time, it seemed that Canada and other major international actors were moving towards more modest and sustainable modes of engagement in FCAS.

Yet other trends pulled Canada and other actors in a different direction. By 2014, two major crises prompted the United States and its allies to partially reconsider their cautious approach to military intervention. Russia's annexation of Crimea and its military interference in other parts of Ukraine compelled NATO to redeploy its forces and the West to greatly increase economic assistance to central Europe.

The territorial expansion of the Islamic State in Iraq and Syria (ISIS) also galvanized new security-development responses by the West. Canada joined that return to robust WOG approaches, as we can see in **Box 14.4**.

Box 14.4

Canada and the Iraq–Syria Complex

Context

In 1990, Iraq invaded its neighbour Kuwait, setting in train the First Gulf War of 1991, in which Iraq was soundly defeated by a US-led coalition. The Iraqi regime of President Saddam Hussein remained in power, however, and tensions between Iraq and the West remained high throughout the 1990s. In 2002, the US and UK accused Iraq of illegally holding weapons of mass destruction. In 2003, a US-led coalition invaded Iraq and toppled the Hussein regime, opening the door to the election of parties based on the Shiite majority and awakening the genie of democratic movements in the wider Middle East and North Africa region. Far from turning into a stable democratic state as the modernizationists (Chapters 1 and 2) had hoped, Iraq then entered a period of protracted civil strife and instability.

By 2013, the Arab Spring had degenerated into a brutal civil war in Syria, pitting the regime of President Bashar Al-Assad against a complex patchwork of Western-backed and Islamic rebels. After the American military pullout from Iraq at the end of 2011, conflict between the Shiite-based Al-Maliki government in Iraq and a revived rebel movement dominated by Sunni Islamists escalated. In 2014, Syrian and Iraqi Islamic groups joined forces to create the Islamic State in Iraq and Syria (ISIS), or Daesh. They split with Al-Qaeda, and in June 2014, Daesh captured Mosul, a major city in northern Iraq.

While initially cautious about getting sucked back into Iraq, by mid-2014 the Obama

Administration was re-engaging militarily and politically. Other Western countries followed suit, this time with partial support from regional partners Jordan, Saudi Arabia, and Turkey. Critics have suggested that Daesh is a "providential monster" that has revived the sagging fortunes of the military-industrial complex in the post-post-9/11 era (Harling 2014). By 2016 that effort had reversed the expansion of Daesh in Iraq. Meanwhile, Russia's decision to forcefully support the Al-Assad regime changed the balance of power in neighbouring Syria, at enormous human cost.

Canada's renewed WOG involvement

In June 2014, Ottawa added Iraq to its list of 25 top "development partners." By the end of the year, it had pledged $28 million in humanitarian assistance (HA) to Iraq, mainly in the form of "relief supplies, emergency shelter and urgent health care for thousands of civilians in northern Iraq" (DFATD 2014a). That assistance was disbursed largely through Canadian non-governmental organizations such as the Red Cross, Save the Children, and Mercy Corps.

In August 2014, Canadian Forces began airlifting military supplies such as "small-arms ammunition to assist the Iraqi security forces in protecting civilians from the terrorist threat presented by the Islamic State of Iraq ... " (ibid.). On his visit to Baghdad in September 2014, Foreign Minister John Baird (2011–2015) announced a contribution of $15 million in

(Box 14.4 continued on next page)

Box 14.4 (continued)

security assistance—namely "non-lethal" equipment "to assist security forces combating ISIL," as well as support to regional efforts aimed at limiting the movement of foreign fighters into Iraq and Syria (ibid.). A few days later, Prime Minister Harper announced that Canada had deployed several dozen Canadian forces officers to "join the U.S. in advising the Government of Iraq on how to enable security forces to be more effective against the threat posed by ISIL" (DND 2014). After a House of Commons debate in October 2014, the prime minister revealed the participation of Canadian forces in air combat operations "aimed at degrading ISIL's ability to carry out military operations," until April 2015 (ibid.). Ottawa committed further political, military, and humanitarian assistance in early 2015.

After being elected in October 2015, Prime Minister Justin Trudeau's government signalled its intent to reposition Canada's role in the conflicts linking Iraq, Syria, and the wider region. In February 2016, it announced a plan it billed as "comprehensive, integrated and sustained, involving the pursuit of military, diplomatic, stabilization and, separately, humanitarian and development lines of effort to invest in all aspects of a durable solution" (GOC 2016). That plan confirmed that the earlier decision to stop Canadian air combat roles had been implemented, as had the decision to accept 25,000 Syrian refugees. It increased other contributions by, for example, deploying more Canadian Forces personnel to support Coalition planning and intelligence efforts, as well as to train, advise, and assist Iraqi (especially Kurdish) forces conducting operations against Daesh. The plan also included increasing Canadian humanitarian and development assistance to several countries in the region, including Jordan and Lebanon.

Conclusion

Despite the tentative shift away from the highly interventionist, "security-first," perspective reflected in Canada's WOG engagement in Afghanistan, that approach to the security-development nexus still has some currency in Ottawa. Will Canada and its allies stay in the "unending war" mode, as predicted by post-colonial analysts like Duffield (2007)?

It is impossible to answer that question with certainty, but our historical overview suggests that there are reasons to believe that Canadians will stay on that path, just as there are sound reasons on the other hand to think that the government and other stakeholders might opt for a distinct approach. Canada and its partners are at a proverbial fork in the road on FCAS, as they are on other major challenges confronting humanity, such as climate change and sustainable development.

History reminds us that the security-development nexus has deep roots in the formation of modern states, in colonialism, in anti-colonial and post-colonial struggles. (See Chapter 1.) It is hardly a Canadian or even a Western invention, as the example of revolutionary China illustrates clearly. Yet the particular kind of security-development nexus crafted by Western states after 9/11 to address threats in fragile and conflict-affected states/situations remains influential. In his last year as prime minister, Stephen Harper applied a variant of that approach to what he described as a "long-term" engagement against terrorism in Iraq and Syria. If that becomes the dominant way of engaging in FCAS, then post-colonial theorists will have correctly anticipated the West's strategy.

Nonetheless, other theoretical perspectives suggest that history can be more open-ended. Paris (2010) argued that a more mature approach to "liberal peacebuilding" could be constructed in the post-post-9/11 era. That would entail adapting market-oriented economic policies and liberal democratic institutions to the realities of different FCAS; investing much more in fostering genuine national and local ownership rather than imposing solutions from the outside; and remaining engaged for the long run rather than focusing on exit strategies. That is precisely what is envisaged in the New Deal between OECD donors and the g7+ grouping of FCAS, as well as in the Sustainable Development Goals. It is no accident (since Paris was an adviser to Prime Minister Trudeau in 2015–2016) that the Trudeau government elected in 2015 signalled its intent to remain engaged in FCAS while placing more emphasis on UN peace operations, smarter aid, and a more generous approach to refugees, particularly from Syria. The International Assistance Strategy announced in June 2017 promises to focus more of Canada's aid program on appropriate engagement in FCAS.

Yet certain scholars caution that emancipatory or even appropriate international engagement is rare in FCAS. That fact underscores the relevance of continuing to conduct empirically grounded and theoretically informed research on different embodiments of the security-development nexus. It also highlights the importance of engaging in informed dialogue with policy-makers and practitioners working at that nexus, in Canada and elsewhere.

Questions for Further Learning

- There have been differences between Canada's approaches to the security-development nexus in distinct FCAS since 2001. What are they and how can they been explained?

- How does Canada's WOG approach resemble (or not) the approaches of other Western states? How does Canada's WOG approach resemble (or not) the approaches of emerging powers like Brazil and China?

- How has Canada's engagement in FCAS reflected changing approaches to gender?

- To what extent does Canada have leeway to act differently from its allies in Iraq and Syria today? What could Ottawa do differently in those contexts?

- What theories or key concepts shed the most light on Canada's current policies in FCAS?

Key Terms

fragile and conflict-affected states/situations (FCAS), p. 274
peacebuilding, p. 274

peacekeeping, p. 274
securitization, p. 274
security-development nexus, p. 274

whole-of-government (WOG) approaches, p. 274

Suggested Readings

Canadian Foreign Policy Journal: http://www.tand-fonline.com/toc/rcfp20/current
Canadian Journal of Development Studies: http://www.tandfonline.com/toc/rcjd20/current
Conflict, Security and Development: http://www.tandfonline.com/toc/ccsd20/current
Journal of Peacebuilding and Development: http://www.tandfonline.com/toc/rjpd20/current
OECD. 2015. *States of Fragility 2015. Meeting Post-2015 Ambitions.* Paris: OECD-DAC.

Suggested Videos

GAC. (2014). Canada and UNDP: making most of the debris in Haiti. https://www.youtube.com/watch?v=xRSg2sqhinw\.
Gross, P. (2015). Hyena Road. http://www.imdb.com/title/tt4034452/.
International Dialogue (2016). The New Deal. https://www.youtube.com/watch?v=sKSZG3haMk8.
MacGinty, R. (2011). Peacebuilding by the international community. https://www.youtube.com/watch?v=zN8rIxoXqW0.
TheRealNews. (2015). Post-Conflict Fragile States, Will They Overcome? https://www.youtube.com/watch?v=AHiA9hohKr8.

Suggested Websites

Centre for Security Governance: http://www.secgovcentre.org/
Centre d'Études et de recherche international, Université de Montréal: http://www.cerium.ca/
Country Indicators for Foreign Policy Project, Carleton University: http://www4.carleton.ca/cifp/ffs.htm
Centre for International Policy Studies, University of Ottawa: http://cips.uottawa.ca/networks/fsrn/
Fund for Peace, Fragile States Index: http://ffp.statesindex.org/
Government of Canada: Global Affairs Canada (Development Branch): http://www.international.gc.ca/development-developpement/index.aspx?lang=eng
OECD DAC International Network on Conflict and Development: http://www.oecd.org/dac/governanceandpeace/conflictandfragility/theinternationalnetworkonconflictandfragility.htm
United Nations: Department of Peacekeeping Operations: http://www.un.org/en/peacekeeping/about/dpko/
Peacebuilding Support Office: http://www.un.org/en/peacebuilding/pbso/
World Bank: http://www.worldbank.org/en/topic/fragilityconflictviolence

Works Cited

Ashcroft, Bill, Gareth Griffiths, and Helen Tiffin, eds. 2007. *Post-Colonial Studies: Key Concepts.* 2nd ed. London: Routledge.
Baranyi, Stephen. 2005. "Quel avenir pour le Canada et la consolidation de la paix?" In *Faire la paix. Concepts et pratiques de la consolidation de la paix*, edited by Yvan Conoir and Gérard Verna, 442–465. Sainte-Foy, QC: Presses de l'Université de Laval.
———. 2011. "Canada and the Travail of Partnership in Haiti." In *Fixing Haiti: MINUSTAH and Beyond*, edited by Andrew Thompson and Jorge Heine. Tokyo: UNU Press.
———. 2012. "Contested Statehood and State-building in Haiti." *Revista de ciencia politica* 32 (3): 723–738.
———. 2014. "Canada and the Security-Development Nexus in Haiti: The 'dark side' or changing shades of grey?" *Canadian Foreign Policy Journal* 20 (2): 163–175.
Baranyi, Stephen, and Anca Paducel. 2012. "Whither Development in Canada's Approach towards Fragile States?" In *Struggling for Effectiveness: CIDA and Canadian Foreign Aid*, edited by Stephen Brown. Montreal and Kingston: McGill-Queen's University Press.
Brown, Stephen. 2008. "CIDA Under the Gun."

In *Canada among Nations 2007: What Room for Manoeuvre?* edited by Jean Daudelin and Daniel Schwanen, 91–107. Montreal and Kingston: McGill-Queen's University Press.

———. 2012. "Introduction: Canadian Aid Enters the Twentieth Century." In *Struggling for Effectiveness: CIDA and Canadian Foreign Aid,* edited by Stephen Brown, 3–23. Montreal and Kingston: McGill-Queen's University Press.

Chapin, Paul, and John Foster. 2001. "Peacebuilding Policy Consultations and Dialogues: A Study of the Canadian Experience." *Canadian Foreign Policy Journal* 9 (1): 103–142.

Chen, Yun. 2009. *Transition and Development in China.* London: Ashgate.

DFATD (Department of Foreign Affairs, Trade and Development). 2014a. "Canada Responds to the Situation in Iraq." Accessed on December 6, 2014, at http://www.international.gc.ca/development-developpement/humanitarian_response-situations_crises/iraq.aspx?lang=eng.

———. 2014b. "Canada's Ongoing Support for Ukraine—Timeline." Accessed on December 10, 2014, at http://www.international.gc.ca/international/support-ukraine-soutien.aspx?lang=eng.

———. 2015a. *Evaluation of Canada-Haiti Cooperation. 2006–2013—Synthesis Report.* Accessed on July 31, 2015, at http://www.international.gc.ca/department-ministere/evaluation/2015/dev-eval-canada-haiti01.aspx?lang=eng.

———. 2015b. "Backgrounder—Canada's Continued Programming in Response to the Crisis in Syria and Iraq." Accessed on August 6, 2015, at http://www.international.gc.ca/media/aff/news-communiques/2015/07/30a_bg.aspx?lang=eng.

DND (Department of National Defence). 2014. "Operation Impact." Accessed on December 6, 2014, at http://www.forces.gc.ca/en/operations-abroad-current/op-impact.page#tab-1413735967987-2

Dosal, Paul. 2006. *Cuba Libre: A Brief History of Cuba.* Wheeling, IL: Harlan Davidson.

Duffield, Mark. 2001. *Global Governance and New Wars.* London: Zed Books and Palgrave.

———. 2007. *Development, Security and the Unending War: Governing the World of Peoples.* Cambridge: Polity Press.

Engler, Yves. 2012. *The Ugly Canadian: Stephen Harper's Foreign Policy.* Black Point, NS: Fernwood.

GOC (Government of Canada). 2005. "Canada's International Policy Statement: A Role of Pride and Influence in the World." Ottawa: Government of Canada.

———. 2012. *Canada's Engagement in Afghanistan: Fourteenth and Final Report to Parliament.* Ottawa: GOC.

———. 2016. "Prime Minister Sets New Course to Address Crises in Iraq and Syria and Impacts on the Region." 8 February. Ottawa: Prime Minister's Office. http://pm.gc.ca/eng/news/2016/02/08/prime-minister-sets-new-course-address-crises-iraq-and-syria-and-impacts-region

Harling, Peter. 2014. "État islamique, un monstre providentiel." *Le Monde Diplomatique.* Septembre 1, 6–7.

Holmes, John. 1979. *The Shaping of Peace: Canada and the Search for World Order 1943–1957.* Toronto: University of Toronto Press.

Ignatieff, Michael. 2004. *The Lesser Evil: Political Ethics in an Age of Terror.* Toronto: Penguin Canada.

ICISS/International Commission on Intervention and State Sovereignty. 2001. *The Responsibility to Protect.* Ottawa: IDRC.

International Dialogue on Peacebuilding and State-building. 2011. "A New Deal for Engagement in Fragile and Conflict-Affected States." Accessed on July 31, 2015, at http://www.pbsbdialogue.org/documentupload/49151944.pdf.

Levant, Victor. 1986. *Quiet Complicity: Canadian Involvement in the Vietnam War.* Toronto: Between the Lines.

McRae, Rob, and Don Hubert. 2001. *Human Security and the New Diplomacy.* Montreal/Kingston: McGill-Queen's University Press.

McAskie, Carolyn. 2010. "The Global Challenge of Fragile States: Is There a Role for Canada?"

McLeod Group policy paper. Available at http://www.mcleodgroup.ca/mcleod-group-resources/.

Morton, Desmond. 1985. *A Military History of Canada*. Edmonton: Hurtig Press.

Nossal, Kim. 1985. *The Politics of Canadian Foreign Policy*. Scarborough: Prenctice-Hall Canada.

OECD/Organisation of Economic Co-operation and Development. 2004. "OECD Development Assistance Committee Guidelines for Security System Reform and Governance." Paris: OECD.

———. 2010. *Monitoring the Principles for Good International Engagement in Fragile States and Situations. Fragile States Monitoring Survey. Global Report*. Paris: OECD.

———. 2012. "Canada: Development Assistance Committee (DAC) Peer Review 2012." Paris: OECD.

Paris, Roland. 1997. "Peacebuilding and the Limits of Liberal Internationalism." *International Security* 22 (2): 54–89.

———. 2001. "Human security: Paradigm Shift or Hot Air?" *International Security* 26 (2): 87–102.

———. 2010. "Saving Liberal Peacebuilding." *Review of International Studies* 36 (2): 337–365.

Patrick, Stewart, and Kaysie Brown. 2007. *Greater Than the Sum of its Parts? Assessing Whole of Government Approaches to Fragile States*. New York: International Peace Academy.

Picard, Louis, and Terry Buss. 2009. *A Fragile Balance: Re-examining the History of Foreign Aid, Security and Diplomacy*. Sterling, VA: Kumarian Press.

Richmond, Oliver. 2011. *A Post-Liberal Peace*. Milton Park: Routledge.

Rist, Gilbert. 2008. *The History of Development from Western Origins to Global Faith*. 3rd ed. London: Zed Books.

Stein, Janice, and Eugene Lang. 2007. *The Unexpected War: Canada in Kandahar*. Toronto: Viking.

Te-Sheng. 2011. *Warriors of the Rainbow*. Well GO USA Entertainment.

Tiessen, Rebecca, and Krystel Carrier. 2014. "The Erasure of 'Gender' in Canadian Foreign Policy under the Harper Conservatives: The Significance of the Discursive Shift from 'Gender Equality' to 'Equality Between Women and Men'." *Canadian Foreign Policy Journal* 21 (2): 95–111.

Tiessen, Rebecca, and Stephen Baranyi, eds. 2017. *Omissions and Obligations: Canada's Ambiguous Actions on Gender Equality*. Montreal and Kingston: McGill-Queen's University Press.

Truman, Harry. 1949. "Inaugural Address." Delivered at Washington, D.C., on 20 January. https://www.trumanlibrary.org/whistlestop/50yr_archive/inagural20jan1949.htm.

Turenne-Sjolander, Claire, and Kathryn Trevenen. 2010. "Constructing Canadian Foreign Policy: Myths of Good International Citizens, Protectors and the War in Afghanistan." In *Canadian Foreign Policy in Critical Perspective*, edited by J. Marshall Beier and Lana Wylie. Toronto: Oxford University Press.

UNSG (UN Secretary-General). 1992. *An Agenda for Peace*. New York: United Nations.

Walby, K. and Monaghan, J., 2011. "Haitian paradox" or dark side of the security-development nexus? Canada's role in the securitization of Haiti, 2004–2009. *Alternatives: Global, Local, Political* 36 (4), 273–287. doi: 10.1177/0304375411431760

World Bank. 2011. *World Development Report 2011: Conflict, Security and Development*. Washington and Oxford: World Bank and Oxford University Press.

Zürcher, Christoph, Carrie Manning, Kristie D. Evenson, Rachel Hayman, Sarah Riese, and Nora Roehner. 2013. *Costly Democracy: Peacebuilding and Democratization after War*. Stanford, CA: Stanford University Press.

Part IV

Ethical Issues and Globality

15 Our Role

A Moral Case for Helping or an Ethical Duty to Strive for Justice?

Mahmoud Masaeli

Key Terms

duty for justice

development ethics

ethics of duty

moral responsibility to help

the principle of humanity

Overview

Against the appeal of *moral responsibility to help* address poverty, development ethicists have raised the concern that development is a matter of freedom and people's right to self-determination; hence it involves an *ethics of duty for justice* to eliminate the causes of poverty. Deriving from moral conscience, the former conviction requests sympathy and care for fellow human beings. In contrast, the latter draws on empathy; to be with others and their struggle to end injustice. Moral responsibility to help derives from the responsibility for humanity: acknowledging the hardship and then assisting in the lowering of suffering. The duty to justice requires taking measures to end suffering. This chapter primarily analyzes the intellectual roots of the two types of moral obligation. In the third line of argument, the chapter appeals for a change in the essence of the question by drawing on the ethics of development beyond the dichotomy of the two moral traditions.

Learning Objectives

By the end of this chapter, students will be able to:

- understand the main ideas and conceptions of morality and ethical thought related to the development.
- compare the strengths and failures of both the moral responsibility to help and the ethics of justice.
- comprehend and argue our moral obligation for eliminating inequality.
- present human development as the alternative perspective in development theory.
- illustrate the inextricable tie between development and democratic participation as the essential feature of curing inequality.

On the Way of Curing Inequalities: Moral Responsibility to Help or Duty for Justice?

The mainstream tradition in development studies tends to look for the causes of poverty in the interior barriers against development. This tradition of thought, including the branches of modernization theory in sociology and economic development theories, takes note that development results from a process of scientific spirit and technological innovations that progressively moves societies from a stagnant condition toward productivity and market planning. (See Chapter 2.) Countries that are incapable of growing themselves endogenously should be assisted by advanced countries. This assistance derives from a moral responsibility to help underdeveloped societies in their process of economic growth. Responsibility to help, in its original conviction, stems from the moral ties between the privileged and underprivileged classes. This obligation is accomplished through voluntary charities assisting those who have a hard time or need help from affluent people in meeting their basic needs. Indeed, the have-nots bear an essential right to demand assistance, while the haves hold a voluntary obligation to help them. By removing the obstacles against the capability of the have-nots in their success, this help improves their condition of life. The outcome of the link between the right of the disadvantaged to receive help and the moral obligation of the advantaged to help would be the creation of a healthy social fabric promising prosperity for all members.

The moral belief in assisting the have-nots in Western modern philosophy traces its roots back to classical liberal thought at the dawn of modern time. Classical liberal thinkers of the seventeenth to nineteenth centuries assumed that the road to prosperity passed through the exercise of individual freedom in open societies, with rights such as the freedom of exchange in the economic sphere. But this freedom, which originates from the equal worth of individuals, must not be mistaken for equality in the sharing of wealth. Instead, freedom is a capacity that allows individuals to choose their own path to success. Accordingly, uneven growth is caused by the obstacles against individual freedom. Facing such causes, Adam Smith (1723–1790) introduced the moral justifications for helping eliminate obstacles to people's enjoyment of freedom.

Adam Smith is known for introducing a market-based economy that favours the interests of the entrepreneurs rather than the defence of the miserable. Without any doubt, his masterpiece, *An Inquiry into the Causes of the Wealth of Nations* (1776), presents a brilliant account of an economic system based on the competitive nature of human beings as both self-interest seekers and social players. In the free marketplace, fair opportunity is provided to everyone to compete over the production of better and cheaper goods and services, and therefore everyone benefits from the exchange. Benefit making improves the productive capacity of society. However, a healthy society is not formed based on the mere humanity of the competitors. Rather, their self-loving attitude and their private interests are the true stimulus in the advancement of social progress and prosperity. The very fact that *The*

Wealth of Nations is intended to introduce guidance for creating a process of free competition in economic exchange that generates goods and services has definite implications for today's economic thinking. Smith invents the idea of free competition as the stimulation of more production leading to higher gross domestic product, which is the indicator of economic progress of nations. The most interesting idea of the book is that if the economic system is left free in its capacity, it can regulate itself without being dropped into the extreme self-love of the competitors. This self-regulation is referred to as the "invisible hand." In fact, if people industriously contribute in the production of better goods to others, and by exchange get their own desired goods and service, it is as if the common interest of the whole society is indirectly served. In defending the invisible hand, Smith reasons that in free societies, competitors employ their talents, time, and capital to direct the industry towards the greatest values for the whole society. Correspondingly, economic progress and the process of common prosperity rest on guaranteeing freedom in market-based societies (Smith 1776, Book IV, Chapter II, Paragraph IX).

In a deeper reflection, in *The Theory of Moral Sentiments* (1759), Smith had formulated a theory of natural justice based on the argument that people's self-regarding attitude will naturally result in socially desirable ends. In this work, once again Smith uses the "invisible hand" metaphor to argue that the uneven division of the wealth would, in the end, result in the common good of society. That is, although the rich look for luxury articles, their spending distributes the wealth to those who need it. Indeed, the overconsumption of the rich does not inflict harm on those who are not able to have a luxurious life style because the rich not only provide employment for them, but also the spending of the rich would be beneficial for others. Hence, on the condition that everyone gets their share of the necessities of life, everyone will be happy in the end. Naturally, the outcome of this exchange would be the advancement of

the interests of society. This is where the invisible hand metaphor becomes a panacea for the advancement of the interests of society (Smith 2002, 184–85).

Smith's theory of the invisible hand might have the potential for addressing poverty, but it is intrinsically unable to respond to inequality. This theory also conflicts with his own account of human freedom, since Smith regards inequality as a natural social status. In the *Theory of Moral Sentiments*, this uneven divide between the landlord and the labourer is attributed to Providence, and hence gets its justification from God's will to divide opportunities unevenly among social classes (2002, ibid.). This statement is unlike today's belief in equality of status, since it treats the existing inequalities as being not the matter of concern. Instead, what is important is the happiness of the unevenly divided social classes regardless of whether or not they get an equal portion of the benefits of production or enjoy equality of social status.

It is critical to note that in Smith's invisible hand there is no clear insight into justice in its contemporary sense. Indeed, either caused by lack of capability to function in the proper manner, or originating from the monopolizing of economic and political resources, or even lack of resolution to decide properly, injustice as a social phenomenon has been ignored by Smith. To a certain extent, Smith has devoted his thoughts to reminding the advantaged people of his time to fulfil their moral obligation in helping the poor. In the view of Smith, the poor are neglected since the moral sentiments are rotted by too much attention to and admiration for the success of the rich. Accordingly, the poor individual is ashamed of his poverty and perhaps feels that it "places him out of the sight of mankind" (ibid., 52). It must be noted that, in Smith's view, being poor means to be in a status that is more severe than being a have-not. It is more than hunger, servitude, and starvation. Poverty involves social exclusion and the suppression of the poor. The disposition to worship wealth has led society toward an inhumane stratification. In today's political language, the institutionalization of competition in the pursuit of interest making in capitalist societies has led to too much concentration on the maximization of benefits and too little attention to moral sentiments and feeling of sympathy with the poor.

In a sense, poverty is caused by a dual disposition in our perspective of life. We tend to be more oriented toward success and wealth and, and, and as we despise weakness, this disposition impacts our moral sentiments negatively. That is the reason why we become indifferent toward the poor. The social implication of this construction is widespread poverty fuelled by a sense of social inferiority by the have-nots. It would be strange to realize that in addressing poverty Smith suggests short-range measures by the government, while in his economic theory in *The Wealth of Nations* he favours the minimum involvement of the government in the private business of individuals. But, for Smith, help programs must be short-term, because eradication of poverty requires social ambitions and self-interest plans. In other words, poverty will be cured only by economic growth; very much like today's outlook that the prosperous life depends on economic progress. However, economic growth itself needs the removal of the obstacles to the benefit making of individuals. That is, there is a definite need to support the freedom of interest seekers to pursue their economic plans.

In a striking argument, Smith holds that the support of the poor by the government may result in the elimination of absolute poverty. However, the social dimension of poverty, the sense of inferiority and powerlessness, must include individuals and their own plans for their life; in today's lexicon, this is equal to self-reliance and self-esteem. That is why from Smith's perspective the government must only provide public goods to supplement free economic transactions. Only in this way can markets produce wealth by individuals' entrepreneurial spirit and hard work. Indeed, Smith

teaches that the feeling of inferiority is sometimes a positive factor in the life of society, since the poor may work harder to be rewarded. Reminiscent of the invisible hand metaphor, hard work is required to expand out of the vortex of inferiority: work harder to be rewarded.

It is no wonder that Smith ignores the root causes of enormous inequality, especially at the international sphere. Nor did he explain that the wealth of the European nations was basically accumulated from British imperial policies abroad. He simply argued that free trade increases peace and friendly relations among different peoples, without providing empirical evidence for the accuracy of the argument.

Challenging Smith's account of the moral responsibility to help, and criticising the failure of the liberal account of morality to address the widespread inequality in the eighteenth and nineteenth centuries, socialist thinkers opened an objection against the mere moral responsibility to help and argued in favour of a duty for justice. In contrast to the liberal assumptions of self-interest/self-love and individual liberty as the necessary means for success in the market economy, socialist thinkers favoured a communal account of human life, which is now called utopian socialism. Utopian socialism is a constellation of perspectives for futuristic and imaginary ideal societies. In their perspective, human beings by their nature are social beings, and therefore no sense of selfhood will be attained in isolation and away from being in relationships. People's personalities will not be actualized in loneliness. Success cannot be achieved through competition and self-interest seeking. Rather, human beings are social agents who act through a process of cooperation to make a prosperous and just life for all. The condition of life must be determined based on an actualized conception of equality. So, beyond moral responsibility to help, the enormous inequality can only be healed by an ethics of justice: distribution of opportunities, wealth, and power throughout society. To put it a bit differently, although socialists share the liberal idea of equality, for them equality must be understood in the real condition of life, *equality of condition* and not *equality of opportunity/status*. To better comprehend this contention, mere individual liberty and equality are not sufficient for justice. Morality cannot improve the unequal conditions of life. What is required, liberal socialists claim, is to have the two sorts of equality completing each other; there is no chance of equal condition of life without equality of status, and no equality of status without equality of condition. In other words, equality of opportunity exists only in an atmosphere that confirms the equal qualification of individuals.

Not to be mistaken for Marxism (see Chapter 1), early socialism rejects relying on the sole equality of opportunity and insists that, without the equality of condition, not even moral equality can be conceived. Morality without justice in social life is meaningless. Justice involves the equality of condition. Being a witness to the miserable life of workers in the eighteenth century, Claude Henri de Saint-Simon (1760–1825) is one of the first socialist thinkers who stressed the importance of equality of condition. Although he was influenced by the revolutionary anti-aristocratic slogans of the Enlightenment, especially John Locke's philosophy of liberty and individual rights, he could not be indifferent to the impoverished condition of life of the labourers of his time. Saint-Simon was striving for justice by moving attention away from equality understood in terms of liberty and individualist rights (equality of status) toward defining equality in accordance with socialist principles. In the socialist society, although different classes accomplish diverse tasks, their dignity and equal worth is acknowledged in a harmonious whole. The key to this harmony is the scientific spirit. Saint-Simon argued that certainty in morality and politics emerges from the application of a scientific method to the social order. He called for the establishment of a class of scientific experts and elites whose members would use their skills to end the strife caused by warring classes and instead address society's most pressing problem: inequality and poverty.

He knew inequality was caused by rampant profit-making, where real equality was dissolved. In this perspective, the commercial society defined by classical liberals such as Smith disharmonized society; normal life dropped into the vortex of social strife and class conflict over the sources of wealth. In a later work, Saint-Simon criticized the ills of his time that had resulted from the domination of idlers who, without taking any part in the productive economy, lived on incomes generated from investment. Against this background of human selfishness, Saint-Simon insisted that in the new industrial societies led by experts, inequality would be eliminated. However, given the complexity of tasks and functions in the new societies, the conception of individualism is rendered obsolete, since individuals become a part of a whole "complex we." This new "we" that socialism introduces is a system of life that is not only more efficient than commercial society, but also demonstrates justice.

In search of justice, Robert Owen (1771–1858) introduced socialism as the means of improving the quality of life of the disadvantaged classes. Appalled by the social costs of capitalism, such as widespread poverty and inequality, Owen (1991) developed a systematic account of egalitarianism as a new alternative to the capitalist account of morality for helping the poor. He sought to cure the evil of capitalism in a new system of production for public interests endorsed by an alternative system of education. He was convinced that capitalism was generating more selfishness and hence was morally bankrupt. Therefore, there was a need for a visible distribution of the benefits of production. First in New Lanark in Britain (1825), he created a village store offering the workers their necessary goods at fair prices. Then he created a nursery and day school for the children of the workers in Lanark Cotton Mills. Later Owen moved to New Harmony in Indiana (1826) and established his model factory with the highest standards of working conditions. His aim was to achieve communities of equality in the capitalist societies of Britain and America.

Owen (1991), a mill owner, tried to convince his fellow capitalists that there are advantages to justice. Central to his thought is the Enlightenment idea of reason and its importance in dispersing selfishness from the minds of people and replacing it with the importance of self-knowledge and economic and social progress for greater happiness. He explains that the essays are not the outcome of a mere speculation, but instead represent a practicable remedy for societies replete with poverty, inequality, and human misery. He conceived distrust, theft, and drunkenness as the malaises of the capitalist system, which transmits the wrong messages to youth and adult alike. The cure for the decadent society is to strive for justice by providing the excluded people with their needs as well as giving them a proper education.

Although more names can be referred to in the quest for justice, we need to dedicate a few sentences to Charles Fourier (1772–1837). As with other proponents of utopian socialism, Fourier diagnosed the industrial capitalist societies with the massive challenges of deception, selfishness, and the shortcomings and injustice of individualism. He noticed that poverty and inequality were born in industrial civilization; hence they must be eradicated by re-organizing society around a cooperative system. The individualist culture disharmonized human passions, since it encouraged people to compete over maximization of benefits and thereby divided human society. So, harmonization handled through a cooperative society removes evils from human beings' behaviour and instead improves the common good. Indeed, in contrast to Smith. who sees the invisible hand in the free competition for benefit making as the determinant of the common good, Fourier (1967) finds the "visible hand" of justice latent in the cooperative model of social harmonization.

By the mid-twentieth century, ethical thoughts in response to poverty and inequality remained locked in the dichotomy of the *moral responsibility to help* and the *duty for justice*. However, and without delving into the nuances of the two competing moral outlooks, the quest for the ideal society did not expand beyond the confines of domestic life in capitalist free societies and the socialist collective countries. (See Chapter 2.) There is no reference to the pervasive injustice in non-Western societies. In other words, the *ideal* invisible hand of liberalism and the *practical* visible hand of socialism were the metaphors depicting only a portrayal of the just societies in the West. None of these moral traditions remained seriously sensitive to the unequal development structure of the world system inherited from colonialism and imperialism.

The same question revisited internationally

The post–Second World War order urged reflecting a second time upon the same question: *Moral responsibility to help* or *duty for justice*? It was, however, still slightly problematic to decide which option was more rigorous, given the complex context of international life. Entering a normative phase, members of the international community reordered themselves under the general banner of the United Nations and reaffirmed their faith in the importance of "human rights," "equality," and "social progress" as the means of building a new peaceful international life. (See Case Study 1.) But the novelty of the reaffirmation was that equality was defined beyond its individual meaning; the preamble to the UN Charter (1945) proclaimed it as the *equality of all nations large and small*. Considering this new attitude, the international community prepared itself to answer the same question by a wider insight into the malaises of international life: unequal development on a global scale. This shift in outlook required a move away from answering the question with domestic concentration toward responding to inequality in the international sphere. Indeed, the choice of new life in the emerging networked world of internationalism and interdependency required that the space between national and international moral thoughts be eliminated.

In this changing context, four ideas regarding the problem of inequality dominated the early post–Second World War ethical thinking. The first was that developed nations have a moral obligation to reduce the gap between the haves and have-nots at the international level. This obligation had instrumental merits, since it could consolidate the dominant position of triumphant liberal societies in international life. The second was that economic interdependence urged deeper cooperation between the major industrialized countries and the underdeveloped nations. Cooperation improves mutual understanding; hence it is influential for strengthening and securing international justice. This contention is especially endorsed by liberal internationalism. (See Chapter 14.) The third idea was that internationalism must have a humane characteristic, since the very idea of international life requires assisting underdeveloped nations to join the new normative international order, promising friendly relationships among all states in the world. The fourth was that humane internationalism entails an indivisible union between the peaceful life for all and social and economic progress for all in the world. In truth, the post–Second World War normative thoughts affirmed a re-articulated version of the invisible hand that licensed moral responsibility to help underdeveloped nations as a way of guaranteeing the international common good.

The United Nations system was apparently a manifestation of this re-articulated invisible hand metaphor. The UN Charter (1945) expresses in the preamble the idea that preventing "the scourge of war, which twice in our lifetime has brought untold sorrow to mankind," rests on

1. promoting human rights and equality on both individual and national levels,
2. establishing conditions for international justice, and,
3. improving social progress and better standards of life in larger freedom.

Soon after, and while the post–Second World War period was rapidly dropping into a new fault line over the same question of moral responsibility to help or duty for justice, the UN reaffirmed the importance of individual human rights, freedom, dignity, and equality in a number of international legal instruments. The UN Charter and the *Universal Declaration of Human Rights* (UN 1948) are two of the most important legal documents that confirmed the newly re-articulated invisible hand doctrine. Unavoidably, the new metaphor conflated the two moral outlooks. The synthesized perspective suggested that *moral responsibility to help the underdeveloped nations improves international justice*. In reality, the normative attitude of the second half of the twentieth century ended the quarrel over our moral role in addressing the persisting inequality:

Recognition of the inherent dignity and of the equal and inalienable rights of all members of the human family is the foundation of freedom, justice and peace in the world (UN 1948, Preamble).

What is innovative in this new outlook is its extension beyond national borders. Concrete measures were adopted to align this new outlook with the new normative international order. In his inaugural address in 1949, US President Harry Truman pointed to the condition of misery prevailing over half of the people of the world and argued that poverty was a threat both to them and to more prosperous areas (Truman 1949). He argued that the improvement of science and technology had provided humanity with the ability to relieve suffering of the people of underdeveloped societies, saying that the awareness of the miserable condition of life of others and modern inexhaustible technical knowledge required that the advanced nations embark on a bold new program for making the benefits of their scientific advances and industrial progress available for the improvement and growth of underdeveloped areas. Truman reasoned that, if the people of the world received help they could, through their own efforts, make their own life better. Truman concluded that the obligation to help would result in justice: "To that end we will devote our strength, our resources, and our firmness of resolve. With God's help, the future of mankind will be assured in a world of justice, harmony, and peace" (Truman 1949).

Notable in synthesizing the two moral views was the process of legalization and institutionalization of the *moral responsibility to help for justice*, which started in the 1960s. In addressing the tension between the Western advocacy of liberal values and the Marxist subversive perspectives during the Cold War (1946–1989), and the impacts of this rivalry on the underdeveloped countries, UN diplomacy strove to consolidate the synthesized moral account. In 1966, the International Covenants on Civil and Political Rights and on Economic, Social, and Cultural Rights were adopted, again reaffirming the synthesized account of moral responsibility to help for justice already set out in the Universal Declaration of Human Rights:

> In accordance with the principles proclaimed in the Charter of the United Nations, recognition of the inherent dignity and of the equal and inalienable rights of all members of the human family is the foundation of freedom, justice and peace in the world (UN 1966a and 1966b: Preamble).

More institutionalized weight was added to the moral responsibility to help underdeveloped countries. The United Nations General Assembly passed Resolution 1710 (XVI) to establish the 1960s as the United Nations Development

Decade, which called for the intensification of efforts to mobilize and to sustain support for the measures required on the part of both developed and developing countries to accelerate progress towards self-sustaining growth of the economies of individual nations and their social advancement. In line with this initiative, US President John F. Kennedy, in his 1961 inaugural address, acknowledged the importance of the moral responsibility to help for justice: "To those peoples in the huts and villages of half the globe struggling to break the bonds of mass misery, we pledge our best efforts to help them help themselves" (Kennedy, 1961). To follow up on this moral pledge, the United States Agency for International Development was created in the same year. Later, the Development Assistance Committee was set up in the Organisation for Economic Co-operation and Development, with the aim of harmonizing foreign aid flows for the economic progress of the developing countries. In these harmonized initiatives, liberal thought played the defining role; it is the moral responsibility to help that improves justice.

Questioning the Synthesized Moral Doctrine

The striking question on duty for justice remained unanswered for the scholars whose perspectives formed the non-liberal outlooks. At least four critical strands of dissatisfaction with the moral responsibility to help for justice appeared in the literature of international development in the 1970s and 1980s. The first critical perspective is the dependency approach, including dependency theory and its variations, and world system theory and its variants. (See Chapters 1 and 2). Dependency theory essentially criticizes the moral responsibility to help for being ignorant of the systemic and structural reasons for the prevalent unequal development caused from the sixteenth century onward by Europe's drive for capitalist accumulation, colonialism, and imperialist policies stripping down developing countries' resources. For the scholars of the dependency approach, in the condition of structural dependency, which might be called imperialism, moral responsibility to help cannot result in justice. Justice requires breaking down dependency through the subversion of the whole system.

The second critical strand against the moral responsibility to help is the regularization theory, which originates from within dependency theory but follows a distinctive intellectual argument borrowed from Gramscian scholarship. In this scholarship, the Italian neo-Marxist Antonio Gramsci (1891–1937) replaces the mechanism of direct/physical control, of domination, with hegemony, which is the ideological control of the masses. Domination by ideology, or controlling the worldview of the masses, is the best means of suppressing any other ways of explaining reality. Hegemony notably consists of the ways through which the beliefs of people are formed. It also involves the institutions that uphold those beliefs, such as education, knowledge making, and the media. Through those institutions, certain kinds of normative behaviours are held up as true, right, and moral. Indeed, hegemony is implanted in the minds and beliefs of people in such a way that alternative ways of envisioning the real world are very hard to imagine. That is, hegemony is created based on people's consent through the manipulation of their worldview: domination by consent.

Gramsci added another dimension to his idea of hegemony: confusion about the conceptions of good and bad. Having prevailed from the beginning of the post–Second World War period, the moral responsibility to help for justice is then a way of normalizing worldviews and values that the capitalist world desires. Under hegemony, the moral responsibility to help cannot result in justice, given the fact that global capitalism is strictly maintaining the existing exploitative and oppressive international system.

The third critical strand is the early postcolonial scholarship (see Chapter 1) represented in the book *Black Skin, White Masks* by Frantz Fanon (1967). In this perspective, underdevelopment has been caused by colonial dehumanizing policies, resulting in the formation of the otherness, the non-European "inferior" people. And, even in a postcolonial era, neocolonialism still sets a double policy of "containment" and "denial" on the former colonies. The former may be depicted in terms of today's terms of world trade and other means of interaction in international life. It contains physical, economic, social, and psychological elements. It basically comes with the racist policies of the colonial forces. But, the latter, the denial, is more sophisticated. Denial entails a process of alienating people of former colonies from their history, culture, and identity. This is a denial of the soul of people and communities from themselves, which is more complicated than the negation from their homeland. The negation of the soul of people of former colonies is, indeed, not just a material or social act, but an act of depersonalization, that is, emptying people of their own sense of identity.

Imposed inequality has been caused by the "White Masks," denoting a link between the colonizers and colonized in a hierarchical sense of who they are and to what culture and identity they belong. Since colonialism has been established through violence, and has created its own puppet state in the postcolonial era, the whole process of depersonalization under the Whiteness must be reversed through revolutionary violence, according to Fanon. Indeed, in contrast to Gandhi's non-violence approach, Fanon believed that there was no other way to overcome inequality in the colonial context other than by fighting for justice. Reforms and aid flows are not the right solutions. What is required is to depict a link between emancipation and people's prosperity. To Fanon, it is only through the struggle for restoration of people's humanity that justice can be achieved for African and Caribbean societies.

Following in the footsteps of the poststructuralist movement of the 1980s, the post-development and fourth critique against the moral responsibility to help for justice proposes that such morality is political. Inspired by the post-modernist French philosopher Michel Foucault (1926–1984), post-development theorists argue that power relations determine the foundation of society. (See Chapter 1.) This power dynamic shapes our cognitive and scientific capacities. The ways through which we see, understand, and decide, and especially the whole knowledge of development has been notified by power relations. In this perspective power is disciplinary, meaning it monitors, regulates and normalizes social relations. The outcome is that society unconsciously and unquestioningly accepts disciplinary control. It follows that knowledge becomes the means of monitoring, controlling and even suppressing people.

Considering these critical standpoints, post-development scholars appeal for a change in thoughts and programs of development. The idea of development is hegemonic—a given historical conjuncture sets the parameters of how we think. Thus, the idea of moral responsibility to help is inherently deceptive because it springs from the very hegemonic knowledge of development. That is the reason why post-development thinkers quarrel with the foundations of the moral responsibility to help by inquiring as to what the meaning of development is and who is benefiting from it.

Post-development scholars also call for a change in the methodology of development to replace Western interventionist development with contextualized and participatory models. Arturo Escobar (b. 1952), a leading post-development theorist, casts a critical light on the idea and practice of development by arguing that the historical roots of the idea of development are to be found in the political rearrangement that occurred after the Second World War. The notions of "underdevelopment" and "Third World" emerged as the working concepts to describe the process by which not only the West, but also the East (i.e., the Soviet bloc) redefined themselves and the global power structures. That is why the moral responsibility to

help that came into existence through Truman's fourth point is essentially fraudulent, because its result is a gamut of ills and evils: environmental destruction, dehumanizing the experience of development for much of the world's population, and the continual reproduction of neo-imperialism, neo-capitalism, and patriarchal structures of domination and exploitation.

The road to justice passes through alternative perspectives: improving self-examination, and the re-thinking of self-reliance and the status of subaltern groups. In this vision of justice, alternative perspectives embrace the experience of people living on the margins with the aim of addressing the ills and evils that affect those people. Reminiscent of José Ortega's dictum "I am I and my circumstances" (Weigert 1983), the alternative approach to development embraces the condition of life of people and encourages them to find out what the causes of inequality are and how they must be resolved. Only people who experience their own problems are in the best position to determine how to improve their own condition of life. Then, through a participatory model, they can learn how to build confidence and how to gain the basic research skills that are required for a good development. To do justice to the inferior status of underdeveloped societies we must encourage them to increase their level of ownership of the process of their own development.

Changing the Substance of the Question: Toward the Ethics of Duty

The 1970s literature on ethics and development showed an interest in reflecting on the nature of the question already raised, but wanted to go beyond the dichotomy. This is a fundamentally different position from that expressed by development ethicists. Although development ethicists do not represent a unified perspective, they share a unified question that is directly related to the principal enquiry of this chapter. What is good development? This is a question not only about the theoretical foundations of development, but also, and more decisively, related to the ethical implications of the *idea* of development. The question is striking because it asks who is addressed by development. If development is to be for prosperity, greater well-being and human flourishing, it must be a living idea capable of moving in time in order to address the needs of people in their cultural context and horizon of meanings. Correspondingly, although it must address humanity in its application, it must be renewable in time horizons and contextual frameworks. Notable to this view of development is its suitability in the current age of global transformation. Good development is, then, more than either the theory or practice. Instead, it is a matter of reflective doing; the *praxis*. (See **Figure 15.1**.)

It must be noted that development as praxis is not a matter of reflection and theorization. It involves, rather, an obligation for the improvement of human well-being, flourishing, and respect for others. In this sense, good development is creative, other-regarding, and dialogical. Still, the precise meanings of these characteristics of good development are contested and ambiguous, given that it is a complex term. Thus, to achieve this view of development, an engaged view of our moral role is required. This engaged view must be grounded on the three following minimum movements in our perspective of development:

- A shift away from the comprehensive ideas on development to a constructed and agreed-upon account of development,
- A move beyond the mere moral arguments on development toward the formation of a political will for change,
- A movement and commitment toward a *perfect duty* for addressing and alleviating inequality.

Figure 15.1
Development as Praxis

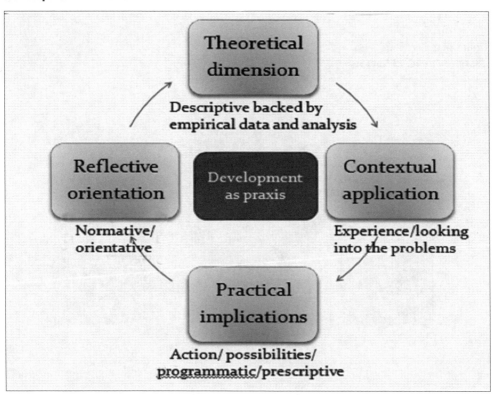

Development ethicists have in one way or another addressed this view of development by highlighting the importance of good development. From its early appearance, **development ethics** has gone through a process of evolution. We suggest that there are three generations to be discerned in the maturing of development ethics.

The first generation of development ethicists include social critics and activists of the mid-twentieth century, heralded by Mahatma Gandhi (1869–1948), whose non-violent disobedience against British colonialism in India and South Africa laid the basis for civil resistance movements in the modern era. However, Gandhi must be considered as a development ethicist because of the emphasis on human-centred thoughts in his account of development: effective participation, importance of harmony, deep equality including gender, basic needs as means for a higher goal *and* a humanistic and egalitarian social order. What especially gives a greater humanist tone to this approach is the weight he accords to human rights and the participatory role of citizens in

the process of development, the importance of harmony in the life of society, and a demand for deep equality. Thus, good development involves people's autonomous will to determine their own model of development. Integrating these elements of his thought into a non-violent culture, with his egalitarianism policy, the ideal society is formed. Justice exists in this model of society. See **Figure 15.2**.

A second generation of development ethics was largely brought forward by Peter Berger and Denis Goulet. The striking characteristic of the works of this generation of ethicists is that, for them, good development must improve the quality of life. For this purpose, the theory and practice of development from the beginning must be morally evaluated to know in what areas those practices have improved the life of people and in what domains people's lives have been affected negatively. Only in this way can a good representation of development be portrayed.

By the same token, Des Gasper (2004) suggests three different accounts of the meaning,

Figure 15.2
Justice: The Ideal Society

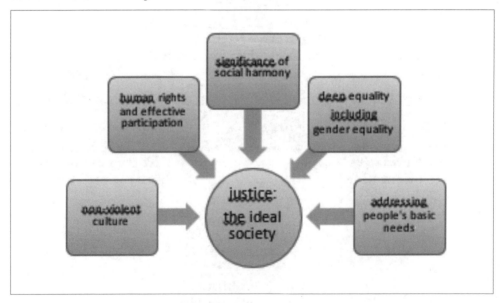

functioning, and implication of development for the condition of life. The first is a non-evaluative conception that envisions the meaning of development in terms of structural changes in the stagnant context of underdeveloped societies, economic growth, and modernization—which was long the predominant approach in scholarship—and industrialization and urbanization. There were hesitations as to whether changes and economic growth necessarily resulted in a better condition of life. The second is an understanding of development managed through the interventionist policies of advanced societies. Even in the most optimistic outlook, it is not clear just how inspiration and intervention drawn from such very different societies can provide meaningful guidance to find solutions to the domestic causes of underdevelopment in developing countries. (See Chapter 1.) The third view looks at development in terms of its ability to improve the condition of life of people in underdeveloped societies. In this third view, development is associated with good changes that are created and good end results (Gasper 2004).

To Gasper, development must bring nations to their own desirable growth, the fulfilment of good potentials, and cultural maturation for fulfilment. This view of development changes our perception and understanding of development by opening our eyes to an evaluative vision of development as good development. Development in this sense certainly goes beyond the dichotomy of the two moral perspectives discussed earlier in this chapter. It gives a fundamentally different answer to the question because it changes the question itself. The question would not be about our moral role for either helping others or striving for justice. In its place, the question changes to how we may assist others to improve their own desirable condition of life, to fulfil their own potential for a just society. From Gasper's perspective, development would certainly consist of a process of advantageous changes involving the active contribution of people in restructuring their self-esteem and identity. This perspective gives us a view of a just development whose justness would be inextricable from people's choices.

The human development and capability approach presents the third generation of development ethics with a newer outlook regarding our moral duty. It is based in part on the idea of development as the fulfilment of people's basic needs (food, clothing, shelter, education, health care, nutrition, dignity). This theory was very popular in the 1970s and was even embraced by the World Bank under the presidency of Robert McNamara (1968–1980). In effect, McNamara and his chief economist Paul Streeten argued against the then-prevailing view of development in both the Western aid donors and the receiving countries by stating that the reality of poverty in the world implies a new conceptual framework for development. This framework was the forerunner of human development.

Mahbub ul Haq, Special Advisor to the United Nations Development Program in the 1990s, argued that development meant enlarging people's choices. It is not about enlarging the quantity of income or disharmonized production in a society, but rather about the people themselves. While the theory of basic needs accentuated providing the deprived with the opportunity for a full life, human development draws on all needs of all human beings for attaining their sense and actualization of their humanness. Having extended the scope of the needs to all human beings, the human development approach goes on to address the needs of disadvantaged people in advanced societies as well. Human development is a human-centred approach concerned with how to advance the richness of human life, rather than just the richness of the economy. In this view, the prime question of this chapter loses its essence, since the whole reflection of development has been fundamentally changed.

The Indian philosopher and economist Amartya Sen expanded on this framework by introducing the notion of human capabilities. Bringing together a range of ideas that had previously been excluded from development theories, the capability approach draws on what individuals are truly capable of doing. To start with, Sen exhorts his readers to understand the link between the space of justice and its criteria. Space refers to the domain in which resources, commodities, and opportunities are divided. Criteria provide the means of assessment of human well-being. Sen suggests viewing well-being in terms of the capabilities of people to function properly. The capability approach then adds another novelty to the idea of human development; freedom to achieve the desirable life will eventually result in a person's well-being.

The capability approach has been grounded on five assumptions. The first is agency, which is the ability of human beings to act and change in accordance with their own values and objectives. In this sense agency involves being socially engaged, enjoying actualized freedoms and bearing responsibilities. The second is the importance of human freedom, understood as the real opportunity to accomplish different functioning combinations (being and doing) that we value. Freedom is the core characteristic of agency; hence it must have a substantive meaning. That is, one's determined will and the availability of the opportunity to achieve desirable functioning. The third assumption derives from the conception of freedom: the actualized freedom of people or their capability. Capability means peoples' potential for the proper functioning required for a decent life, a life worth living. The fourth element is to emphasize judgement on the well-being of people in accordance with their capability and not the availability of commodities and goods. Finally, the fifth

element of the capability approach pertains to the space where people can pursue their own valuable goals and achieve them. This means that, for the capabilities to be actualized, there is a dependency on the availability of opportunities for people to participate in the definition of their own well-being. In other words, capability must be interwoven with a participatory model of democracy. Good development stems from this participatory potential being accessible to people.

The capability approach provided a new framework for addressing the question of our moral role in eradicating or altering inequality. This approach, as already explained, stresses the freedom of people to improve or achieve the functioning they value, and could further elevate the significance of humanity as the central focus of development. "The focus here is on the freedom that a person actually has to do this or be that—things that he or she may value doing or being" (Sen 2009, 232). The obvious implication of this approach for development is that it ties good development to genuine choice for people, and binds development to elevating authentic self-direction and people's self-esteem. Only in this way would people be able to shape their own desirable life, both as individual persons and as part of the community. In this respect, we must help others in improving and strengthening the endogenous factors in their own authentic development. Note that this is not intervention. Instead, we act from the ethics of duty, motivated by an obligation to humanity.

Conclusion

Although the modern era, and especially the commencement of industrialization, gradually terminated human suffering and instead brought about commodities and goods for a happy life, it also caused poverty, deprivation, inequality, and injustice. That is why questions were posed by thinkers as to how to cure the malaises of modern social relations and industrialization. Moral philosophers most notably posed specific questions about our role: Do we have a duty to end inequality? If so, what would that duty be? Is it a moral responsibility to help or an ethical duty for justice? These questions preoccupied the minds of ethicists and social and political thinkers alike. Beginning in the eighteenth century, thinkers diagnosed and prescribed solutions for inequality in two different, and to a certain extent incongruous, ways. Classical liberals endorsed the moral responsibility to help as the solution. Early socialists depicted the causes of inequality in the structure of the young European capitalism and advocated structural justice.

The process of internationalization and afterward the splitting of the world into "developed" and "underdeveloped" societies basically caused by neo-colonialism and imperialism further intensified the question: What would be our role in ending uneven development in the world? Responses to the question divided thinkers, and this time politicians joined them in the same division, given the conditions of the Cold War and the ideological confrontation between the liberal and socialist worlds. Liberals synthesized the two answers and created the *moral responsibility to help for justice,* backed by concrete measures to alleviate inequality and poverty. Drawing once again on the structural causes of inequality, socialists favoured justice as the sole role. However, the new debate in the post–Second World War era split over our role to alleviate inequality is the attitude and political plans by both liberal democracies and socialist countries to penetrate developing countries. Accordingly, the solutions to world inequality turned into an ideological rivalry between the two political poles in the Cold War era.

By the 1980s, alternative perspectives emerged in development studies that essentially changed the direction and moved beyond the political/ideological rivalry. Development ethicists, the pioneers of human development and scholars of the capability approach, changed the essence of the question by asking what good development would be. Indeed, they extended beyond the inherent dichotomy latent in the question, and opened up a new horizon to understand and design policies for ending inequality. The novelty of this school of ethical thought is that it leaves the gates open for a communicative exchange, and better to say integration, between moral responsibility to help and ethics of duty for justice under the superior direction of the *ethics of duty for humanity*. This duty is not the same as the response of either capitalism or socialism, and goes beyond their limitations. This initiative has brought about promising insights into theorizing, as well as putting policies into force that have the potential to reduce inequality and improve the quality of life.

Questions for Future Learning

- What should be our role as Canadians in regards to widespread inequality and deprivation in the world? Does this role stop at our national borders or must it be expanded over the world geography of inequality and poverty?
- While critical approaches such as dependency theory provide insights into the structural causes of inequality, how might we take the advantage of that argument to bring about peaceful and collaborative changes in the structure of the world?
- What is the right response to underdevelopment and poverty, given the collapsing of the normative importance of borders?
- What is new in the arguments of development ethicists?
- If we have not been involved in creating unequal development, do we still have any negative duty towards the others? Why and how?

Key Terms

duty for justice, p. 296

development ethics, p. 304

ethics of duty, p. 306

moral responsibility to help, p. 294

the principle of humanity, p. 303

Suggested Readings

Berger, Peter. 1974. *Pyramids of Sacrifice: Political Ethics and Social Change*. New York: Basic Books.

Chauffour, Jean-Pierre. 2009. *The Power of Freedom: Uniting Human Rights and Development*. Washington, D.C.: Cato Institute.

Crocker, David. 2008. *Ethics of Global Development: Agency, Capability, and Deliberative Democracy*. Cambridge, UK: Cambridge University Press.

Deneulin, Severine. 2014. *Wellbeing, Justice and Development Ethics*. London: Routledge.

Gill, Stephan. 2008. *Power and Resistance in the New World Order*. New York: Palgrave Macmillan.

Goulet, Denis. 1995. *Development Ethics: A Guide to Theory and Practice*. New York: The Apex Press.

Isbester, John. 2006. *Promises Not Kept*. Bloomfield, IL: Kumarian Press.

Sen, Amartya. 1999. *Development as Freedom*. New York: Anchor Books.

Ufford, Philip Quarles, and Ananta Kumar Giri, eds.

2003. *A Moral Critique of Development*. London, New York: Routledge.

Vizard, Polly. 2006. *Poverty and Human Rights*. Oxford: Oxford University Press.

Waigani Seminar. 1986. *The Ethics of Development*. Port Moresby: University of Papua New Guinea Press.

Wilber, Charles K. and Amitava Krishna Dutt, eds. 2010. *New Directions in Development Ethics*. Notre Dame, IN: University of Notre Dame Press.

Suggested Videos

Global Ethics Forum: The UN's Efforts in International Development: Relevant or Not?: https://www.youtube.com/watch?v=hqgkG2IHlBc

Hegemony and Gramsci: https://www.youtube.com/watch?v=js8E6C3ZnJo

How does equality link to global sustainability? Richard Wilkinson: http://www.futureearth.org/blog/2013-aug-13/how-does-equality

-link-global-sustainability-richard
-wilkinson-interview

Invisible Hand in Economics: Definition and
Theory: http://study.com/academy/lesson/
invisible-hand-in-economics-definition-theory
.html

Socialism: Definition and Leaders: http://
study.com/academy/lesson/socialism
-definition-leaders.html

Suggested Websites

International Development Ethics Association:
http://developmentethics.org/

International Institute for Sustainable Development: http://www.iisd.org/

Human Development and Capabilities Association:
https://hd-ca.org/

International Development Evaluation Association:
http://www.ideas-int.org/home/

International Development Alliance:
http://www.idanetwork.eu/

Center for Global Development:
http://www.cgdev.org/

Development Classifieds: http://www.comminit
.com/ci-classifieds/classifieds

Works Cited

Crocker, David. 2008. *Ethics of Global Development:
Agency, Capability, and Deliberative Democracy.*
New York: Cambridge University Press.

Escobar, Arturo. 1994. *Encountering Development:
The Making and Unmaking of the Third World.*
Princeton, NJ: Princeton University Press.

Fanon, Frantz. 1967. *Black Skin, White Masks.* New
York: Grove Press.

Fourier, Charles. 1967. *Collected Works of Charles
Fourier.* Paris: Editions Anthropos.

Frank, Andre. 1996. *The Underdevelopment of
Development: Essays in Honor of Andre Gunder
Frank.* Thousand Oaks, CA: Sage Publications.

Gasper, Des. 2004. *The Ethics of Development: From
Econonism to Human Development.* Edinburgh:
Edinburgh University Press.

Gramsci, Antonio. 1971. *Selections from the Prison
Notebooks of Antonio Gramsci.* New York:
International Publishers.

Kennedy, John F. 1961. "Inaugural Address."
Delivered at Washington, D.C., on 20 January.
https://www.jfklibrary.org/Asset-Viewer/
BqXIEM9F4024ntFl7SVAjA.aspx

McNaughton, Frank. 1991. *Harry Truman:
President.* New York: McGraw-Hill.

Owen, Robert. 1991. *A New View of Society and other
Writings.* London: Penguin Books.

Sen, Amartya. 2009. *The Idea of Justice.* Cambridge,
Belknap Press of Harvard University Press.

Smaldone, William. 2014. *European Socialism: A
Concise History with Documents.* Lanham, MD:
Rowman and Littlefield Publishers, Inc.

Smith, Adam. 1776/2003. *Enquiry into the Nature
and Causes of the Wealth of Nations.* New York:
Bantam Classics.

———. 2002. *The Theory of Moral Sentiments.*
Cambridge, UK, New York: Cambridge
University Press.

Truman, Harry 1949. "Inaugural Address."
Delivered at Washington, D.C., on 20 January.
https://www.trumanlibrary.org/whistlestop/
50yr_archive/inagural20jan1949.htm

ul Haq, Mahbub. 1995. *Reflections on Human
Development.* New York: Oxford University
Press.

UN. 1945. *Charter of the United Nations.* New York:
United Nations.

———. 1948. *Universal Declaration of Human
Rights.* New York: United Nations.

———. 1966a. *International Covenant on Civil and
Political Rights.* New York: United Nations.

———. 1966b. *International Covenant on Economic,
Social and Cultural Rights.* New York: United
Nations.

Weigert, Andrew. 1983. *Life and Society: A Medita-
tion on the Social Thought of Jose Ortega y Gasset.*
New York: Irvington Publishers.

Part V

Case Studies in Canada's Engagement with Developing Countries

Case Study 1

Canada and the Shaping of the International Order, 1942–2017

Lauchlan T. Munro

Issue

Between circa 1911 and 1945, the world, and especially the then-dominant powers in Europe, went through a crisis so violent and so profound that something had to be done about it. Two world wars (1914–1918 and 1939–1945) and a series of smaller wars killed tens of millions of people, and tens of millions more died in the chaos that followed. In most of these wars, civilians were deliberately targeted; each world war included a genocide. Civil wars, violent revolutions, and/or counter-revolutions shook China, Germany, Hungary, Iran, Ireland, Italy, Mexico, Russia, Spain, and Turkey. Two great empires, the Austro-Hungarian and the Ottoman, disappeared almost overnight, and the royal dynasties that had ruled for centuries in Austro-Hungary, China, Germany, the Ottoman Empire, and Russia were toppled in the space of seven years, from 1912 to 1919. Hitherto unknown, violent political movements like fascism and communism took power in Germany, Hungary, Italy, Japan, Manchuria, Mongolia, Russia, and Spain. There was a global recession from 1919 to 1921; in 1929 came the decade-long Great Depression, which impoverished hundreds of millions of people. National and international policy makers seemed powerless to deal with these multiple crises; indeed much of what they did only made matters worse. "The absence of international agreements and multilateral institutions" (Singer 1995) inhibited the concerted action that was so desperately needed.

As the Second World War reached its peak around 1942 to 1944, the UK, the US, and other Allied Powers, including Canada, realized that they had to create a better post-war international order if the world were to avoid in future the political, military, and economic catastrophes of the previous three decades. The organizations that they created as the cornerstones of that post-war international order are still with us today, most notably the United Nations (UN), the World Bank, and the International Monetary Fund (IMF). These and other international organizations continue to play key roles in the international order. But in many ways, these organizations reflect the world as it was in the mid-twentieth century. Much has changed since then, including the disappearance of the large colonial empires and the rise of the so-called "emerging economies." (See Chapter 13.) It is no longer clear that the international organizations that we have inherited from the mid-twentieth century are still appropriate to the demands of the twenty-first century. Many of the emerging countries like Brazil, China, India and South Africa resent the Western world's continuing dominance of these international organizations; these countries are seeking a bigger role in managing the international order.

Action

Canada played an important part in creating the post-war international order. Canadian diplomat Lester Pearson took a leading role in creating the UN; Canadian legal scholar John Humphrey was the main author of the Universal Declaration of Human Rights, which serves as the foundation of the international human rights system. During the Cold War (1946–1989) that followed the Second World War, the liberal capitalist democracies like Canada, France, the UK, and the US created other international organizations in response to the challenges of their ideological and military struggle with the Communist bloc, led by the Soviet Union and (later) China. These Cold War organizations included the North Atlantic Treaty Organization (NATO), where Pearson again played a role, the Organisation for Economic Co-operation and Development (OECD), and the G7 group of leading liberal capitalist democracies. (See Case Study 5.)

Canada also pioneered the invention of peacekeeping (1956), and treaties banning landmines (1997) and the use of child soldiers (2000). In environmental matters, Canada led the way to the Montreal Protocol (1987) on ozone depletion and was an early adherent to the Kyoto Protocol on climate change (1997), though successive Liberal and Conservative governments did not implement Kyoto. (See Case Studies 5, 7, and 8.)

The organizations created at the end of the Second World War and during the early Cold War have been, for good or evil, the dominant actors in the international order since 1945. For many decades, the World Bank was the major provider of development financing and policy advice for developing countries. The International Monetary Fund (IMF) works to keep the international payments system running smoothly and to manage disequilibria in the balance of payments of individual countries. The General Agreement on Tariffs and Trade (GATT) and its successor, the World Trade Organization (WTO), have promoted international trade by reducing both tariff and non-tariff barriers to trade. The UN provides the often invisible infrastructure for international cooperation on everything from disease control to international air transport. The UN Security Council is the world's highest authority for international peace and security issues. At the OECD, the liberal capitalist democracies of Australasia, Japan, North America, and Western Europe share their experiences and decide on "best practices" in policy areas as varied as social security, foreign aid, employment policy, and macroeconomic management.

The structure of international organizations thus still reflects the political and economic concerns of the pre-1945 era: international peace and security, international trade and finance, and international economic cooperation. These issues are still important, of course, and will continue to be. But the leading issues of the twenty-first century may require a different organizational structure. The UN agencies dealing with climate change, gender issues, international organized crime, and urbanization, for example, are amongst the least well-funded and least influential UN agencies.

The main international organizations have been dominated in their thinking and leadership by the governments of the leading Western liberal democracies. The World Bank president, for example, has always been American and the IMF's managing director has always been from Western Europe. The OECD, a group of donor countries, sets the standards for the effectiveness of foreign aid (OECD 2005). The UN's funds, programs, and agencies get most of their money from the governments of the liberal capitalist democracies; the citizens of these countries have historically been over-represented in the staff of these UN agencies compared to citizens of developing countries. The heads of UN bodies usually come from donor countries. Of the eight heads of the UN Development Program since 1966, for example, only one has been from a developing country. Every head of the UN Children's Fund since 1946 has been American. The five great powers that won the Second World War in 1945 still today form the permanent and veto-wielding members of the UN Security Council: China, France, Russia, the UK, and the US. Many emerging countries want changes to the Security Council's permanent membership and veto powers, but the incumbents will not agree to it.

The liberal capitalist democracies like Canada continue to prop up the post-1945 international order in many ways (Freeland 2017). In 2011 and 2012, for example, the US and Western Europe refused to allow open competitions when it came time to name new heads of the World Bank and the IMF, preferring instead to impose their own candidates. Canada and its allies still provide material and ideological support to the IMF, the OECD, and the World Bank as the leading suppliers of economic and social policy advice, despite growing evidence of the inadequacy of their approach to economic policy (Ciuriak 2016). While the major Western powers have acceded to the creation of the G20 meeting of the heads of government of the 20 largest economies in the world, including the major emerging economies, the leaders of Canada, France, Germany, Italy, Japan, the UK and the US still continue to meet separately as the G7. Canada in particular wants to preserve the G7. Our influence is much greater inside the G7 than it is in the larger G20. Indeed, our membership in the G7 forms the basis for Canada's claim to be a major power.

Impact

As Chapter 13 shows, the emerging powers have increasing levels of wealth and technical and scientific capacity. They have the ability and the desire to contribute to managing the international order, but they are still told by Canada and its allies to accept second-class status in most parts of that international order. The governments and citizens of the emerging countries are increasingly resentful of the G7's

attitudes, and they are pushing back. When the US and Europe imposed their own candidates as heads of the World Bank and the IMF a few years ago, the emerging economies revolted. They demanded, and got, several of their own nationals hired in other senior positions; citizens of Brazil, China, and Egypt now predominate amongst the senior managers of the World Bank and the IMF.

Not satisfied with claiming their place in existing international organizations, the emerging countries are now creating their own (Munro, 2017). The New Development Bank, for example, promises to offer an alternative to the World Bank, and is owned by Brazil, China, India, and South Africa. The Shanghai Cooperation Organisation brings together China and Russia, along with India, Pakistan, and the central Asian states, in an organization that explicitly rejects the political and economic models proposed by the liberal capitalist democracies. The South American Union is being established in direct competition with the Organization of American States (OAS), which has traditionally been dominated by the US. In other areas, however, the needed organizational change is lagging. The international organizations charged with key elements of the global policy agenda like climate change, gender issues, international organized crime, and urbanization have not fully risen to the challenge.

It is still too early to see how these new organizations will fare or how the older international organizations will adapt to changing circumstances. With Brexit, the rise of nativist and xenophobic movements in many countries, and the election of Trump as US president, the prospects for international cooperation have worsened since 2016. Whether Canada will play a constructive role in the reform of the international order to meet the challenges of the twenty-first century or whether it will insist on maintaining its current privileges also remains to be seen. But it is clear that the South will no longer accept without question the leadership of countries like Canada.

Suggested Readings

Ciuriak, Dan. 2016. *An Opportunity for Europe? The McKinsey Global Institute 2016 Europe Essay Prize*. McKinsey Global Institute.

Freeland, Chrystia. 2017. "Address by Minister Freeland on Canada's foreign policy priorities." Address to the House of Commons. Ottawa: House of Commons. 6 June.

Munro, Lauchlan T. 2017. "Strategies to Shape the International Order: Exit, Voice and Innovation vs. Expulsion, Maintenance and Absorption." *Canadian Journal of Development Studies* 39 (2).

OECD. 2005. *Paris Declaration on Aid Effectiveness.* Paris: Organisation for International Cooperation and Development.

Singer, Hans W. 1995. "An Historical Perspective." In *The UN and the Bretton Woods Institutions,* edited by Mahbub ul Haq, Richard Jolly, Paul Streeten, and Khadija Haq. Macmillan: London and New York.

Case Study 2

Canada and South Africa under Apartheid

Stanley Uche Anozie

Issue

Apartheid as an official policy of racial segregation and discrimination started in South Africa after the National Party gained a majority in the 1948 elections. Only whites were allowed to vote in that election, a fact that illustrates the lost history of racial segregation and discrimination that pervaded South Africa even before apartheid. Apartheid literally emphasized the "apartness" of the whites from the blacks and other "races." The South African government established a social structure that ensured blacks and other ethnic groups (termed "Coloureds" and "Asians") were kept in inferior social, political, and economic status compared to whites. Indeed, "South Africa was struggling with the question of whether blacks even deserved human rights" (Crompton 2007, 6). Apartheid involved a systematic classification and regulation of individuals along racial lines.

Most South Africans were opposed to apartheid. This opposition was exemplified by the African National Congress (ANC), an anti-apartheid group turned political party led by Nelson Mandela. Their objective was to "struggle for the right to live (a life) ... in which all persons live together in harmony and with equal opportunity" (Crompton 2007, 9). However, in the eyes of the South African government and many Western countries, the ANC was a terrorist organization, since it engaged in an armed struggle against apartheid. On 11 June 1964, Justice Quartus de Wet sentenced

Mandela and eight other ANC members to 27 years in prison for their anti-apartheid struggle.

As a core member of the postwar Western alliance (see Chapter 5 and Case Study 1), Canada had to deal with apartheid as a foreign policy issue, especially after the newly independent nations of sub-Saharan Africa put apartheid on the international agenda in the 1960s. Some Canadian governments, notably the Progressive Conservative ones, cared deeply about ending apartheid, while others, mostly the Liberal governments, did little. Canada is and was then a middle power on the global stage, with little hard (i.e., military or economic) power. But under the Diefenbaker (1957–1963) and Mulroney (1984–1993) governments, Canada did use soft power (i.e., the power of ideas, persuasion, shaming, and advocacy, as well as targeted funding) as an effective tool of foreign policy in the fight against apartheid.

Action

The notion of "soft power" involves using public and private diplomacy rather than a show of economic and military power. Canada's soft power diplomacy was done in collaboration with other countries and international agencies supporting the end of apartheid, and often with the democratic forces in South Africa themselves. Canada used soft power public diplomacy to "create followers through the power of its ideas, ideals and less on its economic and military might ... In many ways, the struggle to dismantle apartheid was a quintessential public diplomacy project . . . to use public forms of pressure to force the South African government to create a more just society" (Potter 2006).

Despite its own history of internal colonialism and discrimination toward Indigenous peoples in Canada (see Chapters 9 and 10 and Case Study 9), Canada was widely seen on the international stage as a pluralist liberal democracy and, hence, found itself well positioned to assist in the struggle against apartheid. Canada used its historically close ties with the UK and the US, who were more favourable towards apartheid during the Cold War (1946–1989), to increase its influence on the anti-apartheid agenda. Arguing against apartheid from inside the Western camp made Canada more influential.

As African nations gained independence in the late 1950s and early 1960s, they demanded that the fundamental injustice of apartheid be eradicated. Canadian Prime Minister John Diefenbaker convincingly argued for the expulsion of South Africa from the Commonwealth in 1961. Subsequent Liberal governments under Lester Pearson (1963–1968) and Pierre Trudeau (1968–1979 and 1980–1984) did little to fight apartheid. The short-lived Progressive Conservative government of Joe Clark (1979–1980) did, however, play a useful role in ending white minority rule in South Africa's neighbour, Zimbabwe.

In 1984, Brian Mulroney became prime minister of Canada. Mulroney aligned Canada more closely with the UK and the US on most matters, especially the Cold War. This close alignment on most issues gave Mulroney the room and the credibility to differ from his closest allies over apartheid. Mulroney's secretary of state for external affairs, Joe Clark, made an important statement on apartheid to the House of Commons on September 13, 1985. He said, "Canadians are offended by and abhor the practice of institutionalising racism by a society (i.e., South Africa) that claims to share our values" and that "Canadians' influence (over

South Africa) is limited, but real" (in Blanchette 2000, 188). Clark nominated A. F. Hart, a former Canadian diplomat previously posted to Ghana, to become the administrator of the Canadian Code of Conduct for Employment Practices of Canadian Companies Operating in South Africa. Clark also informed the House of Commons that Canada would give $1 million to assist the families of South African political prisoners and those denied justice by the South African government (ibid.). In addition, Canada demanded the release of detainees and prisoners belonging to the African National Congress and the United Democratic Front. Canada insisted that all South Africans should be "unimpeded by arbitrary restrictions" adopted by their government (ibid.).

Canada's influence on South Africa was largely in the form of firm public diplomacy. It became a moral imperative for Canada in the comity of nations to stand by black South Africans whose freedoms and rights were violated. Clark insisted, as a moral imperative or a duty for justice (see Chapter 15), on instituting "common citizenship (for all races) in South Africa" (ibid.). He also demanded a process of consultation and negotiations, as well as a process of reform that would be devoid of compulsion or intimidation (in Blanchette 2000, 189). The apartheid regime in South Africa responded by accusing Clark of not knowing enough about South Africa. Clark took the opportunity in 1987 to visit South Africa for a familiarization tour (Schiller 2013), which only confirmed his convictions about the evil of apartheid.

But Canada's support for the fight to end apartheid was not confined to mere words. Through a Canadian arm's-length Crown corporation, the International Development Research Centre (see Case Study 6), Canada provided financial and technical support to the ANC and its ally, the Mass Democratic Movement. The aim of this program was to help the ANC make the transition from an opposition movement to a democratic political party that was capable of taking on the complex tasking of governing a large and diverse nation (Sutherland 1999; Hirsch 2005; Van Ameringen 2013). Over half of the members of the first post-apartheid cabinet in South Africa in 1994 had taken part in this program. The architects of South Africa's post-apartheid constitution also studied the Canadian constitution closely, especially the Charter of Rights and Freedoms and aspects of Canadian federalism. In these respects, the South African constitution bears important similarities to Canada's constitution.

In February 1990, when the ANC had its official meeting in Lusaka, Zambia, Clark attended. He received plaudits from Zambian President Kenneth Kaunda, a notable foe of apartheid, on that occasion. After the apartheid authorities released Mandela from prison in February 1990, the first place he visited in North America was Canada, to show appreciation for the support that he and the ANC had received. Mandela was subsequently given honorary Canadian citizenship.

Impact

In May 1994, Nelson Mandela was inaugurated as the first president of a democratic South Africa under a non-racial constitution. Overwhelmingly, the success of the anti-apartheid movement was of course due to the struggles of the South Africans themselves. But international support for the struggle was also important, as has often been acknowledged by the leaders of the anti-apartheid movement. The Canadian government under Brian Mulroney played an important part in supporting the democratic forces in South Africa and in undermining the international legitimacy of apartheid, especially in the UK and the US.

According to one observer, it was "a time when Canada truly stood tall. It spearheaded a key international committee leading the fight against apartheid. It gave moral and financial support to apartheid's opponents on the ground . . . Canada's distinguished fight against apartheid should make every Canadian proud" (Schiller 2013). Canada's international reputation flourished following its contributions to end apartheid in South Africa. This episode also offered Canada the opportunity to become conscious of its own poor record on human rights with respect to Indigenous peoples in Canada.

One of the key elements of South Africa's transition from apartheid to non-racial democracy was its Truth and Reconciliation Commission. That Commission laid bare the evils of apartheid; it has widely been considered a success story following the divisiveness of apartheid. It is no doubt appropriate then that, when Canada launched its own Truth and Reconciliation Commission to look into its treatment of First Nations, Métis, and Inuit peoples, Canada looked at other countries' commissions for inspiration, including South Africa's.

Suggested Readings

Allen, John. 2005. *Apartheid South Africa*. Lincoln, NE: iUniverse.

Blanchette, Arthur. 2000. *Canadian Foreign Policy: 1945-2000 (Major Documents and Speeches)*. Toronto: Dundurn Press.

Crompton, Samuel. 2007. *Nelson Mandela: Ending Apartheid in South Africa*. New York: Chelsea House.

Hirsch, Alan. 2005. *Season of Hope: Economic Reform under Mandela and Mbeki*. Durban: University of Kwazulu-Natal Press.

Potter, Evan. 2006. "Public Diplomacy in South Africa: A Comparison of the Canadian and British Experiences." Paper presented at the Annual Meeting of the International Studies Association, San Diego, CA. Retrieved from http://citation.allacademic.com/meta/p100169_index.html

Schiller, Bill. 2013. "Nelson Mandela: Canada Helped Lead International Fight Against Apartheid." Retrieved from http://www.thestar.com/news/world/2013/12/06/nelson_mandela_canada_helped_lead_international_fight_against_apartheid.html

Sutherland, Sharon. 1999. *Supporting Democracy: The South Africa-Canada Program on Governance*. Ottawa: International Development Research Centre. https://www.idrc.ca/en/book/supporting-democracy-south-africa-canada-program-governance

Van Ameringen, Mark. 2013. "A Time to Reflect on Mandela and Canada's Role in South Africa." http://www.huffingtonpost.com/marc-van-ameringen/a-time-to-reflect-on-mand_b_4412747.html

Suggested Websites

Canada-South Africa Relations. Retrieved from http://www.canadainternational.gc.ca/southafrica-afriquedusud/bilateral_relations_bilaterales/canada_sa-as.aspx?menu_id=7&menu=L&lang=eng

Canada and South Africa Share a Dark Past. http://www.rcinet.ca/english/archives/column/The-Link-Africa/TruthandReconciliationCanada-SouthAfricaResidentialSchoolsAbuses/

Schiller, Bill. 2013. Nelson Mandela on Canada. http://www.thestar.com/news/world/2013/12/06/nelson_mandela_canada_helped_lead_international_fight_against_apartheid.html

Case Study 3

Canada and the Responsibility to Protect

Omid B. Milani

Issue

In a relatively recent development, the sovereignty of states has ceased to be the most sacred principle in international law. In response to the failure of the UN Security Council to prevent the genocide in Rwanda and other mass atrocities in the Balkans and elsewhere in the post-war world, the international community learned that the existing mechanisms are not sufficient for pursuing universal peace. Since the turn of the millennium, there has thus been the beginning of a significant shift from a culture of reaction to one of prevention (Schabas 2006, 63). In particular, the UN General Assembly (UNGA) has declared that "each individual State has the responsibility to protect (R2P) its populations from genocide, war crimes, ethnic cleansing and crimes against humanity" (UNGA 2009). Furthermore, "the international community, through the United Nations, also has the responsibility to use appropriate diplomatic, humanitarian and other peaceful means, in accordance with Chapters VI and VIII of the [UN] Charter, to help to protect populations from genocide, war crimes, ethnic cleansing and crimes against humanity" (ibid.). Canada played a lead role in getting the international community to adopt the R2P doctrine, especially under the Liberal governments of Jean Chrétien (1993–2003) and Paul Martin (2003–2006). However, the relatively short history of the R2P has been replete with inconsistencies, shortcomings, and hypocrisy, primarily from the major powers' side, including Canada's. This Case Study is a critical-legal analysis of Canada's recent impact in relation to R2P. For a general analysis of the R2P, see Knight (2011).

Action

Canada has often played a pivotal role in international peace. (See Chapter 5, Case Studies 1 and 7.) Following the lamentable international response to the 1994 Rwandan genocide and the Balkan wars of the 1990s (see Chapters 5 and 14), Canada pushed for the creation of the International Commission on Intervention and State Sovereignty (ICISS). The Commission's secretariat was housed in a Canadian Crown corporation, the International Development Research Centre. (See Case Study 6.) The Commission's report (ICISS 2001) helped popularize the concept of humanitarian intervention. It asserted that a state's sovereignty depended on its willingness and ability to protect and provide basic services to its populations. If a state is unable or unwilling to protect its populations, then an escalating series of actions is proposed, up to and including military intervention under the auspices of the UN Security Council. R2P is said to rest on three "pillars":

1. the protection responsibilities of the state,
2. international assistance and capacity-building, and
3. timely and decisive response to crisis.

In 2005, Canada led the effort to enshrine this R2P doctrine in a major UNGA resolution (UNGA 2005).

Soon after the ICISS report came out, American conservatives were using R2P to justify the US intervention in Afghanistan (see Case Study 4) and the US-led war in Iraq. However, the Iraq War lacked legality and the military intervention was launched without a UN Security Council resolution. Such actions made the R2P doctrine unpopular with many developing country governments. Following the Arab Spring, Canada has been actively involved in military missions in the Middle East (see Chapter 5 and Case Study 10) that have been justified using R2P-like language. However, its role has been largely limited to military engagement in the region's conflicts. This over-militarized approach has been in contradiction of the principles of the R2P and global peace. In Libya, "the glaring omission of any Canadian voice for, or significant multilateral attempt at, preventive diplomacy and mediation through R2P will remain a lost opportunity for the doctrine itself, for the people of Libya, for Canada and for the international community" (Rashid 2013 46).Though the Canadian-led military intervention succeeded in removing President Muamar Ghaddafi from power (see Chapter 5), it has not brought peace or security to Libya. Rather, it has paved the path for the emergence of extremist militias. Prioritizing military actions over diplomacy and other peaceful means stems from a classic misconception of peace that reduces peace to the absence of war.

In other cases where the state has been manifestly unable or unwilling to protect its citizens from war crimes, ethnic cleansing, and/or crimes against humanity, the R2P doctrine has not, however, been invoked by anyone. This is the case most notably in the current Syrian crisis, but other cases can also be invoked, such as South Sudan, Ukraine, and Yemen. The reasons for this lack of recourse to R2P lie in great-power politics and in the lack of support from one or more of the veto-wielding five permanent members of the UN Security Council.

Impact

Reducing R2P to military engagement is a horrible inclination, which builds upon short-sighted policies, a misunderstanding of peace and, consequently, a misunderstanding of R2P. The mainstream (and perhaps dominant academic) understanding of R2P has distorted the proper understanding of "prevention" from genocide, crimes against humanity, war crimes, and ethnic cleansing. However, using the term "protect" and juxtaposing it with genocide and other crimes can imply a *passive approach* and may become problematic. In other words, in order for an atrocity or a mass killing to be qualified as one of the four above-mentioned crimes, it seems that the international community and states have to remain inactive until the problem escalates to one of those crimes, then "when a state was manifestly failing to protect its population from the *four specified crimes*, the international community [will be] prepared to take collective action in a timely and decisive manner" (UNGA 2009). This inconsistency stems from a misconception in understanding international peace. For thousands of years, *peace* has been defined as being synonymous with absence of war. By reducing peace to the mere absence of war, we tend to blind ourselves to the main causes of war; in fact, peace is better conceived of as the "absence of violence" (Galtung 1969, 167). To put it another way, by redefining peace in a positive (not negative) fashion and linking it to violence of any kind (ibid. 183), our interpretation of the R2P will be transformed. A proactive strategy is more compatible with the intent and philosophy behind the R2P. Nevertheless, the R2P struggles with an inherent fundamental inconsistency, which will be elaborated on shortly.

The shift from a culture of reaction to prevention sees a big obstacle on its way, namely the principle of sovereignty. In other words, the R2P tries to reconcile recognizing states' sovereignty with a universal moral responsibility to protect (Douzinas 2002, 451). One may argue that these two are not, by nature, reconcilable. The state's overwhelming sovereignty can impede any effective effort for protection. This argument is legitimate to a large extent. The failure of liberal internationalism (see Chapters 11 and 14) and the international human rights regime to prevent genocides, war crimes, and so forth is so glaring that "such comprehensive ineffectiveness cannot be dismissed as merely unfortunate failure of implementation" (Gassama 2012, 428). The reason for such failures lies in a paradox between human rights and international law.

One of the paradoxes between human rights and international law, manifest in the three pillars of the UN report on the R2P, is the one between the existence of the state (and recognition of the state's sovereignty as the sacred foundation of international law) and the universality of human rights that transcends political borders and local authorities (Douzinas 2002, 448). Government and authorities exercise power based on their interests; their territories have been their backyard in which to perpetuate the institutions of power. Nationals are subject to national laws. On the other hand, in human rights law, fundamental freedoms, rights, and responsibilities are not bound to the decisions of states; all individuals must be able to enjoy their rights and freedoms regardless of their nationality, race, religion, etc. However, the literature, documents, and instruments regarding the R2P strive to satisfy the demands of classic international law and the emerging (and ever-growing) calls for universal R2P. But to what extent is this gap bridgeable? And a more important query is: how many more lives is this inconsistency going to claim?

Moreover, the double standard exercised by the major powers in terms of their recourse to R2P, and the drastic inconsistency of how those states have been behaving with regard to very similar situations, can also demonstrate a deeper flaw within international law and the protection of the dignity of human beings, which seems to be the basis of the R2P and "the common mission of human rights law and international humanitarian law" (Schabas 2006, 63).

Complicated problems require sophisticated solutions. It might be too naïve to think that the R2P can protect all individuals from mass killings and atrocities. The legal and political capacities of R2P are high and they can be utilized to effect positive change, especially through diplomacy. But due to the inherent inconsistencies and the over-politicized status quo, it might be too wishful an expectation to envisage a world devoid of genocides, war crimes, and the like through the mere actualization of the R2P. The four crimes of genocide, crimes against humanity, ethnic cleansing, and war crimes occur mostly if an armed conflict takes place, and no conflict of any kind happens in a vacuum. The preliminary stages, which can result in wars, genocides, and so on are enumerated in human rights law. However, human rights law and the international community are not mature enough, or are "too cautious" (Schabas 2006, 63), to enter the area of criminalizing those acts of violence.

Unfortunately, human rights alone cannot provide a solution either. Human rights, whether during colonialism or more recently, have been used selectively for satisfying political objectives. For example, while heinous crimes in African countries are often not appealing enough for other states to engage and take any decisive and timely measures, similar crimes in other parts of the world can unite a great number of states against a select militia or a government, as if some are lesser humans in our world. The efforts to achieve any comprehensive success through the R2P, as long as it is solely the responsibility of the states, will be in vain.

Associating peace with violence and defining peace in a positive fashion can be a turning point for the R2P. Although there has been a shift from reaction to prevention, the approach is still too reactive and passive. Instead of focusing on elimination of the smoke (the four crimes), we ought to get rid of the fire that causes the smoke, that is, violence. Needless to say, this approach is more sophisticated, and perhaps more difficult than simply bombarding a country to protect its people! Our understanding of violence should be inclusive of individual and structural forms (Galtung 1969, 183); the real protection will be possible through protecting individuals from all forms of violence, namely ethnocentrism, sexism, poverty, intolerance, inequality, and so forth. They are indeed the elements of *all* wars. Then, with a new understanding of peace, it will be our responsibility, all of us, to protect one another from any form of violence; it will be our collective duty to react.

Works Cited

Douzinas, Costas. 2002. "The end(s) of human rights." *Melbourne University Law Review* 26 (2).

Galtung, Johan. 1969. "Violence, Peace and Peace Research." *Journal of Peace Research* 3 (1).

Gassama, Ibrahim J. 2012. "A World Made of Violence and Misery: Human Rights as a Failed Project of Liberal Internationalism." *Brooklyn Journal of International Law*, no. 37.

Knight, Andy. 2011. "The Development of the Responsibility to Protect: From Evolving Norm to Practice." *Global Responsibility to Protect* 3 (1): 3–36.

Marcel, Gabriel. 1964. *Creative Fidelity*. New York: Noonday Press.

Rashid, Sid. 2013. "Preventive Diplomacy, Mediation and the Responsibility to Protect in Libya: A Missed Opportunity for Canada?" *Canadian Foreign Policy Journal* 13 (1).

Schabas, William. 2006. "Preventing Genocide and Mass Killing: From a Culture of Reaction to Prevention." *UN Chronicle* 43 (1).

United Nations General Assembly (UNGA). 2005. *2005 World Summit Outcome*. A/60/L.1. New York: United Nations.

———. 2009. *Implementing the Responsibility to Protect*. A/63/677. New York: United Nations.

Case Study 4

Canada and Afghanistan 2001–2014

Salamat Ali Tabbasum

Issue

After the 1988 defeat of the Soviet Union in Afghanistan by Mujahideen forces supported by the US and its allies, Afghanistan descended into chaos. Under the Taliban regime (1995–2001) Afghanistan became a safe haven for the terrorist group Al-Qaeda. The attacks on the World Trade Centre and the Pentagon on September 11, 2001 (known as "9/11"), were conducted by Al-Qaeda out of its bases in Afghanistan. Having been attacked, the United States invoked Article 5 of the NATO Treaty (see Chapter 5), which meant that other NATO members such as Canada were called upon to fight the common enemy. The US invaded Afghanistan and, in late 2001, the Taliban government was overthrown. Canada became a staunch ally of the US in what became known as the War on Terror. Canada committed troops, civilian experts, and economic aid to the reconstruction of Afghanistan.

The major problems Afghanistan faced after 2001 were poverty and insecurity, complicated by the almost complete collapse of government structures and an extreme lack of skilled personnel in non-military areas, especially in health, education, and public administration. Afghanistan's lack of technical capacity was a major hindrance in the country's development efforts; donor countries like Canada responded by sending large numbers of their own staff and consultants as "technical assistance." But rural poverty, continuing injustice and inequalities,

corruption in the new Afghan government, the perceived loss of national sovereignty after the American invasion, religious fundamentalism, and the backlash against the counter-insurgency mounted by the Western powers in Afghanistan prompted many young Afghans to join terrorist groups and militias. The United States and its allies, including Canada, realized that security was pivotal to achieving the long-term goal of development in Afghanistan. However, there have been important debates over whether development should take precedence over security in Afghanistan, or vice versa, and what the relationship is between international community's development efforts and that same community's efforts to promote greater peace and security. This terrain is called the security-development nexus. (See Chapter 14.) This case study looks at these debates about the security-development nexus in Afghanistan since 2001.

Action

Canadian aid to Afghanistan increased from $5 million per annum in 2001 to $150 million six years later (Staples and MacDonald 2009) as Afghanistan quickly became a policy priority for the Government of Canada. By 2009, Canada had allocated $1.1 billion to aid projects in Afghanistan and the cost of Canada's military operations in that country had reached $17.8 billion (Staples and MacDonald 2009). Canada had four priorities in Afghanistan:

1. education and health;
2. security, the rule of law, and human rights,
3. promoting regional diplomacy, and
4. helping to deliver humanitarian assistance (Government of Canada 2014).

As these priority areas suggest, Canada's involvement in Afghanistan was not based solely on humanitarian or developmental concerns; rather, security was a significant part of Canada's involvement in Afghanistan.

The dual civil-military character of the Afghan mission was controversial. Under the governments of Prime Ministers Paul Martin (Liberal, 2004–2006) and Stephen Harper (Conservative, 2006–2015), Canada adopted a "whole-of-government approach" (see Chapter 14) to managing the Afghan mission, integrating defence, diplomacy, and development aid. The issue became acute after 2005, when explicit links were established between the Canadian Forces' efforts to improve security in Kandahar Province and the Canadian aid program, which came to be concentrated in that province. Canada's military—like their other Western counterparts—took an increasing role in delivering aid and in protecting aid workers. From 2005 to 2012, Canada's military strategy in Afghanistan became more offensive and Canadian development projects became components of the broader counter-insurgency strategy, intended to win the hearts and minds of ordinary Afghans (Holland 2010). The whole-of-government approach has been criticized by some as hijacking development in favour of security concerns (Baranyi and Paducel 2012; Beal et al. 2006; Turenne-Sjolander 2010). Others have worried that the international legal principle of neutrality in the distribution of humanitarian aid was jeopardized by using the Canadian military, a combatant, to help deliver aid in a war zone (UNESCO 2011). But the Organisation for Economic Co-operation and Development stated that "Canada shows good practice in implementing whole-of-government approaches in fragile states, particularly in Afghanistan. Its

assistance in other partner countries would be more effective if it applied the relevant programme considerations emerging from Afghanistan in those contexts" (OECD/DAC 2012, 12).

Canada's presence in Afghanistan was legitimized on the grounds that it improved the security of the Afghan people (Boucher 2009). Canada contributed to the multilateral security efforts in Afghanistan, including the International Security Assistance Force, starting in 2003. Over the past decade, Canada has not only contributed troops and weapons to Afghanistan but also a significant amount of civilian aid to improve governance in the country (Government of Canada 2014; see also Chapter 11.) To support security, the rule of law, and human rights, Canada provided military trainers and Canadian civilian police to help train the Afghan National Security Forces. Canada also provided a number of civilian experts on governance, human rights, gender, and public administration. Despite the large sums spent, security has not improved in Afghanistan and the stabilization agenda in Afghanistan has come under criticism.

Some suggest that official development assistance (see Chapter 4) should mainly contribute to peacebuilding, which is a stepping-stone to development; according to this view, security agendas should take precedence over development (Beall, Goodfellow, and Putzel 2006). Undoubtedly, security is instrumental for development, but the overemphasis on the former may hurt the effectiveness of our aid programs. McAskie (2010) and Brown (2012) argue that Canadian aid has been ineffective because it has privileged the donor's security priorities in Afghanistan and elsewhere, and does not match local development needs.

Additionally, many Canadian (and other) aid projects bypassed Afghan state institutions, undermining the state's legitimacy and its ability to deliver core public services to its people (Banerjee 2009). Canada's supply-driven approach to aid delivery in Afghanistan may have raised Canada's visibility but could not foster national ownership or empower the Afghan state. The main reason for a lack of national ownership may be the Western donors' market-oriented economic policies, which undermined the emergence of a viable Afghan state (Goodhand and Sedra 2010).

Poverty reduction and development programs in Afghanistan, however, have a mixed record. Some development indicators, such as school enrolments and nutrition rates, have improved enormously since 2001. Primary school enrolment increased to 97.4 percent in 2011 from less than 10 percent in 2001. But secondary school enrolment rate was only at 51.8 percent in 2011 (World Bank 2014), which means that almost 50 percent of children drop out of school sometime after primary school. Many aid projects in Afghanistan were unsustainable and short-term (Banerjee 2013); for instance, Canada spent more than $50 million on building 50 schools which were poorly built, with many being non-functional. Such projects reflect the donor's "window dressing" approach, whereby putting the donor country's flag on a project for short-term publicity purposes takes precedence over long-term development concerns.

Impact

Afghanistan today presents a bleak picture. Real achievements in social and economic development are threatened by a weak state and a fragile security situation, even though a considerable amount of aid money from Canada and other donor has been injected into the country. Meanwhile, Canada and other donors in the country continue to prioritize security over development under the security-development nexus. In view of the poor security situation and fragile nature of the development results to date, several questions could be raised, for instance: what have been the outcomes of the security and stabilization agenda of Canada in Afghanistan? Should Canada continue to prioritize security over development?

Undoubtedly, security is imperative for development, and the relationship between the two is symbiotic. However, the way Canada and other donors have approached development and security in Afghanistan can be questioned. Canada's overemphasis on security compromised the main objective of economic and social development in Afghanistan. Under the guise of securitization in Afghanistan, Canada served the security interests of the US rather than the people of Afghanistan (Échec à la Guerre 2009; Warnock 2009). Our focus on window-dressing projects and easily countable "results" like number of schools built masked a much more complex reality. The ineffectiveness of Canadian aid in Afghanistan was due to a lack of political will and an inefficient and ill-informed bureaucracy (Brown and Raddatz 2012) caught in the whole-of-government trap. The donors' decision to bypass the Afghan state in so many development projects undermined the authority and capacity of the very state we claimed to be trying to build.

Suggested Readings

Banerjee, Nipa. 2009. "Afghanistan: No Security, No Governance." *Options Politiques.*

———. 2010. "Time to Learn from Past Afghan Mistakes." *Options Politiques.*

———. 2013. "An Ex-CIDA Officer's Reflections on Afghanistan: Looking Back, Looking Forward." Available at: http://cips.uottawa.ca/an-ex-cida-officers-reflections-on-afghanistan-looking-back-looking-forward/. Accessed on 12 December, 2014.

Baranyi, Stephen, and Anca Paducel. 2012. "Whither Development in Canada's Approach to Fragile States?" In *CIDA and Canadian Aid Policy* edited by Stephen Brown. Montreal: McGill-Queen's University Press.

Beall, Jo, Thomas Goodfellow, and James Putzel. 2006. "Introductory Article: On the Discourse of Terrorism, Security and Development." *Journal of International Development* 18 (1).

Beaudet, Pierre. 2009. "Canada and the Crisis in Afghanistan." In *Afghanistan and Canada*, edited by Lucia Kowaluk and Steven Staples. Montreal: Black Rose Books.

Boucher, Jean-Christophe. 2009. "Selling Afghanistan: A Discourse Analysis of Canada's Military Intervention, 2001–08." *International Journal*, Summer 2009.

Brown, Stephen, ed. 2012. *Struggling for Effectiveness: CIDA and Canadian Foreign Aid*. Montreal: McGill-Queen's University Press.

Brown, Stephen, and Rosalind Raddatz. 2012. "Taking Stock, Looking Ahead." In *Struggling for Effectiveness: CIDA and Canadian Foreign Aid*, edited by Stephen Brown. Montreal: McGill-Queen's University Press.

Échec à la Guerre. 2009. "Canada's Role in the Occupation of Afghanistan." In *Afghanistan and Canada*, edited by Lucia Kowaluk and Steven Staples. Montreal: Black Rose Books.

Goodhand, Jonathan, and Mark Sedra. 2010. "Who Owns the Peace? Aid, Reconstruction, and Peacebuilding in Afghanistan." *Disasters* 34 (S1): S78–S102.

Government of Canada. 2014. "Canada's Engagement in Afghanistan." Available at: http://www.afghanistan.gc.ca/canada-afghanistan/index.aspx. Accessed on September 9, 2014.

Holland, Kenneth. 2010. "The Canadian Provincial Reconstruction Team: The Arm of Development in Kandahar Province." *American Review of Canadian Studies* 40 (2).

McAskie, Carolyn. 2010. "The Global Challenge of Fragile States: Is There a Role for Canada?" McLeod Group. Available at: http://www.mcleodgroup.ca/docs/fragilestates.html. Accessed on November 20, 2014.

Mullen, Rani. 2009. "Afghanistan in 2008: State Building at the Precipice." *Asian Survey*, 49 (1).

OECD/DAC. 2012. *Canada: Development Assistance Committee (DAC), Peer Review 2012*. Paris: OECD.

Staples, Steven, and David MacDonald. 2009. "How Much Is this War Costing Canadians?" In *Afghanistan and Canada*, edited by Lucia Kowaluk and Steven Staples Montreal: Black Rose Books.

Turenne-Sjolander, Claire. 2010. "The Obama Charm? Canada and Afghanistan under a New US Administration." *American Review of Canadian Studies* 40 (2): 292–304.

UNESCO. 2011. "Education Can Suffer When Line Between Security and Development Is Blurred." Available at: http://www.unesco.orginew/fileadmin/MULTIMEDIAMQ/ED/pdfigmr2011-press-release-militarization.pdf. Accessed on October 20, 2014.

Warnock, John. 2009. "What Is Canada Promoting in Afghanistan? A Brief History." In *Afghanistan and Canada*, edited by Lucia Kowaluk and Steven Staples. Montreal: Black Rose Books.

World Bank. 2014. "School Enrollment, Primary: Afghanistan." Available at: http://data.worldbank.org/indicator/SE.PRM.ENRR. Accessed on January 12, 2015.

Case Study 5

The Ebbs and Flows of Canada's Multilateral Commitments since 1945

Katelyn L.H. Cassin

Issue

Since the creation of the United Nations (UN) at the end of the Second World War (1939–1945), multilateral diplomacy has increasingly impacted the foreign policies of nations worldwide. There are several ways to define multilateralism. One common definition sees multilateralism as "the practice of co-coordinating national policies in groups of three or more states" (Keohane 1990, 732). Another view says that multilateralism implies "generalized principles of conduct," namely "diffuse reciprocity, i.e., an expectation of rough equivalence in benefits over time" (MacDonald 2010, 113; Ruggie 1992, 567, 571). These definitions limit multilateralism to coordination among states. Robert Cox (1992) expands multilateralism to include transborder cooperation involving non-state actors: civil society, business, and transnational social movements. He also argues that multilateralism is "embedded in the unequal . . . relations among states and civil society actors in the global capitalist economy" (Cox 1992, 164). These definitions ground this analysis of Canadian engagement in multilateralism, and offer a glimpse of the challenges associated with collaborative foreign policy.

States and non-state actors collaborate multilaterally for a number of reasons. Small states like Canada seek an international system where the powerful are constrained by rules; such rules can only be constructed multilaterally (Freeland 2017). "Multilateralism . . . is a

leveling exercise. It dilutes the absolute power of the economic giants because it entails diplomacy and deal-making, compromise and consensus, where smaller players like Canada can wield influence out of proportion to their actual economic clout" (Herman, quoted in Keating 2010, 12). Larger and more powerful states join multilateral institutions in an attempt to extend their influence by helping to define those rules. Non-state actors collaborate multilaterally to make their voices heard beyond their national borders. Most importantly, some problems are of truly global importance. Issues such as climate change, nuclear proliferation, disease control, international financial stability, international air and maritime transport, refugee flows, and international organized crime must be managed multilaterally.

Support for multilateralism amongst states has generally declined since 2000, often due to the perception that multilateral institutions are poorly adapted to the challenges of the twenty-first century (Brown and Olender 2013, 158; see Case Study 1). Nations may prefer bilateral action where they think it suits their interests better; for example, they often channel their aid programs through bilateral (i.e., country-to-country) relationships in order to exert "control over planning of projects, and [for the] ability to target aid to countries of highest political or commercial priority" (Pratt 1994, 27; see also Chapter 4). In addition, some nations have become disenchanted with the inefficiencies in the multilateral system. In seeking consensus between members, multilateral institutions can fail to provide conclusive and binding resolutions on issues of paramount global concern. Finally, the hubris of some international organizations, especially the international financial institutions in the 1980s and 1990s, has proven unfounded, which has undermined their credibility in later years (Best 2014; see also Chapters 2 and 3).

Despite these challenges, multilateralism remains important to global governance and the ability of the international community to address issues that are transnational in nature. In the twenty-first century, new actors, both state and non-state, must be incorporated into multilateral frameworks to address important global issues. (See Chapter 3.) Canada played a large part in building the post-1945 multilateral system (see Case Study 1) and much of our self-image as an "honest broker" in international affairs is built on our multilateral tradition. Yet Canada spent much of the last 25 years withdrawing from multilateral engagements. The new Liberal government has recently committed to a re-engagement with multilateralism (Freeland 2017). This case study explores the factors driving Canada's on-and-off relationship with multilateralism.

Action

Canada's multilateral record dates back to the League of Nations (1920) and the Imperial (later Commonwealth) Conferences of the 1920s through the 1940s. From 1945 to the end of the twentieth century, Canada's foreign policy can broadly be described as "the middle-power ideal—that of a financially supportive, initiative-taking, mediating actor with a moderately progressive development philosophy in the multilateral system" (Pratt 1994, 30).

Canada contributed significantly to the creation of the Bretton Woods institutions (the World Bank and the International Monetary Fund), and to the UN and several of its funds and programs, and has at times been active

in UN peacekeeping missions. Canada is an active member of three defence cooperation pacts (NATO, NORAD, and the "Five Eyes"), numerous regional development banks (e.g., the African Development Bank), economic collaborations such as the G7, G20, and the Organisation for Economic Co-operation and Development (OECD), and regional bodies like the Organization of American States, as well as being a leading member of the Commonwealth and La Francophonie. Indeed, Canada is said to be an inveterate "joiner" of international organizations of all sorts (Gurría 2011).

The 1970s were a strong decade for Canadian multilateralism. Multilateral agencies received increased funding from Canada, reaching 32 percent of Canadian official development assistance (ODA) in 1978. Canada also began to make soft loans through regional development banks such as the African Development Fund and set ambitious targets for multilateral ODA in the latter part of the decade (Pratt 1994, 28–29). Part of Canada's motivation toward multilateralism in the 1970s was to counterbalance the US (MacDonald 2010, 114).

The OECD is an important vehicle for Western liberal democracies in coordinating their economic policies and their official development assistance (ODA or "aid"). Canada was the first nation to ratify the Convention of the OECD in 1961, and was followed by 17 other countries the same year. Today the OECD is made up of 34 member states and associates. The Development Assistance Committee (DAC; see Chapter 4) of the OECD is responsible for tracking Official Development Assistance (ODA) expended by member nations through both multilateral and bilateral channels. The OECD Council operates on a basis of consensus. Canada led the OECD in adapting its ODA approach in the late 1960s, encouraging members to abandon patronizing relations between donors and recipients in favour of more equitable partnerships (Gurría 2011). In return, Canada has benefited from the policy advice generated by the peer review process, the

OECD databases and statistics for international comparative purposes, and the wisdom generated by OECD research into best practices in donorship. (See Chapter 4.)

Canada's commitment to multilateralism began to falter during the recession in the early 1980s. This downturn characterized the main policy priorities of the decade, which were funding to multilateral organizations conditional on management reform and development aid conditional on policy reform in recipient countries.

Canada did, however, show its multilateral commitment in 1985, when Progressive Conservative Prime Minister Brian Mulroney (1984–1993) came to the defence of multilateralism and the United Nations specifically, which was facing severe criticism from the United States and other allies at the time. (See Case Study 2.) "History shows that the solitary pursuit of self-interest outside the framework of broader international cooperation is never enough to increase our freedom, safeguard our security, or improve our standard of living" (quoted in Keating 2010, 14). Under Mulroney, Canada did pursue several multilateral initiatives, notably the Montreal Protocol (see Case Study 8), the fight against apartheid in South Africa (see Case Study 2), and the World Summit for Children. All three initiatives were high profile but cost little money.

Nonetheless, the 1989 federal budget instituted general aid cuts, with multilateral aid cut disproportionately. This stance signalled the coming "gradual erosion of [Canada's] reputation as a serious player" in the 1990s (McAskie 2011, 6). Despite Canada's previous position as a top-five multilateral donor in the 1980s and early 1990s, it fell from the top-ten list through the 1990s as its aid and diplomacy budgets were cut. (See Chapter 4.) Canada became increasingly risk-averse, favoured bilateral over multilateral aid, shifted its focus to domestic priorities, and reduced international contributions generally (Pratt 1994, 25; McAskie 2011, 6).

The downward trend continued into the 2000s, with aid to multilateral organizations reaching a low of 21 percent of ODA in 2009. Canada increasingly adopted an "issue-by-issue approach to multilateralism, engaging when the government determined it was in its interest to do so"; this approach has been called "à la carte multilateralism," or "cherry picking" (Brown and Olender 2013, 158; Keating 2010, 20; McAskie 2011, 8). While Canada's declining status in the international community has been widely attributed to the government of Conservative Prime Minister Stephen Harper (2006–2015), many of Canada's failures in the multilateral system predate his leadership. An example is Harper's 2011 decision to withdraw Canada from the Kyoto Protocol (see Case Study 8), a decision which was facilitated by the complete failure of previous Liberal governments to implement Kyoto. The biggest reductions in Canada's aid budget came under the Liberal government of the 1990s, not under Harper. Throughout the 1990s, Canada's commitment to UN peacekeeping also declined, and skepticism was "bred in the troubled times of Rwanda, Somalia, and Bosnia," which has been reignited by the Conservative Party's military patriotism (Kinsman 2014, 14; Keating 2010, 19; McAskie 2011, 8; see Chapters 5 and 14).

Harper characterized his government's foreign policy as "enlightened sovereignty," described as "the natural extension [abroad] of enlightened self-interest" (quoted in Black and Donaghy 2010, 2). The next year, in an address to the UN General Assembly, Harper's Foreign Minister John Baird quoted Margaret Thatcher, stating "Consensus seems to be the process of abandoning all beliefs, principles, values and policies. So it is something in which no-one believes," thus expressing antagonism toward the foundational principle of multilateralism—consensus (quoted in McAskie 2011, 3). Not only did Canada withdraw from the Kyoto Protocol, but it adopted an antagonistic position toward climate change negotiations, arguing that commitments to curb emissions could "jeopardize job creation in difficult economic times" (Brown and Olender 2013, 175). Harper did, however, set more modest goals regarding greenhouse gas reduction and committed $1.2 billion to financing clean energy adaptation in the poorest and most vulnerable nations through the Copenhagen Accord in 2009.

During the 2000s, Canada engaged in what has been termed the "bilateralization of multilateral aid" and "the multilateralization of bilateral aid"— in other words, channelling aid that has been earmarked for specific countries and programs through multilateral organizations (OECD 2011, 28). Since 2005, Canada has been explicit in applying greater scrutiny to multilateral donorship and engagement, prioritizing effectiveness and efficiency (Brown and Olender 2013, 163).

What Canada's increasing ambivalence toward multilateralism has demonstrated is an increasingly utilitarian approach to development and global affairs, prioritizing Canada's economic and political interests to the detriment of its international relationships and image. This approach is characteristic of "hegemonic global powers, not middle powers like Canada," threatening its legacy as a champion of multilateralism and undermining the effectiveness of the international community to deliver aid based on global need (Brown and Olender 2013, 181, 172; Kinsman 2014, 13).

Impact

Canada's commitment to multilateralism has earned it a reputation as an inveterate "joiner," as a reliable and responsible global citizen. This active participation in multilateral cooperation is based on wide public support, to such an extent that it has been considered by some as a symbol of Canadian identity. (Gurría 2011)

The presence of multilateral diplomacy in Canadian identity is popularly articulated in Canadians' self-perception as peacekeepers, defenders of human rights, and generous contributors to international development (Keating 2010, 10). Considering Canada's recent record

with regard to multilateralism, there is incongruence between Canada's policy reality and the values of many of its citizens.

Aside from the impact on Canadian identity and the perception of Canada internationally, multilateralism presents several advantages to international development work. These include the capacity to sustain longer-term projects than is possible in bilateral agreements; the ability to distribute aid according to need, thus preventing the creation of "aid orphans," that is, countries where needs are great but no bilateral donor is interested; the ability to coherently address international issues such as climate change, refugee flows, and epidemics; enabling more inclusive dialogue with states often absent in decision-making processes at the global level; and significantly, multilateral donorship, particularly through the World Bank, provides an avenue for nations to influence "the economic policies of recipient governments to accord with Western preferences, thereby buttressing the world trade and financial order" (Pratt 1994, 26–27). This final point reflects an important note, that despite their inclusiveness, multilateral organizations are subject to unequal power relations and hierarchy, potentially entrenching systems of domination and exclusion that have historical roots in colonialism (Black and Donaghy 2010, 3).

Multilateralism has been a crucial Canadian foreign policy tool to promote its interests, augment its political voice, promote international order and its own security, assert its sovereignty, and foster political and economic relations (Keating 2010, 11). Multilateral engagement has been and remains in Canada's best interest. The new government under Liberal Prime Minister Justin Trudeau has expressed its commitment to re-engage with multilateralism (Freeland 2017). "The adult reality is that Canada abroad has to represent and operate on a composite policy level of economic interest; creative multilateralism and community citizenship; and consistency in values" (Kinsman 2014, 16).

Suggested Videos

Canadian multilateralism and engagement, McGill
Institute for the Study of Canada, McGill
University
https://www.youtube.com/
watch?v=J1HX1T1esk8

Contested multilateralism, Centre for International
Policy Studies, University of Ottawa
https://www.youtube.com/
watch?v=dJManRBp8MU

Declining multilateralism, The German Marshall
Fund of the United States
https://www.youtube.com/
watch?v=uPVa8JYBlfo

Prime Minister Justin Trudeau's Address to the UN
General Assembly September 20, 2016
https://www.youtube.com/
watch?v=ulDYH87K_VU

Understanding multilateralism, Council on Foreign
Relations
https://www.youtube.com/
watch?v=3v3A5CJ7gdM

Suggested Readings

Best, Jacqueline. 2014. *Governing Failure*. Cambridge: Cambridge University Press.

Black, David. 2010. "Canada and the Commonwealth: The Multilateral Politics of a 'Wasting
Asset'." *Canadian Foreign Policy Journal* 16 (2):
61–77.

Black, David, and Greg Donaghy. 2010. "Manifestations of Canadian Multilateralism." *Canadian
Foreign Policy Journal* 16 (2): 1–8.

Brown, Stephen, and Michael Olender. 2013.
"Canada's Fraying Commitment to Multilateral

Development Cooperation." In *Multilateral
Development Cooperation in a Changing Global
Order*, edited by Hany Besada and Shannon
Kindornay. London: Palgrave Macmillan.

Cox, Robert W. 1992. "Multilateralism and World
Order." *Review of International Studies* 18 (2):
161–180.

Freeland, Chrystia. 2017. "Address by Minister
Freeland on Canada's Foreign Policy Priorities."
Address to the House of Commons. Ottawa:
House of Commons. 6 June.

Gurría, Angel. 2011. "Canada and the OECD: 50
Years of Converging Interests." Paris: OECD.

Keating, Tom. 2010. "Multilateralism: Past Imperfect, Future Conditional." *Canadian Foreign
Policy Journal* 16 (2): 9–25.

Keohane, Robert Owen. 1990. "Multilateralism: An
Agenda for Research." *International Journal* 45
(4): 731–764.

Kinsman, Jeremy. 2014, February. "The Legacy of
the Honest Broker." *Policy Magazine*.

MacDonald, Laura. 2011. "A Fine Balance: Multilateralism and Bilateralism in Canadian Policy in
the North American Region." *Canadian Foreign
Policy Journal* 16 (2): 111–124.

McAskie, Carolyn. 2011. "Canada and Multilateralism: Missing in Action." Ottawa: The McLeod
Group.

OECD. 2011. *2011 DAC Report on Multilateral Aid*.
Paris: OECD.

Pratt, Cranford. 1994. *Canadian International
Development Assistance Policies: An Appraisal*.
Montreal: McGill-Queen's University Press.

Ruggie, John Gerard. 1992. "Multilateralism:
The Anatomy of an Institution." *International
Organization* 46 (3): 561–598.

Case Study 6

Canada's Scientific Cooperation with Developing Countries

Bruce Currie-Alder

Issue

The recent era of foreign aid began with American President Harry Truman's inaugural address in 1949, in which he called for "making the benefits of our scientific advances and industrial progress available for the improvement and growth of underdeveloped areas." Science, technology, and innovation promised to provide new opportunities to satisfy the needs of people living in newly independent states. All societies require the capacity to absorb and adapt scientific and technical knowledge, to ensure that research meets their own needs and solves their own problems. Yet the global distribution of scientific capacity remains uneven. Just ten countries in North America, Europe, and Asia account for 80 percent of the world's research expenditures, investing up to 4 percent of their national income in these activities. In comparison, most of the developing world invests less than 0.5 percent of their much smaller national income into research. Worldwide, the distribution of scientists and research publications is even more unequal than income distribution. Developing countries have a meagre share of global income, and yet an even smaller share of the world's scientific talent.

The location of scientific talent matters less than opportunities for developing countries to access global knowledge and garner attention for local challenges. Development challenges vary in time horizon and geographic scale:

responding to pandemic disease is short-term and global, while improving crops in poor soil conditions is longer-term and local. Both require the ability to design, develop, and carry out scientific cooperation, of international quality, that connects global talent and local experience.

There are diverse approaches to scientific cooperation with the developing world, ranging from mobilizing existing talent to design technology that serves poor and vulnerable people, to building capability in poorer countries to conduct science for their own benefit. The Rockefeller and Ford philanthropic foundations were early pioneers in this area, championing the development of the polio vaccine and the green revolution technologies that dramatically decreased child mortality and increased food production. The Bill & Melinda Gates Foundation has carried on this tradition, while Canada has crafted its own unique approach to becoming a world leader in scientific cooperation with the developing world.

Action

Canada's International Development Research Centre (IDRC) was created in 1970 "to initiate, encourage, support and conduct research into the problems of the developing regions of the world and into the means for applying and adapting scientific, technical and other knowledge to the economic and social advancement of those regions" (IDRC Act, s4.1). Modest in size compared to most foreign aid agencies, IDRC accounts for less than 4 percent of Canada's official development assistance. Yet it is among the world's top funders of scientific cooperation with developing countries. When Canada's Parliament passed the *IDRC Act*, it recognized that scientific cooperation required a distinct approach, one predicated on engaging research communities and research users rather than nurturing bilateral relations between governments; this is a very different approach from that taken by most bilateral aid agencies, including CIDA. Such an approach also requires persistence, as it can take years to develop and spread new technologies and solutions that enhance the lives of poor and vulnerable people. Based on years of working alongside scientists and farmers in India, IDRC's first president, David Hopper, imbued IDRC with the conviction that lasting change depended on supporting local societies' control of their own development.

IDRC has retained this tradition of working directly with developing world scientists, bringing in—but not imposing—views from outside where appropriate. At any one time, IDRC supports three to four research priorities, which have included agriculture, water, information sciences, governance, youth employment, women's economic empowerment, health systems, and non-communicable diseases. IDRC tackles problems of regional or global relevance, engaging not only governments, but universities, civil society, and the private sector. A key strength is the expertise of IDRC staff and their involvement in the research process. In the 1970s and 1980s, IDRC program officers scouted developing countries to identify their needs and spot talented people and organizations to address these needs. IDRC staff offered mentoring in research techniques and access to academic literature that was not available locally, and brokered contact with peers abroad. This role has evolved with the spread of the Internet since the mid-1990s, yet IDRC staff remain engaged with individual researchers, monitoring progress, understanding the context in which scientists work, and evaluating their own efforts to improve the lives of poor and vulnerable people. Support from IDRC has enhanced the credibility of local scientists in their own countries, improving their access to policy makers and their ability to inform public debate.

Impact

The lasting impact of IDRC's work can be measured in results that improve the lives of poor and vulnerable people, including new technology, a cleaner environment, and better health.

Technology: IDRC was instrumental in bridging the digital divide, bringing the first Internet connections to Bhutan, Cambodia, Laos, Mongolia, Sri Lanka, and Vietnam. Research supported by IDRC demonstrated the economic benefits to be gained from greater competition among telecommunication providers in Mozambique, Senegal, South Africa, and Uganda. In coastal India, thousands of lives were saved through a tsunami alert conveyed through a village Internet centre. IDRC also funded work that digitized Asian languages, including Dari, Dzongkha, Khmer, Lao, Singhalese, and Tamil. In Senegal, farmers increased their incomes up to 30 percent using smartphones to access market information and choose among competing offers for their produce. More recently, IDRC supported digital innovations to enhance access to education for Syrian refugees and host communities in the Middle East.

Environment: IDRC funded innovations in urban agriculture and greywater treatment in Africa and the Middle East, and helped establish the fields of environmental economics and human-environmental health in developing countries. In Mexico, targeted use of larvicide and public education to remove standing water helped the country to eradicate malaria while eliminating the use of DDT, a requirement of the North American free trade agreement. In Morocco, research helped commercialize argan oil production, helping to preserve endangered trees while generating income that lifted 2,500 women out of poverty. More recently, IDRC has delivered on Canada's commitment under the climate agreements by helping developing countries to tackle climate change, including world-class consortia addressing the needs of poor and vulnerable people in climate hotspots, and economic assessment of changing land use due to sea-level rise and flooding.

Health: In Tanzania, IDRC tested new tools for better targeting of health care to the local burden of disease, resulting in a 40 percent decline in child deaths. IDRC also championed the use of open-source software to allow African countries to adopt electronic health information systems, providing more real-time information and saving costs over previous paper-based reporting. IDRC also invested in clinical and laboratory capacity in Africa to carry out HIV prevention trials, and funded work to improve the rollout of antiretroviral treatment in South Africa. In Asia, research identified practical actions that enabled backyard poultry producers to lower the risk of transmitting avian flu. In 2015, IDRC worked with government partners to support clinical trials of a promising vaccine against Ebola. As part of Canada's commitment to improve the health of women and children, IDRC hosts a centre of excellence dedicated to improving civil registration and vital statistics.

Beyond these contributions of new knowledge and solutions, IDRC has provided talented people with an opportunity to refine their ideas and skills. An important number of researchers supported by IDRC at an early stage in their careers, went on to become progressive leaders within their own countries. Other IDRC-supported researchers became leaders in world science, including Nobel laureates Muhammad Yunus and Elinor Ostrom, and World Food Prize laureates Sir Fazle Hasan Abed, Gebisa Ejeta, Daniel Hillel, Modadugu Gupta, and M. S. Swaminathan.

IDRC also incubated new organizations that built a foundation for science in the developing world, including the African Economic Research Consortium based in Kenya, the Telecentre. org Foundation, and the African Institutes for Mathematical Sciences. The Micronutrient Initiative started in 1992 as a program within IDRC to address deficiencies in vitamin A, iron, and iodine in the diets of people in developing countries. The initiative attracted support from the World Bank and others to become an independent organization in 2002.

IDRC also launched the Canadian International Food Security Research Fund in 2009 to promote innovations in agriculture and nutrition that benefit women and smallholder farmers. Early results between developing country scientists and Canadian researchers enhanced the production and quality of millet, mangos, chickpeas, and livestock. The Canadian Mennonite University helped increase millet production in South Asia by improving de-hulling technology. Compared to rice, this traditional, high-fibre crop needs just one-fifth as much water and is well suited for marginal lands. The University of Guelph and its partners used a natural compound emitted by damaged plants to slow the ripening of mangos, reducing post-harvest loss and prolonging shelf life, enabling a 15 percent increase in farmer income. The University of Saskatchewan helped enhance the productivity of lentils and chickpeas in Ethiopia, leading to improved soil fertility and addressing nutritional deficiencies in zinc and iron. The University of Alberta helped develop a new heat-stable, single-dose vaccine that provides protection against five viral diseases affecting sheep, goats, and cattle.

Looking Forward: Canada's relationship with the developing world must embrace cooperation in science and innovation to achieve the Sustainable Development Goals. At the same time, as Canada is responsible for just 3 percent of world science, the country needs to tap into global talent and engage in the diplomacy of knowledge. Global science has become much more networked as individuals reach out to share funding, data, tasks, and infrastructure. Even as Canada merged CIDA into the Department of Foreign Affairs in 2013, the government wisely retained IDRC as a strategic asset for global development. Canada and Peru cohosted the Global Research Council in 2017, a network of research-granting councils fostering collaboration across continents to benefit both developing and developed nations.

Research for the developing world is at a critical juncture. As donors review public expenditure and narrow the geographic and thematic coverage of foreign aid, science-leading countries are expanding cooperation to respond to the societal challenges at home and abroad. The initial design for the European Union's Horizon 2020 earmarked nearly 40 percent of funding for such societal challenges, and in 2015 the United Kingdom created a £1.5 billion Global Challenge Research Fund. Research is appreciated for providing knowledge and solutions for such challenges, and informs public debate on how to deal with them. Canada's leadership in innovation and research with the developing world is a tremendous asset, as highlighted in the 2017 feminist international-assistance policy and as the world learns how to deliver on the global goals towards 2030.

Suggested Readings

Currie-Alder, Bruce. 2015. *Research for the Developing World: Public Funding from Australia, Canada and the United Kingdom.* Oxford: Oxford University Press.

Muirhead, Bruce, and Ron Harpelle. 2010. *IDRC: 40 Years of Ideas, Innovation, and Impact.* Waterloo: Waterloo University Press.

Royal Society. 2011. *Knowledge, Networks and Nations: Global Scientific Collaboration in the 21st century.* London, UK: Royal Society.

Schneegans, Susan, ed. 2015. *UNESCO Science Report: Towards 2030.* Paris: UNESCO.

Wagner, Caroline. 2008. *The New Invisible College: Science for Development.* Washington, D.C.: Brookings.

Suggested Videos

David O'Brien interview on funding international science collaboration https://youtu.be/a7C2TyY1OEQ

IDRC in 3 minutes https://youtu.be/EjfobysdVJY

Knowledge and Innovation in Africa https://youtu.be/qzI8MU8_FoQ

Naser Faruqui interview at Canadian Science Policy Conference 2015 https://youtu.be/iAzWuf6QbkI

Science and innovation for development Gordon Conway and Jeff Waage https://youtu.be/jXfUHBwfFLs

Canada and the International Criminal Court

Omid B. Milani

Issue

It once seemed a far-fetched dream to bring justice to the abuses committed by the powerful at the international level. The Second World War featured enormous atrocities by all the major powers. The post-war anti-colonial struggles were often violent and the Cold War (1946–1989) saw proxy wars fought between East and West in places as diverse as Angola, Ethiopia, Nicaragua, and Vietnam. At the same time, a growing consciousness of the importance and universality of human rights led people to assert that the atrocities committed in these and other conflicts were unconscionable and deeply repugnant. Something had to be done to hold the criminals accountable before a tribunal.

Since July 1, 2002, the dream of bringing the perpetrators of such crimes to trial has come true in the form of a permanent international court, the International Criminal Court (ICC). Occasional prosecutions of state officials and war criminals through ad hoc tribunals like the Nuremberg tribunals (1946–1949) have occurred for a century or so. "At least since the time of the ancient Greeks, and probably well before that" (Schabas 2007), under the overwhelming sovereignty of the post-Westphalian order, certain acts had been considered illegal, but not criminal. However, with the birth of the ICC, a number of judicial and political questions have been raised, in terms of jurisdiction, political motivations, and so forth, and certain acts have been defined as criminal in international law, and can be prosecuted according to the provisions of the international legal system.

Action

The 1998 Rome Conference, which was attended by hundreds of non-governmental organizations (see Chapter 7) and state delegates, is the cornerstone of the ICC foundation. Out of 161 states attending the Rome Conference, 120 voted for the establishment of the ICC. Led by then-Foreign Minister Lloyd Axworthy (1996–2000), Canada played a pivotal role throughout the conference in drafting the final proposal and in negotiating and facilitating an unprecedented approval for the Rome Statute.

During the Rome conference, the enthusiasm of the state delegations and NGOs was "quite astonishing" (Schabas 1999, 18). Canada chaired a diverse coalition of over 60 countries called the "Like-minded Caucus." However, "Canada relinquished the chair of the 'like-minded' when the legal advisor to its foreign ministry, Philippe Kirsch, was elected president of the Conference's Committee of the Whole" (ibid., 19). Only two weeks before the end of the conference, Kirsch issued a draft, hoping to provide a workable common ground to stimulate the support of the majority. On July 17, the day that the conference was schedule to conclude, despite the efforts of the US to rally opposition, the Rome Statute was adopted. Along with the

Rome Statute, the conference also adopted a Final Act, in which the establishment of a Preparatory Commission by the United Nations General Assembly was provided. The Commission was assigned a number of tasks, of which defining the elements of offences was perhaps the most difficult one. Drafting the rules of procedure and evidence was another task before the Commission. In July 2000, Canada became one of the first countries to ratify the Rome Statute, but it was on July 1, 2002, that the ICC became operational in The Hague.

The ICC's first president was Canadian Philippe Kirsch (2003–2009) and the current president of the ICC is Argentine lawyer and diplomat Silvia Fernández de Gurmendi. In addition to the presidency (consisting of the president and two vice-presidents), the ICC has 18 judges in the Pre-trial, Trial, and Appeal divisions. Crimes punishable in accordance with the Rome Statute are limited to genocide, war crimes, and crimes against humanity. Nevertheless, the Rome Statute allows for the ICC's jurisdiction to be expanded in the future; for instance, inclusion of the crime of aggression has been widely debated during and after the 2010 Kampala Review Conference.

In the field of international criminal law, jurisdiction is understood to be based on five basic elements: territory (the most common basis for exercising jurisdiction), protection, nationality of offender (active personality), nationality of victim (passive personality), and universality. It should be noted that the ICC is created with the consent of the member countries to prosecute crimes that are committed by their nationals and/or on their territory. Moreover, the ICC jurisdiction is secondary to domestic remedies. This is what the Statute refers to as *admissibility*; only when the domestic justice system is "unwilling" or "unable" to prosecute can the ICC prosecute. Universal jurisdiction of the ICC is an effort towards universal realization of peace. Although this type of jurisdiction was initially limited to piracy, the slave trade, and human trafficking, today universal jurisdiction is recognized for offences such as hijacking and other threats to air travel, terrorism, apartheid, and enforced disappearances. Universal jurisdiction is applicable to genocide, crimes against humanity, and war crimes, i.e., the core crimes of the Rome Statute (Schabas 2007, 68).

Several key countries, however, have refused to ratify the Rome Statute of the ICC, including China, Ethiopia, India, Indonesia, Israel, Russia, Saudi Arabia, Sudan, and the United States. Because of their refusal to ratify, they and their citizens are not subject to the jurisdiction of the ICC.

Impact

Since its establishment, the ICC has conducted a number of prosecutions of high profile cases involving war crimes, crimes against humanity, and genocide. As of June 2017, the ICC is pursuing "10 preliminary examinations, 10 situations under investigations (and) 24 cases (with) 14 defendants at large" (ICC 2017). Most of the accused at the ICC have been high-ranking members of governments or militias accused of perpetrating crimes under the Rome Statute; no ordinary "foot soldiers" and very few mid-ranking officers in such governments or militias have been brought to the ICC. The court has only enough investigators, prosecutors, judges, and other court officials to pursue a limited number of cases at a time. In pursuing high-ranking officials, the ICC seeks to create a deterrence effect; leaders, it is hoped, will think twice before ordering or committing atrocities, lest they be "sent to the Hague."

Most of the accused brought before the ICC have been African. This fact has not gone unnoticed in Africa, where both independent observers and some African governments accuse the ICC of racism. In response, the ICC's defenders point to the high number of ratifications of the Rome Statute by African governments, the inability of many of those countries to bring perpetrators to justice, and the prevalence of crimes under the ICC's jurisdiction that have taken place in Africa in recent decades; they also point out the ICC's pursuit of cases outside of Africa.

Many war crimes and crimes against humanity fall outside the ICC's jurisdiction, since the accused are citizens of countries that have not ratified the Rome Statute. For this reason there have been and will be no ICC prosecutions for American actions in Iraq, Indian actions in Kashmir, Israeli actions in Gaza or Lebanon, Russian actions in Ukraine, or Saudi Arabian actions in Yemen. There is an obvious imbalance of justice here.

Genocide, the most aggravated form of crime against humanity (Schabas 2009), has been a classic obsession for international lawyers and legal scholars. Defining genocide, staying coldly faithful to the definitions, and trying to hierarchize such crimes through distinguishing genocide from crimes against humanity has turned into a linguistic and rhetorical game, a game that is played with legal jargon and eloquent phrases at the cost of the lives of individuals. The term genocide is stereotypically associated with the Jewish Holocaust during the Second World War, and a few other more recent examples in Africa, such as the Rwandan Genocide of 1994.

It is rare to speak of Canada as a perpetrator of genocide in the international criminal law literature. However, in 2001, a report was published under the title of *Hidden from History: The Canadian Holocaust. The Untold Story of the Genocide of Aboriginal Peoples by Church and State in Canada* (Annett 2001), which brought unsettling stories to the conscience of Canadians. The report was issued by the Truth Commission into Genocide in Canada. In this report, the author alleges that various crimes that took place in Indian Residential Schools can fall under the 1948 Genocide Convention (ibid., 9). The report points out that the killing of Aboriginal Peoples, causing serious harm on them, inflicting conditions calculated to cause the destruction of Aboriginals, imposing measures

to prevent births, and the like have been systematically undertaken by the Canadian state and various Christian churches. (See Chapters 9 and 10 and Case Study 9.) Whether a genocide did happen in Canada or not, and the applicability of the ICC's jurisdiction, may appear to be appealing topics for academic works. Not the least of these issues to be dealt with is the fact that many of these crimes happened before Canada ratified the Rome Statute.

But such questions are virtually irrelevant to the main purpose of existence of the ICC, i.e., the implementation of justice. The voice of the oppressed and those who have suffered from states' atrocities can only be heard if we drop our "perverse and fetishistic involvement with definitions" (Charny 1994, 64–68), in which the reality of the subject under discussion is lost and the scholars can no longer experience the subject emotionally and "the real enormity of the subject no longer guides or impacts the deliberations" (ibid., 91). With the birth of the ICC, there arose high hopes for bringing power to justice, but those high hopes soon vanished through objectifying the discourse on human suffering. In fact, pursuing universal justice through the ICC and its definitionalism is but a wishful thought. Payam Akhavan, a former Canadian prosecutor at the ICC, notes that "reducing genocide to a rare commodity in a market of competitive suffering does little to promote intersubjective understanding and empathy with the *other*" (Akhavan 2012, 128).

Should we wait for the ICC, or perhaps another triumph of international law, to save individuals from the claws of states? Instead of putting our hopes and trust in the ICC and other similar organizations to punish the perpetrators, perhaps we can take a different path and play an active role to pursue justice. (See Chapter 15.) How many more stories, in Canada or elsewhere, are waiting to be told by another truth commission? And what role will Canada play?

Suggested Readings

Akhavan, Payam. 2012. *Cambridge Studies in International and Comparative Law: Reducing Genocide to Law*. Cambridge: Cambridge University Press.

Annett, Kevin D. 2001. *Hidden from History: The Canadian Holocaust. The Untold Story of the Genocide of Aboriginal Peoples by Church and State in Canada*. Vancouver: The Truth Commission into Genocide in Canada.

Charny, Israel W. 1994. "Towards a Generic Definition of Genocide." In *Genocide: Conceptual and Historical Dimensions*, edited by George J. Andreopoulous. Philadelphia: University of Pennsylvania Press.

ICC. 2017. "Situations and Cases." https://www.icc-cpi.int/. Accessed on 12 June 2017.

Schabas, William A. 2007. *An Introduction to the International Criminal Court*. Cambridge: Cambridge University Press.

———. 2009. *Genocide in International Law: The Crime of Crimes*, 2nd ed. Cambridge: Cambridge University Press.

Case Study 8

Canada and Climate Change

John M.R. Stone

Issue

The presence in the atmosphere of greenhouse gases (GHGs) affects the climate and creates conditions favourable to human existence on this planet. The problem is that today we are increasing the concentration of these gases in the atmosphere faster than the Earth's natural systems can absorb them. This is changing the climate. Science has established that human activities are the dominant cause of climate change. Most of the GHGs we create are through the burning of fossil fuels like oil and coal. Canada is a major emitter of GHGs, both because we rely on fossil fuels to heat our buildings and run our cars, but also because we are a major producer and exporter of oil, coal, and natural gas.

Climate change poses a threat to society, the economy, and the environment worldwide. The poor people in developing countries may be the most at risk from climate change, especially those who live in arid or low-lying areas. The more we allow the unlimited emission of GHGs, the greater will be the danger. Governments have agreed that, in order to avoid dangerous interference with the climate system, we need to limit temperature increases to no more than 2°C above pre-industrial levels. In order to achieve this target, the concentration of GHGs needs to be stabilized, which implies that emissions have to peak and then decline significantly.

GHG emissions have been increasing, despite two decades of Canadian and international discussions, resolutions, and plans. It is now very unlikely that the world will achieve the 2°C target. If we continue along the business-as-usual trajectory, by the end of the twenty-first century, GHG concentrations could be more than three times pre-industrial levels and global temperatures could rise as much as 4°C.

Action

Canada has been significantly engaged in scientific work on climate change for many decades, while Canada's policy engagement has ebbed and flowed over the years under both Liberal and (Progressive) Conservative governments. Several Canadian scientists were central in putting climate change on the international policy agenda in the 1970s and 1980s. Following the First World Climate Conference in 1979, Environment Canada created the Canadian Climate Centre. Shortly afterwards, one of the world's first climate modelling and analysis groups was established in Environment Canada.

In 1988, Canada organized the Conference on the Changing Atmosphere, which brought together governments and scientists from around the world. It was addressed by Progressive Conservative Prime Minister Brian Mulroney (1984–1993). The conference statement concluded that climate change was "an unintended, uncontrolled, globally pervasive experiment . . . the consequences of which would be second only to those of a global nuclear war" (WMO 1988). It adopted an aspirational target of a 20 percent cut in emissions by 2005.

The establishment of the Intergovernmental Panel on Climate Change (IPCC) in 1988 was led by a Canadian, Jim Bruce, who was then working at the World Meteorological Organization (WMO). The IPCC has been an extraordinary success in bringing together the scientific and government communities. Over the years, Canadians have served in many senior positions on the Panel. In 2014, the IPCC completed its *Fifth Assessment Report*.

The first IPCC assessment report was completed in 1990 and presented to the Second World Climate Conference. The Conference, which was organized by Canadian Howard Ferguson, created a committee to develop what became the United Nations Framework Convention on Climate Change (UN/FCCC). This Convention, which was adopted at the Rio Earth Summit in 1992, set a target for industrialized countries to reduce GHG emissions to 1990 levels by 2000.

Reflecting a wave of concern for the environment, the Canadian government created the Green Plan in 1990. This committed an additional $3 billion in federal funding. The government also established in 1990 a "National Action Strategy on Global Warming." It stated that "the limitation of emissions must begin now" (Environment Canada 1990). Canada ratified the UN/FCCC in December 1992. However, Canada's first National Report under the UN/FCCC in 1994 admitted that our energy-related GHG emissions would be 11 percent above the 1990 level in 2000, and that additional measures were needed.

In response, the federal government established a multi-stakeholder Climate Change Task Group to develop a National Action Program. In 1995 it put forward recommendations to reduce Canada's GHG emissions. Media coverage of climate change intensified in 1997 in the run-up to the Third Conference of the Parties under the UN/FCCC in Kyoto, Japan. Federal,

provincial, and territorial energy and environment ministers meeting in Regina in November agreed to try to reduce GHG emissions in Canada back to 1990 levels by around 2010. However, during the Kyoto negotiations, Liberal Prime Minister Jean Chrétien (1993–2003) unilaterally strengthened Canada's commitment to 6 percent below 1990 levels by 2010. Following the Kyoto meeting, Canada established the Climate Change Secretariat, reporting to the Deputy Ministers of Natural Resources Canada and Environment Canada. This arrangement put the Secretariat between a department responsible for fossil fuel development and one responsible for the environment, and thereby created tensions that a weak Secretariat had difficulty adjudicating without strong leadership from the Prime Minister's Office.

Beyond that, the Chrétien government did little by way of follow-up, other than signing the Kyoto Protocol in April 1998. As the Commissioner of the Environment and Sustainable Development (1998) stated in his annual report, many of the elements of the National Action Program were missing or incomplete. Furthermore, according to Environment Canada's own projections, emissions were expected to be 27 percent higher in 2010 than in 1990, rather than 6 percent lower, as committed to in Kyoto.

This unsatisfactory situation lasted until the Conservative Stephen Harper became prime minister. Then the level of activity declined significantly. At best, climate change was an issue that the Harper government (2006–2015) preferred to ignore. While in Opposition in 2002, Harper had written to members of his then Canadian Alliance party that "Kyoto is essentially a socialist scheme to suck money out of wealth-producing nations" (*Toronto Star* 2007) and he questioned the science of climate change. Under Harper's government, climate change scientists and activists were publicly vilified. The Conservative government argued that Canada's economy would be crippled if Canada was forced to meet the Kyoto target. Canada withdrew from the Kyoto Protocol in 2011 (Environment

Canada 2011), the first country to do so. The Climate Change Secretariat and almost all the climate change programs were wound down during the Harper government. The National Round Table on the Environment and the Economy was closed in 2013 after its reports proved unpalatable to the government.

In the 2008 federal election, Liberal leader Stephane Dion promised to introduce a carbon tax if he formed the next government. The idea was to tax GHG emissions and reduce other taxes so that over all the policy would be revenue-neutral. However, the proposal was not well explained and it was portrayed by the Conservative Party as a "tax on everything." Not only did Dion's initiative contribute to the Liberal Party being defeated in 2008 and again in 2011, but it effectively stymied any discussion of carbon pricing for at least a decade.

The UN/FCCC Fifteenth Conference of the Parties, held in Copenhagen in December 2009, was expected to provide a plan to follow up the Kyoto Protocol. It produced a document, called the Copenhagen Accord, that "recognises the scientific view that increases in global temperatures should be kept below 2°C" (UN/FCC 2009). The Copenhagen meeting represented an international low point in addressing the threat from climate change.

Impact

Canada, having an economy dependent of the exploitation of its natural resources (particularly fossil fuels) and being among the highest emitters of GHGs, faces an understandable challenge in reducing emissions. Furthermore, effective action demands political leadership. But the traditionally weak position of the Minister of the Environment (compared to, say, the Minister of Industry or Finance) inside the federal cabinet has long been an impediment to decisive action under both Liberal and (Progressive) Conservative governments.

Canada has had no lack of climate change plans in the last three decades. Canada's reputation on climate change had been largely positive in the 1980s and early 1990s under the Mulroney government. But inaction under the Chrétien government, the aggressive exploitation of the bitumen sands in Alberta, and the inexorable increase in Canadian GHG emissions meant that our reputation was already in decline before the Harper government withdrew from the Kyoto Protocol in 2011. As time passed, it became increasingly clear that Canada was not going to meet its GHG targets. As a result, under Harper, Canada resorted to ploys to make our emissions look smaller. Such manoeuvres earned Canada repeated "fossil of the day" awards by environmental non-governmental organizations at several UN/FCCC meetings.

The situation in Canada changed dramatically in 2015, when the new Liberal Prime Minster, Justin Trudeau, provided the political leadership that had been missing for two decades. Within weeks of being appointed, the new Minister for the Environment and Climate Change, Catherine McKenna, went to a preparatory meeting for the Paris climate change talks with the announcement that "Canada is back!" The Paris conference was a remarkable success, brilliantly engineered by the French government. It basically saved the UN/FCCC process. Paris built on the Lima conference of 2014, where countries had agreed to submit by 2015 their "intended nationally determined contributions" to address the threat of climate change. The Lima process indicates that the Kyoto Protocol's top-down approach has been abandoned. Canada played a constructive role in Paris. Canada was one of the countries that not only reaffirmed the long-term goal of keeping the increase in global average temperature to below 2°C above pre-industrial levels, but also committed to limit the increase to 1.5°C.

Following the Paris conference, the Trudeau government held consultations with the provinces and achieved a pan-Canadian framework for combating climate change. The overarching goal is to set a comparable price on carbon across the Canadian economy. Some provinces, such as British Columbia, have chosen to achieve this through a carbon tax, whereas others, like Ontario and Quebec, chose to use a cap-and-trade approach.

The Trudeau government has recommitted to the Harper government's target of reducing emissions to 30 percent below 2005 levels by 2030. Canada, along with most other countries, recognized that this is insufficient to reach the 2°C target. On a less-positive note, the Trudeau government is still committed to building new pipelines, particularly to the Alberta bitumen sands, which would increase the associated GHG emissions.

Globally, there are encouraging signs that the transition to a new economy based on renewable energy has become irreversible. Investments in energy sources with lower carbon footprints are growing rapidly. There is a growing sense that green technologies offer considerable economic opportunities. And the International Energy Agency recently reported that energy emissions are not increasing, even as the global economy grows.

Suggested Readings

Environment Canada. 1990. *National Action Strategy on Global Warming*. Ottawa: Environment Canada.

Commissioner for the Environment and Sustainable Development. 1998. *1998 Report of the Commissioner for Environment and Sustainable Development*. Ottawa: Office of the Auditor General of Canada.

Environment Canada. 2011. "Canada's Withdrawal from Kyoto Protocol." Press release, 15 December. http://www.ec.gc.ca/Publications/default.asp?lang=En&n=EE4F06AE-1&xml=EE4F06AE-13EF-453B-B633-FCB3BAECEB4F&offset=3&toc=show.

Toronto Star. 2007. "Harper Letter Called Kyoto 'Socialist Scheme'." *Toronto Star*. 30 January.

UN/FCC. 2009. *Copenhagen Accord*. United Nations Framework Convention on Climate Change. FCCC/CP/2009/L.7.

WMO. 1988. *The Changing Atmosphere: Implications for Global Security Conference Statement*. Geneva: World Meteorological Organization.

Case Study 9

Canada and the Arctic

Ketevan Tadiashvili

Issue

Canada has the largest Arctic landmass in the world, comprising 40 percent of the country. The Arctic is a fundamental signifier of the Canadian national identity. The Canadian North includes the administrative regions of the Northwest Territories, Nunavut, and Yukon. As of 2013, more than 100,000 people live in the Arctic, predominantly the Inuit (Government of Canada 2015). The Inuit are a traditionally nomadic group who have inhabited the Canadian Arctic since time immemorial. The contact between the Europeans and the Inuit was mainly established throughout the nineteenth century. The entrance of whalers and Hudson's Bay Company traders was followed by the Northwest Mounted Police and missionaries, who established churches, schools, and other social institutions in the North. This process began the cultural assimilation of the Inuit and increased the presence of the Canadian government, which actively sought to establish Arctic sovereignty (Pigott 2011).

Arctic sovereignty has been a Canadian concern since the nineteenth century, and it is an issue once more gaining political momentum considering the warming effects of climate change and the melting of sea ice, which presents the Northwest Passage through the Canadian Arctic as a navigable sea route between the Atlantic and the Pacific. In 1880, an Order-in-Council was passed to confirm Canadian title and ownership of the Arctic Archipelago;

Canada thereby took responsibility from Britain for the surveillance of the islands. The Inuit settlement in the North and the Order-in-Council form the basis for Canada's historic claim to sovereignty over the North. Canada's jurisdiction over the Arctic mainland and the Arctic Archipelago are uncontested, except for the tiny Hans Island, which is also claimed by Denmark. But Canada's further claims to the internal archipelago waterways, including the Northwest Passage, are questioned internationally (Bravo and Triscott 2011). If clear of ice, the Northwest Passage would be the fastest maritime trade route between Asia and Europe. Thus, there is a significant incentive for the route to be contested by such powers as the United States that want free, unrestrained access to the Northwest Passage. Faced with the prospect that Arctic waters were becoming navigable for commercial traffic, the Parliament of Canada renamed these waterways the "Canadian Northwest Passage" in 2008 (Chung and Hyslop 2008), thus establishing Canadian sovereignty over the Northern waterways as a policy priority of the Canadian government. Developing and establishing a federal presence in the Arctic has long been a Canadian government priority, which is now, more than ever, being brought to the forefront due to new climate change realities (Griffiths 2011).

Action

In 1920, the Imperial Oil Company discovered oil at Fort Norman in the Northwest Territories, and this drove the Canadian government to create a civil service in the North. Simultaneously, the government relocated many Inuit to populate and develop the region. Arctic development really took hold during and after the Second World War (1939–1945), when Canadian economic development accelerated through greater resource extraction and the construction of infrastructure for national defence. Moreover, the Canadian North became a strategic location during the Cold War (1946–1989) due to its proximity to the Soviet Union (Bravo and Triscott 2011). Involuntary relocations of the Inuit to populate the region and the construction of defence installations were the principal government policies used to establish Canadian Arctic sovereignty and pursue development during the 1940 and 1950s.

In 1953, 93 Inuit from northern Quebec were forcefully relocated to the High Arctic, at Resolute Bay and Grise Fiord, where they suffered greatly in a new environment and without any adequate support. In 1993, a Royal Commission investigated claims against the government made by the relocated Inuit and their descendants. The Commission concluded that forced relocations took place to fulfil Canadian sovereignty and economic aspirations. By establishing sedentary settlements in the High North, the government sought to "facilitate" its operational capacities, and increase development initiatives such as "agricultural expansion and land reclamation, urban development and hydroelectric projects" (Dussault and Erasmus 1996, 398). This policy marked another stage in the practice of assimilating the Inuit, using education and wage labour. Having sedentary, acculturated Inuit communities was seen by the Canadian government as an important precondition for social and economic development of the North.

In the 1940s, infrastructure projects such as the Alaska Highway, the Northwest Staging Route, and the Canadian oil pipeline were carried out. Subsequently, the Cold War brought additional security concerns for the Canadian Arctic because of its proximity to the Soviet Union. From 1954 to 1957, Canada and the United States built the Distant Early Warning Line of radar stations across the Arctic to give 24-hour warning of potential Soviet airborne attacks. Thus, infrastructure development in the Arctic was mostly concerned with security and resource extraction. The Canadian government has been criticised for disregarding human and social development in the Arctic. Moreover, it is important to note that the Inuit were not consulted on the building of defence projects, which has caused significant environmental degradation and social change in the North (Branch 2010).

On an international level, the Arctic Council was created in 1996, following the end of the Cold War, and membership includes all eight Arctic states: Canada, Denmark with Greenland, Finland, Iceland, Norway, Russia, Sweden, and the United States. The Council is a forum for cooperation, coordination, and involvement of Indigenous Arctic communities. Canada was recently the chair of the Arctic Council, from 2013 to 2015. The Arctic Council actively discusses such issues as the effects of climate change, and seeks to reach a consensus on policy matters among its member states (Foreign Affairs, Trade and Development Canada 2015).

Impact

The Inuit communities congregated around the defence sites to access employment opportunities. Long-term effects of the defence projects include the development of housing, transportation, communications, and physical infrastructure in the Arctic, also accessed by the Inuit communities. As well, the adoption of such programs as the Canadian Rangers, which incorporated the Inuit into the Canadian Forces and used traditional Inuit survival skills and knowledge for Arctic operations, is an example of a social development policy (Branch 2010). Furthermore, after decades of refusing to apologize and acknowledge the wrongful forced relocations of 1953, an official government apology was issued on 18 August 2010 for the inhumane treatment and suffering caused by the relocation (Duncan 2010).

The negative outcomes of the government policy once more include the lack of social development in the North. Since 1970, the crime rates in the Northern administrative regions have surpassed the rates of any other region in Canada. The Inuit are highly represented in crime statistics, and this has been attributed to such factors as high levels of unemployment, the dominance of non-Inuit in the policing and justice system, the disintegration of traditional community leadership and social fabric, overcrowded housing, and more (Oliver, Finès, Bougie, and Kohen 2014). Moreover, climate change is affecting the migration routes of caribou and other animals and causing pack ice to melt throughout the North, thus reducing the environmental capacity for animals like polar bears, seals, and walrus. These changes in turn significantly affect the Inuit cultural identity, which is intrinsically tied to the physical ecology of the Arctic, and also alters such traditional practices as hunting (Leduc 2010).

Recent Canadian foreign and domestic policy has had a significant focus on the Arctic. The development strategy under Stephen Harper's Conservative government (2006–2015) centred primarily around building defence projects, building a research centre, and exploiting the Arctic natural resource base. For example, mining activities, such as investments in diamond mining and extractive projects, including the Mackenzie Gas Project, were a significant focus of Harper's Arctic policy (Government of Canada 2009). The current Liberal government under Justin Trudeau (2015–) has thus far committed to increasing Arctic defence and the number of the Canadian Rangers for surveillance and territorial control purposes (Department of Finance 2015).

Canadian Arctic policy is still largely defence- and extraction-centred, and lacking social development. In light of recent climate change realities, basing the Arctic economic development on extractive industry advancement has received criticism and pressure from activist groups (Ozkan and Schott 2013). To sum up, due to climate change and the rapid melting of glaciers, which is making the Arctic more accessible than ever, the Arctic region is attracting global attention and for Canada it is a major domestic and foreign policy priority.

Suggested Readings

Bonesteel, Sarah. 2008. *Canada's Relationship with Inuit: A History of Policy and Program Development*. Ottawa: Indian and Northern Affairs Canada. https://www.aadnc-aandc.gc.ca/eng/1100100016900/1100100016908

Bravo, Michael, and Nicola Triscott. 2011. *Arctic Geopolitics and Autonomy*. Ostfildern, Germany: Hatje Cantz.

Chung, Talia, and Caroline Hyslop. 2008. "The Arctic: A Canadian Parliamentary Chronology." PRB 08-11E. Ottawa: Parliament of Canada. http://www.parl.gc.ca/Content/LOP/researchpublications/prb0811-e.htm.

Department of Finance. 2015. *Strong Leadership: A Balanced Budget, Low Tax Plan for Jobs, Growth and Security. Budget Speech by the Hon. Joe Oliver, Minister of Finance*. Ottawa: Department of Finance. http://www.budget.gc.ca/2015/docs/speech-discours/2015-04-21-eng.html.

Duncan, John. 2010. "Apology for the Inuit High Arctic Relocation." Speech made at Inukjuak, Nunavik: Indigenous and Northern Affairs Canada. 18 August. http://www.aadnc-aandc.gc.ca/eng/1100100016115/1100100016116

Dussault, Rene, and George Erasmus. 1996. *Report of the Royal Commission on Aboriginal Peoples. Vol. 1, Looking Forward, Looking Back*. Ottawa. Indian and Northern Affairs Canada.

Foreign Affairs, Trade and Development Canada. 2015. "The Arctic Council." http://www.international.gc.ca/arctic-arctique/council-conseil.aspx?lang=eng

Government of Canada. 2015. "The Canadian Arctic." December 16. http://www.canadainternational.gc.ca/united_kingdom-royaume_uni/bilateral_relations_bilaterales/arctic-arctique.aspx?lang=eng

Griffiths, Franklyn. 2011. *Canada and the Changing Arctic: Sovereignty, Security, and Stewardship*. Waterloo: Wilfrid Laurier University Press.

Leduc, Timothy. 2010. *Climate, Culture, Change: Inuit and Western Dialogues with a Warming North*. Ottawa: University of Ottawa Press.

Oliver, L., Philippe Fines, Evelyne Bougie, and D. Kohen. 2014. "Intentional injury hospitalizations in geographical areas with a high percentage of Aboriginal-identity residents, 2004/2005 to 2009/2010." *Chronic Diseases and Injuries in Canada* 34 (2–3): 82–93.

Ozkan, Umat, and Stephan Schott. 2013. "Sustainable development and capabilities for the polar region." *Social Indicators Research* 114 (3): 1259–1283.

Pigott, Peter. 2011. *From Far and Wide: A Complete History of Canada's Arctic Sovereignty*. Toronto: Dundurn Press.

Case Study 10

Canada and the Middle East

Laura Grant and Taryn Husband-Ceperkovic

Issue

No one who reads the news can doubt the political, social, and economic importance of the Middle East. Canada has been involved with the region since we supported the UN's 1947 resolution to partition Palestine into the states of Israel and Jordan (Bell et al. 2007, 23). Since then, Canada has continued its engagement with the region through political, diplomatic, military, trade, and aid relations. Canada has provided humanitarian assistance, counter-terrorism support, knowledge sharing, and technical assistance. For many decades, Canada was deeply involved in the Palestinian-Israeli peace process. Today, the Middle East region contains two of Canada's main bilateral aid recipients, Jordan and West Bank and Gaza). Canada participates in UN peacekeeping missions in Egypt and Lebanon.

Since the 9/11 terrorist attacks on the United States in 2001, however, Western countries have increasingly seen the Middle East region through the lens of security issues. Tensions are high and conflicts affect large parts of the region, especially Iraq, Syria, Libya, and Yemen. The common perception is that the policies of nations outside the region have often contributed to radicalization rather than reconciliation (Funk 2007, 25). Historically, Canada's Middle East policies have promoted Canadian values of tolerance, democracy, human rights and rule of law. In recent years, Canada's approach too has changed and we now provide military assistance in the fight against the Islamic State in Iraqi Kurdistan; in 2011, Canada led the air war to overthrow Libyan President Muammar Gaddafi.

Canada's capacity to act alone in the Middle East is limited, but there have been and there remain many creatively pragmatic options available to Canadian policy makers that draw on Canada's strong history of humanitarianism and diplomacy.

Action

Canada's deep and systematic involvement in the Middle East began in 1947 with the partition of Palestine into Israel and Jordan. Canada helped establish the world's first peacekeeping operation, between Egypt and Israel, in 1956, and has contributed to UN peacekeeping missions in the region since then, though with decreasing levels of participation in recent decades. Canada was invited in 1991 to chair the Refugee Working Group (DFATD 2013), a multilateral (see Case Study 5) effort to deal with the Palestinian refugee crisis that started in 1947. More recently, Canada has been involved in strengthening the electoral process in the Palestinian territories, by assisting in the creation of a voter registry for the elections that took place in 2006, and through establishing and managing the Palestinian Election Support Fund between 2004 and 2007. This initiative aimed to increase both civil society involvement and participation by women (Clark 2007, 94). Canada's political involvement waned somewhat in the 1990s in favour of more limited technical assistance and other development projects (Bell et al. 2007, 24). A Canadian Crown corporation, the International Development Research Centre (IDRC; see Case Study 6) funded the Scholarship Fund for Palestinian Refugee Women and the Middle East Good Governance Fund (Muirhead and Harpelle 2007, 152). The rise of terrorism following 9/11 and the increasing association of development and security concerns (see Chapter 14) have since drawn Canadian attention back to the region.

Though Canada was always a strong supporter of Israel, Canada also long acted as an "honest broker" in the Israeli-Palestinian peace process. The Conservative government of Stephen Harper (2006–2015) dramatically altered course, heavily favouring Israel on every issue (Robinson 2011; Hibbard 2012) and downsizing its dealings with the Palestinian Authority. The Harper policy meant that Canada had only one real friend in the Middle East, Israel, while losing the trust of many others (Martin 2011). When Canada lost its bid for a seat on the UN Security Council in 2010, it was widely believed that Harper's Middle East policy lost Canada many votes in that region.

Since Justin Trudeau became prime minister in 2015, there has been little change from Harper's Middle East policy, except for one notable occurrence. In 2016, International Development Minister Marie-Claude Bibeau announced that Canada would provide $25 million to the United Nations Relief and Works Agency for Palestinian Refugees (GAC 2016a). The UN agency had been cut off by the previous Conservative government for allegedly having

Figure CS10.1

Canadian Official Development Aid Flows to the Middle East and North Africa

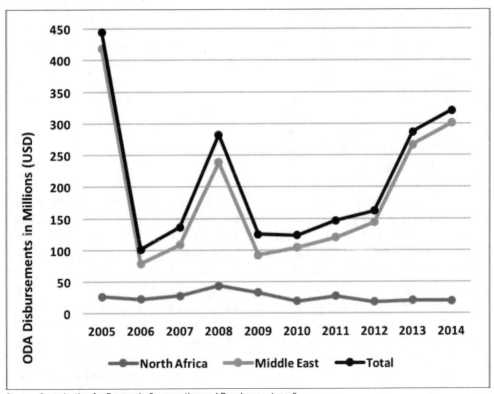

Source: Organisation for Economic Co-operation and Development, 2016.

ties to Hamas (*Globe and Mail* 2016). While this announcement was met with much controversy, it may signal a shift in Canadian government thinking on the Middle East.

Today, the main Canadian government actors in the Middle East are Global Affairs Canada (aid, trade, and diplomacy), the Department of National Defence (counter-terrorism, military operations, and peacekeeping; see Chapter 5), and IDRC (research and scientific cooperation; see Case Study 6). Canada's aid has varied drastically over the past decade, with levels climbing since 2012. See **Figure CS10.1** (previous page).

Global Affairs Canada manages most of Canada's aid to the Middle East; its emphasis in the region is humanitarian assistance (principally for the Syrian crisis), promoting access to quality education, maternal and child health, supporting sustainable economic growth, increasing food security, and state-building, including efforts to foster good governance and democratic norms.

Gender equality is a priority across Canada's international development efforts, including in the Middle East. A Canadian project supports women in parliaments and other decision-making roles in the region, including a project in partnership with the Forum of Federations. In keeping with Canada's commitment to knowledge sharing and skill building, the project will support more than 5,000 women in Jordan, Tunisia, and Morocco in developing the skills necessary to take political roles in their communities (GAC 2016b).

In humanitarian assistance, Canada provided $1.6 million to assist international NGO Handicap International in 2014–2015 to address the health and security needs of displaced persons in Yemen. The project aims to provide rehabilitative healthcare services to people injured by conventional weapons and other persons with disabilities, to strengthen the capacity of Yemeni health care providers to deliver such services, and to create a system to respond to the needs of persons

with disabilities and conflict-related injuries (DFATD 2016).

The growth of violent extremism and the rise of the so-called Islamic State are seen by the Canadian government as development concerns. Under both Harper and Trudeau, the fight against the Islamic State and other terrorist actors has been a priority. Both governments prioritized efforts to contribute to security and stability in the region, including legal, institutional, and governance reforms (see Chapter 11), as well as military action. To this end, development funds are being provided to increase the capacity of the governments of countries neighbouring Syria to respond to the growing number of refugees fleeing that country. The resettlement of almost 30,000 Syrian refugees in Canada in 2015–2016 has been financed by Canadian development funds. (See Chapter 6).

The third pillar of Canadian development efforts in the Middle East is IDRC, which is dedicated to increasing the capacity of researchers in the global south by financing development-related applied and policy research. IDRC-supported research projects are focused on finding and testing solutions to insecurity, conflict, desertification, water scarcity, and food insecurity, and on reducing reliance on the oil industry.

Impact

Canada's engagement with the Middle East has involved political, economic, and military endeavours. Our involvement with the region has also waxed and waned over the decades. In the 1950s and 1960s, Canada pioneered peacekeeping in the region. From the 1980s to the early 2000s, Canada played a key role in the Israeli-Palestinian peace process. However, in the 2000s, Canada's domestic issues preoccupied Ottawa, resulting in a decline in Canada's profile as a reliable global player in peace and development (see Chapter 4 and Case Study 5), until security concerns brought us back to the region once again.

Canada is still having an impact in the region through the activities of Global Affairs Canada, IDRC, and the Department of National Defence. Canada's involvement in increasing access to and quality of education, promoting gender equality, and improving food security are helping some of the most vulnerable portions of the population. Knowledge sharing and technical assistance remain a large part of Canada's development profile in the Middle East region, to provide capacity building and training programs to help foster economic and social growth and development. Canada's capacity to act alone in the region is limited. Many Middle Eastern countries are "emerging countries" with high levels of wealth and technical capacity and they do not need our aid. (See Chapter 13.) But there is still scope for Canada to deploy creative diplomatic and other policy tools in the region.

Suggested Readings

Bell, Michael, Michael Molly, David Sultan, and Sallama Shaker. 2007. "Practitioners' Perspectives on Canada-Middle East Relations." In *Canada and the Middle East: In Theory and Practice*, edited by Paul Heinbecker and Bessma Momani. Waterloo: Wilfrid Laurier University Press.

Clark, Janine A. 2007. "Canadian Interests and Democracy Promotion in the Middle East." In *Canada and the Middle East: In Theory and Practice*, edited by Paul Heinbecker and Bessma Momani. Waterloo: Wilfrid Laurier University Press.

Foreign Affairs, Trade and Development Canada. 2013. "Middle East Peace Process." April 29. Retrieved February 4, 2016, from http://www.international.gc.ca/name-anmo/peace_process-processus_paix/refugees-refugies/index.aspx?lang=eng.

DFATD. 2015. "Canada and the Middle East and North Africa." December 21. Retrieved February 4, 2016, from http://www.international.gc.ca/name-anmo/index.aspx?lang=eng.

———. 2016. "Project Profile: Emergency Rehabilitation Services in Yemen - Handicap International 2014 (D000617001)." Retrieved February 4, 2016, from http://www.acdi-cida.gc.ca/cidaweb/cpo.nsf/vWebCSAZEn/ED700CFE8721045E85257F00003F18C2.

Funk, Nathan C. 2007. "Applying Canadian Principles to Peace and Conflict Resolution in the Middle East." In *Canada and the Middle East: In Theory and Practice*, edited by Paul Heinbecker and Bessma Momani. Waterloo: Wilfrid Laurier University Press.

Global Affairs Canada. 2016a. "Backgrounder: Support for Vulnerable Palestinian Refugees." November 16. Retrieved December 5, 2016, from http://news.gc.ca/web/article-en.do?mthd=advSrch&crtr.page=4&crtr.dpt1D=6673&nid=1154809.

———. 2016b. "Canada Supports Women in Parliaments in the Middle East and North Africa." June 7. Retrieved December 5, 2016, from http://www.international.gc.ca/development-developpement/stories-histoires/Middle_East_and_North_Africa-Moyen_Orient_Afrique/women-femmes.aspx?lang=eng.

Globe and Mail. 2016. "Liberals Restore Funding to Controversial Palestinian Aid Agency." November 16. Retrieved December 7, 2016, from http://www.theglobeandmail.com/news/politics/liberals-restore-funding-to-controversial-palestinian-aid-agency/article32877755/.

Hibbard, Steve. 2012. *Canada's Middle East Policy: The End of Fair-Minded Idealism or a New Beginning?* Published by Canadians for Justice and Peace in the Middle East.

Martin, Patrick. 2011. "Canada and the Middle East." In *Canada Among Nations 2009–2010: As Others See Us*, edited by Fen Osler Hampson and Paul Heinbeck. Montreal: McGill-Queen's University Press.

Muirhead, Bruce, and Ron Harpelle. 2007. "The International Development Research Centre and the Middle East: Issues and Research." In *Canada and the Middle East: In Theory and Practice*, edited by Paul Heinbecker and Bessma Momani. Waterloo: Wilfrid Laurier University Press.

Organisation for Economic Co-operation and Development. 2016. "Aid (ODA) Disbursements to Countries and Regions [DAC2a]." Retrieved February 4, 2016, from http://stats.oecd.org/Index.aspx?QueryId=42231&lang=en#.

Robinson, Andrew. 2011. "Canada's Credibility as an Actor in the Middle East Peace Process: The Refugee Working Group, 1992–2000. *International Journal* 66 (3): 695–718.

Case Study 11

Overseas Volunteering and Voluntourism

Lauchlan T. Munro[1]

Issue

"In contrast with almost any other walk of life, many Canadians think that development in poor countries can be managed inexpensively, on a part-time basis and by amateurs" with no specialist knowledge, skills, experience, or qualifications, Smillie and Sánchez point out in Chapter 7. Short-term volunteering stints in developing countries by young and inexperienced citizens of rich Western countries like Canada are an increasingly common manifestation of the phenomenon that Smillie and Sánchez identify. Many readers of this case study will have participated in such short-term volunteering trips. This chapter seeks to understand this phenomenon historically and to critically analyse its ethical stance and its practical effects.

Action

Volunteering has a long history in Canada. The earliest Canadians to volunteer in what we now call developing countries were Christian missionaries of the nineteenth century who, though driven by a genuine desire to help, also believed that white, Christian civilization must export its values and way of life to the "heathens" of Africa, Asia, Latin America, and the Canadian North. (See Chapters 8 and 9.)

In the 1950s and 1960s, several Canadian organizations were formed to send volunteers overseas in response to the shortage of skilled technical personnel in developing countries. Crossroads International, CUSO, SUCO, and the World University Service of Canada were amongst these organizations; similar organizations were established in the US, the UK, and other rich countries. After initial (and unsatisfactory) experiences of sending untrained Canadians abroad, these organizations soon got more professional. They started hiring only Canadians who had relevant qualifications, such as a university degree, a professional designation, or a trade certificate. Increasingly, the role of volunteers was not so much to do the work of development, but to help local counterparts to learn the skills needed to do the work of development. Terms like "skills transfer," "technical assistance," and "capacity building" came into vogue. Later, other NGOs emerged to send Canadians with highly specialized qualifications, like trauma surgeons and physiotherapists, on short-term voluntary missions, often as part of disaster relief efforts. It is important to note, however, that the ultimate goal of all these organizations was to help developing countries, not to help Canadians.

But another view of volunteering was also present. Starting in the 1960s, organizations like Canada World Youth, the Company of Young Canadians, and Katimavik were created primarily to provide young, inexperienced, and unskilled Canadians with an inspirational

1. From 1985 to 1987, the author was a WUSC volunteer in Bhutan, where he taught economics.

work experience through volunteering. The difference in ultimate objectives is important; while these organizations claimed to be raising social consciousness, their primary objective was to help young Canadians build their careers.

Since the 1990s, a new generation of volunteer-sending organizations targeting inexperienced young people has emerged. Many of these are for-profit companies. They typically send young Canadian volunteers, including those in high school, to developing countries for short periods of time, sometimes as little as a week or two. In contrast to the professional volunteer-sending organizations who try to select qualified individuals and send them for extended periods of time, these new organizations often compete to provide their volunteers with the most attractive volunteering experience. This new phenomenon of non-professional, short-term volunteering is known as "voluntourism," a mixture of "volunteering" and "tourism." Voluntourists often do tasks like building a clinic, working in an orphanage, or teaching in a school, regardless of whether they have any qualifications, skills, or experience in those fields. In most cases, little or no vetting beyond a medical check-up or a police clearance is required. Often, the voluntourists must pay their own travel and living expenses. In the end, the qualifications for participating in most such short-term voluntourism assignments are a willingness to help, sufficient free time, and the ability to raise enough money. Most of the voluntourists on such schemes are young white females from the suburban middle class (Quenville 2015; Schwartz 2015).

Impact

Like all social phenomena, voluntourism should be critically examined. As Smillie and Sánchez suggest in Chapter 7, the increasing skill levels in developing countries, including in the poorest ones, pose serious challenges to the older, professional volunteer-sending organizations. Such organizations are having to ask what their role should be, now that the skill shortage in developing countries that these organizations were created to fill has to a large extent been filled by qualified people from the global south. The same question is even more relevant to the newer voluntourism organizations that send young, inexperienced, and unqualified volunteers overseas.

There are basically four justifications for such voluntourism programs. The first is that they are good for the voluntourists, who gain valuable work and life experience. The second is that such programs help the developing world by building schools, teaching children, and tending to orphans. The third is that such programs serve as expressions of international solidarity; they are the training ground for the next generation of global advocates for social justice. The fourth, more mercenary, justification is that the for-profit voluntourism firms are legitimate businesses trying to make a profit by responding to demands for placements from would-be volunteers. Of these four answers, only the third and fourth are substantially true.

The first two justifications for voluntourism are in most cases false, on both ethical and practical grounds. That the volunteers get an important life experience is undeniable; whether that experience serves them well is another question. The fact is that voluntourism usually reinforces a view that sees the citizens of the developing world primarily, or even solely, as people who need "our" help. (See Chapter 15.) And that help can be provided in short-term doses by inexperienced amateurs. No one doubts that most people in developing countries have a lower material standard of living than most Canadians. But to see the people of the global south only as objects of our charity, and not as agents of their own development, reinforces harmful colonial stereotypes while claiming to elevate the moral status of the person who "helps" these people (Harris 2017). Just as important, voluntourism overlooks the structures of local and global power relations that make some people and countries poor. Voluntourism is paternalistic, condescending, and politically naïve.

More seriously, voluntourists sometimes perform tasks in developing countries that would be illegal for them to perform in their home countries unless they had relevant professional designations; examples include providing medical care or teaching primary school (Quenville 2015). The legal issue is a serious one, but the ethical issue is just as problematic. When they engage in such practices, voluntourists effectively treat people of colour in the global south as objects on which the voluntourist may practise with impunity. Since it promotes the view that "we," no matter how unskilled and inexperienced, can and must help "them," many see voluntourism as a manifestation of white privilege (Schwartz 2015).

Voluntourism is also inefficient and ineffective in promoting development. The cost of sending voluntourists abroad for short periods dwarfs any good that they could do; one commentator remarks sarcastically that "venturing to the other side of the world is said to be the most efficient way of helping the needy" (Harris 2017). The literature is also replete with stories of volunteers going south to build a school or clinic; having no training in construction, the walls they build are not straight or structurally sound and have to be re-built by trained local masons and carpenters (Quenville 2015; Biddle 2016). Besides, the voluntourists are rarely invited to ask who will pay to run the school, how the teachers will be hired and supervised, or whether the school will be accredited with the local ministry of education. Voluntourism thus encourages a simplistic view of development as

the accumulation of things (e.g., school buildings), rather than as the process of people taking control over their own lives. (See Chapters 1, 2, and 15.)

In other cases, voluntourists who pay to volunteer in apparently worthy enterprises like wildlife reserves may inadvertently be contributing to scams whose motive is to profit from unwitting do-gooders (Quenville 2015). Voluntourists who work in orphanages may form close emotional ties with the orphans and then leave them after a few weeks or months. As emotionally wrenching as they are for the voluntourist, the long-term psychological effects on the orphans of such repeated attachments and separations are likely to be devastating (Biddle 2016; Quenville 2015). In such cases, voluntourism may do more harm than good.

Combining the ethical and practical worries about voluntourism, Tiessen and Huish (2014) have raised important questions about how several forms of international experiential learning, including voluntourism, provide not only an inadequate, but an often misleading basis for future work in development. Unless they are properly designed, voluntourism programs can reinforce stereotypes reflecting the West's purported intellectual and moral superiority (Schwartz 2015). (See Chapter 9.) Volunteering abroad programs should provide volunteers with adequate pre-departure training, emotional and professional support while the volunteer is abroad, and a debriefing upon return. Ideally, the assignment should be for at least six months, so that the volunteer has time to learn how best to contribute, while still having enough time to contribute meaningfully. Without such measures, volunteers, especially young and inexperienced volunteers, will not be equipped to contribute meaningfully and may not be able to process what they have learned. Volunteer programs must also promote critical thinking about both the ethical and the practical dimensions of development. Instead of assuming that working in an orphanage is a noble thing to do, a critical thinker will ask why so many children are warehoused in orphanages.

A volunteer who thinks critically will ask:

- Why am I interested in volunteering?
- What are the limits of my competence?
- What things should I *not* do, even if asked?

- How can I contribute effectively?
- What harms might I inadvertently create?
- Who is bearing the cost of my wonderful learning experience in a developing country?

These are tough questions, but they need to be asked.

Suggested Readings

Biddle, Pippa. 2016. "The Voluntourist's Dilemma: What's the Cost of Giving Back?" See https://www.gooverseas.com/industry-trends/voluntourist-dilemma.

Harris, John. 2017. "We Carry On Giving, But Isn't Charity an Offence to Basic Dignity?" *The Guardian*. 21 April. https://www.theguardian.com/commentisfree/2017/apr/21/charities-omnipresent-where-next-begging-bowl.

Quenville, Brad. 2015. "Volunteers Unleashed." Documentary aired 10 October 2015 on CBC TV's *Doc Zone*. Available on www.cbc.ca/doczone/episodes/volunteers-unleashed.

Schwartz, Kaylan C. 2015. "Encounters with Discomfort: How Do Young Canadians Understand (Their) Privilege And (Others') Poverty in the Context of an International Volunteer Experience?" *Comparative and International Education* 44 (1).

Tiessen, Rebecca, and Robert Huish, eds. 2014. *Globetrotting or Global Citizenship? Perils and Potential of International Experiential Learning.* Toronto: University of Toronto Press.

List of Acronyms

$	Canadian dollars
3D	Diplomacy, defence, development
AFN	Assembly of First Nations
AMC	Advanced market commitment
BRICS	Brazil, Russia, India, China, South Africa
CAF	Canadian Armed Forces
CIDA	Canadian International Development Agency (1968-2013)
CSO	Civil society organization
CSR	Corporate social responsibility
DFAIT	Department of Foreign Affairs and International Trade (2003-13)
DFATD	Department of Foreign Affairs, Trade and Development (2013-15)
DND	Department of National Defence
EAO	External Aid Office (predecessor to CIDA 1959-68)
FCAS	Fragile and conflict-affected situations/states
FNMI	First Nations, Métis and Inuit
G7	Group of seven leading liberal democracies (Canada, France, Germany, Italy, Japan, UK, US)
G8	G7 plus Russia
GAC	Global Affairs Canada (2015– present)
GHG	Greenhouse gases
GNP	Gross national product
GOC	Government of Canada
HDI	Human development index
ICC	International Criminal Court
ICHRDD	International Centre for Human Rights and Democratic Development (aka "Rights and Democracy")
IDRC	International Development Research Centre
IFI	International financial institution
IMF	International Monetary Fund
LDC	Least developed country/countries
IPCC	Intergovernmental Panel on Climate Change
MDGs	Millennium Development Goals
MIC	Middle income country/countries
NAFTA	North American Free Trade Agreement
NATO	North Atlantic Treaty Organization
NGO	Non-governmental organization
NORAD	North American Air Defence Command
ODA	Official development assistance
OECD	Organisation for Economic Co-operation and Development
OECD-DAC	OECD-Development Co-operation Directorate (formerly the OECD Development Assistance Committee)
PPP	Public–private partnership
R2P	Responsibility to Protect
RCMP	Royal Canadian Mounted Police
SDGs	Sustainable Development Goals
UK	United Kingdom of Great Britain and Northern Ireland
UN	United Nations
UNAMIR	UN Assistance Mission in Rwanda
UNDP	United Nations Development Program
UN/FCCC	UN Framework Convention on Climate Change
UNISOM	UN Operation in Somalia
UNPROFOR	UN Protection Force (former Yugoslavia)
UNSC	United Nations Security Council
UNSG	United Nations Secretary-General
US	United States of America
US$	United States dollars
WID	Women in development
WOG	Whole of government
WTO	World Trade Organization

Author Biographies

STEPHEN BARANYI is an Associate Professor at the University of Ottawa, where he teaches and conducts research on development and security. His recent work has appeared in several books as well as in these journals: *Third World Thematics*; *Third World Quarterly*; *Canadian Foreign Policy Journal*; *Conflict, Development and Security*; and the *Journal of Peacebuilding and Development*. See some of his blogs at: http://cips.uottawa.ca/author/stephen-baranyi/.

TRYCIA BAZINET is of white French settler background. She grew up in Abitibi-Témiscamingue, in what is known as Northern Quebec. She has a bachelor in Women's Studies from Concordia University and a master's degree in Globalization and International Development from the University of Ottawa. She currently is a PhD student in Indigenous and Canadian studies at Carleton University. She is also a local community organizer.

PIERRE BEAUDET is Professor in the Department of Social Sciences at the Université du Québec en Outaouais. He was until 2017 Deputy Director of the School of International Development and Global Studies, University of Ottawa. He is co-editor (with Paul Haslam and Jessica Schafer) of *Introduction to International Development: Approaches, Actors, Issues and Practice*, 3rd edition (Oxford University Press, 2017). He was previously active with NGOs and social movements in Canada, Africa, Asia, and Latin America.

CASEY BRUNELLE is a graduate of the School of International Development and Global Studies at the University of Ottawa. In 2015, he completed a contract at United Nations headquarters in New York City, specializing in humanitarian response. Casey is currently an intelligence advisor, with more than six years' experience in both the public and private sectors.

KATELYN L. H. CASSIN is a PhD candidate in International Development at the University of Ottawa, with expertise in peacebuilding, international development, and the anthropology of religion. Her research investigates the role of religion in bridging barriers between United Nations peacekeepers and local populations in Lebanon. She has written on Canadian multilateralism, security sector reform in Iraq, the comprehensive approach, and the experiences of Muslim Canadian military personnel in the Canadian Armed Forces.

TRACY COATES is a Professor (long-term appointment) in the Institute of Canadian and Aboriginal Studies at the University of Ottawa. A strategic and creative educator and consultant in the areas of critical theory, law, Indigenous knowledges, and Indigenizing the academy, her work focuses on community mobilization and facilitating community-proponent partnerships. Tracy is of mixed Mohawk and European ancestry and uses her experience in urban Aboriginal and remote communities to inform her approach to Indigegogy/pedagogy, research, and decolonization. Tracy holds a Juris Doctor from Osgoode Hall, and a Masters in Environmental Studies from York University.

BRUCE CURRIE-ALDER is Program Leader for Climate Adaptation in Africa and Asia in Canada's International Development Research Centre (IDRC). His expertise spans environmental science, international development, and research policy. He was previously IDRC's director for the Middle East and North Africa (2013–2017), and Chief of Staff (2008–2013). His works include *Research for the Developing World* and *International Development: Ideas, Experience and Prospects* (Oxford University Press, 2013 and 2015). He holds a PhD in public policy from Carleton University.

KATHLEAN C. FITZPATRICK PhD, LSE (2008) is an international relations scholar with a specific research focus on the intersections of political theory, gender, and Indigenous studies. Her doctoral research was a holistic analysis of Eurocentric new world empire and the colonial policies and practices and early state formation of the newly emergent settler societies of British/French/Dutch/Spanish North America. Her personal, academic, and professional development path has lead her to be a scholar/activist/artist dedicated to the (re-)newal of the Treaty relationship between newcomers and the Indigenous people(s) across Turtle Island. Dr. Fitzpatrick practices transformative education with the spirit and intent of re-building positive peace with All Our Relations. She is a Senior Fellow at the School of International Development and Global Studies at the University of Ottawa.

BRUNO GÉLINAS-FAUCHER is a lawyer and Lecturer at the Université de Montréal, Faculty of Law. He previously served as Law Clerk to The Honourable Thomas Cromwell at the Supreme Court of Canada, where he worked on immigration cases brought to Canada's highest court. He completed graduate studies in law at the University of Cambridge, where he focused on public international law, including migration and refugee issues.

LAURA GRANT is a doctoral candidate in International Development at the University of Ottawa. Her research focuses on civil-military relations in complex peace operations in conflict and post-conflict states. In particular, she explores the effectiveness of the comprehensive approach as employed in Provincial Reconstruction Teams in Afghanistan. She holds a master's degree from the University of Amsterdam in International Development, focused on civil society advocacy.

TARYN HUSBAND-CEPERKOVIC is a doctoral candidate in the School of International Development and Global Studies at the University of Ottawa. His research takes a critical perspective on new institutionalist frameworks, focusing on the role of legal institutions in gender equality efforts and how they can be leveraged by social movements to include a broader definition of gender. He completed his MA in Global Governance at the University of Waterloo, where his research focused on widowhood and social policy in post-conflict contexts.

SHANNON KINDORNAY is an Adjunct Research Professor at the Norman Paterson School of International Affairs at Carleton University and an independent consultant. Her research focuses on development cooperation, global governance, and aid and the private sector. She was previously a researcher at the North-South Institute, where she worked on multilateral development cooperation, Canada's development cooperation program, and the role of the private sector in development. She has also worked at the Canadian International Development Agency.

MAHMOUD MASAELI teaches global ethics and international development at the University of Ottawa. His research and teaching interests focus on global ethics, ethics of globality, dialogical ethics, ethics and human rights, modern political philosophy, and hermeneutics of the selfhood. He holds a special interest in spirituality and global ethics. Mahmoud is the founding president and CEO of Alternative Perspectives and Global Concerns (www.ap-gc.net). He is also the ambassador of the Parliament of the World's Religions.

STEPHEN MCBRIDE is Professor of Political Science and Canada Research Chair in Public Policy and Globalization at McMaster University. His most recent books are, co-authored with Heather Whiteside, *Private Affluence, Public Austerity: Economic Crisis and Democratic Malaise in Canada* (Halifax: Fernwood, 2011); co-edited with Donna Baines, *Orchestrating Austerity: Impacts and Resistance* (Halifax: Fernwood, 2014); co-edited with Carla Lipsig-Mummé, *Work in a Warming World* (Montreal: McGill-Queen's University Press, 2015); and co-edited with Rianne Mahon and Gerard W. Boychuk, *After '08: Social Policy and the Global Financial Crisis* (Vancouver: UBC Press, 2015).

HUNTER MCGILL is Senior Fellow at the University of Ottawa's School of International Development and Global Studies. He has worked in international development for 40 years, as a Canadian public servant, as a consultant, and with the World Bank, Irish Aid, and GTZ. After many years with the Canadian International Development Agency, he moved to the Organisation for Economic Co-operation and Development, where he was responsible for peer reviews done by the member countries of the Development Assistance Committee. He is a member of the boards of Heritage Ottawa, Friends of the Rideau, and the Rideau Waterway Land Trust.

OMID B. MILANI is a cartoonist, a PhD candidate in law, and a part-time professor at the University of Ottawa. His research interests include a wide range of interdisciplinary areas, such as law and philosophy, arts and law, and law and psychology. His current research project touches upon the question of violence in legal and political contexts. Omid is a member of the Human Rights Research and Education Centre at the University of Ottawa.

LAUCHLAN T. MUNRO is Associate Professor and former Director (2012–2016 and 2018) of the University of Ottawa's School of International Development and Global Studies. From 2003 to 2012, he worked at Canada's International Development Research Centre, serving as Vice President from 2009 to 2012. Before that, he worked for 13 years for UNICEF, including as Chief of Strategic Planning from 2000 to 2003. From 1985 to 1987, he was a member of the Royal Bhutanese Civil Service.

DELPHINE NAKACHE is an Associate Professor at the University of Ottawa's School of International Development and Global Studies, where she teaches in public international law and migration and refugee law. Her research interests include securitization of migration, refugee and citizenship policies, migration and human rights standards, and employment standards in a migration/mobility context. With Yves Le Bouthilier, she is the author of *Le droit de la citoyenneté au Canada* (Montreal: Éditions Yvon Blais, 2016).

RODNEY NELSON is an advocate for economic development for Indigenous communities worldwide and is passionate about retaining traditional knowledge. He is a professor at Carleton University and CEO for the Global Governance Group. Rodney holds a PhD in Indigenous/Canadian Studies (Carleton/Trent), an MA in anthropology, and bachelor's degrees in psychology and anthropology. He is a Certified Aboriginal Professional Administrator (CAPA), and a Professional Aboriginal Economic Developer (PAED). Rodney is Anishinabe. He is active in the community as a traditional teacher, fire keeper, and musician.

SYED SAJJADUR RAHMAN has been a Senior Fellow and Visiting Professor at the University of Ottawa's School of International Development and Global Studies since 2014. Before that, for many years he was a senior executive at the Canadian International Development Agency, now part of Global Affairs Canada. He is now part of a research project on development partnerships with middle-income economies in association with researchers in Canada, Bangladesh, and Colombia. He holds a PhD in economics from Carleton University.

FRASER REILLY-KING is the Senior Policy Analyst at the Canadian Council for International Co-operation, where he focuses on Canadian aid and development and broader global trends. He sits on the Management Committee of the Reality of Aid Network as Vice-Chair, and is the former North American representative to the CSO Partnership for Development Effectiveness. Over the past 15 years, he has produced numerous reports, peer-reviewed articles, op-eds, and commentaries for various organizations and media outlets. He holds an MSc in Development Studies from the London School of Economics.

JULIA SÁNCHEZ is President-CEO of the Canadian Council for International Co-operation (CCIC). At CCIC, she has focused on promoting an enabling environment for civil society participation in international development and development policy in Canada and abroad. She sits on the boards or advisory groups of several Canadian and international CSOs, including the CSO Partnership for Development Effectiveness and the Community of Democracies. She holds a BA in political science and an MA in economics from McGill.

GERD SCHÖNWÄLDER works for the Research and Innovation Directorate-General of the European Commission. He has been a guest researcher at the Centre for International Policy Studies and the German Development Institute, working on external democracy support with a focus on emerging democracies as well as Canada. For several years, Gerd was the Director of Policy and Planning at the International Development Research Centre. He holds a PhD in Political Science from McGill University.

IAN SMILLIE is an international development practitioner, teacher, and writer. He has lived and worked in Asia and Africa, was a founder of Inter Pares, and was Executive Director of CUSO. He is the author of several books, including *Freedom from Want* (2008), *Blood on the Stone: Greed, Corruption and War in the Global Diamond Trade* (2010), and *Diamonds* (2014). He helped develop the "Kimberley Process," a global certification system designed to halt the traffic in conflict diamonds. He chairs the Board of the Diamond Development Initiative and is Past President of the Canadian Association for the Study of International Development. He received the Order of Canada in 2003.

JOHN M.R. STONE is Adjunct Professor in the Department of Geography and Environmental Studies at Carleton University. He received his PhD in Chemical Spectroscopy from the University of Reading in 1969 and worked for many years for the Canadian Public Service. Since retiring in 2005, he has been a Visiting Fellow at the International Development Research Centre. He was a Member of the Bureau of the Intergovernmental Panel on Climate Change and a Lead Author for the IPCC Fifth Assessment Report. He is Board Member of the Pembina Institute.

SALAMAT ALI TABBASUM teaches part time at the School of International Development and Global Studies and the Graduate School of Public and International Affairs at the University of Ottawa. Dr. Tabbasum completed his PhD in Politics and International Studies at the Department of Politics and International Studies, University of Cambridge, UK. Dr. Tabbasum's main areas of research interest include international relations, conflict, security and development, international development, and international political economy.

KETEVAN TADIASHVILI is completing her master's program in International Development and Global Studies at the University of Ottawa. Her thesis topic focuses on anti-dam activism in the Svaneti region of post-Soviet Georgia, and on the whole on exploring post-Soviet energy politics.

STEPHANIE TOMBARI is Research Manager for the World Green Building Council, which works with green building councils around the world to achieve net-zero carbon in the construction and building sector. She has taught courses at Ontario universities on international development, comparative politics, public policy, and professional communication, and worked for seven years in international development. Stephanie holds a PhD in comparative public policy from McMaster University and was a postdoctoral fellow with the Automotive Policy Research Centre.

STANLEY UCHE ANOZIE teaches philosophy, logic, and critical thinking at William Paterson University and Felician University in New Jersey. Anozie taught Introduction to Philosophy/ Creative Thinking from 2001 to 2002. In 2007, he was awarded a Master's Scholarship from Social Sciences and Humanities Research Council of Canada (SSHRC), and received a Doctoral Fellowship from Ontario Graduate Scholarship (Canada) for 2011–2012. He obtained his MA and PhD in philosophy from Dominican University College, Ottawa, Canada.

Studies in International Development and Globalization

Series editor: Lauchlan T. Munro

The *Studies in International Development and Globalization* series presents new perspectives on a range of topics in development and globalization studies—including Indigenous peoples, women, social movements, labour issues, agriculture, governance, and migration—revealing the tensions and conflicts that occur in the wake of development and highlighting the quest for social justice in global contexts.

Previous titles in this collection

Stephen Brown, Molly den Heyer and David R. Black (eds.), *Rethinking Canadian Aid*,
    Second Edition, 2016.

Henry Veltmeyer (dir.), *Des outils pour le changement*, 2015.

Pierre Beaudet et Paul A. Haslam (dir.), *Enjeux et défis du développement international*, 2014.

Andrea Martinez, Pierre Beaudet et Stephen Baranyi (dir.), *Haïti aujourd'hui, Haïti demain.*
    Regards croisés, 2011.

Daniel C. Bach et Mamoudou Gazibo (dir.), *L'État néopatrimonial. Genèse et*
    trajectoires contemporaines, 2011.

Jacques Fisette et Marc Raffinot (dir.), *Gouvernance et appropriation locale du développement.*
    Au-delà des modèles importés, 2010.

Pierre Beaudet, Jessica Schafer et Paul Haslam (dir.), *Introduction au développement international.*
    Approches, acteurs et enjeux, 2008.

Isabelle Beaulieu, *L'État rentier. Le cas de la Malaysia*, 2008.

Saturnino M. Borras, *Pro-Poor Land Reform. A Critique*, 2007.

www.press.uottawa.ca

Printed in August 2018
by Gauvin Press,
Gatineau, Québec